12/08
Repl.

REASON AND REVOLUTION

Reason and Revolution

Hegel and the Rise of Social Theory

Herbert Marcuse

100th Anniversary Edition

Humanity Books

an imprint of Prometheus Books

59 John Glenn Drive, Amherst, New York 14228-2119

Published 1999 by Humanity Books, an imprint of Prometheus Books

Inquiries should be addressed to
Humanity Books
59 John Glenn Drive
Amherst, New York 14228–2119.
VOICE: 716–691–0133, ext. 210. FAX: 716–691-0137.

11 10 09 08 11 10 9

Library of Congress Cataloging-in-Publication Data

Marcuse, Herbert, 1898–1979.
Reason and revolution : Hegel and the rise of social theory / by Herbert Marcuse. — 100th anniversary ed.
p. cm.
Reprint. Originally published: London : Oxford University Press, 1941.
Includes bibliographical references.
ISBN-13: 978–1–57392–718–5
ISBN-10: 1–57392–718–X(pbk. : alk. paper)
1. Hegel, Georg Wilhelm Friedrich, 1779–1831—Contributions in sociology. 2. Sociology—Germany—History. 3. Sociology—Methodology—History. 4. Dialectic. 5. Positivism. I. Title.
HM22.G3H43 1999
301—dc21 99–13602
CIP

Printed in the United States of America on acid-free paper

TO

MAX HORKHEIMER

AND THE

INSTITUTE OF SOCIAL RESEARCH

Preface to the Anniversary Edition

THIS book is being reissued by Humanity Books in 1998, the 100th anniversary of the birth of Herbert Marcuse.

Marcuse was born on July 19, 1898, in Berlin, Germany. He studied at universities in Berlin and Freiburg, where he knew philosophers Edmund Husserl and Martin Heidegger. Marcuse fled Nazi Germany for the United States in 1934 and became a naturalized American citizen in 1940. He taught philosophy and politics at Columbia University, Brandeis University, and the University of California at San Diego. He died July 29, 1979.

Marcuse was noted as a scholar of Hegel, Marx, and Freud. He was a key figure in the "Frankfurt School," a group of anti-Stalinist neo-Marxists who helped to formulate thought on the intellectual and political left. He inspired many leaders of the "Rebellion of 1968" and the New Left. He took part in sit-ins and was lionized by his students. His advocacy of revolution and emancipation resonated with the *zeitgeist.* He criticized capitalism for reducing the masses to mere consumers.

Among his most important books are *Eros and Civilization: A Philosophical Inquiry into Freud* (1955); *Soviet Marxism: A Critical Analysis* (1958); *One-Dimensional Man: Studies in the Ideology of Advanced Industrial Societies* (1965); *An Essay on Liberation* (1969); and *Counter-Revolution and Revolution* (1972).

Reason and Revolution: Hegel and the Rise of Social Theory was first published in 1941 and is now considered a classic. This augmented edition was first published in 1954 by Humanities Press International and has been one of Marcuse's most influential works.

Preface

THE content of a truly philosophical work does not remain unchanged with time. If its concepts have an essential bearing upon the aims and interests of men, a fundamental change in the historical situation will make them see its teachings in a new light. In our time, the rise of Fascism calls for a reinterpretation of Hegel's philosophy. We hope that the analysis offered here will demonstrate that Hegel's basic concepts are hostile to the tendencies that have led into Fascist theory and practice.

We have devoted the first part of the book to a survey of the structure of Hegel's system. At the same time, we have tried to go beyond mere restatement and to elucidate those implications of Hegel's ideas that identify them closely with the later developments in European thought, particularly with the Marxian theory.

Hegel's critical and rational standards, and especially his dialectics, had to come into conflict with the prevailing social reality. For this reason, his system could well be called a *negative philosophy*, the name given to it by its contemporary opponents. To counteract its destructive tendencies, there arose, in the decade following Hegel's death, a *positive philosophy* which undertook to subordinate reason to the authority of established fact. The struggle that developed between the negative and positive philosophy offers, as we have attempted to show in the second part of this book, many clues for understanding the rise of modern social theory in Europe.

There is in Hegel a keen insight into the locale of progressive ideas and movements. He attributed to the American rational spirit a decisive role in the struggle for an adequate order of life, and spoke of 'the victory of some future and intensely vital rationality of the American nation . . .' Knowing far better than his critics the forces that threatened freedom and reason, and recognizing these forces to have been bound up with the social system Europe had acquired, he once looked beyond that continent to this as the only 'land of the future.'

In the use of texts, I have frequently taken the liberty of citing an English translation and changing the translator's rendering where I thought it necessary, without stipulating that the change was made. Hegelian terms are often rendered by different English equivalents, and I have attempted to avoid confusion on this score by giving the German word in parenthesis where a technical term was involved.

The presentation of this study would not have been possible without the assistance I received from Mr. Edward M. David who gave the book the stylistic form it now has. I have drawn upon his knowledge of the American and British philosophic tradition to guide me in selecting those points that could and that could not be taken for granted in offering Hegel's doctrine to an American and English public.

I thank the Macmillan Company, New York, for granting me permission to use and quote their translations of Hegel's works, and I thank the following publishers for authorizing me to quote their publications: International Publishers, Longmans, Green and Co., Charles H. Kerr and Co., The Macmillan Co., The Viking Press, The Weekly Foreign Letter (Lawrence Dennis).

My friend Franz L. Neumann, who was gathering material for his forthcoming book on National Socialism, has given me constant advice, especially on the political philosophy.

Professor George H. Sabine was kind enough to read the chapter on Hegel's Philosophy of Right and to offer valuable suggestions.

I am particularly grateful to the Oxford University Press, New York, which encouraged me to write this book and undertook to publish it at this time.

HERBERT MARCUSE

Institute of Social Research
Columbia University
New York, N. Y.

March 1941.

Contents

PART I

THE FOUNDATIONS OF HEGEL'S PHILOSOPHY

PART II

THE RISE OF SOCIAL THEORY

CONCLUSION

THE END OF HEGELIANISM

PART I

The Foundations of Hegel's Philosophy

Introduction

1. The Socio-Historical Setting

GERMAN idealism has been called the theory of the French Revolution. This does not imply that Kant, Fichte, Schelling, and Hegel furnished a theoretical interpretation of the French Revolution, but that they wrote their philosophy largely as a response to the challenge from France to reorganize the state and society on a rational basis, so that social and political institutions might accord with the freedom and interest of the individual. Despite their bitter criticism of the Terror, the German idealists unanimously welcomed the revolution, calling it the dawn of a new era, and they all linked their basic philosophical principles to the ideals that it advanced.

The ideas of the French Revolution thus appear in the very core of the idealistic systems, and, to a great extent, determine their conceptual structure. As the German idealists saw it, the French Revolution not only abolished feudal absolutism, replacing it with the economic and political system of the middle class, but it completed what the German Reformation had begun, emancipating the individual as a self-reliant master of his life. Man's position in the world, the mode of his labor and enjoyment, was no longer to depend on some external authority, but on his own free rational activity. Man had passed the long period of immaturity during which he had been victimized by overwhelming natural and social forces, and had become the autonomous subject of his own development. From now on, the struggle with nature and with social organization was to be guided by his own progress in knowledge. The world was to be an order of reason.

The ideals of the French Revolution found their resting place in the processes of industrial capitalism. Napoleon's empire liquidated the radical tendencies and at the same time consolidated the economic consequences of the revolution. The French philosophers of the period interpreted the realization of reason as the liberation of industry. Expanding industrial production seemed capable of providing all the necessary means to gratify human wants. Thus, at the same time that Hegel elaborated his system, Saint-Simon in France was exalting industry as the sole power that could lead mankind to a free and rational society. The economic process appeared as the foundation of reason.

Economic development in Germany lagged far behind that in France and England. The German middle class, weak and scattered over numerous territories with divergent interests, could hardly contemplate a revolution. The few industrial enterprises that existed were but small islands within a protracted feudal system. The individual in his social existence was either enslaved, or was the enslaver of his fellow individuals. As a thinking being, however, he could at least comprehend the contrast between the miserable reality that existed everywhere and the human potentialities that the new epoch had emancipated; and as a moral person, he could, in his private life at least, preserve human dignity and autonomy. Thus, while the French Revolution had already begun to assert the reality of freedom, German idealism was only occupying itself with the idea of it. The concrete historical efforts to establish a rational form of society were here transposed to the philosophical plane and appeared in the efforts to elaborate the notion of reason.

The concept of reason is central to Hegel's philosophy.

He held that philosophical thinking presupposes nothing beyond it, that history deals with reason and with reason alone, and that the state is the realization of reason. These statements will not be understandable, however, so long as reason is interpreted as a pure metaphysical concept, for Hegel's idea of reason has retained, though in an idealistic form, the material strivings for a free and rational order of life. Robespierre's deification of reason as the *Être suprême* is the counterpart to the glorification of reason in Hegel's system. The core of Hegel's philosophy is a structure the concepts of which—freedom, subject, mind, notion—are derived from the idea of reason. Unless we succeed in unfolding the content of these ideas and the intrinsic connection among them, Hegel's system will seem to be obscure metaphysics, which it in fact never was.

Hegel himself related his concept of reason to the French Revolution, and did so with the greatest of emphasis. The revolution had demanded that 'nothing should be recognized as valid in a constitution except what has to be recognized according to reason's right.' [1] Hegel further elaborated this interpretation in his lectures on the Philosophy of History: 'Never since the sun had stood in the firmament and the planets revolved around it had it been perceived that man's existence centres in his head, i.e. in Thought, inspired by which he builds up the world of reality. Anaxagoras had been the first to say that Νοῦς governs the World; but not until now had man advanced to the recognition of the principle that Thought ought to govern spiritual reality. This was accordingly a glorious mental dawn. All thinking beings shared in the jubilation of this epoch.' [2]

In Hegel's view, the decisive turn that history took with

[1] *Ueber die Verhandlung der Württembergischen Landstände*, in *Schriften zur Politik und Rechtsphilosophie*, ed. Georg Lasson, Leipzig 1913, p. 198.

[2] *Philosophy of History*, trans. J. Sibbree, New York 1899, p. 447.

the French Revolution was that man came to rely on his mind and dared to submit the given reality to the standards of reason. Hegel expounds the new development through a contrast between an employment of reason and an uncritical compliance with the prevailing conditions of life. 'Nothing is reason that is not the result of thinking.' Man has set out to organize reality according to the demands of his free rational thinking instead of simply accommodating his thoughts to the existing order and the prevailing values. Man is a thinking being. His reason enables him to recognize his own potentialities and those of his world. He is thus not at the mercy of the facts that surround him, but is capable of subjecting them to a higher standard, that of reason. If he follows its lead, he will arrive at certain conceptions that disclose reason to be antagonistic to the existing state of affairs. He may find that history is a constant struggle for freedom, that man's individuality requires that he possess property as the medium of his fulfillment, and that all men have an equal right to develop their human faculties. Actually, however, bondage and inequality prevail; most men have no liberty at all and are deprived of their last scrap of property. Consequently the 'unreasonable' reality has to be altered until it comes into conformity with reason. In the given case, the existing social order has to be reorganized, absolutism and the remainders of feudalism have to be abolished, free competition has to be established, everyone has to be made equal before the law, and so on.

According to Hegel, the French Revolution enunciated reason's ultimate power over reality. He sums this up by saying that the principle of the French Revolution asserted that thought ought to govern reality. The implications involved in this statement lead into the very center of his philosophy. Thought ought to govern reality. What men think to be true, right, and good ought to be realized in the actual organization of their societal and individual life. Thinking, however, varies among individuals, and the resulting diversity of individual opinions cannot provide a guiding principle for the common organization of life. Unless man possesses concepts and principles of thought that denote universally valid conditions and norms, his thought cannot claim to govern reality. In line with the tradition of Western philosophy, Hegel believes that such objective concepts and principles exist. Their totality he calls reason.

The philosophies of the French Enlightenment and their revolutionary successors all posited reason as an objective historical force which, once freed from the fetters of despotism, would make the world a place of progress and happiness. They held that 'the power of reason, and not the force of weapons, will propagate the principles of our glorious revolution.' [3] By virtue of its own power, reason would triumph over social irrationality and overthrow the oppressors of mankind. 'All fictions disappear before truth, and all follies fall before reason.' [4]

The implication, however, that reason will immediately show itself in practice is a dogma unsupported by the course of history. Hegel believed in the invincible power of reason as much as Robespierre did. 'That faculty which man can call his own, elevated above death and decay, . . . is able to make decisions of itself. It announces itself as reason. Its law-making depends on nothing else, nor can it take its standards from any other authority on earth or in heaven.' [5] But to Hegel, reason cannot govern reality unless reality has become rational in itself.

[3] Robespierre, quoted by Georges Michon, *Robespierre et la guerre révolutionnaire*, Paris 1937, p. 134.

[4] Robespierre in his report on the cult of the Être suprême, quoted by Albert Mathiez, *Autour de Robespierre*, Paris 1936, p. 112.

[5] Hegel, *Theologische Jugendschriften*, ed. H. Nohl, Tübingen 1907, p. 89.

This rationality is made possible through the subject's entering the very content of nature and history. The objective reality is thus also the realization of the subject. It is this conception that Hegel summarized in the most fundamental of his propositions, namely, that Being is, in its substance, a 'subject.'[6] The meaning of this proposition can only be understood through an interpretation of Hegel's *Logic,* but we shall attempt to give a provisional explanation here that will be expanded later.[7]

The idea of the 'substance as subject' conceives reality as a process wherein all being is the unification of contradictory forces. 'Subject' denotes not only the epistemological ego or consciousness, but a mode of existence, to wit, that of a self-developing unity in an antagonistic process. Everything that exists is 'real' only in so far as it operates as a 'self' through all the contradictory relations that constitute its existence. It must thus be considered a kind of 'subject' that carries itself forward by unfolding its inherent contradictions. For example, a stone is a stone only in so far as it remains the same thing, a stone, throughout its action and reaction upon the things and processes that interact with it. It gets wet in the rain; it resists the axe; it withstands a certain load before it gives way. Being-a-stone is a continuous holding out against everything that acts on the stone; it is a continuous process of becoming and being a stone. To be sure, the 'becoming' is not consummated by the stone as a conscious subject. The stone is changed in its interactions with rain, axe, and load; it does not change itself. A plant, on the other hand, unfolds and develops itself. It is not now a bud, then a blossom, but is rather the whole movement from bud through blossom to decay. The plant constitutes and preserves itself in this movement. It comes much nearer to being an actual

[6] See Hegel, *Phenomenology of Mind,* trans. J. B. Baillie, London (The Macmillan Company, New York), 1910, p. 15.
[7] See below, pp. 63 ff., 123 ff.

'subject' than does the stone, for the various stages of the plant's development grow out of the plant itself; they are its 'life' and are not imposed upon it from the outside.

The plant, however, does not 'comprehend' this development. It does not 'realize' it as its own and, therefore, cannot reason its own potentialities into being. Such 'realization' is a process of the true subject and is reached only with the existence of man. Man alone has the power of self-realization, the power to be a self-determining subject in all processes of becoming, for he alone has an understanding of potentialities and a knowledge of 'notions.' His very existence is the process of actualizing his potentialities, of molding his life according to the notions of reason. We encounter here the most important category of reason, namely, freedom. Reason presupposes freedom, the power to act in accordance with knowledge of the truth, the power to shape reality in line with its potentialities. The fulfillment of these ends belongs only to the subject who is master of his own development and who understands his own potentialities as well as those of the things around him. Freedom, in turn, presupposes reason, for it is comprehending knowledge, alone, that enables the subject to gain and to wield this power. The stone does not possess it; neither does the plant. Both lack comprehending knowledge and hence real subjectivity. 'Man, however, knows what he is,—only thus is he real. Reason and freedom are nothing without this knowledge.' [8]

Reason terminates in freedom, and freedom is the very existence of the subject. On the other hand, reason itself exists only through its realization, the process of its being made real. Reason is an objective force and an objective reality only because all modes of being are more or less modes of subjectivity, modes of realization. Subject and

[8] *Vorlesungen über die Geschichte der Philosophie*, ed. J. Hoffmeister, Leipzig 1938, p. 104.

object are not undered by an impassable gulf, because the object is in itself a kind of subject and because all types of being culminate in the free 'comprehensive' subject who is able to realize reason. Nature thus becomes a medium for the development of freedom.

The life of reason appears in man's continuous struggle to comprehend what exists and to transform it in accordance with the truth comprehended. Reason is also essentially a historical force. Its fulfillment takes place as a process in the spatio-temporal world, and is, in the last analysis, the whole history of mankind. The term that designates reason as history is mind (*Geist*) which denotes the historical world viewed in relation to the rational progress of humanity—the historical world not as a chain of acts and events but as a ceaseless struggle to adapt the world to the growing potentialities of mankind.

History is organized into different periods, each marking a separate level of development and representing a definite stage in the realization of reason. Each stage is to be grasped and understood as a whole, through the prevailing ways of thinking and living which characterize it, through its political and social institutions, its science, religion and philosophy. Different stages occur in the realization of reason, but there is only one reason, just as there is only one whole and one truth: the reality of freedom. 'This final goal it is, at which the process of the world's history has been continually aiming, and to which the sacrifices that have ever and anon been laid on the vast altar of the earth, through the long lapse of ages, have been offered. This is the only final aim that realizes and fulfills itself; the only pole of repose amid the ceaseless chain of events and conditions, and the sole true reality in them.' [9]

An *immediate* unity of reason and reality never exists. The unity comes only after a lengthy process, which be-

[9] *Philosophy of History*, pp. 19-20.

gins at the lowest level of nature and reaches up to the highest form of existence, that of a free and rational subject, living and acting in the self-consciousness of its potentialities. As long as there is any gap between real and potential, the former must be acted upon and changed until it is brought into line with reason. As long as reality is not shaped by reason, it remains no reality at all, in the emphatic sense of the word. Thus reality changes its meaning within the conceptual structure of Hegel's system. 'Real' comes to mean not everything that actually exists (this should rather be called appearance), but that which exists in a form concordant with the standards of reason. 'Real' is the reasonable (rational), and that alone. For example, the state becomes a reality only when it corresponds to the given potentialities of men and permits their full development. Any preliminary form of the state is not yet reasonable, and, therefore, not yet real.

Hegel's concept of reason thus has a distinctly critical and polemic character. It is opposed to all ready acceptance of the given state of affairs. It denies the hegemony of every prevailing form of existence by demonstrating the antagonisms that dissolve it into other forms. We shall attempt to show that the 'spirit of contradicting' is the propulsive force of Hegel's dialectical method.[10]

In 1793, Hegel wrote to Schelling: 'Reason and freedom remain our principles.' In his early writings, no gap exists between the philosophical and the social meaning of these principles, which are expressed in the same revolutionary language the French Jacobins used. For example, Hegel says the significance of his time lies in the fact that 'the halo which has surrounded the leading oppressors and gods of the earth has disappeared. Philosophers demon-

[10] Hegel himself once characterized the essence of his dialectic as the 'spirit of contradicting' (Eckermann, *Gespräche mit Goethe in den letzten Jahren seines Lebens,* October 18, 1827).

strate the dignity of man; the people will learn to feel it and will not merely demand their rights, which have been trampled in the dust, but will themselves take them, —make them their own. Religion and politics have played the same game. The former has taught what despotism wanted to teach, contempt for humanity and the incapacity of man to achieve the good and to fulfill his essence through his own efforts.'[11] We even encounter more extreme statements, which urge that the realization of reason requires a social scheme that contravenes the given order. In the *Erstes Systemprogramm des Deutschen Idealismus,* written in 1796, we find the following: 'I shall demonstrate that, just as there is no idea of a machine, there is no idea of the State, for the State is something mechanical. Only that which is an object of freedom may be called an idea. We must, therefore, transcend the State. For every State is bound to treat free men as cogs in a machine. And this is precisely what it should not do; hence, the State must perish.'[12]

However, the radical purport of the basic idealistic concepts is slowly relinquished and they are to an ever increasing extent made to fit in with the prevailing societal form. This process is, as we shall see, necessitated by the conceptual structure of German idealism, which retains the decisive principles of liberalistic society and prevents any crossing beyond it.

The particular form, however, that the reconciliation between philosophy and reality assumed in Hegel's system was determined by the actual situation of Germany in the period when he elaborated his system. Hegel's early philosophical concepts were formulated amid a decaying German Reich. As he declared at the opening of his pamphlet

[11] Hegel, Letter to Schelling, April 1795, in *Briefe von und an Hegel,* ed. Karl Hegel, Leipzig 1887.

[12] *Dokumente zu Hegels Entwicklung,* ed. J. Hoffmeister, Stuttgart 1936, p. 219 f.

on the German Constitution (1802), the German state of the last decade of the eighteenth century was 'no longer a State.' The remains of feudal despotism still held sway in Germany, the more oppressive because split into a multitude of petty despotisms, each competing with the other. The Reich 'consisted of Austria and Prussia, the Prince-Electors, 94 ecclesiastical and secular princes, 103 barons, 40 prelates, and 51 Reich towns; in sum, it consisted of nearly 300 territories.' The Reich itself 'possessed not a single soldier, its yearly income amounting to only a few thousand florins.' There was no centralized jurisdiction; the Supreme Court (*Reichskammergericht*) was a breeding ground 'for graft, caprice, and bribery.' [13] Serfdom was still prevalent, the peasant was still a beast of burden. Some princes still hired out or sold their subjects as mercenary soldiers to foreign countries. Strong censorship operated to repress the slightest traces of enlightenment.[14] A contemporary depicts the current scene in the following words. 'Without law and justice, without protection from arbitrary taxation, uncertain of the lives of our sons, and of our freedom and our rights, the impotent prey of despotic power, our existence lacking unity and a national spirit . . .—this is the status quo of our nation.' [15]

In sharp contrast to France, Germany had no strong, conscious, politically educated middle class to lead the struggle against this absolutism. The nobility ruled without opposition. 'Hardly anyone in Germany,' remarked Goethe, 'thought of envying this tremendous privileged mass, or of begrudging them their happy advantages.' [16]

[13] T. Perthes, *Das Deutsche Staatsleben vor der Revolution,* Hamburg 1845, pp. 19, 34, 41. See also W. Wenck, *Deutschland vor hundert Jahren,* Leipzig 1887.

[14] K. T. von Heigel, *Deutsche Geschichte vom Tode Friedrichs des Grossen bis zur Auflösung des alten Reichs,* Stuttgart 1899 ff., vol. I, p. 77.

[15] J. Müller, in von Heigel, op. cit., p. 115.

[16] *Dichtung und Wahrheit,* in: *Werke, Cottasche Jubiläumsausgabe,* vol. XXII, p. 51.

The urban middle class, distributed among numerous townships, each with its own government and its own local interests, was impotent to crystallize and effectuate any serious opposition. To be sure, there were conflicts between the ruling patricians and the guilds and artisans. But these nowhere reached the proportions of a revolutionary movement. Burghers accompanied their petitions and complaints with a prayer that God protect the Fatherland from 'the terror of revolution.' [17]

Ever since the German Reformation, the masses had become used to the fact that, for them, liberty was an 'inner value,' which was compatible with every form of bondage, that due obedience to existing authority was a prerequisite to everlasting salvation, and that toil and poverty were a blessing in the eyes of the Lord. A long process of disciplinary training had introverted the demands for freedom and reason in Germany. One of the decisive functions of Protestantism had been to induce the emancipated individuals to accept the new social system that had arisen, by diverting their claims and demands from the external world into their inner life. Luther established Christian liberty as an internal value to be realized independently of any and all external conditions. Social reality became indifferent as far as the true essence of man was concerned. Man learned to turn upon himself his demand for the satisfaction of his potentialities and 'to seek within' himself, not in the outer world, his life's fulfillment.[18]

German culture is inseparable from its origin in Protestantism. There arose a realm of beauty, freedom, and morality, which was not to be shaken by external realities and

[17] von Heigel, op. cit., pp. 305-6.

[18] See *Studien über Autorität und Familie. Forschungsberichte aus dem Institut für Sozialforschung*, Paris 1936, p. 136 ff., and *Zeitschrift für Sozialforschung*, Paris 1936, vol. v, p. 188 ff.

struggles; it was detached from the miserable social world and anchored in the 'soul' of the individual. This development is the source of a tendency widely visible in German idealism, a willingness to become reconciled to the social reality. This reconciliatory tendency of the idealists constantly conflicts with their critical rationalism. Ultimately, the ideal that the critical aspects set forth, a rational political and social reorganization of the world, becomes frustrated and is transformed into a spiritual value.

The 'educated' classes isolated themselves from practical affairs and, thus rendering themselves impotent to apply their reason to the reshaping of society, fulfilled themselves in a realm of science, art, philosophy, and religion. That realm became for them the 'true reality' transcending the wretchedness of existing social conditions; it was alike the refuge for truth, goodness, beauty, happiness, and, most important, for a critical temper which could not be turned into social channels. Culture was, then, essentially idealistic, occupied with the *idea* of things rather than with the things themselves. It set freedom *of thought* before freedom *of action,* morality before practical justice, the inner life before the social life of man. This idealistic culture, however, just because it stood aloof from an intolerable reality and thereby maintained itself intact and unsullied, served, despite its false consolations and glorifications, as the repository for truths which had not been realized in the history of mankind.

Hegel's system is the last great expression of this cultural idealism, the last great attempt to render thought a refuge for reason and liberty. The original critical impulse of his thinking, however, was strong enough to induce him to abandon the traditional aloofness of idealism from history. He made philosophy a concrete historical factor and drew history into philosophy.

History, however, when comprehended, shatters the idealistic framework.

Hegel's system is necessarily associated with a definite political philosophy and with a definite social and political order. The dialectic between civil society and the state of the Restoration is not incidental in Hegel's philosophy, nor is it just a section of his *Philosophy of Right;* its principles already operate in the conceptual structure of his system. His basic concepts are, on the other hand, but the culmination of the entire tradition of Western thought. They become understandable only when interpreted within this tradition.

We have thus far attempted in brief compass to place the Hegelian concepts in their concrete historical setting. It remains for us to trace the starting point of Hegel's system to its sources in the philosophical situation of his time.

2. The Philosophical Setting

German idealism rescued philosophy from the attack of British empiricism, and the struggle between the two became not merely a clash of different philosophical schools, but a struggle for philosophy as such. Philosophy had never ceased to claim the right to guide man's efforts towards a rational mastery of nature and society, or to base this claim upon the fact that philosophy elaborated the highest and most general concepts for knowing the world. With Descartes, the practical bearing of philosophy assumed a new form, which accorded with the sweeping progress of modern technics. He announced a 'practical philosophy by means of which, knowing the force and the action of fire, water, air, the stars, heavens and all other bodies that environ us . . . we can employ them in all those uses to which they are adapted, and thus render ourselves the masters and possessors of nature.'[19]

The achievement of this task was, to an ever increasing extent, bound up with the establishment of universally valid laws and concepts in knowledge. Rational mastery of nature and society presupposed knowledge of the truth, and the truth was a universal, as contrasted to the multifold appearance of things or to their immediate form in the perception of individuals. This principle was already alive in the earliest attempts of Greek epistemology: the truth is universal and necessary and thus contradicts the ordinary experience of change and accident.

The conception, that the truth is contrary to the matters of fact of existence and independent of contingent individuals, has run through the entire historical epoch in which man's social life has been one of antagonisms among conflicting individuals and groups. The universal has been hypostatized as a philosophical reaction to the historical fact that, in society, only individual interests prevail, while the common interest is asserted only 'behind the back' of the individual. The contrast between universal and individual took on an aggravated form when, in the modern era, slogans of general freedom were raised and it was held that an appropriate social order could be brought about only through the knowledge and activity of emancipated individuals. All men were declared free and equal; yet, in acting according to their knowledge and in the pursuit of their interest, they created and experienced an order of dependence, injustice and recurring crises. The general competition between free economic subjects did not establish a rational community which might safeguard and gratify the wants and desires of all men. The life of men was surrendered to the economic

[19] *Discourse on Method*, part VI, in: *Philosophical Works*, ed. E. S. Haldane and G. R. T. Ross, Cambridge 1931, vol. I, p. 119.

mechanisms of a social system that related individuals to one another as isolated buyers and sellers of commodities. This actual lack of a rational community was responsible for the philosophical quest for the unity (*Einheit*) and universality (*Allgemeinheit*) of reason.

Does the structure of individual reasoning (the subjectivity) yield any general laws and concepts that might constitute universal standards of rationality? Can a universal rational order be built upon the autonomy of the individual? In expanding an affirmative answer to these questions, the epistemology of German idealism aimed at a unifying principle that would preserve the basic ideals of individualistic society without falling victim to its antagonisms. The British empiricists had demonstrated that not a single concept or law of reason could lay claim to universality, that the unity of reason is but the unity of custom or habit, adhering to the facts but never governing them. According to the German idealists, this attack jeopardized all efforts to impose an order on the prevailing forms of life. Unity and universality were not to be found in empirical reality; they were not given facts. Moreover, the very structure of empirical reality seemed to warrant the assumption that they could never be derived from the given facts. If men did not succeed, however, in creating unity and universality through their autonomous reason and even in contradiction to the facts, they would have to surrender not only their intellectual but also their material existence to the blind pressures and processes of the prevailing empirical order of life. The problem was thus not merely a philosophical one but concerned the historical destiny of humanity.

The German idealists recognized the concrete historical manifestations of the problem; this is clear in the fact that all of them connected the theoretical with the *practical* reason. There is a necessary transition from Kant's analysis of the transcendental consciousness to his demand for the community of a *Weltbürgerreich,* from Fichte's concept of the pure ego to his construction of a totally unified and regulated society (*der geschlossene Handelsstaat*); and from Hegel's idea of reason to his designation of the state as the union of the common and the individual interest, and thus as the realization of reason.

The idealistic counterattack was provoked not by the empiricist approaches of Locke and Hume, but by their refutation of general ideas. We have attempted to show that reason's right to shape reality depended upon man's ability to hold generally valid truths. Reason could lead beyond the brute fact of what is, to the realization of what ought to be, only by virtue of the universality and necessity of its concepts (which in turn are the criteria of its truth). These concepts the empiricists denied. General ideas, said Locke, are 'the inventions and creatures of the understanding, made by it for its own use, and concern only signs . . . When therefore we quit particulars, the generals that rest are only the creatures of our own making . . .' [20] For Hume, general ideas are abstracted from the particular, and 'represent' the particular and the particular only.[21] They can never provide universal rules or principles. If Hume was to be accepted, the claim of reason to organize reality had to be rejected. For as we have seen, this claim was based upon reason's faculty to attain truths, the validity of which was not derived from experience and which could in fact stand against experience. ''Tis not . . . reason, which is the guide of life, but custom.' [22] This conclusion of the empiricist investigations did more than

[20] *Essay Concerning Human Understanding,* book III, ch. 3, section ii, in: *Philosophical Works,* ed. J. A. St. John, London 1903, vol. II, p. 14.

[21] *A Treatise of Human Nature,* book I, part I, section VII, ed. L. A. Selby-Bigge, Oxford 1928, pp. 17 ff.

[22] Hume, *An Abstract of A Treatise of Human Nature,* published for the first time in 1938, Cambridge University Press, p. 16.

undermine metaphysics. It confined men within the limits of 'the given,' within the existing order of things and events. Whence could man obtain the right to go beyond not some particular within this order, but beyond the entire order itself? Whence could he obtain the right to submit this order to the judgment of reason? If experience and custom were to be the sole source of his knowledge and belief, how could he act against custom, how act in accordance with ideas and principles as yet not accepted and established? Truth could not oppose the given order or reason speak against it. The result was not only skepticism but conformism. The empiricist restriction of human nature to knowledge of 'the given' removed the desire both to transcend the given and to despair about it. 'For nothing is more certain, than that despair has almost the same effect upon us as enjoyment, and that we are no sooner acquainted with the impossibility of satisfying any desire, than the desire itself vanishes. When we see, that we have arrived at the utmost extent of human reason, we sit down contented.' [28]

The German idealists regarded this philosophy as expressing the abdication of reason. Attributing the existence of general ideas to the force of custom, and the principles by which reality is understood, to psychological mechanisms, was, to them, tantamount to a denial of truth and reason. Human psychology, they saw, is subject to change—is, in fact, a domain of uncertainty and chance from which no necessity and universality could be derived. And yet, such necessity and universality were the sole guarantee of reason. Unless, the idealists declared, the general concepts that claimed such necessity and universality could be shown to be more than the product of imagination, could be shown to draw their validity neither from experience nor from individual psychology, unless,

[28] Hume, *Treatise*, Introduction, p. xxii.

in other words, they were shown applicable to experience without arising from experience, reason would have to bow to the dictates of the empirical teaching. And if cognition by reason, that is, by concepts that are not derived from experience, means metaphysics, then the attack upon metaphysics was at the same time an attack upon the conditions of human freedom, for the right of reason to guide experience was a proper part of these conditions.

Kant adopted the view of the empiricists that all human knowledge begins with and terminates in experience, that experience alone provides *the material* for the concepts of reason. There is no stronger empiricist statement than that which opens his *Critique of Pure Reason.* 'All thought must, directly or indirectly, . . . relate ultimately to intuitions, and therefore, with us, to sensibility, because in no other way can an object be given to us.' Kant maintains, however, that the empiricists had failed to demonstrate that experience also furnishes the means and modes by which this empirical material is organized. If it could be shown that these principles of organization were the genuine possession of the human mind and did not arise from experience, then the independence and freedom of reason would be saved. Experience itself would become the product of reason, for it would then not be the disordered manifold of sensations and impressions, but the comprehensive organization of these.

Kant set out to prove that the human mind possessed the universal 'forms' that organized the manifold of data furnished to it by the senses. The forms of 'intuition' (space and time) and the forms of 'understanding' (the categories) are the universals through which the mind orders the sense manifold into the continuum of experience. They are *a priori* to each and every sensation and impression, so that we 'get' and arrange impressions under these forms. Experience presents a necessary and universal order only by virtue of the *a priori* activity of the human mind, which perceives all things and events in the form of space and time and comprehends them under the categories of unity, reality, substantiality, causality, and so on. These forms and categories are not derived from experience, for, as Hume had pointed out, no impression or sensation can be found that corresponds to them; yet experience, as an organized continuum, originates in them. They are universally valid and applicable because they constitute the very structure of the human mind. The world of objects, as a universal and necessary order, is produced by the subject—not by the individual, but by those acts of intuition and understanding that are common to all individuals, since they constitute the very conditions of experience.

This common structure of the mind Kant designates as 'transcendental consciousness.' It consists of the forms of intuition and of understanding, which, in Kant's analysis, are not static frames, but forms of operation that exist only in the act of apprehending and comprehending. The transcendental forms of intuition or outer sense synthesize the manifold of sense data into a spatio-temporal order. By virtue of the categories, the results of this are brought into the universal and necessary relations of cause and effect, substance, reciprocity, and so on. And this entire complex is unified in the 'transcendental apperception,' which relates all experience to the thinking ego, thereby giving experience the continuity of being 'my' experience. These processes of synthesis, *a priori* and common to all minds, hence universal, are interdependent and are brought to bear *in toto* in every act of knowledge.

What Kant calls the 'highest' synthesis, that of transcendental apperception, is the awareness of an 'I think,' which accompanies every experience. Through it, the thinking ego knows itself as continuous, present, and active throughout the series of its experiences. The transcendental apperception, therefore, is the ultimate basis for the unity of the subject and, hence, for the universality and necessity of all the objective relations.

Transcendental consciousness depends on the material received through the senses. The multitude of these impressions, however, becomes an organized world of coherent objects and relations only through the operations of transcendental consciousness. Since, then, we know the impressions only in the context of the *a priori* forms of the mind, we cannot know how or what the 'things-in-themselves' are that give rise to the impressions. These things-in-themselves, presumed to exist outside of the forms of the mind, remain completely unknowable.

Hegel regarded this skeptical element of Kant's philosophy as vitiating to his attempt to rescue reason from the empiricist onslaught. As long as the things-in-themselves were beyond the capacity of reason, reason remained a mere subjective principle without power over the objective structure of reality. And the world thus fell into two separate parts, subjectivity and objectivity, understanding and sense, thought and existence. This separation was not primarily an epistemological problem for Hegel. Time and again he stressed that the relation between subject and object, their opposition, denoted a concrete conflict in existence, and that its solution, the union of the opposites, was a matter of practice as well as of theory. Later, he described the historical form of the conflict as the 'alienation' (*Entfremdung*) of mind, signifying that the world of objects, originally the product of man's labor and knowledge, becomes independent of man and comes to be governed by uncontrolled forces and laws in which man no longer recognizes his own self. At the same time, thought becomes estranged from reality and the truth becomes an impotent ideal preserved in thought while the actual world is calmly left outside its influence. Unless man succeeds in reuniting the separated parts of his world and in bringing nature and society within the scope of his reason, he is forever doomed to frustration. The task of philosophy in this period of general disintegration is to demonstrate the principle that will restore the missing unity and totality.

Hegel sets forth this principle in the concept of reason. We have attempted to sketch the socio-historical and the philosophical roots of this concept which effect a tie between the progressive ideas of the French Revolution and the prevailing currents of philosophical discussion. Reason is the veritable form of reality in which all antagonisms of subject and object are integrated to form a genuine unity and universality. Hegel's philosophy is thus necessarily a system, subsuming all realms of being under the all-embracing idea of reason. The inorganic as well as the organic world, nature as well as society, are here brought under the sway of mind.

Hegel considered philosophy's systematic character to be a product of the historical situation. History had reached a stage at which the possibilities for realizing human freedom were at hand. Freedom, however, presupposes the reality of reason. Man could be free, could develop all his potentialities, only if his entire world was dominated by an integrating rational will and by knowledge. The Hegelian system anticipates a state in which this possibility has been achieved. The historical optimism that it breathes provided the basis for Hegel's so-called 'pan-logism' which treats every form of being as a form of reason. The transitions from the *Logic* to the *Philosophy of Nature,* and from the latter to the *Philosophy of Mind* are made on the assumption that the laws of nature spring from the rational structure of being and lead in a continuum to the laws of the mind. The realm of mind achieves in freedom what the realm of nature achieves in blind necessity—the fulfillment of the potentialities inherent in reality. It is this state of reality which Hegel refers to as 'the truth.'

Truth is not only attached to propositions and judgments, it is, in short, not only an attribute of thought, but of reality in process. Something is true if it is what it can be, fulfilling all its objective possibilities. In Hegel's language, it is then identical with its 'notion.'

The notion has a dual use. It comprehends the nature or essence of a subject-matter, and thus represents the true thought of it. At the same time, it refers to the actual realization of that nature or essence, its concrete existence. All fundamental concepts of the Hegelian system are characterized by the same ambiguity. They never denote mere concepts (as in formal logic), but forms or modes of being comprehended by thought. Hegel does not presuppose a mystical identity of thought and reality, but he holds that the right thought represents reality because the latter, in its development, has reached the stage at which it exists in conformity with the truth. His 'pan-logism' comes close to being its opposite: one could say that he takes the principles and forms of thought from the principles and forms of reality, so that the logical laws reproduce those governing the movement of reality. The unification of opposites is a process Hegel demonstrates in the case of every single existent. The logical form of the 'judgment' expresses an occurrence in reality. Take, for example, the judgment: this man is a slave. According to Hegel, it means that a man (the subject) has become enslaved (the predicate), but although he is a slave, he still remains man, thus essentially free and opposed to his predicament. The judgment does not attribute a predicate to a stable subject, but denotes an actual process of the subject whereby the latter becomes something other than itself. The subject *is* the very process of becoming the predicate and of contradicting it. This process dissolves into a multitude of antagonistic relations the stable subjects that traditional logic had assumed. Reality appears as a dynamic in which all fixed forms reveal themselves to be mere abstractions. Consequently, when in Hegel's logic concepts pass from one form to another, this refers to the fact that, to correct thinking, one form of being passes to another, and that every particular form can be determined only by the totality of the antagonistic relations in which this form exists.

We have emphasized the fact that, to Hegel, reality has reached a stage at which it exists in truth. This statement now needs a correction. Hegel does not mean that everything that exists does so in conformity with its potentialities, but that the mind has attained the self-consciousness of its freedom, and become capable of freeing nature and society. The realization of reason is not a fact but a task. The form in which the objects immediately appear is not yet their true form. What is simply given is at first negative, other than its real potentialities. It becomes true only in the process of overcoming this negativity, so that the birth of the truth requires the death of the given state of being. Hegel's optimism is based upon a destructive conception of the given. All forms are seized by the dissolving movement of reason which cancels and alters them until they are adequate to their notion. It is this movement that thought reflects in the process of 'mediation' (*Vermittlung*). If we follow the true content of our perceptions and concepts, all delimitation of stable objects collapses. They are dissolved into a multitude of relations that exhaust the developed content of these objects and terminate in the subject's comprehensive activity.

Hegel's philosophy is indeed what the subsequent reaction termed it, a negative philosophy. It is originally motivated by the conviction that the given facts that appear to common sense as the positive index of truth are in reality the negation of truth, so that truth can only be established by their destruction. The driving force of the dialectical method lies in this critical conviction. Dialectic in its entirety is linked to the conception that all forms of being are permeated by an essential negativity, and that this negativity determines their content and movement. The dialectic represents the counterthrust to any form of positivism. From Hume to the present-day logical positivists, the principle of this latter philosophy has been the ultimate authority of the fact, and observing the immediate given has been the ultimate method of verification. In the middle of the nineteenth century, and primarily in response to the destructive tendencies of rationalism, positivism assumed the peculiar form of an all-embracing 'positive philosophy,' which was to replace traditional metaphysics. The protagonists of this positivism took great pains to stress the conservative and affirmative attitude of their philosophy: it induces thought to be satisfied with the facts, to renounce any transgression beyond them, and to bow to the given state of affairs. To Hegel, the facts in themselves possess no authority. They are 'posited' (*gesetzt*) by the subject that has mediated them with the comprehensive process of its development. Verification rests, in the last analysis, with this process to which all facts are related and which determines their content. Everything that is given has to be justified before reason, which is but the totality of nature's and man's capacities.

Hegel's philosophy, however, which begins with the negation of the given and retains this negativity throughout, concludes with the declaration that history has achieved the reality of reason. His basic concepts were still bound up with the social structure of the prevailing system, and in this respect, too, German idealism may be said to have preserved the heritage of the French Revolution.

However, the 'reconciliation of idea and reality,' proclaimed in Hegel's *Philosophy of Right,* contains a decisive element that points beyond mere reconciliation. This element has been preserved and utilized in the later doctrine of the negation of philosophy. Philosophy reaches its end when it has formulated its view of a world in which reason is realized. If at that point reality contains the conditions necessary to materialize reason in fact, thought can cease to concern itself with the ideal. The truth now would require actual historical practice to fulfill it. With the relinquishment of the ideal, philosophy relinquishes its critical task and passes it to another agency. The final culmination of philosophy is thus at the same time its abdication. Released from its preoccupation with the ideal, philosophy is also released from its opposition to reality. This means that it ceases to be philosophy. It does not follow, however, that thought must then comply with the existing order. Critical thinking does not cease, but assumes a new form. The efforts of reason devolve upon social theory and social practice.

* * *

Hegel's philosophy shows five different stages of development:

1. The period from 1790 to 1800 marks the attempt to formulate a religious foundation for philosophy, exemplified in the collected papers of the period, the *Theologische Jugendschriften.*

2. 1800-1801 saw the formulation of Hegel's philosophical standpoint and interests through critical discussion of contemporary philosophical systems, especially those of Kant, Fichte, and Schelling. Hegel's main works of this period are the *Differenz des Fichteschen und Schellingschen Systems der Philosophie, Glauben und Wissen,* and other articles in the *Kritische Journal der Philosophie.*

3. The years 1801 to 1806 yielded the *Jenenser* system, the

earliest form of Hegel's complete system. This period was documented by the *Jenenser Logik und Metaphysik, Jenenser Realphilosophie,* and the *System der Sittlichkeit.*

4. 1807, the publication of the *Phenomenology of Mind.*

5. The period of the final system, which was outlined as early as 1808-11 in the *Philosophische Propädeutik,* but was not consummated until 1817. To this period belong the works that make up the bulk of Hegel's writing: *The Science of Logic* (1812-16), the *Encyclopaedia of the Philosophical Sciences* (1817, 1827, 1830), the *Philosophy of Right* (1821), and the various Berlin lectures on the Philosophy of History, the History of Philosophy, Esthetics, and Religion.

The elaboration of Hegel's philosophic system is accompanied by a series of political fragments that attempt to apply his new philosophical ideas to concrete historical situations. This process of referring philosophical conclusions to the context of social and political reality begins in 1798 with his historical and political studies; is followed by his *Die Verfassung Deutschlands* in 1802; and continues right through to 1831, when he wrote his study on the English Reform Bill. The connecting of his philosophy with the historical developments of his time makes Hegel's political writings a part of his systematic works, and the two must be treated together, so that his basic concepts are given philosophical as well as historical and political explanation.

I

Hegel's Early Theological Writings (1790-1800)

If we wish to partake of the atmosphere in which Hegel's philosophy originated, we must go back to the cultural and political setting of Southern Germany in the closing decades of the eighteenth century. In Württemberg, a country under the sway of a despotism that had just consented to some slight constitutional limitations on its power, the ideas of 1789 were beginning to exert a strong impact, particularly on intellectual youth. The period of that earlier cruel despotism seemed to have passed: the despotism under which the whole country was terrorized by constant military conscriptions for foreign wars, heavy arbitrary taxations, the sale of offices, the establishment of monopolies that plundered the masses and enriched the coffers of an extravagant prince, and sudden arrests that followed the slightest suspicions or stirrings of protest.[1] The conflicts between Duke Charles Eugene and the estates were mitigated by an agreement in 1770, and the most striking obstacle to the functioning of a centralized government was thus removed; but the result was only to divide absolutism between the personal rule of the duke and the interests of the feudal oligarchy.

The German enlightenment, however, this weaker counterpart of the English and French philosophy that had shattered the ideological framework of the absolutist state, had filtered into the cultural life of Württemberg: the

[1] See Karl Pfaff, *Geschichte des Fürstenhauses und Landes Wirtemberg*, Stuttgart 1839, Part III, section 2, pp. 82 ff.

duke was a pupil of the 'enlightened despot,' Frederick II of Prussia, and in the latter period of his rule he indulged in an enlightened absolutism. The spirit of the enlightenment went forward in the schools and universities that he promoted. Religious and political problems were discussed in terms of eighteenth century rationalism, the dignity of man was extolled, as was his right to shape his own life against all obsolete forms of authority and tradition, and tolerance and justice were praised. But the young generation that was then attending the theological University of Tübingen—among them Hegel, Schelling, and Hölderlin—was above all impressed by the contrast between these ideals and the miserable actual condition of the German Reich. There was not the slightest chance for the rights of man to take their place in a reorganized state and society. True, the students sang revolutionary songs and translated the *Marseillaise;* they perhaps planted liberty trees and shouted against the tyrants and their henchmen; but they knew that all this activity was an impotent protest against the still impregnable forces that held the fatherland in their grip. All that could be hoped for was a modicum of constitutional reform, which might better balance the weight of power between the prince and the estates.

In these circumstances, the eyes of the young generation turned longingly towards the past and particularly to those periods of history in which unity had prevailed between the intellectual culture of men and their social and political life. Hölderlin drew a glowing picture of ancient Greece, and Hegel wrote a glorification of the ancient city-state, which at points even outshone the exalted description of early Christianity that the theological student set down. We find that a political interest time and again broke into the discussion of religious problems in Hegel's early theological fragments. Hegel ardently strove to recapture the power that had produced and maintained, in the ancient republics, the living unity of all spheres of culture and that had generated the free development of all national forces. He spoke of this hidden power as the *Volksgeist:* 'The spirit of a nation, its history, religion and the degree of political freedom it has reached cannot be separated one from the other, neither as regards their influence nor as regards their quality; they are interwoven in one bond . . .'[2]

Hegel's use of the *Volksgeist* is closely related to Montesquieu's use of the *esprit général* of a nation as the basis for its social and political laws. The 'national spirit' is not conceived as a mystical or metaphysical entity, but represents the whole of the natural, technical, economic, moral, and intellectual conditions that determine the nation's historical development. Montesquieu's emphasis on this historical basis was directed against the unjustifiable retention of outmoded political forms. Hegel's concept of the *Volksgeist* kept these critical implications. Instead of following the various influences of Montesquieu, Rousseau, Herder, and Kant on Hegel's theological studies, we shall limit ourselves to the elaboration of Hegel's main interest.

Hegel's theological discussion repeatedly asks what the true relation is between the individual and a state that no longer satisfies his capacities but exists rather as an 'estranged' institution from which the active political interest of the citizens has disappeared. Hegel defined this state with almost the same categories as those of eighteenth century liberalism: the state rests on the consent of individuals, it circumscribes their rights and duties and protects its members from those internal and external dangers that might threaten the perpetuation of the whole. The individual, as opposed to the state, possesses the in-

[2] *Theologische Jugendschriften,* p. 27.

alienable rights of man, and with these the state power can under no circumstances interfere, not even if such interference may be in the individual's own interest. 'No man can relinquish his right to give unto himself the law and to be solely responsible for its execution. If this right is renounced, man ceases to be man. It is not the state's business, however, to prevent him from renouncing it, for this would mean to compel man to be man, and would be force.'[3] Here is nothing of that moral and metaphysical exaltation of the state which we encounter in Hegel's later works.

The tone slowly changed, however, within the very same period of Hegel's life and even within the same body of his writings, and he came to consider it as man's historical 'fate,' a cross to be borne, that he accept social and political relations that restrict his full development. Hegel's enlightened optimism and his tragic praise of a lost paradise were replaced by an emphasis on historical necessity. Historical necessity had brought about a gulf between the individual and the state. In the early period they were in a 'natural' harmony, but one attained at the expense of the individual, for man did not possess conscious freedom and was not master of the social process. And the more 'natural' this early harmony was, the more easily could it be dissolved by the uncontrolled forces that then ruled the social world. 'In Athens and Rome, successful wars, increasing wealth, and an acquaintance with luxury and greater convenience of life produced an aristocracy of war and wealth' that destroyed the republic and caused the complete loss of political liberty.[4] State power fell into the hands of certain privileged individuals and groups, with the vast mass of the citizens pursuing only their private interest without regard for the common

[3] Ibid., p. 212.

[4] Ibid., p. 222.

good; 'the right to security of property' now became their whole world.[5]

Hegel's efforts to comprehend the universal laws governing this process led him inevitably to an analysis of the role of the social institutions in the progress of history. One of his historical fragments, written after 1797, opens with the sweeping declaration that 'security of property is the pivot on which the whole of modern legislation turns,' [6] and in the first draft to his pamphlet on *Die Verfassung Deutschlands* (1798-9), he states that the historical form of 'bourgeois property' (*bürgerliches Eigentum*) is responsible for the prevailing political disintegration.[7] Moreover, Hegel maintained that the social institutions had distorted even the most private and personal relations between men. There is a significant fragment in the *Theologische Jugendschriften*, called *Die Liebe*, in which Hegel states that ultimate harmony and union between individuals in love is prevented because of the 'acquisition and possession of property as well as rights.' The lover, he explains, 'who must look upon his or her beloved as the owner of property must also come to feel his or her particularity' militating against the community of their life—a particularity that consists in his or her being bound up with 'dead things' that do not belong to the other and remain of necessity outside of their unity.[8]

The institution of property Hegel here related to the fact that man had come to live in a world that, though molded by his own knowledge and labor, was no longer his, but rather stood opposed to his inner needs—a strange world governed by inexorable laws, a 'dead' world in which human life is frustrated. The *Theologische Jugendschriften* present in these terms the earliest formulation

[5] Ibid., p. 223.
[6] *Dokumente zu Hegels Entwicklung*, p. 268.
[7] Ibid., p. 286.
[8] *Theologische Jugendschriften*, pp. 381-2.

of the concept of 'alienation' (*Entfremdung*), which was destined to play a decisive part in the future development of the Hegelian philosophy.

Hegel's first discussion of religious and political problems strikes the pervasive note that the loss of unity and liberty—a historical fact—is the general mark of the modern era and the factor that characterizes all conditions of private and societal life. This loss of freedom and unity, Hegel says, is patent in the numerous conflicts that abound in human living, especially in the conflict between man and nature. This conflict, which turned nature into a hostile power that had to be mastered by man, has led to an antagonism between idea and reality, between thought and the real, between consciousness and existence.[9] Man constantly finds himself set off from a world that is adverse and alien to his impulses and desires. How, then, is this world to be restored to harmony with man's potentialities?

At first, Hegel's answer was that of the student of theology. He interpreted Christianity as having a basic function in world history, that of giving a new 'absolute' center to man and a final goal to life. Hegel could also see, however, that the revealed truth of the Gospel could not fit in with the expanding social and political realities of the world, for the Gospel appealed essentially to the individual as an individual detached from his social and political nexus; its essential aim was to save the individual and not society or the state. It was therefore not religion that could solve the problem, or theology that could set forth principles to restore freedom and unity. As a result, Hegel's interest slowly shifted from theological to philosophical questions and concepts.

Hegel always viewed philosophy not as a special science but as the ultimate form of human knowledge. The need

[9] Ibid., p. 244.

for philosophy he derived from the need to remedy the general loss of freedom and unity. He explicitly stated this in his first philosophical article. 'The need for philosophy arises when the unifying power [*die Macht der Vereinigung*] has disappeared from the life of men, when the contradictions have lost their living interrelation and interdependence and assumed an independent form.' [10] The unifying force he speaks of refers to the vital harmony of the individual and common interest, which prevailed in the ancient republics and which assured the liberty of the whole and integrated all conflicts into the living unity of the *Volksgeist*. When this harmony was lost, man's life became overwhelmed by pervasive conflicts that could no longer be controlled by the whole. We have already mentioned the terms in which Hegel characterized these conflicts: nature was set against man, reality was estranged from 'the idea' and consciousness opposed to existence. He next summarized all these oppositions as having the general form of a conflict between subject and object,[11] and in this way he connected his historical problem to the philosophical one that had dominated European thought since Descartes. Man's knowledge and will had been pushed into a 'subjective' world, whose self-certainty and freedom confronted an objective world of uncertainty and physical necessity. The more Hegel saw that the contradictions were the universal form of reality, the more philosophical his discussion became—only the most universal concepts could now grasp the contradictions, and only the ultimate principles of knowledge could yield the principles to resolve them.

At the same time, even the most abstract of Hegel's concepts retained the concrete denotation of his questions.

[10] 'Differenz des Fichteschen und Schellingschen Systems,' in *Erste Druckschriften*, ed. Georg Lasson, Leipzig 1913, p. 14.

[11] Ibid., p. 13.

Philosophy was charged with a historical mission—to give an exhaustive analysis of the contradictions prevailing in reality and to demonstrate their possible unification. The dialectic developed out of Hegel's view that reality was a structure of contradictions. The *Theologische Jugendschriften* still covered the dialectic over with a theological framework, but even there the philosophical beginnings of the dialectical analysis can already be traced.

The first concept Hegel introduces as the unification of contradictions is the concept of life.

We might better understand the peculiar role Hegel attributed to the idea of life if we recognize that for him all contradictions are resolved and yet preserved in 'reason.' Hegel conceived life as mind, that is to say, as a being able to comprehend and master the all-embracing antagonisms of existence. In other words, Hegel's concept of life points to the life of a rational being and to man's unique quality among all other beings. Ever since Hegel, the idea of life has been the starting point for many efforts to reconstruct philosophy in terms of man's concrete historical circumstance and to overcome thereby the abstract and remote character of rationalist philosophy.[12]

Life is distinguished from all other modes of being by its unique relation to its determinations and to the world as a whole. Each inanimate object is, by virtue of its particularity and its limited and determinate form, different from and opposed to the genus; the particular contradicts the universal, so that the latter does not fulfill itself in the former. The living, however, differs from the non-living in this respect, for life designates a being whose different parts and states (*Zustände*) are integrated into a complete unity, that of a 'subject.' In life, 'the particular . . . is at the same time a branch of the infinite tree of

[12] See Wilhelm Dilthey, *Die Jugendgeschichte Hegels*, in *Gesammelte Schriften*, Leipzig 1921, vol. IV, pp. 144 ff.

Life; every part outside the whole is at the same time the whole, Life.' [13] Each living individual is also a manifestation of the whole of life, in other words, possesses the full essence or potentialities of life. Furthermore, though every living being is determinate and limited, it can supersede its limitations by virtue of the power it possesses as a living subject. Life is at first a sequence of determinate 'objective' conditions—objective, because the living subject finds them outside of its self, limiting its free self-realization. The process of life, however, consists in continuously drawing these external conditions into the enduring unity of the subject. The living being maintains itself as a self by mastering and annexing the manifold of determinate conditions it finds, and by bringing all that is opposed to itself into harmony with itself. The unity of life, therefore, is not an immediate and 'natural' one, but the result of a constant active overcoming of everything that stands against it. It is a unity that prevails only as the result of a process of 'mediation' (*Vermittlung*) between the living subject as it is and its objective conditions. The mediation is the proper function of the living self as an actual subject, and at the same time it *makes* the living self an actual subject. Life is the first form in which the substance is conceived as subject and is thus the first embodiment of freedom. It is the first model of a real unification of opposites and hence the first embodiment of the dialectic.

Not all forms of life, however, represent such a complete unity. Only man, by virtue of his knowledge, can achieve 'the idea of Life.' We have already indicated that for Hegel a perfect union of subject and object is a prerequisite to freedom. The union presupposes a knowledge of the truth, meaning thereby a knowledge of the potentialities of both subject and object. Man alone is able to transform objective conditions so that they become a medium

[13] *Theologische Jugendschriften*, p. 307.

for his subjective development. And the truth he holds frees not only his own potencies, but those of nature as well. He brings the truth into the world, and with it is able to organize the world in conformity with reason. Hegel illustrates this point in the mission of John the Baptist, and for the first time advances the view that the world is in its very essence the product of man's historical activity. The world and all 'its relations and determinations are the work of the ἀνθρώπου φωτός, of man's self-development.' [14] The conception of the world as a product of human activity and knowledge henceforth persists as the driving force of Hegel's system. At this very early stage, we can already discover the features of the later dialectical theory of society.

'Life' is not the most advanced philosophic concept that Hegel attained in his first period. The *Systemfragment,* in which he gives a more precise elaboration of the philosophic import of the antagonism between subject and object and between man and nature, uses the term mind (*Geist*) to designate the unification of these disparate domains. Mind is essentially the same unifying agency as life—'Infinite Life may be called a Mind because Mind connotes the living unity amid the diversity . . . Mind is the living law that unifies the diversity so that the latter becomes living.' [15] But although it means no more than life, the concept mind lays emphasis on the fact that the unity of life is, in the last analysis, the work of the subject's free comprehension and activity, and not of some blind natural force.

The *Theologische Jugendschriften* yield yet another concept that points far into Hegel's later logic. In a fragment entitled *Glauben und Wissen,* Hegel declares, 'Unification and Being [*Sein*] are equivalent; the copula "is"

[14] Ibid., p. 307.

[15] P. 347.

in every proposition expresses a unification of subject and predicate, in other words, a Being.'[16] An adequate interpretation of this statement would require a thorough discussion of the basic developments in European philosophy since Aristotle. We can here only intimate some of the background and content of the formulation.

Hegel's statement implies that there is a distinction between 'to be' (*Sein*) and being (*Seiendes*), or, between determinate being and being-as-such. The history of Western philosophy opened with the same distinction, made in answer to the question, What is Being? which animated Greek philosophy from Parmenides to Aristotle. Every being around us is a determinate one: a stone, a tool, a house, an animal, an event, and so on. But we predicate of every such being that it *is* thus and so; that is, we attribute being to it. And this being that we attribute to it is not any particular thing in the world, but is common to all the particular beings to which it can be attributed. This points to the fact that there must be a being-as-such that is different from every determinate being and yet attributable to every being whatsoever, so that it can be called the real 'one' in all the diversity of determinate beings. Being-as-such is what all particular beings have in common and is, as it were, their substratum. From this point, it was comparatively easy to take this most universal being as 'the essence of all being,' 'divine substance,' 'the most real,' and thus to combine ontology with theology. This tradition is operative in Hegel's *Logic*.

Aristotle was the first to regard this being-as-such that is attributed alike to every determinate being not as a separate metaphysical entity but as the process or movement through which every particular being molds itself into what it *really* is. According to Aristotle, there is a distinction that runs through the whole realm of being

[16] P. 383.

between the essence (οὐσία) and its diverse accidental states and modifications (τὰ συμβεβηκότα). Real being, in the strict sense, is the essence, by which is meant the concrete individual thing, organic as well as inorganic. The individual thing is the subject or substance enduring throughout a movement in which it unifies and holds together the various states and phases of its existence. The different modes of being represent various modes of unifying antagonistic relations; they refer to different modes of persisting through change, of originating and perishing, of having properties and limitations, and so on. And Hegel incorporates the basic Aristotelian conception into his philosophy: 'The different modes of being are more or less complete unifications.'[17] Being means unifying, and unifying means movement. Movement, in turn, Aristotle defines in terms of potentiality and actuality. The various types of movement denote various ways of realizing the potentialities inherent in the essence or moving thing. Aristotle evaluates the types of movement so that the highest type is that in which each and every potentiality is fully realized. A being that moves or develops according to the highest type would be pure ἐνέργεια. It would have no material of realization outside of or alien to itself, but would be entirely itself at every moment of its existence. If such a being were to exist, its whole existence would consist in thinking. A subject whose self-activity is thought has no estranged and external object; thinking 'grasps' and holds the object as thought, and reason apprehends reason. The veritable being is veritable movement, and the latter is the activity of perfect unification of the subject with its object. The true Being is therefore thought and reason.

Hegel concludes his presentation in the *Encyclopaedia of the Philosophical Sciences* with the paragraph from Aristotle's *Metaphysics* in which the veritable being is

[17] P. 384.

explained to be reason. This is significant as more than a mere illustration. For, Hegel's philosophy is in a large sense a re-interpretation of Aristotle's ontology, rescued from the distortion of metaphysical dogma and linked to the pervasive demand of modern rationalism that the world be transformed into a medium for the freely developing subject, that the world become, in short, the reality of reason. Hegel was the first to rediscover the extremely dynamic character of the Aristotelian metaphysic, which treats all being as process and movement—a dynamic that had got entirely lost in the formalistic tradition of Aristotelianism.

Aristotle's conception that reason is the veritable being is carried through by sundering this being from the rest of the world. The νους-θεός is neither the cause nor creator of the world, and is its prime mover only through a complicated system of intermediaries. Human reason is but a weak copy of this νους-θεός. Nevertheless, the life of reason is the highest life and highest good on earth.

The conception is intimately connected with a reality offering no adequate fulfillment of the proper potentialities of men and things, so that the fulfillment was located in an activity that was most independent of the prevailing incongruencies of reality. The elevation of the realm of mind to the position of the sole domain of freedom and reason was conditioned by a world of anarchy and bondage. The historical conditions still prevailed in Hegel's time; the visible potentialities were actualized in neither society nor nature, and men were not free subjects of their lives. And since ontology is the doctrine of the most general forms of being and as such reflects human insight into the most general structure of reality, there can be little wonder that the basic concepts of Aristotelian and Hegelian ontology were the same.

II

Towards the System of Philosophy (1800-1802)

1. The First Philosophical Writings

In 1801, Hegel began his academic career in Jena, then the philosophic center of Germany. Fichte had taught there until 1799, and Schelling was appointed professor in 1798. Kant's social and legal philosophy, his *Metaphysik der Sitten,* had been published in 1799, and his revolutionizing of philosophy in his three *Critiques of Reason* still exerted a prime influence on intellectual life. Quite naturally, therefore, Hegel's first philosophical articles centered about the doctrines of Kant, Fichte, and Schelling, and he formulated his problems in terms of the currents of discussion among the German idealists.

As we have seen, Hegel took the view that philosophy arises from the all-embracing contradictions into which human existence has been plunged. These have shaped the history of philosophy as the history of basic contradictions, those between 'mind and matter, soul and body, belief and understanding, freedom and necessity,' contradictions that had more recently appeared as those between 'reason and sense' (*Sinnlichkeit*), 'intelligence and nature,' and, in the most general form, 'subjectivity and objectivity.'[1] These were the very concepts that lay at the root of Kant's *Critique of Pure Reason,* and the ones Hegel now dissolved in his dialectical analysis.

The first concept Hegel subjected to dialectical re-interpretation was that of reason. Kant had made the basic

[1] *Erste Druckschriften,* p. 13.

distinction between reason (*Vernunft*) and understanding (*Verstand*). Hegel gave both concepts new meaning and made them the starting point of his method. For him, the distinction between understanding and reason is the same as that between common sense and speculative thinking, between undialectical reflection and dialectical knowledge. The operations of the understanding yield the usual type of thinking that prevails in everyday life as well as in science. The world is taken as a multitude of determinate things, each of which is demarcated from the other. Each thing is a distinct delimited entity related as such to other likewise delimited entities. The concepts that are developed from these beginnings, and the judgments composed of these concepts, denote and deal with isolated things and the fixed relations between such things. The individual determinations exclude one another as if they were atoms or monads. The one is not the other and can never become the other. To be sure, things change, and so do their properties, but when they do so, one property or determination disappears and another takes its place. An entity that is isolated and delimited in this way Hegel calls 'finite' (*das Endliche*).

Understanding, then, conceives a world of finite entities, governed by the principle of identity and opposition. Everything is identical with itself and with nothing else; it is, by virtue of its self-identity, opposed to all other things. It can be connected and combined with them in many ways, but it never loses its own identity and never becomes something other than itself. When red litmus paper turns blue or day changes to night, a here and now existent ceases to be here and now, and some other thing takes its place. When a child becomes a man one set of properties, those of childhood, is replaced by another, those of manhood. Red and blue, light and dark, childhood and manhood, eternally remain irreconcilable oppositions. The operations of understanding thus divide the world into numberless polarities, and Hegel uses the expression 'isolated reflection' (*isolierte Reflection*) to characterize the manner in which understanding forms and connects its polar concepts.

The rise and spread of this kind of thinking Hegel connects with the origin and prevalence of certain relationships in human life.[2] The antagonisms of 'isolated reflection' express real antagonisms. Thinking could come to understand the world as a fixed system of isolated things and indissoluble oppositions only when the world had become a reality removed from the true wants and needs of mankind.

Isolation and opposition are not, however, the final state of affairs. The world must not remain a complex of fixed disparates. The unity that underlies the antagonisms must be grasped and realized by reason, which has the task of reconciling the opposites and 'sublating' them in a true unity. The fulfillment of reason's task would at the same time involve restoring the lost unity in the social relations of men.

As distinguished from the understanding, reason is motivated by the need 'to restore the totality.' [3] How can this be done? First, says Hegel, by undermining the false security that the perceptions and manipulations of the understanding provide. The common-sense view is one of 'indifference' and 'security,' 'the indifference of security.' [4] Satisfaction with the given state of reality and acceptance of its fixed and stable relations make men indifferent to the as yet unrealized potentialities that are not 'given' with the same certainty and stability as the objects of sense. Common sense mistakes the accidental appearance of things for their essence, and persists in believing that there is an immediate identity of essence and existence.[5]

[2] Ibid., pp. 14-15. [3] P. 16. [4] P. 22. [5] Pp. 22-3.

The identity of essence and existence, *per contra,* can only result from the enduring effort of reason to create it. It comes about only through a conscious putting into action of knowledge, the primary condition for which is the abandonment of common sense and mere understanding for 'speculative thinking.' Hegel insists that only this kind of thinking can get beyond the distorting mechanisms of the prevailing state of being. Speculative thinking compares the apparent or given form of things to the potentialities of those same things, and in so doing distinguishes their essence from their accidental state of existence. This result is achieved not through some process of mystical intuition, but by a method of conceptual cognition, which examines the process whereby each form has become what it is. Speculative thinking conceives 'the intellectual and material world' not as a totality of fixed and stable relations, but 'as a becoming, and its being as a product and a producing.' [6]

What Hegel calls speculative thinking is in effect his earliest presentation of dialectical method. The relation between dialectical thinking (reason) and isolating reflection (understanding) is clearly defined. The former criticizes and supersedes the fixed oppositions created by the latter. It undermines the 'security' of common sense and demonstrates that 'what common sense regards as immediately certain does not have any reality for philosophy.' [7] The first criterion of reason, then, is a distrust of matter-of-fact authority. Such distrust is the real skepticism that Hegel designates as 'the free portion' of every true philosophy.[8]

The form of reality that is immediately given is, then, no final reality. The system of isolated things in opposition, produced by the operations of the understanding,

[6] P. 14. [7] Ibid., p. 22.
[8] 'Verhältnis des Skeptizismus zur Philosophie,' in op. cit., p. 175.

must be recognized for what it is: a 'bad' form of reality, a realm of limitation and bondage. The 'realm of freedom,' [9] which is the inherent goal of reason, cannot be achieved, as Kant and Fichte thought, by playing off the subject against the objective world, attributing to the autonomous person all the freedom that is lacking in the external world, and leaving the latter a domain of blind necessity. (Hegel is here striking against the important mechanism of 'internalizing' or introversion, by which philosophy and literature generally have made liberty into an inner value to be realized within the soul alone.) In the final reality there can be no isolation of the free subject from the objective world; that antagonism must be resolved, together with all the others created by the understanding.

The final reality in which the antagonisms are resolved Hegel terms 'the Absolute.' At this stage of his philosophical development he can describe this absolute only negatively. Thus, it is quite the reverse of the reality apprehended by common sense and understanding; it 'negates' common-sense reality in every detail, so that the absolute reality has no single point of resemblance to the finite world.

Whereas common sense and the understanding had perceived isolated entities that stood opposed one to the other, reason apprehends 'the identity of the opposites.' It does not produce the identity by a process of connecting and combining the opposites, but transforms them so that they cease to exist as opposites, although their content is preserved in a higher and more 'real' form of being. The process of unifying opposites touches every part of reality and comes to an end only when reason has 'organized' the whole so that 'every part exists only in relation to the whole,' and 'every individual entity has meaning and significance only in its relation to the totality.' [10]

[9] 'Differenz des Fichteschen und Schellingschen Systems,' p. 18.
[10] Ibid., p. 21.

The totality of the concepts and cognitions of reason alone represents the absolute. Reason, therefore, is fully before us only in the form of an all-embracing 'organization of propositions and intuitions,' that is, as a 'system.' [11] We shall explain the concrete import of these ideas in the next chapter. Here, in his first philosophical writings, Hegel intentionally emphasizes the negative function of reason: its destruction of the fixed and secure world of common sense and understanding. The absolute is referred to as 'Night' and 'nothing,' [12] to contrast it to the clearly defined objects of everyday life. Reason signifies the 'absolute annihilation' of the common-sense world.[13] For, as we have already said, the struggle against common sense is the beginning of speculative thinking, and the loss of everyday security is the origin of philosophy.

Hegel gives further clarification to his position in the article 'Glauben und Wissen,' in which he contrasts his conclusions to those of Kant's *Critique of Pure Reason.* The empirical principle that Kant retained by making reason dependent on 'given' objects of experience is here rejected completely. In Kant, Hegel declares, reason is limited to an inner realm of the mind and is made powerless over 'things-in-themselves.' In other words, it is not really reason but the understanding that holds sway in the Kantian philosophy.

On the other hand, Hegel makes special mention of the fact that Kant did overcome this limitation at many points. For example, the notion of an 'original synthetic unity of apperception' recognizes Hegel's own principles of the original identity of opposites,[14] for the 'synthetic unity' is properly an activity by which the antagonism between subject and object is produced and simultaneously overcome.

[11] Pp. 25, 34-5. [12] P. 16. [13] P. 17.
[14] 'Glauben und Wissen,' in op. cit., p. 240.

Kant's philosophy therefore 'contains the true form of thought' as far as this concept is concerned, namely, the triad of subject, object, and their synthesis.[15]

This is the first point at which Hegel makes the claim that the triad (*Triplizität*) is the true form of thought. He does not state it as an empty schema of thesis, antithesis, and synthesis, but as the dynamic unity of opposites. It is the proper form of thought because it is the proper form of a reality in which every being is the synthetic unity of antagonistic conditions.

Traditional logic has recognized this fact in setting forth the form of the judgment as *S* is *P*. We have already hinted at Hegel's interpretation of this form. To know what a thing really is, we have to get beyond its immediately given state (*S* is *S*) and follow out the process in which it turns into something other than itself (*P*). In the process of becoming *P*, however, *S* still remains *S*. Its reality is the entire dynamic of its turning into something else and unifying itself with its 'other.' The dialectical pattern represents, and is thus 'the truth of,' a world permeated by negativity, a world in which everything is something other than it *really* is, and in which opposition and contradiction constitute the laws of progress.

2. The First Political Writings

The critical interests of dialectical philosophy are clearly illustrated by Hegel's important political pamphlets of this period. These show that the condition in which the German Reich found itself after its unsuccessful war with the French Republic had a place at the root of Hegel's early works.

The universal contradictions that, according to Hegel,

[15] Ibid., p. 247.

animate philosophy concretely exist in the antagonisms and disunity among the numerous German states and estates and between each of these and the Reich. The 'isolation' that Hegel had demonstrated in his philosophical articles is manifest in the stubborn way in which not only each estate but practically each individual pursues his own particular interest without any consideration for the whole. The consequent 'loss of unity' has reduced the Imperial power to complete impotence and left the Reich an easy prey to any aggressor.

> Germany is no longer a state . . . If Germany were still to be called a state, its present condition of decay could only be called anarchy, were it not for the fact that her component parts have constituted themselves as states. It is only the remembrance of a past tie and not any actual union that gives them the appearance of unity . . . In her war with the French Republic Germany has come to realize that she is no longer a state . . . The obvious results of this war are the loss of some of the most beautiful of the German lands, and of some millions of her population, a public debt (even larger in the south than in the north) which carries the agonies of the war into peace-time, and the result that besides those who have fallen under the power of conquerors and foreign laws and morals, many states will lose their highest good in the bargain, that is, their independence.[16]

Hegel goes on to cxamine the basis for the disintegration. The German constitution, he finds, no longer corresponds to the actual social and economic state of the nation. The constitution is a vestige of an old feudal order that has long since been replaced by a different order, that of individualistic society.[17] The retention of the old form of constitution in the face of the radical change that has taken place in all social relations is tantamount to maintaining a given condition simply because it is given. Such

[16] 'Die Verfassung Deutschlands,' in *Schriften zur Politik und Rechtsphilosophie*, pp. 3-4.

[17] Ibid., p. 7, *note*.

a practice is opposed to every standard and dictate of reason. The prevailing ordering of life is in sharp conflict with the desires and needs of society; it has lost 'all its power and all its dignity' and has become 'purely negative.' [18]

And, Hegel continues, that which persists in this 'merely empirical manner,' without being 'adapted to the idea of reason,' cannot be regarded as 'real.' [19] The political system has to be destroyed and transformed into a new rational order. Such a transformation cannot be made without violence.

The extreme realism of Hegel's position shows through the idealistic framework and terminology. 'The notion of and insight into necessity are much too weak to effect action. The notion and the insight are accompanied by so much distrust that they have to be justified by violence; only then does man submit to them.' [20] The notion can be justified by violence only in so far as it expresses an actual historical force that has ripened in the lap of the existing order. The notion contradicts reality when the latter has become self-contradictory. Hegel says that a prevailing social form can be successfully attacked by thought only if this form has come into open contradiction with its own 'truth,' [21] in other words, if it can no longer fulfill the demands of its own contents. This is the case with Germany, Hegel holds. There, the champions of the new order represent historical forces that have outgrown the old system. The state, which should perpetuate the common interest of its members in an appropriate rational form—for such alone would be its 'truth'—does not do this. For this reason, the rulers of the state speak falsely when they defend their position in the name of the common interest.[22] Their foes, not they, represent the common

[18] P. 139. [19] P. 3. [20] P. 136. [21] P. 140. [22] Ibid.

interest, and their notion, the idea of the new order they uphold, is not merely an ideal but the expression of a reality that no longer endures in the prevailing order.

Hegel's point is that the old order has to be replaced by a 'true community' (*Allgemeinheit*). *Allgemeinheit* means at one and the same time, first, a society in which all particular and individual interests are integrated into the whole, so that the actual social organism that results accords with the common interest (community), and, second, a totality in which all the different isolated concepts of knowledge are fused and integrated so that they receive their significance in their relation to the whole (universality). The second meaning is obviously the counterpart of the first. Just as the conception of disintegration in the sphere of knowledge expresses the existing disintegration of human relations in society, so the philosophical integration corresponds to a social and political integration. The universality of reason, represented by the absolute, is the philosophical counterpart of the social community in which all particular interests are unified into the whole.

A real state, Hegel holds, institutionalizes the common interest and defends it in all external and internal conflicts.[23] The German Reich, Hegel declares, does not have this character.

> Political powers and rights are not public offices set up to accord with the organization of the whole, nor are the acts and duties of the individual determined by the needs of the whole. Each particular part of the political hierachy, each princely house, each estate, town, corporation, and so on, in short, everyone who has rights in or duties toward the state has acquired them through his own power. The state, in view of the encroachment on its own power, can do no more than confirm that it has been deprived of its power . . .[24]

[23] Pp. 13, 17-18.

[24] P. 10.

Hegel explains the breakdown of the German state by contrasting the feudal system with the new order of individualist society that succeeded it. The rise of the latter social order is explained in terms of the development of private property. The feudal system proper integrated the particular interests of the different estates into a true community. The freedom of the group or of the individual was not essentially opposed to the freedom of the whole. In modern times, however, 'exclusive property has completely isolated the particular needs from each other.'[25] People speak of the universality of private property as if it were common to all of society and therefore, perhaps, an integrating unity. But this universality, says Hegel, is only an abstract legal fiction; in reality, private property remains 'something isolated' that has no relation to the whole.[26] The only unity that can be achieved among property owners is the artificial one of a universally applied legal system. Laws, however, stabilize and codify only the existing anarchic conditions of private ownership and thus transform the state or the community into an institution that exists for the sake of particular interests. 'Possession existed prior to law and did not originate from law. That which had already been privately appropriated was made a legal right . . . German constitutional law is therefore in the proper sense private law, and political rights are legalized forms of possession, property rights.'[27] A state wherein the antagonistic private interests are thus made pre-eminent in all fields may not be called a true community. Moreover, Hegel declares, 'The struggle to make the state power into private property dissolves the state and brings about the destruction of its power.'[28]

The state, taken over by private interests, must nevertheless at least assume the appearance of a true community

[25] P. 9, *note*. [26] P. 11, *note*. [27] Ibid. [28] P. 13.

in order to put down general warfare and to defend equally the property rights of all its members. The community thus becomes an independent power, elevated above the individuals. 'Each individual wishes to live, through the state's power, with his property secure. The power of the state appears to him . . . as something alien that exists outside of him.' [29]

Hegel in this period carried his criticism of the structure of modern society so far that he obtained an insight into the mechanism by which the state becomes an independent entity over and above the individuals. He reworked the pamphlet on the German Constitution several times, and its final form shows a distinct weakening of his critical attitude. Gradually, the 'higher' form of state that is to replace the outmoded one (exemplified by Germany) takes form as an absolute or power state. The reforms Hegel demands are the creation of an effective Reich army, wrested from the control of the estates and placed under the unified command of the Empire, and the centralization of all bureaus, finance, and law. The idea of a strong centralized state, we must note, was at that time a progressive one, which aimed to set free the available productive forces that were being hampered by the existing feudal forms. Four decades later, Marx emphasized in his critical history of the modern state that the centralized absolutistic state was a material advance over the feudal and semi-feudal state forms. Consequently, the proposal that such an absolute state be set up is not itself a sign that Hegel's critical attitude was weakening. We note the weakening, rather, in the consequences Hegel draws from his conception of the absolute state. We shall develop these briefly.

In the article on the German Constitution, there appears, for the first time in Hegel's formulations, a distinct

[29] P. 18, *note*.

subordination of right to might. Hegel was eager to free his centralized state from any and all limitations that might hinder its efficiency, and he therefore made the state interest superior to the validity of right. The fact is clearly shown in Hegel's remarks on the foreign policy of his ideal state:

Right, he says, pertains to 'the state's interest,' laid down for and granted to the state by contracts with other states.[30] In the continuously changing constellations of power, one state's interest must sooner or later clash with that of another. Right then confronts right. War, 'or whatever it might be,' must then decide not which right is true and just, 'for both sides have a true right, but which right shall yield to the other.' [31] We shall find the same thesis, greatly elaborated, in the *Philosophy of Right*.

A further consequence drawn from the conception of the power state is a new interpretation of freedom. The basic idea is retained, that the ultimate freedom of the individual will not contradict the ultimate freedom of the whole, but will be fulfilled only within and through the whole. Hegel had placed great stress on this point in his article on the difference between Fichte's and Schelling's systems, in which he said that the community that conforms to reason's standard must be conceived 'not as a limitation on the individual's true freedom but as an expansion of it. The highest community is the highest freedom, in its power and in its exercise of it.' [32] Now, however, in the study of the German Constitution, he states: 'The stubbornness of the German character has not permitted the individuals *to sacrifice* their special interests to the society, or to unite in a common interest and find their freedom in fully *submitting* to the higher power of the state.' [33]

[30] P. 100.
[31] P. 101.
[32] *Erste Druckschriften*, p. 65.
[33] *Schriften zur Politik*, pp. 7 f.

The new element of sacrifice and submission now overshadows the earlier idea that the individual's interest is fully to be preserved in the whole. And, as we shall see, Hegel has here in effect taken the first step that leads to his identifying freedom with necessity, or submission to necessity, in his final system.

3. The System of Morality

At about the same time, Hegel wrote the first draft of that part of his system known as the Philosophy of Mind. This draft, the so-called System of Morality (*System der Sittlichkeit*), is one of the most difficult in German philosophy. We shall sketch its general structure and limit the interpretation to those parts that disclose the material tendencies of Hegel's philosophy.

The system of morality, like all the other drafts of the *Philosophy of Mind,* deals with the development of 'culture,' by which is meant the totality of man's conscious, purposive activities in society. Culture is a realm of mind. A social or political institution, a work of art, a religion, and a philosophical system exist and operate as part and parcel of man's own being, products of a rational subject that continues to live in them. As *products* they constitute an objective realm; at the same time, they are subjective, created by human beings. They represent the possible unity of subject and object.

The development of culture shows distinct stages that denote different levels of relation between man and his world, that is, different ways of apprehending and mastering the world and of adapting it to human needs and potentialities. The process itself is conceived as ontological as well as historical; it is an actual historical development as well as a progression to higher and truer modes of being. In the gradual working out of Hegel's philosophy, however, the ontological process gains greater and greater predominance over the historical, and to a large extent is eventually detached from its original historical roots.

The general scheme is as follows. The first stage is an immediate rapport between the isolated individual and given objects. The individual apprehends the objects of his environment as things he needs or desires; he uses them to fulfill his wants, consuming and 'annihilating' them as food, beverages, and so on.[34] A higher level is reached in the cultural process when human labor molds and organizes the objective world, no longer simply annihilating things but preserving them as enduring means for the perpetuation of life. This stage presupposes a conscious association of individuals who have organized their activity on some plane of division of labor so that there is a constant production to replace what is used up. This is the first step towards a community in societal life and towards universality in the sphere of knowledge. To the extent that the individuals associate themselves as having a common interest, their conceptions and volitions become influenced and are guided by the notions they hold in common, and hence approach the universality of reason.

The forms of association differ according to the different degrees of integration that are achieved in them. The integrating agency is first the family, then the social institutions of labor, property, and law, and finally the state.

We shall not deal with the concrete social and economic concepts with which Hegel fills this scheme, since we shall encounter them again in the *Jenenser* drafts of the *Philosophy of Mind*. We only wish to emphasize here that Hegel describes the various social institutions and relations as a system of contradicting forces, originating from the mode

[34] *Schriften zur Politik*, pp. 430 ff.

of social labor. That mode of labor transforms the particular work of the individual, pursued for the gratification of his personal wants, into 'general labor,' which operates to produce commodities for the market.[35] Hegel calls this last 'abstract and quantitative' labor and makes it responsible for the increasing inequality of men and wealth. Society is incapable of overcoming the antagonisms growing out of this inequality; consequently, the 'system of government' has to concentrate on the task. Hegel outlines three different systems of government, in fact, each of which constitutes an advance on the other in fulfilling the task. They are intrinsically related to the structure of the society over which they rule.

The general picture of society is one in which 'the system of wants' is a 'system of mutual physical dependence.' The individual's labor fails to guarantee that his wants will be attended to. 'A force alien to the individual and over which he remains powerless' determines whether or not his needs will be fulfilled. The value of the product of labor is 'independent of the individual and is subject to constant change.'[36] The system of government is itself of this anarchic kind. What governs is nothing but 'the unconscious blind totality of needs and the modes of their fulfillment.'[37]

Society must master its 'unconscious and blind fate.' Such mastery, however, remains incomplete so long as the general anarchy of interests prevails. Excessive wealth goes hand in hand with excessive poverty, and purely quantitative labor pushes man 'into a state of utmost barbarism,' especially that part of the population that 'is subjected to mechanical labor in the factories.'[38]

The next stage in government, represented as a 'system of justice,' balances the existing antagonisms, but does so only in terms of the prevailing property relations. Govern-

[35] Pp. 428-38. [36] P. 492. [37] P. 493. [38] P. 496.

ment here rests upon the administration of justice, but it administers the law with 'complete indifference to the relation in which a thing stands to any particular individual's needs.' [39] The principle of freedom, namely, that 'the governed are identical with the governing,' cannot be fully realized because the government cannot do away with conflicts among particular interests. Liberty therefore appears only in 'the law courts, and in the discussion and adjudication of litigations.' [40]

Hegel barely sketched the third system of government in this series. It is, however, most significant that the main concept in its discussion is 'discipline' (*Zucht*). 'The great discipline is expressed in the general morals . . . and in the training for war, and in the trial of the true value of the individual in war.' [41]

The quest for the true community thus terminates in a society governed by utmost discipline and military preparation. The true unity between the individual and common interest, which Hegel demanded as the sole aim of the state, has led to an authoritarian state that is to suppress the increasing antagonisms of individualistic society. Hegel's discussion of the various stages of government is a concrete description of the development from a liberal to an authoritarian political system. This description contains an immanent critique of liberalist society, for the gist of Hegel's analysis is that liberalist society necessarily gives birth to an authoritarian state. Hegel's article on Natural Law,[42] probably written shortly after the outline of the System of Morality, applies this critique to the field of political economy.

Hegel examines the traditional system of political economy and finds it to be an apologetic formulation of the

[39] P. 499. [40] P. 501. [41] P. 502.

[42] 'Ueber die wissenschaftlichen Behandlungsarten des Naturrechts,' in op. cit., pp. 329 ff.

principles that govern the existing social system. The character of that system, Hegel again says, is essentially negative, for the very nature of the economic structure prevents the establishment of a true common interest. The task of the state, or of any adequate political organization, is to see to it that the contradictions inherent in the economic structure do not destroy the whole system. The state must assume the function of bridling the anarchic social and economic process.

Hegel attacks the doctrine of natural law because, he says, it justifies all the dangerous tendencies that aim to subordinate the state to the antagonistic interests of individualist society. The theory of the social contract, for example, fails to note that the common interest can never be derived from the will of competing and conflicting individuals. Moreover, natural law works with a purely metaphysical conception of man. As he appears in the natural-law doctrine, man is an abstract being who is later equipped with an arbitrary set of attributes. The selection of these attributes changes according to the changing apologetic interest of the particular doctrine. It is, moreover, in line with the apologetic function of natural law that most qualities that characterize man's existence in modern society are disregarded (for example, the concrete relations of private property, the prevailing modes of labor, and so on).

The first draft of Hegel's social philosophy, then, already enunciated the conception underlying his entire system: the given social order, based upon the system of abstract and quantitative labor and upon the integration of wants through the exchange of commodities, is incapable of asserting and establishing a rational community. This order remains essentially one of anarchy and irrationality, governed by blind economic mechanisms—it remains an order of ever repeated antagonisms in which all progress is but a temporary unification of opposites. Hegel's demand for a strong and independent state derives from his insight into the irreconcilable contradictions of modern society. Hegel was the first to attain this insight in Germany. His justification of the strong state was made on the ground that it was a necessary supplement to the antagonistic structure of the individualist society he analyzed.

III

Hegel's First System (1802-1806)

THE *Jenenser* system, as it is called, is Hegel's first complete system, consisting of a logic, a metaphysic, philosophy of nature, and philosophy of mind. Hegel formulated it in his lectures at the University of Jena from 1802 to 1806. These lectures have only recently been edited from Hegel's original manuscripts and published in three volumes, each of them representing a different stage of elaboration. The *Logic* and the *Metaphysics* exist in but one draft each, the *Philosophy of Nature* and the *Philosophy of Mind* in two.[1] The considerable variations between these will be neglected here, since they have no bearing on the structure of the whole.

We have chosen to deal only with the general trend and organization of the whole, and with the principles that guide the development of the concepts. The content of the particular concepts will be discussed when we reach the different sections of the final system.

1. THE LOGIC

Hegel's *Logic* expounds the structure of being-as-such, that is, the most general forms of being. The philosophical tradition since Aristotle designated as categories the concepts that embrace these most general forms: substance,

[1] *Jenenser Logik, Metaphysik und Naturphilosophie* (1802), ed. G. Lasson, Leipzig 1923. Cited here as *Jenenser Logik.—Jenenser Realphilosophie* I (1803-4), ed. J. Hoffmeister, Leipzig 1932. *Jenenser Realphilosophie* II (1805-6), ed. J. Hoffmeister, Leipzig 1931.

affirmation, negation, limitation; quantity, quality; unity, plurality, and so on. Hegel's *Logic* is an ontology in so far as it deals with such categories. But his *Logic* also deals with the general forms of *thought,* with the notion, the judgment, and the syllogism, and is in this respect 'formal logic.'

We can understand the reason for this seeming heterogeneity of content when we remember that Kant, too, treated ontology as well as formal logic in his *Transcendental Logic,* taking up the categories of substantiality, causality, community (reciprocity), together with the theory of judgment. The traditional distinction between formal logic and general metaphysics (ontology) is meaningless to transcendental idealism, which conceives the forms of being as the results of the activity of human understanding. The principles of thought thus also become principles of the objects of thought (of the phenomena).

Hegel, too, believed in a unity of thought and being, but, as we have already seen, his conception of the unity differed from Kant's. He rejected Kant's idealism on the ground that it assumed the existence of 'things-in-themselves' apart from 'phenomena,' and left these 'things' untouched by the human mind and therefore untouched by reason. The Kantian philosophy left a gulf between thought and being, or between subject and object, which the Hegelian philosophy sought to bridge. The bridge was to be made by positing one universal structure of all being. Being was to be a process whereih a thing 'comprehends' or 'grasps' the various states of its existence and draws them into the more or less enduring unity of its 'self,' thus actively constituting itself as 'the same' throughout all change. Everything, in other words, exists more or less as a 'subject.' The identical structure of movement that thus runs through the entire realm of being unites the objective and subjective worlds.

With this point in mind, we can readily see why logic and metaphysics are one in the Hegelian system. The *Logic,* it has often been said, presupposes an identity of thought and existence. The statement has meaning only in so far as it declares that the movement of thought reproduces the movement of being and brings it to its true form. It has also been maintained that Hegel's philosophy puts notions in an independent realm, as if they were real things, and makes them move around and turn into each other. It must be said in reply that Hegel's *Logic* deals primarily with the forms and types of being as comprehended by thought. When, for example, Hegel discusses the passage of quantity into quality, or of 'being' into 'essence' he intends to show how, when actually comprehended, quantitative entities turn into qualitative ones, and how a contingent existence turns into an essential one. He means to be dealing with real things. The interplay and motility of the notions reproduces the concrete process of reality.

There is, however, yet another intrinsic relation between the notion and the object it comprehends. The correct notion makes the nature of an object clear *to us.* It tells us what the thing is in itself. But while the truth becomes evident to us, it also becomes evident that the things 'do not exist in' their truth. Their potentialities are limited by the determinate conditions in which the things exist. Things attain their truth only if they negate their determinate conditions. The negation is again a determination, produced by the unfolding of previous conditions. For example, the bud of the plant is the determinate negation of the seed, and the blossom the determinate negation of the bud. In its growth, the plant, the 'subject' of this process, does not act on knowledge and fulfill its potentialities on the basis of its own comprehending power. It rather endures the process of fulfillment passively. Our notion of the plant, on the other hand, comprehends that the plant's existence is an intrinsic process of development; our notion sees the seed as potentially the bud and the bud as potentially the blossom. The notion thus represents, in Hegel's view, the real form of the object, for the notion gives us the truth about the process, which, in the objective world, is blind and contingent. In the inorganic, plant, and animal worlds, beings differ essentially from their notions. The difference is overcome only in the case of the thinking subject, which is capable of realizing its notion in its existence. The various modes of being may thus be ordered according to their essential difference from their notions.

This conclusion is the source of the basic divisions of Hegel's *Logic.* It starts with the concepts that grasp reality as a multitude of objective things, simply 'being,' free from any subjectivity. They are qualitatively and quantitatively connected with each other, and the analysis of these connections hits upon relations that can no longer be interpreted in terms of objective qualities and quantities but requires principles and forms of thought that negate the traditional concepts of being and reveal the *subject* to be the very substance of reality. The whole construction can be understood only in the mature form Hegel gave it in the *Science of Logic;* we shall limit ourselves here to a brief description of the basic scheme.

Every particular existent is essentially different from what it could be if its potentialities were realized. The potentialities are given in its notion. The existent would have true being if its potentialities were fulfilled and if there were, therefore, an identity between its existence and its notion. The difference between the reality and the potentiality is the starting point of the dialectical process that applies to every concept in Hegel's *Logic.* Finite things are 'negative'—and this is a defining characteristic of them; they never are what they can and ought to be. They always exist in a state that does not fully express their potentialities as realized. The finite thing has as its essence 'this absolute unrest,' this striving 'not to be what it is.'[2]

Even in the abstract formulations of the *Logic* we can see the concrete critical impulses that underlie this conception. Hegel's dialectic is permeated with the profound conviction that all immediate forms of existence—in nature and history—are 'bad,' because they do not permit things to be what they can be. True existence begins only when the immediate state is recognized as negative, when beings become 'subjects' and strive to adapt their outward state to their potentialities.

The full significance of the conception just outlined lies in its assertion that negativity is constitutive of all finite things and is the 'genuine dialectical' moment[3] of them all. It is 'the innermost source of all activity, of living and spiritual self-movement.'[4] The negativity everything possesses is the necessary prelude to its reality. It is a state of privation that forces the subject to seek remedy. As such, it has a positive character.

The dialectical process receives its motive power from the pressure to overcome the negativity. Dialectics is a process in a world where the mode of existence of men and things is made up of contradictory relations, so that any particular content can be unfolded only through passing into its opposite. The latter is an integral part of the former, and the whole content is the totality of all contradictory relations implied in it. Logically, the dialectic has its beginning when human understanding finds itself unable to grasp something adequately from its given quali-

2 *Jenenser Logik*, p. 31.

3 *Science of Logic*, trans. W. H. Johnston and L. G. Struthers, The Macmillan Company, New York 1929, vol. I, p. 66.

4 Ibid., vol. II, p. 477.

tative or quantitative forms. The given quality or quantity seems to be a 'negation' of the thing that possesses this quality or quantity. We shall have to follow Hegel's explanation of this point in some detail.

He begins with the world as common sense views it. It consists of an innumerable multitude of things—Hegel calls them 'somethings' (*Etwas*), each of them with its specific qualities. The qualities the thing has distinguish it from other things, so that if we want to separate it off from other things we simply enumerate its qualities. The table here in this room is being used as a desk; it is finished in walnut, heavy, wooden, and so on. Being a desk, brown, wooden, heavy, and so on, is not the same as just being a table. *The* table is not any of these qualities, nor is it the sum total of them. The particular qualities are, according to Hegel, at the same time the 'negation' of the table-as-such. The propositions in which the table's qualities are predicated of it would indicate this fact. They have the formal logical structure *A* is *B* (that is, not *A*). 'The table is brown' expresses also that the table is other than itself. This is the first abstract form in which the negativity of all finite things is expressed. The very being of something appears as other than itself. It exists, as Hegel puts it, in its 'otherness' (*Anderssein*).

The attempt to define something by its qualities, however, does not end in negativity, but is pushed a step further. A thing cannot be understood through its qualities without reference to other qualities that are actually excluded by the ones it possesses. 'Wooden,' for example, is meaningful only through the relation to some other, non-wooden material. The meaning of 'brown' requires that the meaning of other colors that are contraries of brown be known, and so on. 'The quality is related to what it excludes; for it does not exist as an absolute, for itself, but exists in such a way that it is for itself only in so far as some other [quality] does not exist.'[5] We are at every point led beyond the qualities that should delimit the thing and differentiate it from some other thing. Its seeming stability and clarity thus dissolve into an endless chain of 'relations' (*Beziehungen*).

The opening chapters of Hegel's *Logic* thus show that when human understanding ventures to follow out its conceptions, it encounters the dissolution of its clearly delimited objects. First, it finds it completely impossible to identify any thing with the state in which it actually exists. The effort to uncover a concept that truly identifies the thing for what it is plunges the mind into an infinite sea of relations. Everything has to be understood in relation to other things, so that these relations become the very being of that thing. This infinitude of relations, which seems to portend the failure of any attempt to capture the thing's character, becomes for Hegel, quite to the contrary, the first step in true knowledge of the thing. That is, it is the first step if properly taken.

The process is discussed by Hegel through an analysis of 'infinity.' This is differentiated into two kinds, 'bad' and 'real' infinity. The bad or spurious infinite is, so to speak, the wrong road to the truth. It is the activity of trying to overcome the inadequacy of a definition by going to more and more of the related qualities entailed, in the hope of reaching an end. The understanding simply follows out the relations, as each is entailed, adding one to the next in the vain effort to exhaust and delimit the object. The procedure has a rational core, but only inasmuch as it presupposes that the essence of the object is made up of its relations to other objects. The relations cannot, however, be grasped by the 'spurious infinity' of mere 'added connections' (*Und-Beziehungen*) by which common sense links one object with another.

[5] *Jenenser Logik,* p. 4.

The relations must be apprehended in another way. They must be seen as created by the object's own movement. The object must be understood as one that itself establishes and 'itself puts forth the necessary relation of itself to its opposite.'[6] This would presuppose that the object has a definite power over its own development so that it can remain itself in spite of the fact that every concrete stage of its existence is a 'negation' of itself, an 'otherness.' The object, in other words, must be comprehended as a 'subject' in its relations to its 'otherness.'

As an ontological category, the 'subject' is the power of an entity to 'be itself in its otherness' (*Bei-sich-selbst-sein im Anderssein*). Only such a mode of existence can incorporate the negative into the positive. Negative and positive cease to be opposed to each other when the driving power of the subject makes negativity a part of the subject's own unity. Hegel says the subject 'mediates' (*vermittelt*) and 'sublates' (*aufhebt*) the negativity. In the process the object does not dissolve into its various qualitative or quantitative determinations, but is substantially held together throughout its relations with other objects.

This is the mode of being or existence that Hegel describes as 'real infinity.'[7] Infinity is not something behind or beyond finite things, but is their true reality. The infinite is the mode of existence in which all potentialities are realized and in which all being reaches its ultimate form.

The goal of the *Logic* is herewith set. It consists on the one hand in demonstrating the true form of such a final reality and, on the other, in showing how the concepts that try to grasp that reality are led to the conclusion that it is the absolute truth. Hegel announced in his criticism of the Kantian philosophy that the task of logic was 'to develop' the categories and not merely 'to

[6] Ibid., p. 32.

[7] Ibid., pp. 30-34.

assemble' them. Such an endeavor would be possible of fruition only if the objects of thought have a systematic order. That order, Hegel says, is derived from the fact that all modes of being attain their truth through the free subject that comprehends them in relation to its own rationality. The arrangement of the *Logic* reflects this systematic comprehension. It starts with the categories of immediate experience, which apprehend only the most abstract forms of objective being (of material things, that is), namely, Quantity, Quality, and Measure. These are the most abstract, since they view every object as externally determined by other objects. Simple connection prevails in this case because the various modes of being are here externally connected with each other, and no being is comprehended as having an intrinsic relation to itself and to the other things with which it interacts. For example, an object is taken as constituting itself in the processes of attraction and repulsion. According to Hegel, this is an abstract and external interpretation of objectivity since the dynamic unity of a being is here conceived as the product of some blind natural forces over which it exercises no power. The categories of simple connection are thus farthest from any recognition of the substance as 'subject.'

The categories Hegel treats in the second section of the *Logic* under the general title of Relation (*Verhältnis*) come one step closer to the goal. Substantiality, Causality, and Reciprocity do not denote abstract and incomplete entities (as did the categories of the first section), but real relations. A substance is what it is only in relation to its accidents. Likewise, a cause exists only in relation to its effects, and two interdependent substances only in their relation to each other. The connection is intrinsic. The substance—the all-embracing category of this group—denotes a movement much more intrinsic than the blind force of attraction and repulsion. It possesses a definite power over its accidents and effects, and through its own power it establishes its relation to other things, thus having the ability to unfold its own potentialities. It does not, however, possess knowledge of these potentialities and therefore does not possess the freedom of self-realization. Substantiality still denotes a relation of objects, of material things, or, as Hegel says, a relation of being. To grasp the world in its veritable being we must grasp it with the categories of freedom, which are to be found only in the realm of the thinking subject. A transition is necessary from the relation of being to the relation of thought.

The latter relation refers to that between the particular and the universal in the notion, the judgment, and the syllogism. To Hegel, it is not a relation of formal logic, but an ontological relation, and the true relation of all reality. The substance of nature as well as history is a universal that unfolds itself through the particular. The universal is the natural process of the genus, realizing itself through the species and individuals. In history, the universal is the substance of all development. The Greek city-state, modern industry, a social class—all these universalities are actual historical forces that cannot be dissolved into their components. On the contrary, the individual facts and factors obtain their meaning only through the universal to which they belong. The individual is determined not by his particular but by his universal qualities, for instance, by his being a Greek citizen, or a modern factory worker, or a bourgeois.

Universality, on the other hand, is no 'relation of being' since all being—as we have seen—is determinate and particular. It can be understood only as a 'relation of thought,' that is, as the self-development of a comprehensive and comprehending subject.

In traditional philosophy, the category of universality has been treated as a part of logic, dealt with in the doctrine of the notion, the judgment and the syllogism. To Hegel, however, these logical forms and processes reflect and comprise the actual forms and processes of reality. We have already hinted at Hegel's ontological interpretation of the notion and the judgment. Fundamental in this context is his treatment of the definition. Within the logical tradition, the definition is the relation of thought that grasps the universal nature of an object in its essential distinction from other objects. According to Hegel, the definition can do this only because it reproduces (mirrors) the actual process in which the object differentiates itself from other objects to which it is related. The definition must express, then, the movement in which a being maintains its identity through the negation of its conditions. In short, a real definition cannot be given in one isolated proposition, but must elaborate the real history of the object, for its history alone explains its reality.[8] The real definition of a plant, for instance, must show the plant constituting itself through the destruction of the seed by the bud and of the bud by the blossom. It must tell how the plant perpetuates itself in its interaction and struggle with its environment. Hegel calls the definition 'the self-preservation' and explains this usage: 'In defining living things their characteristics must be derived from the weapons of attack and defense with which these things preserve themselves from other particular things.'[9]

In all these cases, thought seizes the real relations of the objective world and presents us with the knowledge of what the things are 'in themselves.' These real relations thought has to ferret out because they are hidden

[8] Cf. *Science of Logic*, vol. 1, p. 61.
[9] *Jenenser Logik*, p. 109.

by the appearance of things. For this reason, thought is more 'real' than its objects. Moreover, thought is the existential attribute of a being that 'comprehends' all objects, in the twofold sense that it understands and comprises them. The objective world comes to its true form in the world of the free subject, and the objective logic terminates in the subjective logic. In the *Jenenser* system, the latter is treated in the section on Metaphysics. It expounds the categories and principles that comprehend all objectivity as the arena of the developing subject, that is, as the arena of reason.

The rough outlines we have provided of Hegel's main ideas will be more clearly elaborated when we discuss the final system of logic. Hegel's first logic already manifests the endeavor to break through the false fixity of our concepts and to show the driving contradictions that lurk in all modes of existence and call for a higher mode of thought. The *Logic* presents only the general form of the dialectic, in its application to the general forms of being. The more concrete applications appear in Hegel's *Realphilosophie,* particularly in his social philosophy. We shall not dwell now on the difficult transition from the *Logic* and *Metaphysics* to the *Philosophy of Nature* (which will be discussed with the final logic), but shall pass directly to the *Jenenser Philosophy of Mind,* which deals with the historical realization of the free subject, man.

2. The Philosophy of Mind

The history of the human world does not begin with the struggle between the individual and nature, since the individual is really a later product in human history. The community (*Allgemeinheit*) comes first, although in a ready-made, 'immediate' form. It is as yet not a rational community and does not have freedom as its quality. Consequently, it soon splits up into numerous antagonisms. Hegel calls this original unity in the historical world 'consciousness,' thus re-emphasizing that we have entered a realm in which everything has the character of the subject.

The first form consciousness assumes in history is not that of an individual but of a universal consciousness, perhaps best represented as the consciousness of a primitive group with all individuality submerged in the community. Feelings, sensations, and concepts are not properly the individual's but are shared among all, so that the common and not the particular determines the consciousness. But even this unity contains opposition; consciousness is what it is only through its opposition to its objects. To be sure, these, as objects of consciousness, are 'comprehended objects' (*begriffene Objekte*), or objects that cannot be divorced from the subject. Their 'being comprehended' is part of their character as objects. Either side of the opposition, consciousness or its objects, thus has the form of subjectivity, as do all the other types of opposition in the realm of mind. The integration of the opposing elements can only be an integration within subjectivity.

The world of man develops, Hegel says, in a series of integrations of opposites. In the first stage, the subject and its object take the form of consciousness and its concepts; in the second stage, they appear as the individual in conflict with other individuals; and in the final stage they appear as the nation. The last stage alone represents the attainment of a lasting integration between subject and object; the nation has its object in itself; its effort is directed solely towards reproducing itself. Corresponding to the three stages are three different 'media' of integration: language, labor, and property.

	SUBJECT	MEDIUM	OBJECT
1	Consciousness	Language	Concepts
2	Individuals or Groups of Individuals	Labor	Nature
3	Nation Community of Individuals	Property	Nation Community of Individuals

Language is the medium in which the first integration between subject and object takes place.[10] It is also the first actual community (*Allgemeinheit*), in the sense that it is objective and shared by all individuals. On the other hand, language is the first medium of individuation, for through it the individual obtains mastery over the objects he knows and names. A man is able to stake out his sphere of influence and keep others from it only when he knows his world, is conscious of his needs and powers, and communicates this knowledge to others. Language is thus also the first lever of appropriation.

Language, then, makes it possible for an individual to take a conscious position *against* his fellows and to assert his needs and desires against those of the other individuals. The resulting antagonisms are integrated through the process of labor, which also becomes the decisive force for the development of culture. The labor process is responsible for various types of integration, conditioning all the subsequent forms of community that correspond to these types: the family, civil society, and the state (the latter two terms appear only later in Hegel's philosophy). Labor first unites individuals into the family, which appropriates as 'family property'[11] the objects that provide for its

[10] *Jenenser Realphilosophie,* I, pp. 211 ff.
[11] Ibid., pp. 221 f.

subsistence. The family, however, finds itself and its property among other property-owning families. The conflict that develops here is not between the individual and the objects of his desire, but between one group of individuals (a family) and other similar groups. The objects are already 'appropriated'; they are the (actual or potential) property of individuals. The institutionalization of private property signifies, to Hegel, that the 'objects' have finally been incorporated into the subjective world: the objects are no longer 'dead things,' but belong, in their totality, to the sphere of the self-realization of the subject. Man has toiled and organized them, and has thus made them part and parcel of his personality. Nature thus takes its place in the history of man, and history becomes essentially human history. All historical struggles become struggles between groups of property-owning individuals. This far-reaching conception completely influences the subsequent construction of the realm of mind.

With the advent of the various property-owning family units there begins a 'struggle for mutual recognition' of their rights. Since property is looked upon as an essential and constitutive element of individuality, the individual has to preserve and defend his property in order to maintain himself as an individual. The consequent life-and-death struggle, Hegel says, can come to an end only if the opposed individuals are integrated into the community of the nation (*Volk*).

This transition from family to nation corresponds roughly to the transition from 'a state of nature' to a state of civil society, as the political theories of the eighteenth century conceived it. Hegel's interpretation of the 'struggle for mutual recognition' will be explained in our discussion of the *Phenomenology of Mind*, in which it becomes the entering wedge for freedom. The consequence of the struggle for mutual recognition is a first real integration that gives the groups or individuals in conflict an objective common interest. The consciousness that achieves this integration is again a universal (the *Volksgeist*), but its unity is no longer a primitive and 'immediate' one. It is rather a product of self-conscious efforts to make the existing antagonisms work in the interest of the whole. Hegel calls it a mediated (*vermittelte*) unity. The term mediation here manifests its concrete significance. The activity of mediation is no other than the activity of labor. Through his labor, man overcomes the estrangement between the objective world and the subjective world; he transforms nature into an appropriate medium for his self-development. When objects are taken and shaped by labor, they become part of the subject who is able to recognize his needs and desires in them. Through labor, moreover, man loses that atomic existence wherein he is, as an individual, opposed to all other individuals; he becomes a member of a community. The individual, by virtue of his labor, turns into a universal; for labor is of its very nature a universal activity: its product is exchangeable among all individuals.

In his further remarks on the concept of labor, Hegel actually describes the mode of labor characteristic of modern commodity production. Indeed, he comes close to the Marxian doctrine of abstract and universal labor. We encounter the first illustration of the fact that Hegel's ontological notions are saturated with a social content expressive of a particular order of society.

Hegel states, 'the individual satisfies his needs by his labor, but not by the particular product of his labor; the latter, to fill his needs, has to become something other than it is.' [12] The particular object becomes a universal one in the process of labor—it becomes a commodity. The universality also transforms the *subject* of labor, the la-

[12] Ibid., p. 238

borer, and his individual activity. He is forced to set aside his particular faculties and desires. Nothing counts in the distribution of the product of labor but 'abstract and universal labor.' 'The labor of each is, with regard to its content, universal for the needs of all.' Labor has 'value' only as such a 'universal activity' (*allgemeine Tätigkeit*): its value is determined by 'what labor is for all, and not what it is for the individual.' [13]

This abstract and universal labor is connected with concrete individual need through the 'exchange relationships' of the market.[14] By virtue of the exchange, the products of labor are distributed among individuals according to the value of abstract labor. Hegel, therefore, calls exchange 'the return to concreteness'; [15] through it the concrete needs of men in society are fulfilled.

Hegel is obviously striving for an exact understanding of the function of labor in integrating the various individual activities into a totality of exchange relationships. He touches the sphere in which Marx later resumed the analysis of modern society. The concept of labor is not peripheral in Hegel's system, but is the central notion through which he conceives the development of society. Driven by the insight that opened this dimension to him, Hegel describes the mode of integration prevailing in a commodity-producing society in terms that clearly foreshadow Marx's critical approach.

He emphasizes two points: the complete subordination of the individual to the demon of abstract labor, and the blind and anarchic character of a society perpetuated by exchange relationships. Abstract labor cannot develop the individual's true faculties. Mechanization, the very means that should liberate man from toil, makes him a slave of

13 Ibid.

14 *Jenenser Realphilosophie*, II, p. 215.

15 Ibid.

his labor. 'The more he subjugates his labor, the more powerless he himself becomes.' The machine reduces the necessity of toil only for the whole, not for the individual. 'The more mechanized labor becomes, the less value it has, and the more the individual must toil.' [16] 'The value of labor decreases in the same proportion as the productivity of labor increases . . . The faculties of the individual are infinitely restricted, and the consciousness of the factory worker is degraded to the lowest level of dullness.' [17] While labor thus changes from the self-realization of the individual into his self-negation, the relation between the particular needs and labor, and between the needs and the labor of the whole, takes the form of 'an incalculable, blind interdependence.' The integration of conflicting individuals through abstract labor and exchange thus establishes 'a vast system of communality and mutual interdependence, a moving life of the dead. This system moves hither and yon in a blind and elementary way, and like a wild animal calls for strong permanent control and curbing.' [18]

The tone and pathos of the descriptions point strikingly to Marx's *Capital*. It is not surprising to note that Hegel's manuscript breaks off with this picture, as if he was terrified by what his analysis of the commodity-producing society disclosed. The last sentence, however, finds him formulating a possible way out. He elaborates this in the *Realphilosophie* of 1804-5. The wild animal must be curbed, and such a process requires the organization of a strong state.

Hegel's early political philosophy is reminiscent of the origins of political theory in modern society. Hobbes also founded his Leviathan State upon the otherwise unconquerable chaos, the *bellum omnium contra omnes*, of

[16] *Jenenser Realphilosophie*, I, p. 237.

[17] Ibid., p. 239.

[18] Ibid., p. 240.

individualistic society. Between Hobbes and Hegel, however, lies the period in which the absolutist state had unleashed the economic forces of capitalism, and in which political economy had uncovered some of the mechanisms of the capitalist labor process. Hegel had indulged in a study of political economy. His analysis of civil society got to the root structure of modern society and presented elaborate critical analysis, whereas Hobbes got and used intuitive insight. And even more, Hegel discovered in the upsurge of the French Revolution principles that pointed beyond the given framework of individualist society. The ideas of reason and freedom, of a unity between the common and the particular interest, denoted, for him, values that could not be sacrificed to the state. He struggled all his life to render them consonant with the necessity of 'controlling and curbing.' His attempts to solve the problem are manifold, and the final triumph goes not to the Leviathan, but to the rational state under the rule of law.

The second *Jenenser Realphilosophie* goes on to discuss the manner in which civil society is integrated with the state. Hegel discusses the political form of this society under the heading of 'Constitution.' Law (*Gesetz*) changes the blind totality of exchange relations into the consciously regulated apparatus of the state. The picture of the anarchy and confusion of civil society is painted in even darker colors than before.

> [The individual] is subject to the complete confusion and hazard of the whole. A mass of the population is condemned to the stupefying, unhealthy and insecure labor of factories, manufactories, mines, and so on. Whole branches of industry which supported a large bulk of the population suddenly fold up because the mode changes or because the values of their products fall on account of new inventions in other countries, or for other reasons. Whole masses are thus abandoned to helpless poverty. The conflict between vast wealth and vast pov-

erty steps forth, a poverty unable to improve its condition. Wealth becomes . . . a predominant power. Its accumulation takes place partly by chance, partly through the general mode of distribution . . . Acquisition develops into a many-sided system which ramifies into fields from which smaller business cannot profit. The utmost abstractness of labor reaches into the most individual types of work and continues to widen its sphere. This inequality of wealth and poverty, this need and necessity turn into the utmost dismemberment of will, inner rebellion and hatred.[19]

But Hegel now stresses the positive aspect of this degrading reality. 'This necessity which means complete hazard for the individual existence is at the same time the preservative. The State power intervenes; it must see to it that every particular sphere [of life] is sustained, it must search out new outlets, must open channels of trade in foreign lands, and so on . . .'[20] The 'hazard' that prevails in society is not mere chance, but the very process by which the whole reproduces its own existence and that of each of its members. The exchange relations of the market provide the necessary integration without which isolated individuals would perish in the competitive conflict. The terrible struggles within the commodity-producing society are 'better' than those between wholly unrestricted individuals and groups—'better,' because they take place on a higher level of historical development and imply a 'mutual recognition' of individual rights. The 'contract' (*Vertrag*) expresses this recognition as a social reality. Hegel views the contract as one of the foundations of modern society; the society is actually a framework of contracts between individuals.[21] (We shall see, however, that he later takes great pains to restrict the validity of contracts to the sphere of civil society—that is, to the economic and social relations—and to exclude them as having a function

19 *Jenenser Realphilosophie*, II, pp. 232-3.
20 Ibid.
21 Pp. 218 f.

between states.) The assurance that a relation or a performance is secured by a contract—and that the contract will be kept under all circumstances—alone makes the relations and performances in a commodity-producing society calculable and rational. 'My word must be good not for moral reasons,' but because society presupposes that there are mutual obligations on the part of its members. I do my work under the condition that another does likewise.[22] If I break my word, I break the very contract of society and not only hurt a particular person but the community; I place myself outside of the whole which can alone fulfill my right as an individual. Therefore, says Hegel, 'the universal is the substance of the contract.'[23] Contracts not only regulate individual performance, but the operation of the whole. The contract treats individuals as free and equal; at the same time it considers each not in his contingent particularity but in his 'universality,' as a homogeneous part of the whole. This identity of the particular and the universal is, of course, not yet realized. The proper potentialities of individuals are, as Hegel has pointed out before, far from preserved in civil society. Consequently, force must stand behind every contract. The threatened application of force, and not his own voluntary recognition, binds the individual to his contract. The contract thus involves the possibility of breach of the contract and the revolt of the individual against the whole.[24] Crime signifies the act of revolt, and punishment is the mechanism through which the whole restores its right over the rebellious individual. The recognition of the rule of law represents that stage of integration in which the individual reconciles himself with the whole. The rule of law differs from the rule of contracts in so far as it takes into account 'the self of the individual in his existence as well as in his knowledge.'[25] The individual knows that he

[22] Pp. 219-20. [23] P. 226. [24] P. 221. [25] P. 225.

can exist only by force of the law, not only because it protects him, but because he sees it to represent the common interest, which, in the last analysis, is the sole guarantee of his self-development. Individuals perfectly free and independent, yet united in a common interest—this is the proper notion of the law. The individual is 'confident' that he finds 'himself, his essence' in the law and that the law preserves and sustains his essential potentialities.[26]

Such a conception presupposes a state whose laws really manifest the free will of associated individuals, as if they had assembled and decided upon the best legislation for their common interest. The law could not otherwise express the will of each and at the same time 'the general will.' Given that common decision, the law would be a true identity between the individual and the whole. Hegel's conception of law envisages such a society; he is describing a goal to be attained and not a prevailing condition.

The gap between ideal and reality, however, narrows slowly. The more realistic Hegel's attitude towards history becomes, the more he endows the present with the greatness of the future ideal. But whatever the outcome of Hegel's struggle between philosophical idealism and political realism, his philosophy will not accept any state that does not operate by the rule of law. He can accept a 'power state,' but only in so far as the freedom of the individuals prevails therein and the state's power enhances their proper power.[27]

The individual can be free only as a political being. Hegel thus resumes the classical Greek conception that the *Polis* represents the true reality of human existence. Accordingly, the final unification of the social antagonisms is achieved not by the reign of law, but by the political institutions that embody the law: by the state proper. What

[26] P. 248.

[27] See below, pp. 200 ff.

is the form of government that best safeguards this embodiment and is therefore the highest form of unity between the part and the whole?

Preliminary to his answer of this question, Hegel sketches the origin of the state and the historical roles of tyranny, democracy, and monarchy. He repudiates the theory of the social contract [28] on the ground that it assumes that 'the general will' is operative in the isolated individuals prior to their entry into the state. As against the social contract theory he stresses that 'the general will' can arise only out of a long process, which culminates in the final regulation of the social antagonisms. The general will is the result and not the origin of the state; the state originates through an 'outside force' that impels the individuals against their will. Thus, 'all states are founded through the illustrious power of great men.' [29] And Hegel adds, 'not by physical force.' The great founders of the state had in their personality something of the historic power that coerces mankind to follow out its own course and to progress thereby; these personalities reflect and bear the higher knowledge and the higher morality of history even if they as individuals are not conscious of it, or even if they are driven by quite other motives. The idea which Hegel is here introducing appears later to be the *Weltgeist.*

The earliest state is of necessity a tyranny. The state forms Hegel now describes have both a historical and a normative order: tyranny is the earliest and the lowest, hereditary monarchy the latest and highest form.[30] Again, the standard by which the state is evaluated is the success it has in producing a proper integration of individuals into the whole. Tyranny integrates individuals by negating them. But it does have one positive result: it disciplines

[28] *Jenenser Realphilosophie,* II, pp. 245-6.
[29] Ibid., p. 246.
[30] Pp. 246-53.

them, teaches them to obey. Obeying the person of the ruler is preparatory to obeying the law. 'The people overthrow tyranny because it is abject, detestable, and so on; in reality, however, because it has become superfluous.'[81] Tyranny ceases to be historically necessary once the discipline has been accomplished. It is then succeeded by the rule of law, that is, by democracy.

Democracy represents a real identity between the individual and the whole; the government is one with all the individuals, and their will expresses the interest of the whole. The individual pursues his own particular interest, hence he is the 'bourgeois'; but he also occupies himself with the needs and tasks of the whole, hence he is the *citoyen*.[82]

Hegel illustrates democracy by reference to the Greek city-state. There, the unity between the individual and the general will was still fortuitous; the individual had to yield to the majority, which was accidental in its turn. Such a democracy therefore could not represent the ultimate unity between the individual and the whole. 'The beautiful and happy freedom of the Greeks' integrated individuals into an 'immediate' unity only, founded on nature and feeling rather than on the conscious intellectual and moral organization of society. Mankind had to advance to a higher form of the state beyond this one, to a form in which the individual unites himself freely and consciously with others into a community that in turn preserves his real essence.

The best guardian of such a unity, in Hegel's opinion, is hereditary monarchy. The person of the monarch represents the whole elevated above all special interests; monarch by birth, he rules, as it were, 'by nature,' untouched by the antagonisms of society. He is, therefore, the most stable and enduring 'point' in the movement of the

81 Pp. 247-8. 82 P. 249.

whole.[33] 'Public opinion' is the tie that binds the spheres of life and controls their course. The state is neither an enforced nor a natural unity, but a rational organization of society through its various 'estates.' In each estate the individual indulges his own specific activity and yet serves the community. Each estate has its particular place, its consciousness, and its morality, but the estates terminate in the 'universal' estate, that is, in the state functionaries who attend to nothing except the general interest. The functionaries are elected and each 'sphere [town, guild, and so on] administers its own affairs.' [34]

More important than these details are the questions, What qualities does hereditary monarchy possess that justify its place of honor in the philosophy of mind? How does this state form fulfill the principles that guided the construction of that philosophy? Hegel looked upon hereditary monarchy as the Christian state *par excellence,* or, more strictly, as the Christian state that came into being with the German Reformation. To him this state was the embodiment of the principle of Christian liberty, which proclaimed the freedom of man's inner conscience and his equality before God. Hegel thought that without this inner freedom the outer freedom democracy was supposed to institute and protect was of no avail. The German Reformation represented to his mind the great turning point in history that came with the pronouncement that the individual was really free only when he had become self-conscious of his inalienable autonomy.[35] Protestantism had established this self-consciousness, and shown that Christian liberty implied, in the sphere of the social reality, submission and obedience to the divine hierarchy of the state. We shall deal further with this matter when we reach the *Philosophy of Right.*

One question still to be answered affects the whole struc-

[33] P. 250. [34] P. 251. [35] P. 251.

ture of Hegel's system. The historical world, in so far as it is built, organized, and shaped by the conscious activity of thinking subjects, is a realm of mind. But the mind is fully realized and exists in its true form only when it indulges in its proper activity, namely, in art, religion, and philosophy. These domains of culture are, then, the final reality, the province of ultimate truth. And this is precisely Hegel's conviction: the absolute mind lives only in art, religion, and philosophy. All three have the same content in a different form: Art apprehends the truth by mere intuition (*Anschauung*), in a tangible and therefore limited form; Religion perceives it free of such limitation, but only as mere 'assertion' and belief; Philosophy comprehends it through knowledge and possesses it as its inalienable property. On the other hand, these spheres of culture exist only in the historical development of mankind, and the state is the final stage of this development. What, then, is the relation between the state and the realm of absolute mind? Does the rule of the state extend over art, religion, and philosophy, or is it rather limited by them?

The problem has been frequently discussed. It has been pointed out that Hegel's attitude underwent several changes, that he was first inclined to elevate the state above the cultural spheres, that he then co-ordinated it with or even subordinated it to them, and that he then returned to the original position, the predominance of the state. There are apparent contradictions in Hegel's statements on this point even within the same philosophical period. In the second *Jenenser Realphilosophie* he declares that the absolute mind 'is at first the life of a nation in general; however, the Mind has to free itself from this life,' [86] and he says, moreover, that with art, religion, and philosophy, 'the absolute free Mind . . . produces a different world, one in which it has its proper form, where its work is

[86] P. 253.

accomplished, and where the Mind attains the intuition of its own as its own.'[37] Contrary to these statements, Hegel says in his discussion of the relation between religion and the state that 'the government stands above all; it is the Mind which knows itself as the universal essence and reality . . .'[38] Furthermore, he calls the state 'the reality of the kingdom of heaven . . . The State is the spirit of reality, whatever appears within the State must conform to it.'[39] The meaning of these contradictions and their possible solution can be made clear only through an understanding of the constitutive role of history in Hegel's system. Here, we shall attempt but a preliminary explanation.

Hegel's first system already reveals the outstanding traits of his philosophy, especially its emphasis on the universal as the true being. We indicated in our introduction the socio-historical roots of this 'universalism,' showing that its base was the lack of a 'community' in individualist society. Hegel remained faithful to the heritage of the eighteenth century and incorporated its ideals into the very structure of his philosophy. He insisted that the 'truly universal' was a community that preserved and fulfilled the demands of the individual. One might interpret his dialectic as the philosophic attempt to reconcile his ideals with an antagonistic social reality. Hegel recognized the great forward surges that must be generated by the prevailing order of society—the development of material as well as cultural productivity; the destruction of obsolete power relations that hampered the advance of mankind; and the emancipation of the individual so that he might be the free subject of his life. When he stated that every 'immediate unity' (which does not imply an opposition between its component parts) is, with regard to the possibilities of human development, inferior to a unity pro-

[37] P. 263. [38] P. 267. [39] P. 270.

duced by integrating real antagonisms, he was thinking of the society of his own time. The reconciliation of the individual and the universal seemed impossible without the full unfolding of those antagonisms which push the prevailing forms of life to a point where they openly contradict their content. Hegel has described this process in his picture of modern society.

The actual conditions of modern society are the strongest instance of dialectic in history. There is no doubt that these conditions, however they might be justified on the ground of economic necessity, contradict the ideal of freedom. The highest potentialities of mankind lie in the rational union of free individuals, that is, in the universal and not in fixed particularities. The individual can hope to fulfill himself only if he is a free member of a real community.

The enduring quest for such a community amidst the haunting terror of an anarchic society is at the back of Hegel's insistence upon the intrinsic connection between truth and universality. He was thinking of the fulfillment of that quest when he designated the true universality as the end of the dialectical process and as the final reality. Time and again, the concrete social implications of the concept of universality break through his philosophic formulations, and the picture of an association of free individuals united in a common interest comes clearly to light. We quote the famous passage in the *Aesthetics:*

> True independence consists alone in the unity and in the interpenetration of both the individuality and the universality with each other. The universal acquires through the individual its concrete existence, and the subjectivity of the individual and particular discovers in the universal the unassailable basis and the most genuine form of its reality . . .
>
> In the Ideal [state], it is precisely the particular individuality which ought to persist in inseparable harmony with the substantive totality, and to the full extent that freedom and

independence of the subjectivity may attach to the Ideal the world-environment of conditions and relations should possess no essential objectivity apart from the subject and the individual.[40]

The *Philosophy of Mind,* and in fact the whole of the Hegelian system, is a portrayal of the process whereby 'the individual becomes universal' and whereby 'the construction of universality' takes place.

[40] *The Philosophy of Fine Arts,* trans. F. P. R. Osmaston, George Bell and Sons, London 1920, vol. I, pp. 243 f.

IV

The Phenomenology of Mind (1807)

HEGEL wrote the *Phenomenology of Mind* in 1806 in Jena while the Napoleonic armies were approaching that city. He finished it as the battle of Jena sealed the fate of Prussia and enthroned the heir of the French Revolution over the powerless remnants of the old German Reich. The feeling that a new epoch in world history had just begun pervades Hegel's book. It marks his first philosophical judgment on history and draws its final conclusions from the French Revolution, which now becomes the turning point of the historical as well as the philosophical way to truth.

Hegel saw that the result of the French Revolution was not the realization of freedom, but the establishment of a new despotism. He interpreted its course and its issue not as a historical accident, but as a necessary development. The process of emancipating the individual necessarily results in terror and destruction as long as it is carried out by individuals *against* the state, and not *by* the state itself. The state alone can provide emancipation, though it cannot provide *perfect* truth and *perfect* freedom. These last are to be found only in the proper realm of mind, in morality, religion, and philosophy. We have already encountered this sphere as the realization of truth and freedom in Hegel's first *Philosophy of Mind*. There, however, they were founded on an adequate state order and remained in an intrinsic connection with it. This connection is all but lost in the *Phenomenology of Mind*. The state ceases now to have an all-embracing significance. Freedom and reason are made activities of the pure mind and do not require a definite social and political order as a pre-condition, but are compatible with the already existing state.

We may assume that his experience of the breakdown of liberal ideas in the history of his own time drove Hegel to take refuge in the pure mind, and that for philosophy's sake he preferred reconciliation with the prevailing system to the terrible contingencies of a new upheaval. The reconciliation that now takes place between philosophical idealism and the given society announces itself not so much as a change in the Hegelian system as such, but as a change in the treatment and function of the dialectic. In the preceding periods the dialectic was oriented to the actual process of history rather than to the end-product of this process. The sketchy form of the *Jenenser Philosophy of Mind* strengthened the impression that something new could yet happen to the mind, and that its development was far from concluded. Furthermore, the *Jenenser* system elaborated the dialectic in the concrete process of labor and of social integration. In the *Phenomenology of Mind* the antagonisms of this concrete dimension are leveled and harmonized. 'The world becomes Mind' takes on the meaning not only that the world in its totality becomes the adequate arena in which the plans of mankind are to be fulfilled, but also means that the world itself reveals a steady progress towards the absolute truth, that nothing new can happen to mind, or, that everything that does happen to it eventually contributes to its advancement. There are, of course, failures and repulses; progress by no means takes place in a straight line, but is produced by the interplay of ceaseless conflicts. The negativity, as we shall see, remains the source and the motive power of the movement. Every failure and every setback, however, possesses its proper good and its proper truth. Every conflict implies its own solution. The change in Hegel's point of view becomes manifest in the unshakable certainty with which he determines the end of the process. The mind, despite all deviations and defeats, despite misery and deterioration, will attain its goal, or, rather, has attained it, in the prevailing social system. The negativity seems to be a *secure* stage in the growth of mind rather than the force that goads it beyond; the opposition in the dialectic appears as a wilful play rather than a struggle of life and death.

Hegel conceived the *Phenomenology of Mind* as an introduction to his philosophical system. During the execution of the work he altered his original plan, however. Knowing that he would not be able to publish the rest of his system in the near future, he incorporated large parts of it into his introduction. The extreme difficulties that the book offers are, to a great extent, due to this procedure.

As an introductory volume, the work intends to lead human understanding from the realm of daily experience to that of real philosophical knowledge, to absolute truth. This truth is the same that Hegel had already demonstrated in the *Jenenser* system, namely, the knowledge and process of the world as mind.

The world in reality is not as it appears, but as it is comprehended by philosophy. Hegel begins with the experience of the ordinary consciousness in everyday life. He shows that this mode of experience, like any other, contains elements that undermine its confidence in its ability to perceive 'the real,' and force the search to proceed to ever higher modes of understanding. The advance to these higher modes is thus an internal process of experience and is not produced from without. If man pays strict attention to the results of his experience, he will abandon one type of knowledge and proceed to another;

he will go from sense-certainty to perception, from perception to understanding, from understanding to self-certainty, until he reaches the truth of reason.

Hegel's *Phenomenology of Mind* thus presents the immanent history of human experience. This is not, to be sure, the experience of common sense, but one already shaken in its security, overlaid with the feeling that it does not possess the whole truth. It is an experience already en route to real knowledge. The reader who is to understand the various parts of the work must already dwell in the 'element of philosophy.' The 'We' that appears so often denotes not everyday men but philosophers.

The factor that determines the course of this experience is the changing relation between consciousness and its objects. If the philosophizing subject adheres to its objects and lets itself be guided by their meaning, it will find that the objects undergo a change by which their form as well as their relation to the subject alters. When experience begins, the object seems a stable entity, independent of consciousness; subject and object appear to be alien to one another. The progress of knowledge, however, reveals that the two do not subsist in isolation. It becomes clear that the object gets its objectivity from the subject. 'The real,' which consciousness actually holds in the endless flux of sensations and perceptions, is a universal that cannot be reduced to objective elements free of the subject (for example, *quality, thing, force, laws*). In other words, the real object is constituted by the (intellectual) activity of the subject; somehow, it essentially 'pertains' to the subject. The latter discovers that it itself stands 'behind' the objects, that the world becomes real only by force of the comprehending power of consciousness.

This is, however, at first nothing but a re-statement of the case of transcendental idealism, or, as Hegel says, it is a truth only 'for us,' the philosophizing subjects, and not yet a truth manifested in the objective world. Hegel goes further. He says, self-consciousness has yet to demonstrate that it is the true *reality;* it must actually make the world its free realization. Referring to this task, Hegel declares the subject to be 'absolute negativity,' signifying that it has the power to negate every given condition and to make it its own conscious work. This is not an epistemological activity and cannot be carried out solely within the process of knowledge, for that process cannot be severed from the historical struggle between man and his world, a struggle that is itself a constitutive part of the way to truth and of the truth itself. The subject must make the world its own doing if it is to recognize itself as the only reality. The process of knowledge becomes the process of history.

We have already reached this conclusion in the *Jenenser Philosophy of Mind.* Self-consciousness carries itself into the life-and-death struggle among individuals. From here on, Hegel links the epistemological process of self-consciousness (from sense-certainty to reason) with the historical process of mankind from bondage to freedom. The 'modes or forms [*Gestalten*] of consciousness'[1] appear simultaneously as objective historical realities, 'states of the world' (*Weltzustände*). The constant transition from philosophical to historical analysis—which has often been criticized as a confusion, or an arbitrary metaphysical interpretation of history—is intended to verify and demonstrate the historical character of the basic philosophical concepts. All of them comprehend and retain actual historical stages in the development of mankind. Each form of consciousness that appears in the immanent progress of knowledge crystallizes as the life of a given historical epoch. The process leads from the Greek city-state to the French Revolution.

[1] *Phenomenology of Mind,* trans. J. B. Baillie, London (The Macmillan Company, New York), 1910, vol. I, p. 34.

Hegel describes the French Revolution as the unloosing of a 'self-destructive' freedom, self-destructive because the consciousness that strove here to change the world in accordance with its subjective interests had not yet found its truth. In other words, man did not discover his real interest, he did not freely place himself under laws that secure his own freedom and that of the whole. The new state created by the Revolution, Hegel says, only altered the external form of the objective world, making it a medium for the subject, but it did not achieve the subject's *essential* freedom.

The achievement of the latter takes place in the transition from the French revolutionary era to that of German idealist culture. The realization of true freedom is thus transferred from the plane of history to the inner realm of the mind. Hegel says: 'absolute freedom leaves its self-destructive sphere of reality [that is, the historical epoch of the French Revolution] and passes over into another realm, that of the self-conscious mind. Here, freedom is held to be true in so far as it is unreal . . .'[2] This new realm had been a discovery of Kant's ethical idealism. Within it, the autonomous individual gives himself the unconditional duty to obey universal laws that he imposes upon himself of his own free will. Hegel did not, however, regard this 'realm' as the final abode of reason. The conflict that developed from Kant's reconciliation of the individual with the universal, a conflict between the dictate of duty and the desire for happiness, forced the individual to seek the truth in other solutions. He looks for it in art and religion and finally finds it in the 'absolute knowledge' of dialectical philosophy. There, all opposition between consciousness and its object is overcome; the subject possesses and knows the world as its own reality, as reason.

[2] Ibid., p. 604.

The *Phenomenology of Mind* in this way leads up to the *Logic*. The latter unfolds the structure of the universe, not in the changing forms that it has for knowledge that is not yet absolute, but in its true essence. It presents 'the truth in its true form.' [8] Just as the experience with which the *Phenomenology* began was not everyday experience, the knowledge with which it ends is not traditional philosophy, but a philosophy that has absorbed the truth of all previous philosophies and with it all the experience mankind has accumulated during its long trek to freedom. It is a philosophy of a self-conscious humanity that lays claim to a mastery of men and things and to its right to shape the world accordingly, a philosophy that enunciates the highest ideals of modern individualist society.

After this brief preliminary survey of the broad perspective of the *Phenomenology of Mind,* we now turn to a discussion of its principal conceptions in greater detail.

The Preface to the *Phenomenology* is one of the greatest philosophical undertakings of all times, constituting no less an attempt than to reinstate philosophy as the highest form of human knowledge, as 'the Science.' We shall here limit ourselves to its main points.

Hegel starts with a critical analysis of the philosophic currents of the turn of the eighteenth century, and proceeds to develop his concept of philosophy and philosophic truth. Knowledge has its source in the vision that essence and existence are distinct in the various cognitive processes. The objects it gets in immediate experience fail to satisfy knowledge, because they are accidental and incomplete, and it turns to seek the truth in the *notion* of objects, convinced that the right notion is not a mere subjective intellectual form, but the essence *of things*. This,

[8] P. 35.

however, is but the first step of knowledge. Its major effort is to demonstrate and expound the relation between essence and existence, between the truth preserved in the notion and the actual state in which things exist.

The various sciences differ from each other by the way in which the objects they deal with are related to their truth. This is confusing unless one bears in mind that for Hegel truth signifies a form *of existence* as well as of knowledge, and that, consequently, the relation between a being and its truth is an objective relation of things themselves. Hegel illustrates this conception by contrasting mathematical and philosophical knowledge. The essence or 'nature' of the right-angle triangle is that its sides are related just as the Pythagorean proposition has it; but this truth is 'outside' the triangle. The proof of the proposition consists in a process carried on solely by the knowing subject. '. . . the triangle .... is taken to pieces, and its parts made into other figures to which the construction gives rise in the triangle.'[4] The necessity for the construction does not arise from the nature or notion of the triangle. 'The process of mathematical proof does not belong to the object; it is a function that takes place outside of the matter in hand. The nature of a right-angled triangle does not break itself up into factors in the manner set forth in the mathematical construction which is required to prove the proposition expressing the relation of its parts. The entire process of producing the result is an affair of knowledge which takes its own way of going about it.'[5] In other words, the truth about mathematical objects exists outside of themselves, in the knowing subject. These objects, therefore, are in a strict sense untrue and unessential 'external' entities.

The objects of philosophy, on the other hand, bear an intrinsic relation to their truth. For example, the princi-

[4] P. 40.

[5] P. 39.

ple that 'the nature of man requires freedom and that freedom is a form of reason' is not a truth imposed upon man by an arbitrary philosophical theory, but can be proved to be the inherent aim of man, his very reality. Its proof is not advanced by the external process of knowledge but by the history of man. In philosophy, the relation of an object to its truth is an actual happening (*Geschehen*). To come back to the example, man finds that he is *not* free, that he is separated from his truth, leading a fortuitous, untrue existence. Freedom is something he must acquire by overcoming his bondage, and he acquires it when he eventually knows his true potentialities. Freedom presupposes conditions that render freedom possible, namely, conscious and rational mastery of the world. The known history of mankind verifies the truth of this conclusion. The notion of man is his history, as apprehended by philosophy. Thus, essence and existence are actually interrelated in philosophy, and the process of proving the truth there has to do with the existing object itself. The essence arises in the process of existence, and conversely, the process of existence is a 'return' to the essence.[6]

Philosophical knowledge aims only at the 'essentials' that have a constitutive bearing upon man's destiny and that of his world. The sole object of philosophy is the world in its true form, the world as reason. Reason, again, comes into its own only with the development of mankind. Philosophic truth, therefore, is quite definitely concerned with man's existence; it is his innermost prod and goal. This, in the last analysis, is the meaning of the statement that truth is immanent in the object of philosophy. The truth fashions the very existence of the object and is not, as in mathematics, indifferent to it. Existing in truth is a matter of life (and death), and the way to truth is

[6] P. 39.

not only an epistemological but also a historical process.

This relation between truth and existence distinguishes the philosophic method. A mathematical truth may be arrested in one proposition; the proposition is true and its contradictory is false. In philosophy, the truth is a real process that cannot be put into a proposition. 'The abstract or unreal is not its element and content, but the real, what is self-establishing, has life within itself, existence in its very notion. It is the process that creates its own moments in its course, and goes through them all; and the whole of this movement constitutes its positive content, and its truth.' [7] No single proposition can grasp this process. For instance, the proposition, 'The nature of man is freedom in reason,' is, if taken by itself, untrue. It omits all the facts that make up the meaning of freedom and of reason, and that are assembled in the whole historical drive towards freedom and reason. Furthermore, the proposition is false in so far as freedom and reason can only appear as the result of the historical process. The conquest of bondage and irrationality, and hence bondage and irrationality themselves, are essential parts of the truth. Falsehood here is as necessary and real as truth. The falsehood must be conceived as the 'mistaken form' or untruth of the real object—this object in its untrue existence; the false is the '*otherness,* the negative aspect of the substance,' [8] but none the less a part of it and hence constitutive in its truth.

The dialectical method conforms to this structure that the philosophic object has, and attempts to reconstruct and follow its real movement. A philosophic system is true only if it includes the negative state and the positive, and reproduces the process of becoming false and then returning to truth. As a system of this kind, the dialectic is the true method of philosophy. It shows that the object with

[7] Pp. 43-4.

[8] P. 36.

which it deals exists in a state of 'negativity,' which the object, through the pressures of its own existence, throws off in the process of regaining its truth.

If, then, in philosophy, no single proposition is true apart from the whole, in what sense is the whole system true? The dialectical system alters the structure and meaning of the proposition and makes it something quite different from the proposition of traditional logic. The latter logic, to which Hegel alludes as 'the logic of common sense,' meaning the logic of traditional scientific method as well, treats propositions as consisting of a subject, which serves as a fixed and stable base, and a predicate attached to it. The predicates are the accidental properties, or, in Hegel's language, 'determinations' of a more or less fixed substance.

As a contrast to this view of the proposition, Hegel sets the 'speculative judgment' in philosophy.[9] The speculative judgment does not have a stable and passive subject. Its subject is active and develops itself into its predicates. The predicates are various forms of the subject's existence. Or, to state it somewhat differently, what happens is that the subject 'goes under' (*geht zu Grunde*) and turns into the predicate. The speculative judgment thus shakes 'the solid base' of the traditional proposition 'to its foundations, and the only object is this very movement of the subject.'[10] For example, the proposition God is Being, taken as a speculative judgment, does not mean that the subject, God, 'possesses' or 'supports' the predicate 'Being' among many other predicates, but that the subject, God, 'passes' into Being. 'Being' here is 'not predicate but the essential nature' of God. The subject God 'seems to cease to be what He was when the proposition was put forward, viz. a fixed subject,' and to become the predicate.[11] Whereas the traditional judgment and proposition imply

[9] P. 61. [10] P. 59. [11] P. 61.

a clear distinction of subject from predicate, the speculative judgment subverts and destroys 'the nature of judgment or of the proposition in general.' It strikes the decisive blow against traditional formal logic. The subject becomes the predicate without at the same time becoming identical with it. The process cannot be adequately expressed in a single proposition; 'the proposition as it appears is a mere empty form.' [12] The locus of truth is not the proposition, but the dynamic system of speculative judgments in which every single judgment must be 'sublated' by another, so that only the whole process represents the truth.

The traditional logic and the traditional concept of truth are 'shaken to their foundations' not by philosophic fiat but by insight into the dynamic of reality. The speculative judgment has for its content the objective process of reality in its essential, 'comprehended form,' not in its appearance. In this very basic sense, Hegel's change from traditional to material logic marked the first step in the direction of unifying theory and practice. His protest against the fixed and formal 'truth' of traditional logic was in effect a protest against divorcing truth and its forms from concrete processes; a protest against severing truth from any direct guiding influence on reality.

In Germany, idealistic philosophy championed the right of theory to guide practice. For idealistic philosophy represented the most advanced form of consciousness that then prevailed, and the idea of a world permeated with freedom and reason had no securer refuge than was offered by this remote sphere of culture. The subsequent development of European thought cannot be understood apart from its idealist origins.

A thorough analysis of the *Phenomenology of Mind*

[12] P. 65.

would require more than a volume. We may forego that analysis, since the latter parts of the work deal with problems we have already outlined in the discussion of the *Jenenser* system. We shall confine our interpretation to the opening sections, which elaborate the dialectical method in great detail and set the pattern for the entire work.[13]

Knowledge begins when philosophy destroys the experience of daily life. Analysis of this experience is the starting point of the search for truth. The object of experience is first given through the senses and takes the form of sense-knowledge or sense-certainty (*sinnliche Gewissheit*). Characteristic of this kind of experience is the fact that its subject as well as its object appears as an 'individual this,' here and now. I see this house, here at this particular place and at this particular moment. The house is taken as 'real' and seems to exist *per se*. The 'I' that sees it seems to be unessential, 'can as well be as *not* be,' and 'only knows the object because the object exists.'[14]

If we analyze a bit, we see that what is known in this experience, what sense-certainty holds as its invariant own amid the flux of impressions, is not the object, the house, but the Here and the Now. If I turn my head, the house disappears and some other object appears, which, with another turn of my head, will likewise disappear. To keep hold of and to define the actual content of sense-certainty I must refer to the Here and Now as the only elements that remain permanent in the continuous change of objective data. What is the Here and Now? *Here* is a house, but it is likewise not a house but a tree, a street, a man, and so on. Now is daytime, but somewhat later now is night, then morning, and so on. The Now remains identical

[13] Compare J. Loewenberg's excellent analysis in his two articles on the Phenomenology of Mind, in *Mind*, vol. XLIII and XLIV, 1934-5.

[14] P. 92.

throughout the differences of day, night, or morning. Moreover, it is Now just because it is neither day, nor night, nor any other moment of time. It preserves itself through the negation of all other moments of time. In other words, the Now exists as something negative; its being is a non-being. The same holds true for Here. Here is neither the house nor the tree nor the street, but what 'is and remains in the disappearance of the house, tree, and so on, and is indifferently house, tree.' [15] That is to say, the Now and the Here are something *Universal.* Hegel says an entity 'which is by and through negation, which is neither this nor that, which is a *not-this,* and with equal indifference this as well as that—a thing of this kind we call a Universal.' The analysis of sense-certainty thus demonstrates the reality of the universal and develops at the same time the philosophic notion of universality. The reality of the universal is proved by the very content of the observable facts; it exists in their process and can be grasped only in and through the particulars.

This is the first result we obtain from philosophical analysis of sense-certainty: it is not the particular, individual object, but the universal that is 'the truth of sense-certainty, the true content of sense-experience.' [16] The result implies something more astonishing. Sense-experience holds it self-evident that the object is the essential, 'the real,' while the subject is unessential and its knowledge dependent upon the object. The true relation is now found to be 'just the reverse of what first appeared.' [17] The universal has turned out to be the true content of experience. And the locus of the universal is the subject and not the object; the universal exists 'in knowledge, which formerly was the non-essential factor.' [18] The object is not *per se;* it is 'because I know it.' The certainty of sense experi-

[15] P. 94. [16] Ibid. [17] P. 95. [18] Ibid.

ence is thus grounded in the subject; it is, as Hegel says, banished from the object, and forced back into the 'I.'

Further analysis of sense-experience reveals that the 'I' goes through the same dialectical process as the object, showing itself to be something universal. At first, the individual I, my ego, seems the sole stable point in the flux of sense data. 'The disappearance of the particular Now and Here that we mean is prevented by the fact that I keep hold of them.' I assert that it is daytime and that I see a house. I record this truth, and someone else reading it later may assert that it is night and that he sees a tree. 'Both truths have the same authenticity' and both become false with a change of time and place. The truth, therefore, cannot attach to a particular individual I. If I say I see a house here and now, I imply that everyone could take my place as subject of this perception. I assume 'the I *qua* universal, whose seeing is neither the seeing of this tree nor of this house, but just seeing.' Just as the Here and Now are universal as against their individual content, so the I is universal as against all individual I's.

The idea of a universal I is an abomination to common sense, though everyday language makes constant use of it. When I say 'I' see, hear, and so on, I put everybody in my place, substitute any other I for my individual I. 'When I say "I," "this individual," I say quite generally "all I's," everyone is what I say, everyone is "I," this individual I.'

Sense-experience thus discovers that truth lies neither with its particular object nor with the individual I. The truth is the result of a double process of negation, namely, (1) the negation of the 'per se' existence of the object, and (2) the negation of the individual I with the shifting of the truth to the universal I. Objectivity is thus twice 'mediated' or constructed by consciousness and henceforward remains tied to consciousness. The development of the objective world is throughout interwoven in the development of consciousness.

Common sense resents such a destruction of its truth and claims that it can indicate the exact particular Here and Now it means. Hegel accepts the challenge. 'Let us, then, see how that immediate Here and Now which is shown to us is constituted.' [19] When I point to a particular Now, 'it has already ceased to be by the time it is pointed out. The Now that is, is other than the one indicated, and we see that the Now is just this—to be when it no longer is.' Pointing to the Now is thus a process involving the following stages: (1) I point to the Now and assert that it is thus and so. 'I point it out, however, as something that has been.' In so doing, I cancel the first truth and assert (2) that the Now *has been,* and that such is the truth. But what has been, *is not*. Thus, (3) I cancel the second truth, negate the negation of the Now, and assert it again as true. This Now, however, which results from the whole process, is not the Now that common sense first meant. It is indifferent to present or past. It is the Now that is past, the one that is present, and so on, and is in all this one and the same Now. In other words, it is something universal.

Sense-experience has thus itself demonstrated that its real content is not the particular but the universal. 'The dialectic process involved in sense-certainty is nothing else than the mere history of its process—of its experience; and sense-certainty itself is nothing else than simply this history.' [20] Experience itself passes to a higher mode of knowledge, which aims at the universal. Sense-certainty turns into perception.

Perception (*Wahrnehmung*) is distinguished from sense-certainty by the fact that its 'principle' is universality.[21] The objects of perception are things (*Dinge*), and things

[19] P. 98. [20] P. 100. [21] P. 104.

remain identical in the changes of Here and Now. For example, I call this thing I perceive here and now 'salt.' I refer not to the particular heres and nows in which it is present to me but to a specific unity in the diversity of its 'properties' (*Eigenschaften*). I refer to the 'thinghood' of the thing. The salt is white, cubical in shape, and so on. These properties in themselves are universal, common to many things. The thing itself seems to be nothing but the 'simple togetherness' of such properties, their general 'medium.' But it is more than such simple togetherness. Its properties are not arbitrary and exchangeable, but rather 'exclude and negate' other properties. If the salt is white and pungent, it cannot be black and sweet. The exclusion is not an arbitrary matter of definition; on the contrary, the definition is dependent on the data offered by the thing itself. It is the salt that excludes and negates certain properties that contradict its 'being salt.' The thing is thus not a 'unity indifferent to what it is, but . . . an *excluding*, repelling unity.' [22]

So far, the object seems to be a definite one, which perception merely has to accept and to 'take unto itself' passively. Perception, like sense-experience, first gathers the truth from the object. But, like sense-experience also, it discovers that the *subject* itself constitutes the objectivity of the thing. For when perception attempts to determine what the thing really is, it plunges into a series of contradictions. The thing is a unity and at the same time a multiplicity. The contradiction cannot be avoided by assigning the two aspects to each of the two factors of perception, so that unity is attached to the consciousness of the subject and the multiplicity to the object. Hegel shows that this would only lead to new contradictions. Nor does it help to assume that the thing is *really* a unity and that the multiplicity is produced by its relation to other

[22] P. 108.

things.[23] All such attempts to escape the contradiction only serve to demonstrate that it is inescapable and constitutes the very content of perception. The thing is in itself unity and difference, unity in difference. Hegel's further analysis of this relationship leads to a new determination of universality. The real universal contains diversity and at the same time maintains itself as an 'excluding and repelling' *unity* in all particular conditions. In this way, the analysis of perception goes beyond the point reached in the analysis of sense-experience. The universal now denoted as the true content of knowledge bears a different character. The unity of the thing is not only determined but constituted by its relation to other things, and its thinghood consists in this very relation. The salt, for example, is what it is only in relation to our taste, to the food to which it is added, to sugar, and so on. The thing salt, to be sure, is more than the mere 'togetherness' of such relations; it is a unity in and for itself, but this unity exists only in these relations and is nothing 'behind' or outside them. The thing becomes itself through its opposition to other things; it is, as Hegel says, the unity of itself with its opposite, or, of being-for-itself with being-for-another.[24] In other words, the very 'substance' of the thing must be gleaned from its self-established relation to other things. This, however, is not within the power of perception to accomplish; it is the work of (conceptual) *understanding*.

The analysis of perception produced 'unity in difference' or the 'unconditioned universal' as the true form of the object of knowledge, unconditioned because the unity of the thing asserts itself despite and through all delimiting conditions. When perception attempted to grasp the real content of its object, the 'thing' turned out to be a self-constituting unity in a diversity of relations to other

[23] P. 117.

[24] P. 119.

things. Hegel now introduces the concept of force to explain how the thing is held together as a self-determining unity in this process. The substance of the thing, he says, can only be understood as force.

The concept of force takes in all the elements that philosophic analysis has so far found to be characteristic of the real object of knowledge. Force is itself a relation, the elements of which are distinct and yet not separate from each other; it is in all conditions not contingent but necessarily determined by itself.[25] We shall not follow the details of Hegel's discussion of this concept, but shall limit ourselves to its conclusions.

If we take the substance of things to be force, we actually split reality into two dimensions. We transcend the perceptible properties of things and reach something beyond and behind them, which we define as 'the real.' For, force is not an entity in the world of perception; it is not a thing or quality we can point to, such as white or cubical. We can only perceive the effect or expression of it, and for us its existence consists in this expression of itself. Force is nothing apart from its effect; its being consists entirely in this coming to be and passing away. If the substance of things is force, their mode of existing turns out to be appearance. For, a being that exists only as 'vanishing,' one that 'is *per se* straightway non-being, we call . . . a semblance (*Schein*).'[26] The term appearance or semblance has for Hegel a twofold meaning. It means first that a thing exists in such a way that its existence is different from its essence; secondly, it means that that which appears is not *mere* seeming (*blosser Schein*), but is the expression of an essence that *exists* only *as appearing*.

[25] See the *Jenenser Logik*, p. 50. Force 'combines in itself the two sides of the relation, the identity and the difference . . . Conceived as Force, the substance is Cause in itself . . . Force is the very determinateness that makes the substance this determinate substance and at the same time posits it as relating itself to its opposite.'

[26] *Phenomenology of Mind*, p. 136.

In other words, the appearance is not a non-being but is the appearance of the essence.

The discovery that force is the substance of things gives the process of knowledge insight into the realm of essence. The world of sense-experience and perception is the realm of appearance. The realm of essence is a 'supersensible' world beyond this changing and evanescent realm of appearance. Hegel calls this early vision of the essence 'the first and therefore imperfect manifestation of Reason'—imperfect because consciousness still finds its truth, 'in the form of an object,' that is, as something opposed to the subject. The realm of essence comes forth as the 'inner' world of things. It remains 'for consciousness a bare and simple beyond, because consciousness does not as yet find itself in it.'

But truth cannot remain eternally out of reach of the subject if man is to escape from an untrue existence in an untrue world. The ensuing analysis therefore buckles down to the task of showing that behind the appearance of things is the subject itself, who constitutes their very essence. Hegel's insistence that the subject be recognized behind the appearance of things is an expression of the basic desire of idealism that man transform the estranged world into a world of his own. The *Phenomenology of Mind* accordingly follows through by merging the sphere of epistemology with the world of history, passing from the discovery of the subject to the task of mastering reality through self-conscious practice.

The concept of force leads to the transition from consciousness to self-consciousness. If the essence of things is conceived as force, the stability of the objective world dissolves into an interplay of movement. The concept, however, means more than a mere play. A force wields a definite power over its effects and remains itself amid its various manifestations. In other words, it acts according to an inherent 'law,' so that, as Hegel puts it, the truth of force is 'the *law* of Force' (*das Gesetz der Kraft*).[27] The realm of essence is not, as it first seemed, a blind play of forces, but a domain of permanent *laws* determining the form of the perceptible world. While the multiplicity of these forms seems at first to require a corresponding multitude of laws, further analysis discloses that the diversity is but a deficient aspect of the truth, and knowledge, in setting out to unify the many laws into an over-arching single law, succeeds in this early phase in gleaning the general form of such. Knowledge finds that things exist under a law if they have 'gathered and preserved all the moments of their appearance' into their inner essence and are capable of preserving their essential identity in their relations to all things. This identity of the 'substance,' as we have already indicated, must be understood as the specific work of a 'subject' that is essentially a constant process of 'unification of opposites.'[28]

The previous analysis has disclosed that the essence of things is force, and the essence of force, law. Force under law is what characterizes the self-conscious subject. The essence of the objective world thus points to the existence of the self-conscious subject. Understanding finds nothing but *itself* when it seeks the essence behind the appearance of things. 'It is manifest that behind the so-called curtain, which is to hide the inner world, there is nothing to be seen unless *we ourselves* go behind there, as much in order that we may thereby see, as that there may be something behind there which can be seen.'[29] The truth of understanding is self-consciousness. The first chapter of the *Phenomenology* has come to a close and the history of self-consciousness begins.

Before we follow this history, we must evaluate the general significance of the first chapter. The reader learns

[27] Ibid., p. 142. [28] See above, p. 69. [29] Ibid., p. 162.

that behind the curtain of appearance is not an unknown thing-in-itself, but the knowing subject. Self-consciousness is the essence of things. We usually say this is the step from Kant to Hegel, that is, from critical to absolute idealism. But to say only that is to omit the purpose that drove Hegel to make this transition.

The first three sections of the *Phenomenology* are a critique of positivism [80] and, even more, of 'reification.' To begin with the latter, Hegel attempts to show that man can know the truth only if he breaks through his 'reified' world. We borrow the term 'reification' from the Marxist theory, where it denotes the fact that all relations between men in the world of capitalism appear as relations between things, or, that what in the social world seem to be the relations of things and 'natural' laws that regulate their movement are in reality relations of men and historical forces. The commodity, for instance, embodies in all its qualities the *social* relations of labor; capital is the power of disposing over men; and so on. By virtue of the inversion, the world has become an alienated, estranged world, in which man does not recognize or fulfill himself, but is overpowered by dead things and laws.

Hegel hit upon the same fact within the dimension of philosophy. Common sense and traditional scientific thought take the world as a totality of things, more or less existing *per se,* and seek the truth in objects that are taken to be independent of the knowing subject. This is more than an epistemological attitude; it is as pervasive as the practice of men and leads them to accept the feeling that they are secure only in knowing and handling objective facts. The more remote an idea is from the impulses, interests, and wants of the living subject, the more true it becomes. And this, according to Hegel, is the ut-

[80] Positivism is used as a general term for the philosophy of 'common sense' experience.

most defamation of truth. For there is, in the last analysis, no truth that does not *essentially concern* the living subject and that is not the subject's truth. The world is an estranged and untrue world so long as man does not destroy its dead objectivity and recognize himself and his own life 'behind' the fixed form of things and laws. When he finally wins this *self-consciousness,* he is on his way not only to the truth of himself but also of his world. And with the recognition goes the doing. He will try to put this truth into action and *make* the world what it *essentially* is, namely, the fulfillment of man's self-consciousness.

This is the impulse animating the opening sections of the *Phenomenology*. True practice presupposes true knowledge and the latter is endangered above all by the positivist claim. Positivism, the philosophy of common sense, appeals to the certainty of facts, but, as Hegel shows, in a world where facts do not at all present what reality can and ought to be, positivism amounts to giving up the real potentialities of mankind for a false and alien world. The positivist attack on universal concepts, on the ground they cannot be reduced to observable facts, cancels from the domain of knowledge everything that may not yet be a fact. In demonstrating that sense-experience and perception, to which positivism appeals, in themselves imply and mean not the particular observed fact but something universal, Hegel is giving a final immanent refutation of positivism. When he emphasizes time and again that the universal is pre-eminent over the particular, he is struggling against limiting truth to the particular 'given.' The universal is more than the particular. This signifies in the concrete that the potentialities of men and things are not exhausted in the given forms and relations in which they may actually appear; it means that men and things are all they have been and actually are, and yet more than all this. Setting the truth in the universal expressed Hegel's conviction that no given particular form, whether in nature or society, embodies the whole truth. Moreover, it was a way of denouncing the isolation of men from things and of recognizing that their potentialities could not be preserved except in their redintegration.

In the treatment of self-consciousness, Hegel resumes the analysis begun in the *System der Sittlichkeit* and the *Jenenser Philosophy of Mind,*[81] of the relation between the individual and his world. Man has learned that his own self-consciousness lies behind the appearance of things. He now sets out to realize this experience, to prove himself master of his world. Self-consciousness thus finds itself in a 'state of desire' (*Begierde*): man, awakened to self-consciousness, desires the objects around him, appropriates and uses them. But in the process he comes to feel that the objects are not the true end of his desire, but that his needs can be fulfilled only through association with other individuals. Hegel says, 'self-consciousness attains its satisfaction only in another self-consciousness.'[82] The meaning of this rather strange statement is explained in the discussion of lordship and bondage that follows it. The concept of labor plays a central role in this discussion in which Hegel shows that the objects of labor are not dead things but living embodiments of the subject's essence, so that in dealing with these objects, man is actually dealing with man.

The individual can become what he is only through another individual; his very existence consists in his 'being-for-another.' The relation, however, is by no means one of harmonious co-operation between equally free individuals who promote the common interest in the pursuit of their own advantage. It is rather a 'life-and-death struggle'

[81] See above, pp. 57, 77.

[82] *Phenomenology of Mind,* p. 173.

between essentially unequal individuals, the one a 'master' and the other a 'servant.' Fighting out the battle is the only way man can come to self-consciousness, that is, to the knowledge of his potentialities and to the freedom of their realization. The truth of self-consciousness is not the 'I' but the 'We,' 'the ego that is We and the We that is ego.' [33]

In 1844 Marx sharpened the basic concepts of his own theory through a critical analysis of Hegel's *Phenomenology of Mind*. He described the 'alienation' of labor in the terms of Hegel's discussion of master and servant. Marx was not familiar with the stages of Hegel's philosophy prior to the *Phenomenology*, but he nevertheless caught the critical impact of Hegel's analysis, even in the attenuated form in which social problems were permitted to enter the *Phenomenology of Mind*. The greatness of that work he saw in the fact that Hegel conceived the 'self-creation' of man (that is, the creation of a reasonable social order through man's own free action) as the process of 'reification' and its 'negation,' in short, that he grasped the 'nature of labor' and saw man to be 'the result of his labor.' [34] Marx makes reference to Hegel's definitive insight, which disclosed to him that lordship and bondage result of necessity from certain relationships of labor, which are, in turn, relationships in a 'reified' world. The relation of lord to servant is thus neither an eternal nor a natural one, but is rooted in a definite mode of labor and in man's relation to the products of his labor.

Hegel's analysis actually begins with the 'experience' that the world in which self-consciousness must prove itself is split into two conflicting domains, the one in which man is bound to his labor so that it determines his whole

[33] Ibid., p. 174.

[34] *Marx-Engels Gesamtausgabe*, Erste Abteilung, Band 3. Berlin 1932, p. 150.

existence, and the other in which man appropriates and possesses another man's labor and becomes master by the very fact of this appropriation and possession. Hegel denotes the latter as the lord and the former as the bondsman.[85] The bondsman is not a human being who happens to labor, but is essentially a laborer; his labor is his being. He works on objects that do not belong to him but to another. He cannot detach his existence from these objects; they constitute 'the chain from which he cannot get away.'[86] He is entirely at the mercy of him who owns these objects. It must be noted that according to this exposition, dependence of man on man is neither a personal condition nor grounded in personal or natural conditions (viz. inferiority, weakness, and so on), but is 'mediated' by things. In other words, it is the outcome of man's relation to the products of his labor. Labor so shackles the laborer to the objects that his consciousness itself does not exist except 'in the form and shape of thinghood.' He becomes a thing whose very existence consists in its being used. The being of the laborer is a 'being-for-another.'[87]

Labor is, however, at the same time the vehicle that transforms this relationship. The laborer's action does not disappear when the products of his labor appear, but is preserved in them. The things labor shapes and fashions fill the social world of man, and function there as objects of labor. The laborer learns that his labor perpetuates this world; he sees and recognizes himself in the things about him. His consciousness is now 'externalized' in his work and has 'passed into the condition of permanence.' The man who 'toils and serves' thus comes to view the independent being as himself.[88] The objects of his labor are no longer dead things that shackle him to other men, but products of his work, and, as such, part and parcel of his

[85] *Phenomenology of Mind*, p. 182.
[86] Ibid.
[87] Ibid., p. 181.
[88] P. 186.

own being. The fact that the product of his labor is objectified does not make it 'something other than the consciousness moulding the thing through work; for just that form is his pure self-existence, which therein becomes truly realized.' [39]

The process of labor creates self-consciousness not only in the laborer but in the master as well. Lordship is defined chiefly by the fact that the lord commands objects he desires without working on them.[40] He satisfies his type of need through having someone, not himself, work. His enjoyment depends upon his own freedom from labor. The laborer he controls delivers to him the objects he wants in an advanced form, ready to be enjoyed. The laborer thus preserves the lord from having to encounter the 'negative side' of things, that on which they become fetters on man. The lord receives all things as products of labor, not as dead objects, but as things that bear the hallmark of the subject who worked on them. When he handles these things as his property, the lord is really handling another self-consciousness, that of the laborer, the being through whom he attains his satisfaction. The lord in this wise finds that he is not an independent 'being-for-himself,' but is essentially dependent on another being, upon the action of him who labors for him.

Hegel has so far developed the relation of lordship and bondage as a relation each side of which recognizes that it has its essence in the other and comes to its truth only through the other. The opposition between subject and object that determined the forms of mind hitherto described has now disappeared. The object, shaped and cultivated by human labor, is in reality the objectification of a self-conscious subject. 'Thinghood, which received its shape and form through labor, is no other substance than consciousness. In this way, we have a new mode [*Gestalt*]

[39] P. 187.
[40] P. 182.

of self-consciousness brought about. We have now a consciousness which . . . *thinks* or is free self-consciousness.' [41] Why this rather sudden identification of the free self-consciousness with the 'consciousness which thinks'? Hegel goes on to a definition of thinking that answers this question in the basic terms of his philosophy. He says, the subject of thinking is not the 'abstract ego' but the consciousness that knows that it is the 'substance' of the world. Or, thinking consists in knowing that the objective world is in reality a subjective world, that it is the objectification of the subject. The subject that really thinks comprehends the world as 'his' world. Everything in it has its true form only as a 'comprehended' (*begriffenes*) object, namely, as part and parcel of the development of a free self-consciousness. The totality of objects that make up man's world have to be freed from their 'opposition' to consciousness and must be taken up in such a way as to assist its development.

Hegel describes thinking in terms of a definite kind of existence. 'In thinking, I am free, because I am not in an other, but remain simply and solely in touch with myself; and the object . . . is in undivided unity my being-for-myself; and my procedure in comprehending is a procedure within myself.' [42] This explanation of freedom shows that Hegel is connecting this basic concept with the principle of a particular form of society. He says that he is free who, in his existence with others, remains solely with himself, he who holds his existence, as it were, as his own undisputed property. Freedom is self-sufficiency and independence of all 'externals,' a state wherein all externality has been appropriated by the subject. The fears and anxieties of competitive society, seem to motivate this idea of freedom, the individual's fear of losing him-

[41] P. 190. [42] P. 191.

self and his anxiety to preserve and secure his own. It leads Hegel to give the predominant position to the 'element of thought.'

Indeed, if freedom consists in nothing but complete self-sufficiency, if everything that is not entirely mine or myself restricts my freedom, then freedom can only be realized in thinking. We must therefore expect Hegel to treat stoicism as the first historical form of self-conscious freedom. The stoic mode of existence seems to have overcome all the restrictions that apply in nature and society. 'The essence of this consciousness is to be free, on the throne as well as in fetters, throughout all the dependence that attaches to its individual existence . . .'[43] Man is thus free because he 'persistently withdraws from the movement of existence, from activity as well as endurance, into the mere essentiality of thought.'

Hegel goes on to say, however, that this is not real freedom. It is only the counterpart of 'a time of universal fear and bondage.' He thus repudiates this false form of freedom and corrects his statement quoted above. 'Freedom in thought takes only pure thought as its truth, but this lacks the concrete filling of life. It is, therefore, merely the notion of freedom, not living freedom itself.'[44] The sections on stoicism in which these statements appear show the play of conflicting elements in his philosophy. He has demonstrated that freedom rests in the element of thought; he now insists on an advance from freedom in thought to 'living freedom.' He states that the freedom and independence of self-consciousness is therefore but a transitory stage in the development of mind towards real freedom. The latter dimension is reached when man abandons the abstract freedom of thought and enters into the world in full consciousness that it is 'his own' world. The 'hitherto negative attitude' of self-consciousness towards

[43] P. 193.

[44] P. 193.

reality 'turns into a positive attitude. So far it has been concerned merely with its own independence and freedom; it has sought to keep itself "for itself" at the expense of the world or its own actuality . . .'[45] Now, 'it discovers the world as its own new and real world, which in its permanence possesses an interest for it.' The subject conceives the world as its own 'presence' and truth; it is certain of finding only itself there.[46]

This process is the process of history itself. The self-conscious subject attains his freedom not in the form of the 'I' but of the We, the associated We that first appeared as the outcome of the struggle between lord and bondsman. The historical reality of that We 'finds its actual fulfillment in the life of a nation.'[47]

We have indicated the subsequent course of the mind in the first pages of this chapter. At the end of the road, pure thought again seems to swallow up living freedom: the realm of 'absolute knowledge' is enthroned above the historical struggle that closed when the French Revolution was liquidated. The self-certainty of philosophy comprehending the world triumphs over the practice that changes it. We shall see whether this solution was Hegel's last word.

The foundations of the absolute knowledge that the *Phenomenology of Mind* presents as the truth of the world are given in Hegel's *Science of Logic,* to which we now turn.

[45] P. 223. [46] Ibid. [47] P. 341.

V

The Science of Logic
(1812-16)

THE striking difference between Hegel's Logic and the traditional logic has often been emphasized in the statement that Hegel replaced the formal by a material logic, repudiating the usual separation of the categories and forms of thought from their content. Traditional logic treated these categories and forms as valid if they were correctly formed and if their use was in conformity with the ultimate laws of thought and the rules of the syllogism —no matter what the content to which they were applied. Contrary to this procedure, Hegel maintained that the content determines the form of the categories as well as their validity. 'But it is the nature of the content, and that alone, which lives and progresses in philosophic cognition, and at the same time it is the inner reflection of the content which posits and originates its determinations.' [1] The categories and modes of thought derive from the process of reality to which they pertain. Their form is determined by the structure of this process.

It is in this connection that the claim is often made that Hegel's logic was new. Novelty is supposed to consist in his use of the categories to express the dynamic of reality. In point of fact, however, this dynamic conception was not a Hegelian innovation; it occurs in Aristotle's philosophy where all forms of being are interpreted as forms and types of movement. Aristotle attempted exact

[1] *Science of Logic,* trans. W. H. Johnston and L. G. Struthers, The Macmillan Company, New York 1929, vol. I, p. 36.

philosophical formulation in dynamic terms. Hegel simply reinterpreted the basic categories of Aristotle's *Metaphysics* and did not invent new ones.

We must note in addition that a dynamic philosophy was enunciated in German philosophy prior to Hegel. Kant dissolved the static forms of the given reality into a complex of syntheses of 'transcendental consciousness,' while Fichte endeavored to reduce 'the given' to a spontaneous act of the ego. Hegel did not discover the dynamic of reality, nor was he the first to adapt philosophical categories to this process. What he did discover and use was a definite form of dynamic, and the novelty of his logic and its ultimate significance rest upon this fact. The philosophical method he elaborated was intended to reflect the actual process of reality and to construe it in an adequate form.

With the *Science of Logic,* we reach the final level of Hegel's philosophic effort. Henceforward, the basic structure of his system and its ground concepts remain unaltered. It might therefore be appropriate briefly to review this structure and these concepts along the lines of Hegel's exposition of them in the prefaces and the introduction to the *Science of Logic.*

Sufficient notice has not been given to the fact that Hegel himself introduces his logic as primarily a critical instrument. It is, first of all, critical of the view that 'the material of knowledge exists in and for itself in the shape of a finished world apart from Thinking,' that it exists as 'something in itself finished and complete, something which, as far as its reality is concerned, could entirely dispense with thought.' [2] Hegel's first writings have already shown that his attack on the traditional separation of thought from reality involves much more than an epistemological critique. Such dualism, he thinks, is tantamount

[2] Ibid., vol. 1, p. 54.

to a compliance with the world as it is and a withdrawal of thought from its high task of bringing the existing order of reality into harmony with the truth. The separation of thought from being implies that thought has withdrawn before the onslaught of 'common sense.' If, then, truth is to be attained, the influence of common sense must be swept away and with it the categories of traditional logic, which are, after all, the philosophical categories of common sense that stabilize and perpetuate a false reality. And the task of breaking the hold of common sense belongs to the dialectical logic. Hegel repeats over and over that dialectics has this 'negative' character. The negative 'constitutes the quality of dialectical Reason,' [3] and the first step 'towards the true concept of Reason' is a 'negative step'; [4] the negative 'constitutes the genuine dialectical procedure.' [5] In all these uses 'negative' has a twofold reference: it indicates, first, the negation of the fixed and static categories of common sense and, secondly, the negative and therefore untrue character of the world designated by these categories. As we have already seen, negativity is manifest in the very process of reality, so that nothing that exists is true in its given form. Every single thing has to evolve new conditions and forms if it is to fulfill its potentialities.

The existence of things is, then, basically negative; all exist apart from and in want of their truth, and their actual movement, guided by their latent potentialities, is their progress towards this truth. The course of progress, however, is not direct and unswerving. The negation that every thing contains determines its very being. The material part of a thing's reality is made up of what that thing *is not,* of what it excludes and repels as its opposite. 'The one and only thing *for securing scientific progress*

[3] P. 36. [4] P. 56. [5] P. 66.

. . . is knowledge of the logical precept that Negation is just as much Affirmation as Negation, or that what is self-contradictory resolves itself not into nullity, into abstract Nothingness, but essentially only into the negation of its *particular* content . . .'[6]

Contradiction, or the concrete form of it we are discussing, the opposition, does not displace the actual identity of the thing, but produces this identity in the form of a process in which the potentialities of things unfold. The law of identity by which traditional logic is guided implies the so-called law of contradiction. *A* equals *A* only in so far as it is opposed to non-*A*, or, the identity of *A* results from and contains the contradiction. *A* does not contradict an external non-*A*, Hegel holds, but a non-*A* that belongs to the very identity of *A;* in other words, *A* is *self*-contradictory.

By virtue of the negativity that belongs to its nature each thing is linked with its opposite. To be what it *really* is it must become what it is not. To say, then, that everything contradicts itself is to say that its essence contradicts its given state of existence. Its proper nature, which is, in the last analysis, its essence, impels it to 'transgress' the state of existence in which it finds itself and pass over to another. And not only that, but it must even transgress the bounds of its own particularity and put itself into universal relation with other things. The human being, to take an instance, finds his proper identity only in those relations that are in effect the negation of his isolated particularity—in his membership in a group or social class whose institutions, organization, and values determine his very individuality. The truth of the individual transcends his particularity and finds a totality of conflicting relations in which his individuality fulfills itself.

[6] Pp. 64-5.

We are thus led once more to the universal as the true form of reality.

The logical form of the universal is the notion. Hegel says that the truth and essence of things lives in their notion. The statement is as old as philosophy itself, and has even seeped into popular language. We say that we know and hold the truth of things in our ideas about them. The notion is the idea that expresses their essence, as distinguished from the diversity of their phenomenal existence. Hegel draws the consequence of this view. 'When we mean to speak of things, we call the Nature or essence of them their Concept,' but at the same time we maintain that the concept 'exists only for thought.' [7] For, it is claimed, the concept is a universal, whereas all that exists is a particular. The concept is thus 'merely' a concept and its truth merely a thought. In opposition to this view, Hegel shows that the universal not only *exists,* but that it is even more actually a reality than is the particular. There *is* such a universal reality as man or animal, and this universal in fact makes for the existence of every individual man or animal. 'Every human individual, though infinitely unique, is so only *because* he belongs to the class of man, every animal only *because* it belongs to the class of animal. Being-man, or being-animal, is the Prius of their individuality.' [8] The biological and psychological processes of the human and animal individual are, in a strict sense, not its own but those of its species or kind. When Hegel says that every human individual is first man, he means that his highest potentialities and his true existence center in his being-man. Accordingly, the actions, values, and aims of every particular individual or group have to be measured up against what man can and ought to be.

[7] P. 44. [8] P. 45.

The concrete importance of the conception becomes obvious when contrasted with modern authoritarian ideology in which the reality of the universal is denied, the better to subjugate the individual to the particular interests of certain groups that arrogate to themselves the function of the universal. If the individual were nothing but the individual, there would be no justifiable appeal from the blind material and social forces that overpower his life, no appeal to a higher and more reasonable social ordering. If he were nothing but a member of a particular class, race, or nation, his claims could not reach beyond his particular group, and he would simply have to accept its standards. According to Hegel, however, there is no particularity whatsoever that may legislate for the individual man. The universal itself reserves that ultimate right.

The content of the universal is preserved in the notion. If the universal is not just an abstraction but a reality, then the notion denotes that reality. The formation of the notion, too, is not an arbitrary act of thinking, but something that follows the very movement of reality. The formation of the universal, in the last analysis, is a historical process and the universal a historical factor. We shall see, in Hegel's *Philosophy of History,* that the historical development from the Oriental to the modern world is conceived as one in which man makes himself the actual subject of the historical process. Through the negation of every historical form of existence that becomes a fetter on his potentialities, man finally gets for himself the self-consciousness of freedom. The dialectical notion of man comprehends and includes this material process. This notion therefore cannot be put in a single proposition or a series of propositions that claims to define the essence of man in accordance with the traditional law of identity. The definition requires a whole system of propositions that mirror the actual development of mankind. In the different parts of the system the essence of man will appear in different and even contradictory forms. The truth will be no one of these, but the totality, the concrete development of man.

We have outlined the negative aspect of the dialectic. Its positive aspect consists in its shaping of the universal through the negation of the particular, in its construction of the notion. The notion of a thing is 'the Universal immanent in it,' [9] immanent because the universal contains and holds up the proper potentialities of the thing. Dialectical thinking is 'positive because it is the source of the Universal in which the Particular is comprehended.' [10] The process of dissolving and destroying the common-sense stability of the world thus results in constructing 'the Universal which is in itself concrete,' concrete, for it does not exist outside the particular but realizes itself only in and through the particular, or, rather, in the totality of particulars.

We have taken man as an example of the dialectical construction of the universal. Hegel, however, demonstrates the same process for all entities of the objective and subjective world. The *Science of Logic* deals with the general ontological structure these entities have, and not with their individual concrete existence. For this reason, the dialectical process in the *Logic* assumes a most general and abstract form. We have already discussed it in the chapter on the *Jenenser Logic*.[11] The process of thought begins with the attempt to grasp the objective structure of *being*. In the course of the analysis, this structure dissolves into a multitude of interdependent 'somethings,' qualities and quantities. On further analysis thought discovers that these constitute a totality of an-

[9] P. 45.

[10] P. 36.

[11] See above, pp. 62 ff.

tagonistic relations, governed by the creative power of contradiction. These relations appear as the *essence* of being. The essence, therefore, emerges as the process that negates all stable and delimited forms of being and negates as well the concepts of traditional logic which express these forms. The categories Hegel uses to unfold this essence comprehend the actual structure of being as a unification of opposites which requires that reality be interpreted in terms of the 'subject.' The logic of objectivity thus turns into the logic of subjectivity which is the true *'notion'* of reality.

There are several meanings of the term notion that appear in the exposition.

1. Notion is the 'essence' and 'nature' of things, 'that which by thinking is known in and of things' and 'what is really true in them.' [12] This meaning implies a multitude of notions to correspond to the multitude of things they denote.

2. Notion designates the rational structure of being, the world as *Logos,* reason. In this sense, the notion is 'one, and is the essential basis' and the actual content of the *Logic.*[13]

3. Notion in its true form of existence is 'the free, independent and self-determining Subjective, or rather the Subject itself.' [14] It is this sense of the term that Hegel means when he says, 'The character of Subject must be expressly reserved for the Notion.' [15]

The *Science of Logic* opens with the well-known interplay of Being and Nothing. Unlike the *Phenomenology of Mind,* the *Logic* does not begin with the data of common sense, but with the same philosophical concept that brought the *Phenomenology* to a close. Thinking, in its quest for the truth behind the facts, seeks a stable base for orientation, a universal and necessary law amid the endless flux and diversity of things. Such a universal, if

[12] P. 55. [13] P. 48. [14] P. 75. [15] P. 72.

it is really to be the beginning and the basis for all subsequent determinations, must not itself be determinate, for otherwise it would be neither first nor the beginning. The reason it could not be determinate if it is to be a beginning lies in the fact that everything determinate is dependent on that which determines it, and hence is not prior.

The first and indeterminate universal that Hegel posits is being. It is common to all things (for all things are being), therefore, the most universal entity in the world. It has no determination whatsoever; it is pure being and nothing else.

The *Logic* thus begins, as the whole of Western philosophy began, with the concept of being. The question, What is Being? sought that which holds all things in existence and makes them what they are. The concept of being presupposes a distinction between determinate being (something; *Seiendes*) and being-as-such (*Sein*), without determinations.[16] Daily language distinguishes being from determinate being in all the forms of judgment. We say a rose is a plant; he is jealous; a judgment is true; God is. The copula 'is' denotes being, but being that is quite different from a determinate being. The 'is' does not point to any actual thing that could be made the subject of a determinate proposition, for in determining being as such and such a thing, we would have to use the selfsame 'is' which we are attempting to define, a patent impossibility. We cannot define being as some thing since being is the predicate of every thing. In other words, every thing *is,* but being *is not* some thing. And what is not some thing is nothing. Thus, being is 'pure indeterminateness and vacuity'; it is no thing, hence nothing.[17]

In the attempt to grasp being we encounter nothing.

[16] See above, pp. 40 f.

[17] *Science of Logic,* vol. I, p. 94.

Hegel uses this fact as an instrumentality to demonstrate the negative character of reality. In the foregoing analysis of the concept of being, being did not 'turn into' nothing, but both were revealed as identical, so that it is true to say every determinate being contains the being as well as the nothing. According to Hegel, there is not a single thing in the world that does not have in it the togetherness of being and nothing. Everything *is* only in so far as, at every moment of its being, something that as yet *is not* comes into being and something that is now passes into not-being. Things *are* only in so far as they arise and pass away, or, being must be conceived as becoming (*Werden*).[18] The togetherness of being and nothing is thus manifest in the structure of all existents and must be retained in every logical category: 'This unity of Being and Nothing, as being the primary truth, is, once and for all, the basis and the element of all that follows: therefore, besides Becoming itself, all further logical determinations . . . and in short all philosophic concepts, are examples of this unity.'

If this is the case, logic has a task hitherto unheard of in philosophy. It ceases to be the source of rules and forms for correct thinking. In fact, it takes rules, forms, and all the categories of traditional logic to be false because they disregard the negative and contradictory nature of reality. In Hegel's logic the content of the traditional categories is completely reversed. Moreover, since the traditional categories are the gospel of everyday thinking (including ordinary scientific thinking) and of everyday practice, Hegel's logic in effect presents rules and forms of false thinking and action—false, that is, from the standpoint of common sense. The dialectical categories construct a topsy-turvy world, opening with the identity of being and nothing and closing with the notion as the true reality. Hegel

[18] Ibid., p. 118.

plays up the absurd and paradoxical character of this world, but he who follows the dialectical process to the end discovers that the paradox is the receptacle of the hidden truth and that the absurdity is rather a quality possessed by the correct schema of common sense, which, cleansed of their dross, contains the latent truth. For the dialectic shows latent in common sense the dangerous implication that the form in which the world is given and organized may contradict its true content, that is to say, that the potentialities inherent in men and things may require the dissolution of the given forms. Formal logic accepts the world-form as it is and gives some general rules for theoretical orientation to it. Dialectical logic, on the other hand, rejects any claim of sanctity for the given, and shatters the complacency of those living under its rubric. It holds that 'external existence' is never the sole criterion of the truth of a content,[19] but that every form of existence must justify before a higher tribunal whether it is adequate to its content or not.

Hegel said the negativity of being is 'the basis and the element' of all that ensues. Progress from one logical category to another is stimulated by an inherent tendency in every type of being to overcome its negative conditions of existence and pass into a new mode of being where it attains its true form and content. We have already noted that the movement of categories in Hegel's logic is but a reflection of the movement of being. Moreover, it is not quite correct to say that one category 'passes into' another. The dialectical analysis rather reveals one category *as* another, so that the other represents its unfolded content—unfolded by the contradictions inherent in it.

The first category that participates in this process is quality. We have seen that all being in the world is determinate; the first task of the logic is to investigate this

[19] P. 124.

determinacy. Something is determinate when it is qualitatively distinct from any other being. 'By virtue of its quality Something is opposed to an Other: it is variable and finite, and determined as negative, not only in contrast with an Other, but simply in itself.' [20] Every qualitative determination is in itself a limitation and therefore a negation. Hegel gives this old philosophic statement a new content in linking it with his negative conception of reality.[21] A thing exists with a certain quality—this means that it excludes other qualities and finds itself limited by the ones it has. Moreover, every quality is what it is only in relation to other qualities, and these relations determine the very nature of a quality. Thus, the qualitative determinates of a thing are reduced to relations that dissolve the thing into a totality of other things, so that it exists in a dimension of 'otherness.' For instance, the table here in this room is, if analyzed for its qualities, not the table but a certain color, material, size, tool, and so on. It is, Hegel says, in respect of qualities, not being-for-itself, but 'being-for-other' (*Anderssein, Sein-für-Anderes*). As against this otherness stands what the thing is in itself (its being a table), or, as Hegel calls it, its 'Being-in-itself' (*Ansichsein*). These are the two conceptual elements with which Hegel constructs every being. It must be noted that for Hegel these two elements cannot be detached from one another. A thing in itself is what it is only in its relations with others, and, conversely, its relations with others determine its very existence. The traditional idea of a thing-in-itself behind phenomena, an outer world separated from the inner, an essence permanently removed from reality, is rendered absurd by this conception, and philosophy emerges as definitely joined to the concrete reality.

We return to our analysis of quality. Determinate being

[20] P. 121.

[21] See above, pp. 123 f.

is more than the flux of changing qualities. Something preserves itself throughout this flux, something that passes into other things, but also stands against them as a being for itself. This something can exist only as the product of a process through which it integrates its otherness with its own proper being. Hegel says that its existence comes about through 'the negation of the negation.' [22] The first negation is the otherness in which it turns, and the second is the incorporation of this other into its own self.

Such a process presupposes that things possess a certain power over their movement, that they exist in a certain self-relation that enables them to 'mediate' their existential conditions.[23] Hegel adds that this concept of mediation is 'of the utmost importance' because it alone overcomes the old metaphysical abstractions of Substance, Entelechy, Form, and so on, and, by conceiving the objective world as the development of the subject, paves the way for a philosophical interpretation of concrete reality.

Hegel attributes to the thing a permanent relation to itself. 'Something is in itself in so far as it has returned to itself from Being-for-Other.' [24] It is then an 'intro-reflected' being. Intro-reflection is a characteristic of the subject, however, and in this sense the objective 'something' is already 'the beginning of the subject,' [25] though only the beginning. For, the process by which the something sustains itself is blind and not free; the thing cannot manœuver the forces that shape its existence. The 'something' is hence a low level of development in the process that culminates in a free and conscious subject. 'Something determines itself as Being-for-Self and so on, till finally, as Notion, it receives the concrete intensity of the subject.' [26]

22 *Science of Logic*, vol. I, p. 128.
23 Pp. 127-8.
24 P. 132.
25 P. 128.
26 Ibid.

Hegel continues by pointing out that the thing's unity with itself, which is the basis for its determinate states, is really something negative, because it results from the 'negation of the negation.' The objective thing *is* determined; it passes into a new mode of being by *suffering* the action of manifold natural forces; hence, the 'negative unity' that it has is not a conscious or active unity, but a mechanical one. Owing to its lack of real power, the thing simply 'collapses into that simple unity which is Being,'[27] a unity that is not the result of a self-directed process of its own. The thing, engaged though it is in continuous transitions into other things and states, is subject *to* change and not the subject *of* change.

The sections that follow outline the manner in which the unity of a thing may develop. They are difficult to understand because Hegel applies to the objective world categories that find their verification only in the life of the subject. Concepts like determination, mediation, self-relation, ought, and so on, anticipate categories of subjective existence. Hegel nevertheless uses them to characterize the world of objective things, analyzing the existence of things in terms of the existence of the subject. The net result is that objective reality is interpreted as the field in which the subject is to be realized.

Negativity appears as the difference between being-for-other and being-for-self within the unity of the thing. The thing as it is 'in itself' is different from the conditions in which it actually exists. The actual conditions of the thing 'oppose' or stand in the way of its working out its proper nature. This opposition Hegel denotes as that between determination (*Bestimmung*), which now takes on the meaning of the 'proper nature' of the thing, and talification (*Beschaffenheit*), which refers to the actual state or condition of the thing. The determination of a

27 P. 128.

thing comprises its inherent potentialities 'as against the external conditions which are not yet incorporated in the thing itself.'[28]

When, for instance, we speak of the determination of man, and say that that determination is reason, we imply that the external conditions in which man lives do not agree with what man properly is, that his state of existence is not reasonable and that it is man's task to make it so. Until the task is successfully completed, man exists as a being-for-other rather than a being-for-self. His talification contradicts his determination. The presence of the contradiction makes man restive; he struggles to overcome his given external state. The contradiction thus has the force of an 'Ought' (*Sollen*) that impels him to realize that which does not as yet exist.

As we have said, the objective world, too, is now treated as a participant in the same kind of process. The thing's transition from one talification to another, and even its passage into another thing, are interpreted as motivated by the thing's own potentialities. Its transformation does not occur, as first appeared, 'according to its Being-for-other,' but according to its proper self.[29] Within the process of change, every external condition is taken into the thing's proper being, and its other is 'posited in the thing as its own moment.'[30] The concept of negation, too, undergoes revision in Hegel's exposition at this point. We have seen that the various states of a thing were interpreted as various 'negations' of its true being. Now, since the thing is conceived as a kind of subject that determines itself through its relations to other things, its existent qualities or talifications are barriers or limits (*Grenzen*) through which its potentialities must break. The process of existence is simply the contradiction between talifications and potentialities; hence, to exist and to be limited

[28] P. 136. [29] P. 137. [30] P. 138.

are identical. 'Something has its Determinate Being only in Limit' [31] and the 'Limits are the principle of that which they limit.'

Hegel summarizes the result of this new interpretation by saying that the existence of things is 'the unrest of Something in its Limit; it is immanent in the Limit to be the contradiction which sends Something on beyond itself.' [32] We have herewith reached Hegel's concept of finitude. Being is continuous becoming. Every state of existence has to be surpassed; it is something negative, which things, driven by their inner potentialities, desert for another state, which again reveals itself as negative, as limit.

> When we say of things that they are finite, we mean thereby . . . that Not-Being constitutes their nature and their Being. Finite things are; but their relation to themselves is that they are related to themselves as something negative, and in this self-relation send themselves on beyond themselves and their Being. They are, but the truth of this Being is their end. The finite does not only change, . . . it perishes; and its perishing is not merely contingent, so that it could be without perishing. It is rather the very being of finite things that they contain the seeds of perishing as their own Being-in-Self [*Insichsein*], and the hour of their birth is the hour of their death.[33]

These sentences are a preliminary enunciation of the decisive passages in which Marx later revolutionized Western thought. Hegel's concept of finitude freed philosophic approaches to reality from the powerful religious and theological influences that were operative even upon secular forms of eighteenth-century thought. The current idealistic interpretation of reality in that day still held the view that the world was a finite one because it was a created world and that its negativity referred to its sinfulness. The struggle against this interpretation of 'negative' was therefore in large measure a conflict with religion

[31] P. 140. [32] Pp. 140-41. [33] P. 142.

and the church. Hegel's idea of negativity was not moral or religious, but purely philosophical, and the concept of finitude that expressed it became a critical and almost materialistic principle with him. The world, he said, is finite not because it is created by God but because finitude is its inherent quality. Correspondingly, finitude is not an aspersion on reality, requiring the transfer of its truth to some exalted Beyond. Things are finite in so far as they are, and their finitude is the realm of their truth. They cannot develop their potentialities except by perishing.

Marx later laid down the historical law that a social system can set free its productive forces only by perishing and passing into another form of social organization. Hegel saw this law of history operative in all being. 'The highest maturity or stage which any Something can reach is that in which it begins to perish.' [34] It is clear enough from the preceding discussion that when Hegel turned from the concept of finitude to that of infinity he could not have had reference to an infinity that would annul the results of his previous analysis, that is, he could not have meant an infinity apart from or beyond finitude. The concept of the infinite, rather, had to result from a stricter interpretation of finitude.

As a matter of fact, we find that the analysis of objective things has already taken us from the finite to the infinite. For the process in which a finite thing perishes and, in perishing, becomes another finite thing, which repeats the same, is in itself a process *ad infinitum,* and not only in the superficial sense that the progression cannot be broken. When a finite thing 'perishes into' another thing, it has changed itself, inasmuch as perishing is its way of consummating its true potentialities. The incessant perishing of things is thus an equally continuous negation of their finitude. It is infinity. 'The finite in perish-

[34] Vol. II, p. 246.

ing, in this negation of its self, has reached its Being-in-Self [*Ansichsein*], and therefore has gained its proper self . . . Thus it passes beyond itself only to find itself again. This self-identity, or negation of negation, is affirmative Being, is the other of the Finite, . . . is the Infinite.' [35]

The infinite, then, is precisely the inner dynamic of the finite, comprehended in its real meaning. It is nothing else but the fact that finitude 'exists only as a passing beyond' itself.[36]

In an addendum to his exposition Hegel shows that the concept of finitude yields the basic principle of idealism. If the being of things consists in their transformation rather than in their state of existence, the manifold states they have, whatever their form and content may be, are but moments of a comprehensive process and exist only within the totality of this process. Thus, they are of an 'ideal' nature and their philosophical interpretation must be idealism.[37] 'The proposition that the finite is of ideal nature constitutes Idealism. In philosophy idealism consists of nothing else than the recognition that the finite has no veritable being. Essentially every philosophy is an idealism, or at least has idealism for its principle . . .' [38] For, philosophy starts when the truth of the given state of things is questioned and when it is recognized that that state has no final truth in itself. To say 'that the finite has no veritable being' does not mean that the true being must be sought in a transmundane Beyond or in the inmost soul of man. Hegel rejects such flight from reality as 'bad idealism.' His idealistic proposition implies that the current forms of thought, just because they stop short at the given forms of things, must be changed into other

[35] Vol. I, p. 149. [36] P. 159.

[37] Hegel employs the original historical sense of 'ideal.' An existent is 'of an ideal nature' if it exists not through itself, but through something else.

[38] P. 168.

forms until the truth is reached. Hegel embodies this essentially critical attitude in his concept of ought. The 'ought' is not a province of morality or religion, but of actual practice. Reason and law inhere in finitude, they not only ought to, but must be realized on this earth. 'In actual fact, Reason and Law are at no such sorry pass as that they merely "ought" to be; . . .—nor yet is Ought in itself perpetual, nor finitude (which would be the same) absolute.' [39] The negation of finitude is at the same time the negation of the infinite Beyond; it involves the demand that the 'ought' be fulfilled in this world.

Accordingly, Hegel contrasts his concept of infinity with the theological idea of it. There is no reality other than or above the finite; if finite things are to find their true being, they must find it through their finite existence and through it alone. Hegel calls his concept of infinity, therefore, the very 'negation of that beyond which is in itself negative.' His infinite is but the 'other' of the finite and therefore dependent on finitude; it is in itself a finite infinity. There are not two worlds, the finite and the infinite. There is only one world, in which finite things attain their self-determination through perishing. Their infinity is in this world and nowhere else.

Conceived as the 'infinite' process of transformation, the finite is the process of being-for-self (*Fürsichsein*). A thing is for itself, we say, when it can take all its external conditions and integrate them with its proper being. It is 'for itself' if it 'has passed beyond the Barrier and its Otherness in such a manner that, thus negating them, it is infinite return upon itself.' [40] Being-for-itself is not a state but a process, for every external condition must continuously be transformed into a phase of self-realization, and each new external condition that arises must be subjected to this treatment. Self-consciousness, Hegel says, is

[39] P. 149.

[40] P. 171.

the 'nearest example of the presence of infinity.' On the other hand, 'natural things never attain a free Being-for-self'; they remain being-for-other.[41]

This essential difference between the object's mode of existence and that of a conscious being results in limiting the term 'finite' to things that do not exist for themselves and do not have the power, therefore, to fulfill their potentialities through their own free, conscious acts. Owing to their lack of freedom and consciousness, their manifold qualities are 'indifferent' to them,[42] and their unity is a quantitative unit rather than a qualitative unity.[43]

We shall omit the discussion of the category of quantity and turn directly to the transition from being to essence, which brings the First Book of the *Science of Logic* to a close. The analysis of quantity discloses that quantity is not external to the nature of a thing but is itself a quality, namely, measure (*Mass*). The qualitative character of quantity finds expression in Hegel's famous law that quantity passes into quality. Something might change in quantity without the slightest change in quality, so that its nature or properties remain one and the same, while it increases or diminishes in a given direction. Everything 'has some play within which it remains indifferent to this change . . .'[44] There comes a point, however, at which the nature of a thing alters with a mere quantitative change. The well-known examples of a heap of grain which ceases to be a heap if one grain after the other is removed, or of water which becomes ice when a gradual decrease of temperature has reached a certain point, or of a nation which, in the course of its expansion, suddenly breaks down and disintegrates: all these examples do not

[41] *Encyclopædia of the Philosophical Sciences*, § 96, Addition (*The Logic of Hegel*, trans. W. Wallace, Oxford 1892, p. 179).
[42] *Science of Logic*, vol. I, p. 192.
[43] P. 199.
[44] P. 387.

cover the full meaning of Hegel's proposition. We must understand also that he aimed it against the ordinary view that the process of 'arising and passing away' was a gradual (*allmählich*) one, he aimed it at the view that *natura non facit saltum*.[45]

A given form of existence cannot unfold its content without perishing. The new must be the actual negation of the old and not a mere correction or revision. To be sure, the truth does not drop full-blown from heaven, and the new must somehow have existed in the lap of the old. But it existed there only as potentiality, and its material realization was excluded by the prevailing form of being. The prevailing form has to be broken through. 'The changes of Being' are 'a process of becoming other which breaks off graduality and is qualitatively other as against the preceding state of existence.'[46] There is no even progress in the world: The appearance of every new condition involves a leap; the birth of the new is the death of the old.

The *Science of Logic* opened with the question, What is Being? It set afoot the quest for categories that could enable us to grasp the truly real. In the course of the analysis, the stability of being was dissolved into the process of becoming and the enduring unity of things was seen to be a 'negative unity,' which could not be known from quantitative or qualitative aspects but rather involved the negation of all qualitative and quantitative determinates. For, every determinate property was seen to contradict what things are 'for themselves.' Whatever the enduring unity of being 'for itself' may be, we know that it is not a qualitative or quantitative entity that exists anywhere in the world, but is rather the negation of all determinates. Its essential character is therefore negativity; Hegel calls it also 'universal contradiction,' existing

[45] Ibid.

[46] P. 389.

as it does 'by the negation of every existing determinateness.' [47] It is 'absolute negativity' or 'negative totality.' [48] This unity, it appears, is such by virtue of a process wherein things negate all mere externality and otherness and relate these to a dynamic self. A thing is for itself only when it has posited (*gesetzt*) all its determinates and made them moments of its self-realization, and is thus, in all changing conditions, always 'returning to itself.' [49] Hegel calls this negative unity and process of self-relation the essence of things.

The question What is Being? is answered in the statement that 'the truth of Being is Essence.' [50] And to learn what essence is, we have merely to collect the results of the preceding analysis:

1. The essence has 'no determinate Being.' [51] All the traditional proposals about a realm of ideas or substances have to be discarded. The essence is neither something in nor something above the world, but rather the negation of all being.

2. This negation of all being is not nothing, but the 'infinite movement of Being' beyond every determinate state.

3. The movement is not a contingent and external process, but one held together by the power of self-relation through which a subject posits its determinates as moments of its own self-realization.

4. Such a power presupposes a definite being-in-self, a capacity for knowing and reflecting upon the determinate states. The process of the essence is the process of reflection.

5. The subject that the essence reveals itself to be is not outside the process nor is it its unchangeable substratum; it is the very process itself, and all its characters

[47] P. 394. [48] P. 403. [49] P. 404. [50] Vol. II, p. 16. [51] P. 17.

are dynamic. Its unity is the totality of a movement that the Doctrine of Essence describes as the movement of reflection.

It is of the utmost importance to know that for Hegel reflection, like all the characters of essence, denotes an objective as well as subjective movement. Reflection is not primarily the process of thinking but the process of being itself.[52] Correspondingly, the transition from being to essence is not primarily a procedure of philosophical cognition, but a process in reality. Being's 'own nature' 'causes it to internalize itself,' and being, thus 'entering into itself becomes Essence.' This means that objective being, if comprehended in its true form, is to be understood as, and actually is, subjective being. The subject now appears as the substance of being, or being pertains to the existence of a more or less conscious subject, which is capable of facing and comprehending its determinate states and thus has the power to reflect upon them and shape itself. The categories of the essence cover the whole realm of being, which now manifests itself in its true, comprehended form. The categories of the Doctrine of Being reappear; determinate being is now conceived as existence and later as actuality; the 'something' as thing and later as substance, and so on.

Reflection is the process in which an existent constitutes itself as the unity of a subject. It has an essential unity that contrasts with the passive and changeable unity of the something; it is not determinate but determining being. All determination is here 'posited by the Essence itself' and stands under its determining power.

If we examine what Hegel attributes to the process of essence and what he discusses under the heading of Determinations of Reflection, we find the traditional ultimate laws of thought, the laws of identity, variety, and contra-

[52] Vol. II, p. 16.

diction. Added under a separate head is the law of ground. The original meaning of these laws and their actual objective content was a discovery made by the Hegelian logic. Formal logic cannot even touch their sense; the separation of the subject matter of thought from its form cuts the very ground from under truth. Thought is true only in so far as it remains adapted to the concrete movement of things and closely follows its various turns. As soon as it detaches itself from the objective process and, for the sake of some spurious precision and stability, tries to simulate mathematical rigor, thought becomes untrue. Within the *Science of Logic,* it is the Doctrine of Essence that provides the basic concepts that emancipate dialectical logic from the mathematical method. Hegel undertakes a philosophic critique of mathematical method before he introduces the Doctrine of Essence—in his discussion of quantity. Quantity is only a very external characteristic of being, a realm in which the real content of things gets lost. The mathematical sciences that operate with quantity operate with a content-less form that can be measured and counted and expressed by indifferent numbers and symbols. But the process of reality cannot be so treated. It defies formalization and stabilization, because it is the very negation of every stable form. The facts and relations that appear in this process change their nature at every phase of the development. 'Our knowledge would be in a very awkward predicament if such objects as freedom, law, morality, or even God himself, because they cannot be measured and calculated, or expressed in a mathematical formula, were to be reckoned beyond the reach of exact knowledge, and we had to put up with a vague generalized image of them . . .' [53] Since it is not only philosophy but every other true field of inquiry that aims

[53] *Encyclopædia of the Philosophical Sciences,* § 99, Addition (*The Logic of Hegel,* trans. W. Wallace, p. 187).

at knowledge of such contents, the reduction of science to mathematics means the final surrender of truth:

> When mathematical categories are used to determine something bearing upon the method or content of philosophic science, such a procedure proves its preposterous nature chiefly herein, that, in so far as mathematical formulae mean thoughts and conceptual distinctions, such meaning must first report, determine and justify itself in philosophy. In its concrete sciences, philosophy must take the logical element from logic and not from mathematics; it must be a mere refuge of philosophic impotence when it flies to the formations which logic takes in other sciences, of which many are only dim presentiments and others stunted forms of it, in order to get logic for philosophy. The mere employment of such borrowed forms is in any case an external and superficial procedure: a knowledge of their worth and of their meaning should precede their use; but such knowledge results only from conceptual contemplation, and not from the authority which mathematics gives them.[54]

The Doctrine of Essence seeks to liberate knowledge from the worship of 'observable facts' and from the scientific common sense that imposes this worship. Mathematical formalism abandons and prevents any critical understanding and use of facts. Hegel recognized an intrinsic connection between mathematical logic and a wholesale acquiescence in facts, and to this extent anticipated more than a hundred years of the development of positivism. The real field of knowledge is not the given fact about things as they are, but the critical evaluation of them as a prelude to passing beyond their given form. Knowledge deals with appearances in order to get beyond them. 'Everything, it is said, has an Essence, that is, things really are not what they immediately show themselves. There is therefore something more to be done than merely rove from one quality to another and merely to advance from

[54] *Science of Logic,* op. cit., vol. I, p. 231.

qualitative to quantitative, and vice versa; there is a permanent in things, and that permanent is in the first instance their Essence.'[55] The knowledge that appearance and essence do not jibe is the beginning of truth. The mark of dialectical thinking is the ability to distinguish the essential from the apparent process of reality and to grasp their relation. The laws of reflection that Hegel elaborates are the fundamental laws of the dialectic. We pass now to a brief summary of these.

Essence denotes the unity of being, its identity throughout change. Precisely what is this unity or identity? It is not a permanent and fixed substratum, but a process wherein everything copes with its inherent contradictions and unfolds itself as a result. Conceived in this way, identity contains its opposite, difference, and involves a self-differentiation and an ensuing unification. Every existence precipitates itself into negativity and remains what it is only by negating this negativity. It splits up into a diversity of states and relations to other things, which are originally foreign to it, but which become part of its proper self when they are brought under the working influence of its essence. Identity is thus the same as the 'negative totality,' which was shown to be the structure of reality; it is 'the same as Essence.'[56]

Thus conceived, the essence describes the actual process of reality. 'The contemplation of everything that *is* shows, in itself, that in its self-identity it is self-contradictory and self-different, and in its variety or contradiction, self-identical; it is in itself this movement of transition of one of these determinations into the other, just because each in itself is its own opposite.'[57]

Hegel's position involves complete reversal of the tra-

[55] *Encyclopædia of the Philosophical Sciences,* § 112, Addition (*The Logic of Hegel,* trans. W. Wallace, p. 208).
[56] *Science of Logic,* vol. II, p. 38.
[57] Ibid.

ditional laws of thought and of the kind of thinking derived from them. We cannot express this identity of things in a proposition that distinguishes a permanent substratum and its attributes from its opposite or contrary. The variety and the opposites are for Hegel part of the thing's essential identity, and, to grasp the identity, thought has to reconstruct the process by which the thing becomes its own opposite and then negates and incorporates its opposite into its own being.

Hegel returns time and again to accent the importance of this conception. By virtue of the inherent negativity in them, all things become self-contradictory, opposed to themselves, and their being consists in that 'force which can both comprehend and endure Contradiction.' [58] *'All things are contradictory in themselves'*—this proposition, which so sharply differs from the traditional laws of identity and contradiction, expresses for Hegel 'the truth and essence of things.' [59] 'Contradiction is the root of all movement and life,' all reality is self-contradictory. Motion especially, external movement as well as self-movement, is nothing but 'existing contradiction.' [60]

Hegel's analysis of the Determinations of Reflection marks the point at which dialectical thinking can be seen to shatter the framework of the idealist philosophy that uses it. So far, we note that the dialectic has yielded the conclusion that reality is contradictory in character and a 'negative totality.' As far as we have penetrated into the Hegelian logic, dialectic has appeared as a universal ontological law, which asserts that every existence runs its course by turning into the opposite of itself and producing the identity of its being by working through the opposition. But a closer study of the law reveals historical implications that bring forth its fundamentally critical motivations. If the essence of things is the result of such

[58] Vol. II, p. 68. [59] P. 66. [60] P. 67.

process, the essence itself is the product of a concrete development, 'something which has become [*ein Gewordenes*].' [61] And the impact of this historical interpretation shakes the foundations of idealism.

It may very well be that the developed antagonisms of modern society impelled philosophy to proclaim contradiction to be the 'definite fundamental basis of all activity and self-movement.' Such an interpretation is fully supported by the treatment accorded decisive social relationships in Hegel's earlier system (for example, in the analysis of the labor process, the description of the conflict between the particular and the common interest, the tension between state and society). There, the recognition of the contradictory nature of social reality was prior to the elaboration of the general theory of the dialectic.

But in any case, when we do apply the Determinations of Reflection to historical realities, we are driven almost of necessity to the critical theory that historical materialism developed. For, what does the unity of identity and contradiction mean in the context of social forms and forces? In its ontological terms, it means that the state of negativity is not a distortion of a thing's true essence, but its very essence itself. In socio-historic terms, it means that as a rule crisis and collapse are not accidents and external disturbances, but manifest the very nature of things and hence provide the basis on which the essence of the existing social system can be understood. It means, moreover, that the inherent potentialities of men and things cannot unfold in society except through the death of the social order in which they are first gleaned. When something turns into its opposite, Hegel says, when it contradicts itself, it expresses its essence. When, as Marx says, the current idea and practice of justice and equality lead to injustice and inequality, when the free exchange of equiva-

[61] P. 62.

lents produces exploitation on the one hand and accumulation of wealth on the other, such contradictions, too, are of the essence of current social relations. The contradiction is the actual motor of the process.

The Doctrine of Essence thus establishes the general laws of thought as laws of destruction—destruction for the sake of the truth. Thought is herewith installed as the tribunal that contradicts the apparent forms of reality in the name of their true content. The essence, 'the truth of Being,' is held by thought, which, in turn, is contradiction.

According to Hegel, however, the contradiction is not the end. The essence, which is the locus of the contradiction, must perish and 'the contradiction resolve itself.' [62] It is resolved in so far as the essence becomes the ground of existence. The essence, in becoming the ground of things, passes into existence.[63] The ground of a thing, for Hegel, is nothing other than the totality of its essence, materialized in the concrete conditions and circumstances of existence. The essence is thus as much historical as ontological. The essential potentialities of things realize themselves in the same comprehensive process that establishes their existence. The essence can 'achieve' its existence when the potentialities of things have ripened in and through the conditions of reality. Hegel describes this process as the transition to actuality.

Whereas the preceding analysis was guided by the fact that the proper potentialities of things cannot be realized

[62] Vol. II, p. 60.

[63] Ibid., pp. 70-73: Hegel explains this relation in his analysis of the Law of Ground. His discussion has a twofold aim: (1) It shows the Essence operative in the actual existence of things; and (2) it cancels the traditional conception of the Ground as a particular entity or form among others. Hegel acknowledges that the 'principle of sufficient reason [or Ground]' implies the critical view that Being 'in its immediacy is declared to be invalid and essentially to be something posited.' He holds, however, that the reason or Ground for a particular being cannot be sought in another likewise particular being.

within the prevailing forms of existence, the analysis of actuality discloses that form of reality in which these potentialities have come into existence. Essential determinations do not here remain outside of things, in the shape of something that ought to be but is not, but are now materialized in their entirety. Despite this general advance embodied in the concept of actuality, Hegel describes actuality as a process totally permeated by conflict between possibility and reality. The conflict, however, is no longer an opposition between existent and as yet non-existent forces, but between two antagonistic forms of reality that co-exist.

A close study of actuality reveals that it is first contingency (*Zufälligkeit*). That which *is* is not what it is of necessity; it might exist in some other form as well. Hegel does not refer to some empty logical possibility. The multitude of possible forms is not arbitrary. There is a definite relation between the given and the possible. Possible is only that which can be derived from the very content of the real. We are here reminded of the analysis previously made in connection with the concept of reality. The real shows itself to be antagonistic, split into its being and its ought. The real contains the negation of what it immediately is as its very nature and thus 'contains . . . Possibility.' [64] The form in which the real immediately exists is but a stage of the process in which it unfolds its content, or the given reality is 'equivalent to possibility.' [65]

The concept of reality has thus turned into the concept of possibility. The real is not yet 'actual,' but is at first only the possibility of an actual. Mere possibility belongs to the very character of reality; it is not imposed by an arbitrary speculative act. The possible and the real are in a dialectical relation that requires a special condition in order to be operative, and that condition

[64] *Science of Logic*, vol. II, p. 175. [65] Ibid., p. 177.

must be one in fact. For instance, if the existing relations within a given social system are unjust and inhuman, they are not offset by other realizable possibilities unless these other possibilities are also manifested as having their roots within that system. They must be present there, for example, in the form of an obvious wealth of productive forces, a development of the material wants and desires of men, their advanced culture, their social and political maturity, and so on. In such a case, the possibilities are not only real ones, but represent the true content of the social system as against its immediate form of existence. They are thus an even more real reality than the given. We may say in such a case that 'the possibility is reality,' and that the concept of the possible has turned back into the concept of the real.[66]

How can possibility be reality? The possible must be real in the strict sense that it must exist. As a matter of fact, the mode of its existence has already been shown. It exists as the given reality itself taken as something that has to be negated and transformed. In other words, the possible is the given reality conceived as the 'condition' of another reality.[67] The totality of the given forms of existence are valid only as conditions for other forms of existence.[68] This is Hegel's concept of real possibility, set forth as a concrete historical tendency and force, so as definitely to preclude its use as an idealistic refuge from reality. Hegel's famous proposition that 'the fact [*die Sache*] *is* before it *exists*'[69] can now be given its strict meaning. Before it exists, the fact 'is' in the form of a condition within the constellation of existing data. The existing state of affairs is a mere condition for another constellation of facts, which bring to fruition the inherent poten-

[66] Ibid.
[67] *Encyclopædia of the Philosophical Sciences*, § 146.
[68] *Science of Logic*, vol. II, p. 179.
[69] P. 105.

tialities of the given. 'When all the conditions of a fact are present, it enters into existence.' [70] And at such a time, also, the given reality is a real possibility for transformation into another reality. 'The Real Possibility of a case [*einer Sache*] is the existing multiplicity of circumstances which are related to it.' [71] Let us revert to our case of a social system as yet unrealized. Such a new system is really possible if the conditions for it are present in the old, that is, if the prior social form actually possesses a content that tends towards the new system as to its realization. The circumstances that exist in the old form are thus conceived not as true and independent in themselves, but as mere conditions for another state of affairs that implies the negation of the former. 'Thus Real Possibility constitutes the totality of conditions; an Actuality . . . which is the Being-in-Self of some Other . . .' [72] The concept of real possibility thus develops its criticism of the positivist position out of the nature of facts themselves. Facts are facts only if related to that which is not yet fact and yet manifests itself in the given facts as a real possibility. Or, facts are what they are only as moments in a process that leads beyond them to that which is not yet fulfilled in fact.

The process of 'leading beyond' is an objective tendency immanent in the facts as given. It is an activity not in thought but in reality, the proper activity of self-realization. For, the given reality holds the real possibilities as its content, 'contains a duality in itself,' and is in itself 'reality and possibility.' In its totality as well as in its every single aspect and relation, its content is enveloped in an inadequacy such that only its destruction can convert its possibilities into actualities. 'The manifold forms of exist-

[70] Ibid. [71] P. 179. [72] P. 180.

ence are in themselves self-transcendence and destruction, and thus are determined in themselves to be a mere possibility.' [73] The process of destroying existing forms and replacing them by new ones liberates their content and permits them to win their actual state. The process in which a given order of reality perishes and issues into another is, therefore, nothing but the self-becoming of the old reality.[74] It is the 'return' of reality to itself, that is, to its true form.[75]

The content of a given reality bears the seed of its transformation into a new form, and its transformation is a 'process of necessity,' in the sense that it is the sole way in which a contingent real becomes actual. The dialectical interpretation of actuality does away with the traditional opposition between contingency, possibility, and necessity, and integrates them all as moments of one comprehensive process. Necessity presupposes a reality that is contingent, that is, one which in its prevailing form holds possibilities that are not realized. Necessity is the process in which that contingent reality attains its adequate form. Hegel calls this the process of actuality.

Without a grasp of the distinction between reality and actuality, Hegel's philosophy is meaningless in its decisive principles. We have mentioned that Hegel did not declare that reality is rational (or reasonable), but reserved this attribute for a definite form of reality, namely, actuality. And the reality that is actual is the one wherein the discrepancy between the possible and the real has been overcome. Its fruition occurs through a process of change, with the given reality advancing in accordance with the possibilities manifest in it. Since the new is therefore the freed truth of the old, actuality is the 'simple positive unity' of those elements that had existed in disunity within the

73 P. 180. 74 P. 183. 75 P. 184.

old; it is the unity of the possible and the real, which in the process of transformation 'returns only to itself.' [76]

Any purported difference between various forms of the actual is but an apparent one, because actuality develops *itself* in all the forms. A reality is actual if it is preserved and perpetuated through the absolute negation of all contingencies, in other words, if all its various forms and stages are but the lucid manifestation of its true content. In such a reality, the opposition between contingency and necessity has been overcome. Its process is *of necessity*, because it follows the inherent law of its own nature and remains in all conditions the same.[77] At the same time, this necessity is *freedom* because the process is not determined from outside, by external forces, but, in a strict sense, is a self-development; all conditions are grasped and 'posited' by the developing real itself. Actuality thus is the title for the final unity of being that is no longer subject to change, because it exercises autonomous power over all change—not simple identity but 'self-identity.' [78]

Such a self-identity can be attained only through the medium of self-consciousness and cognition. For only a being that has the faculty of knowing its own possibilities and those of its world can transform every given state of existence into a condition for its free self-realization. True reality presupposes freedom, and freedom presupposes knowledge of the truth. The true reality, therefore, must be understood as the realization of a knowing *subject*. Hegel's analysis of actuality thus leads to the idea of the subject as the truly actual in all reality.

We have reached the point where the Objective Logic turns into the Subjective Logic, or, where subjectivity emerges as the true form of objectivity. We may sum up Hegel's analysis in the following schema:

[76] P. 184. [77] P. 184. [78] P. 186.

The true form of reality requires freedom.

Freedom requires self-consciousness and knowledge of the truth.

Self-consciousness and knowledge of the truth are the essentials of the subject.

The true form of reality must be conceived as subject.

We must note that the logical category 'subject' does not designate any particular form of subjectivity (such as man) but a general structure that might best be characterized by the concept 'mind.' Subject denotes a universal that individualizes itself, and if we wish to think of a concrete example, we might point to the 'spirit' of a historical epoch. If we have comprehended such an epoch, if we have grasped its notion, we shall see a universal principle that develops, through the self-conscious action of individuals, in all prevailing institutions, facts, and relations.

The concept of the subject, however, is not the last step of Hegel's analysis. He now proceeds to demonstrate that the subject is *notion.* He has shown that the subject's freedom consists of its faculty to comprehend what is. In other words, freedom derives its content from the knowledge of the truth. But the form in which the truth is held is the *notion.* Freedom is, in the last analysis, not an attribute of the thinking subject as such, but of the truth that this subject holds and wields. Freedom is thus an attribute of the notion, and the true form of reality in which the essence of being is realized is the notion. The notion 'exists,' however, only in the thinking subject. 'The Notion, in so far as it has advanced into such an existence as is free in itself, is just the Ego, or pure self-consciousness.' [79]

Hegel's strange identification of the notion and the ego

[79] P. 217.

or subject can be understood only if we bear in mind that he considers the notion to be the activity of comprehending (*Begreifen*) rather than its abstract logical form or result (*Begriff*). We are reminded of Kant's transcendental logic in which the highest concepts of thought are treated as creative acts of the ego that are ever renewed in the process of knowledge.[80] Instead of dwelling on Hegel's elaboration of this point,[81] we shall attempt to develop some of the implications of his concept of the notion.

According to Hegel, the notion is the subject's activity and, as such, the true form of reality. On the other hand, the subject is characterized by freedom, so that Hegel's Doctrine of the Notion really develops the categories of freedom. These comprehend the world as it appears when thought has liberated itself from the power of a 'reified' reality, when the subject has emerged as the 'substance' of being. Such liberated thought has eventually overcome the traditional separation of the logical forms from their content. Hegel's idea of the notion reverses the ordinary relation between thought and reality, and becomes the cornerstone of philosophy as a critical theory. According to common-sense thinking, knowledge becomes the more unreal the more it abstracts from reality. For Hegel, the opposite is true. The abstraction from reality, which the formation of the notion requires, makes the notion not poorer but richer than reality, because it leads from the facts to their essential content. The truth cannot be gleaned from the facts as long as the subject does not yet live in them but rather stands against them. The world of facts is not rational but has to be *brought* to reason, that is, to a form in which the reality actually corresponds to the truth. As long as this has not been accomplished, the truth rests with the abstract notion and not with the

[80] See above, pp. 21 ff.
[81] *Science of Logic*, vol. II, pp. 280 ff.

concrete reality. The task of abstraction consists in the 'transcendence and reduction of reality [as from mere appearance] to the essential, which manifests itself in the Notion only.' [82] With the formation of the notion, abstraction does not desert, but leads into actuality. What nature and history actually are will not be found in the prevailing facts; the world is not that harmonious. Philosophical knowledge is thus set against reality, and this opposition is expressed in the abstract character of the philosophical notions. 'Philosophy is not meant to be a narrative of what happens, but a cognition of what is true in happenings, and out of the body of truth it has to comprehend that which in the narrative appears as mere happening.' [83]

Philosophical cognition is superior to experience and science, however, only in so far as its notions contain that relation to truth which Hegel grants only to dialectical notions. Mere transpassing of the facts does not distinguish dialectical knowledge from positivistic science. The latter, too, goes beyond the facts; it obtains laws, makes predictions, and so forth. With all the apparatus of its procedure, however, positivistic science stays within the given realities; the future it predicts, even the changes of form to which it leads never depart from the given. The form and content of scientific concepts remain bound up with the prevailing order of things; they are static in character even when they express motion and change. Positivist science also works with abstract concepts. But they originate by abstraction from the particular and changing forms of things and fix their common and enduring characters.

The process of abstraction that results in the dialectical notion is quite different. Here, abstraction is the reduction of the diverse forms and relations of reality to the actual process in which they are constituted. The chang-

[82] P. 222. [83] P. 223.

ing and the particular are here as important as the common and enduring. The universality of the dialectical notion is not the fixed and stable sum-total of abstract characters, but a concrete totality that itself evolves the particular differences of all the facts that belong to this totality. The notion not only contains all the facts of which reality is composed, but also the processes in which these facts develop and dissolve themselves. The notion thus establishes 'the *principle* of its distinctions';[84] the diverse facts that the notion comprehends are to be shown as 'inner distinctions' of the notion itself.[85]

The dialectical method derives all concrete determinations from one comprehensive principle, which is the principle of the actual development of the subject-matter itself. The various states, qualities, and conditions of the subject-matter must appear as its own positive unfolded content. Nothing can be added from outside (any given fact, for instance). Dialectical development is not 'the external activity of subjective thought,' but the objective history of the real itself.[86] Hegel is consequently able to say that in dialectical philosophy it is 'not we who frame the notions,'[87] but that their formation is rather an objective development that we only reproduce.

There is no more adequate example of the formation of the dialectical notion than Marx's concept of capitalism. Just as Hegel, in accordance with the doctrine that the notion is an antagonistic totality, declares it 'impossible and absurd to frame the truth in such forms as positive judgment or judgment in general,'[88] Marx, too, repudiates any definitions that fix the truth in a final body of propositions. The concept of capitalism is no less than

[84] P. 244. [85] P. 249. [86] *Philosophy of Right*, § 31.
[87] *Encyclopædia of the Philosophical Sciences*, § 163, Addition 2 (*The Logic of Hegel*, trans. W. Wallace, p. 293).
[88] *Science of Logic*, vol. II, p. 229.

the totality of the capitalist process, comprehended in the 'principle' by which it progresses. The notion of capitalism starts with the separation of the actual producers from the means of production, resulting in the establishment of free labor and the appropriation of surplus value, which, with the development of technology, brings about the accumulation and centralization of capital, the progressive decline of the rate of profit, and the breakdown of the entire system. The notion of capitalism is no less than the three volumes of *Capital,* just as Hegel's notion of the notion comprises all three books of his *Science of Logic.*

Moreover, the notion constitutes a 'negative totality,' which evolves only by virtue of its contradictory forces. The negative aspects of reality are thus not 'disturbances' or weak spots within a harmonious whole, but the very conditions that expose the structure and tendencies of reality. The extraordinary importance of this method becomes quite clear when we consider the way Marx conceived the crisis as a material moment of the capitalist system, so that this 'negative' moment is the fulfillment of the principle of that system. Crises are necessary stages in the 'self-differentiation' of capitalism, and the system reveals its true content through the negative act of breakdown.

The notion presents an objective totality in which every particular moment appears as the 'self-differentiation' of the universal (the principle that governs the totality) and is therefore itself universal. That is to say, every particular moment contains, as its very content, the whole, and must be interpreted as the whole. For explanation, let us again refer to the field in which dialectical logic has come to fruition, the theory of society.

Dialectical logic holds that every particular content is formed by the universal principle that determines the movement of the whole. A single human relation, for example, that between a father and his child, is constituted by the fundamental relations that govern the social system. The father's authority is buttressed by the fact that he is the provider of the family; the egoistic instincts of competitive society enter his love. The image of his father accompanies the adult and guides his submission to the powers that rule over his social existence. The privacy of the family relation thus opens and leads into the prevailing social relations, so that the private relation itself unfolds its own social content. This development proceeds according to the principle of the 'determinate negation.' That is to say, the family relation produces its contradiction that destroys its original content, and this contradiction, though dissolving the family, fulfills its actual function. The particular *is* the universal, so that the specific content directly turns into the universal content through the process of its concrete existence. Here again, dialectical logic reproduces the structure of a historical form of reality in which the social process dissolves every delimited and stable sphere of life into the economic dynamic.

Owing to its intrinsic relation to every other particular moment of the whole, the content and function of every given aspect changes with every change of the whole. To isolate and fix the particular moments is therefore impossible. The unbridgeable gulf asserted to exist between mathematics and dialectical theory rests on this point; this is why every attempt to frame the truth in mathematical forms inevitably destroys it. For, mathematical objects 'have the peculiar distinction . . . that they are external to one another and have a fixed determination. Now if Notions are taken in this manner, so that they correspond to such [mathematical] symbols, then they cease to be

Notions. Their determinations are not such dead matters as numbers and lines, . . . they are living movements; the different determinateness of one side is also immediately internal to the other; and what would be a complete contradiction with numbers and lines is essential to the nature of the Notion.'[89] The notion, the only adequate form of the truth, 'can essentially be apprehended only by Mind . . . It is in vain that an attempt is made to fix it by means of spatial figures and algebraic symbols for the purpose of the external eye and of a notionless mechanical treatment or calculus.'[90]

The entire doctrine of the notion is perfectly 'realistic' if it is understood and executed as a historical theory. But, as we have already hinted, Hegel tends to dissolve the element of historical practice and replace it with the independent reality of thought. The multitude of particular notions eventually converge in *the* notion, which becomes the one content of the entire Logic.[91] This tendency might still be reconciled with a historical interpretation if we regard the notion as representing the final penetration of the world by reason. Realization of the notion would then mean the universal mastery, exercised by men having a rational social organization, over nature—a world that might indeed be imagined as the realization of the notion of all things. Such a historical conception is kept alive in Hegel's philosophy, but it is constantly overwhelmed by the ontological conceptions of absolute idealism. It is ultimately the latter in which the *Science of Logic* terminates.

We cannot follow the Doctrine of the Notion beyond the point we have reached. Instead of a brief and necessarily inadequate outline of the Subjective Logic, we have chosen to attempt a rough interpretation of its closing paragraphs. They furnish the famous transition from the

[89] P. 251. [90] P. 252. [91] See below, p. 165 f.

Logic to the *Philosophy of Nature and Mind,* and thus close the entire range of the system.

THE notion designates the general form of all being, and, at the same time, the true being which adequately represents this form, namely, the free subject. The subject exists, again, in a movement from lower to higher modes of self-realization. Hegel calls the highest form of this self-realization the idea. Ever since Plato the idea has meant the image of the true potentialities of things as against the apparent reality. It was originally a critical concept, like the concept of essence, denouncing the security of common sense in a world too readily content with the form in which things immediately appeared. The proposition that the true being is the idea and not the reality thus contains an intended paradox.

For Hegel, who knew of no realm of truth beyond the world, the idea is actual and man's task is to live in its actuality. The idea exists as cognition and life. The terms will offer no more difficulties; since Hegel's earliest writings, life has stood for the actual form of true being.[92] It represents the mode of existence that a subject, through the conscious negation of all otherness, has made its own free work. Furthermore, life can be such a free work only by virtue of cognition, since the subject requires the power of conceptual thinking to dispose over the potentialities of things.

The element of practice is still retained in the concluding sections of the *Logic.* The adequate form of the idea is termed the unity of cognition and action, or 'the identity of the Theoretical and the Practical Idea.'[93] Hegel expressly declares that the practical idea, the realization of 'the Good' that alters the external reality, is 'higher

[92] See above, pp. 37 f.

[93] *Science of Logic,* vol. II, p. 466.

than the Idea of Cognition, . . . for it has not only the dignity of the universal but also of the simply actual.' [94]

The manner in which Hegel demonstrates this unity shows, however, that he has made a final transformation of history into ontology. The true being is conceived as a perfectly free being. Perfect freedom, according to Hegel, requires that the subject comprehend all objects, so that their independent objectivity is overcome. The objective world then becomes the medium for the self-realization of the subject, which knows all reality as its own and has no object but itself. As long as cognition and action still have an external object that is not yet mastered and is therefore foreign and hostile to the subject, the subject is not free. Action is always directed against a hostile world and, since it implies the existence of such a hostile world, action essentially restricts the freedom of the subject. Only thought, pure thought, fulfills the requirements of perfect freedom, for thought 'thinking' itself is entirely for itself in its otherness; it has no object but itself.[95]

We recall Hegel's statement that 'every philosophy is an idealism.' We can now understand the critical side of idealism, which justifies this statement. There is, however, another aspect of idealism that ties it up with the reality its critical tendencies strive to overcome. From their origin, the basic concepts of idealism reflect a social separation of the intellectual sphere from the sphere of material production. Their content and their validity had to do with the power and the faculties of a 'leisure class,' which became the guardian of the idea by virtue of the fact that it was not compelled to work for the material reproduction of society. For, its exceptional status freed this class from the inhumane relations that the material reproduction created, and made it capable of transcending them.

[94] P. 460.
[95] See *Philosophy of Right*, § 4, Addition.

The truth of philosophy thus became a function of its remoteness from material practice.

We have seen that Hegel protested this trend in philosophy, considering it the complete abdication of reason. He spoke for the actual power of reason and for the concrete materialization of freedom. But he was frightened by the social forces that had undertaken this task. The French Revolution had again shown that modern society was a system of irreconcilable antagonisms. Hegel recognized that the relations of civil society could, owing to the particular mode of labor on which they were based, never provide for perfect freedom and perfect reason. In this society, man remained subject to the laws of an unmastered economy, and had to be tamed by a strong state, capable of coping with the social contradictions. The final truth had therefore to be sought in another sphere of reality. Hegel's political philosophy was governed throughout by this conviction. The *Logic* also bears the mark of resignation.

If reason and freedom are the criteria of true being, and the reality in which they are materialized is marred by irrationality and bondage, they must again come to rest in the idea. Cognition thus becomes more than action, and knowledge, the knowledge of philosophy, draws closer to the truth than does the social and political practice. Although Hegel says that the stage of historical development attained at his time reveals that the idea has become real, it 'exists' as the comprehended world, *present in thought,* as the 'system of science.' This knowledge is no longer individual, but has the 'dignity' of the 'universal.' Mankind has become conscious of the world as reason, of the true forms of all that it is capable of realizing. Purified as it is of the dross of existence, this system of science is the flawless truth, the absolute idea.

The absolute idea is not added to the results of the

preceding analysis as a separate supreme entity. It is in its content, the totality of the concepts that the *Logic* has unfolded, and in its form the 'method' that develops this totality. 'To speak of the absolute idea may suggest the conception that we are at length reaching the right thing and the sum of the whole matter. It is certainly possible to indulge in a vast amount of senseless declamation about the absolute idea. But its true content is only the whole system of which we have been hitherto studying the development.'[96] Consequently Hegel's chapter on the Absolute Idea gives us a final comprehensive demonstration of dialectical method.[97] Here, again, it is presented as the objective process of being, which preserves itself only through the different modes of the 'negation of the negation.' It is this dynamic that eventually moves the absolute idea and makes the transition from the *Logic* to the *Philosophy of Nature and of Mind.* The absolute idea is the true notion of reality and, as such, the highest form of cognition. It is, as it were, dialectical thought, unfolded in its totality. However, it is *dialectical* thought and thus contains its negation; it is not a harmonious and stable form but a process of unification of opposites. It is not complete except in its otherness.

The absolute idea is the *subject* in its final form, *thought.* Its otherness and negation is the *object, being.* The absolute idea now has to be interpreted as objective being. Hegel's *Logic* thus ends where it began, with the category of being. This, however, is a different being that can no longer be explained through the concepts applied in the analysis that opened the *Logic.* For being now is understood in its notion, that is, as a concrete totality wherein all particular forms subsist as the essential dis-

[96] *Encyclopædia of the Philosophical Sciences,* § 237. Addition (*The Logic of Hegel,* trans. W. Wallace, pp. 374 f.).
[97] *Science of Logic,* vol. II, pp. 468-84.

tinctions and relations of one comprehensive principle. Thus comprehended, being is *nature,* and dialectical thought passes on to the *Philosophy of Nature.*

This exposition covers but one aspect of the transition. The advance beyond the *Logic* is not only the methodological transition from one science (Logic) to another (Philosophy of Nature), but also the objective transition from one form of being (the Idea) to another (Nature). Hegel says that 'the idea freely releases itself' into nature, or, freely 'determines itself' as nature.[98] It is this statement, putting the transition forward as an actual process in reality, that offers great difficulties in the understanding of Hegel's system.

We have stressed that dialectical logic links the form of thought with its content. The notion as a logical form is at the same time the notion as existing reality; it is a thinking subject. The absolute idea, the adequate form of this existence, must therefore contain in itself that dynamic which drives it into its opposite, and, through the negation of this opposite, to its return upon itself. But how can this free transformation of the absolute idea into objective being (Nature) and from there into mind be demonstrated as an actual happening?

At this point, Hegel's Logic resumes the metaphysical tradition of Western philosophy, a tradition that it had abandoned in so many of its aspects. Since Aristotle, the quest for being (as such) had been coupled with the quest for the veritable being, for that determinate being that most adequately expresses the characters of being-as-such. This veritable being was called God. The Aristotelian ontology culminated in theology,[99] but a theology that had nothing to do with religion, since it treated the being of God in exactly the same way that it treated the being of

[98] Ibid., p. 486.
[99] Aristotle, *Metaphysics,* Book Λ, 7.

material things. The Aristotelian God is neither the creator nor judge of the world; his function is purely an ontological, one might even say, mechanical one; he represents a definite type of movement.

In line with this tradition, Hegel too links his Logic with theology. He says that the *Logic* 'shows forth God as he is in his eternal essence before the creation of Nature and of a finite Mind.'[100] God in this formula means the totality of the pure forms of all being, or, the true essence of being that the *Logic* unfolds. This essence is realized in the free subject whose perfect freedom is thought. Up to this point Hegel's logic follows the pattern of the Aristotelian metaphysic. But now, the Christian tradition, in which Hegel's philosophy was deeply rooted, asserts its right and prevents the maintenance of a purely ontological concept of God. The absolute idea has to be conceived as the actual creator of the world; it has to prove its freedom by freely releasing itself into its otherness, that is, nature.

Hegel's view does, however, hold to the rationalistic tendencies of his philosophy. The true being does not reside beyond this world, but exists only in the dialectical process that perpetuates it. No final goal exists outside this process that might mark a salvation of the world. As the *Logic* depicts it, the world is 'totality in itself, and contains the pure idea of truth itself.'[101] The process of reality is a 'circle,' showing the same absolute form in all its moments, namely, the return of being to itself through the negation of its otherness. Hegel's system thus even cancels the idea of creation; all negativity is overcome by the inherent dynamic of reality. Nature achieves its truth when it enters the domain of history. The subject's development frees being from its blind necessity, and nature

[100] *Science of Logic,* vol. I, p. 60. [101] Ibid., vol. II, p. 227.

becomes a part of human history and thus a part of mind. History, in its turn, is the long road of mankind to conceptual and practical domination of nature and society, which comes to pass when man has been brought to reason and to a possession of the world as reason. The index that such a state has been achieved is, Hegel says, the fact that the true 'system of science' has been elaborated, meaning his own philosophical system. It embraces the whole world as a comprehended totality in which all things and relations appear in their actual form and content, that is, in their notion. The identity of subject and object, thought and reality, is there attained.

VI

The Political Philosophy (1816-1821)

THE first volume of the *Science of Logic* had appeared in 1812, the last in 1816. During the four year interim had come the Prussian 'War of Liberation,' the Holy Alliance against Napoleon, the battles of Leipzig and Waterloo, and the victorious entry of the Allies into Paris. In 1816, Hegel, then principal of a high school in Nuremberg, was appointed to a professorship of philosophy at the University of Heidelberg. The next year, he published the first edition of the *Encyclopædia of the Philosophical Sciences* and was chosen Fichte's successor at the University of Berlin. This final goal of his academic career coincides with the end of his philosophical development. He became the so-called official philosopher of the Prussian state and the philosophical dictator of Germany.

We shall not enter further on an account of Hegel's biography, since we are not here dealing with his personal character and motives. The social and political function of his philosophy, and the affinity between his philosophy and the Restoration must be accounted for in terms of the particular situation that modern society found itself in at the end of the Napoleonic era.

Hegel saw Napoleon as the historical hero fulfilling the destiny of the French Revolution; he was, thought Hegel, the one man able to transform the achievements of 1789 into a state order and to connect individual freedom with the universal reason of a stable social system. It was not an abstract greatness he admired in Napoleon, but the quality of expressing the historical need of the time. Napoleon was 'the soul of the world,' in whom the universal task of the time was embodied. That task was to consolidate and preserve the new form of society that stood for the principle of reason. We know that the principle of reason in society meant for Hegel a social order built on the rational autonomy of the individual. Individual freedom, however, had assumed the form of brute individualism; the freedom of each individual was pitted in life-and-death competitive struggle against that of every other. The Terror of 1793 exemplified this individualism and was its necessary outcome. The conflict among feudal estates had once attested that feudalism was no longer capable of uniting the individual and the general interest; the pervasive competitive freedom of individuals now witnessed that middle-class society also was not. Hegel saw in the sovereignty of the state the one principle that would bring unity.

Napoleon had to a large extent crushed the vestiges of feudalism in Germany. The Civil Code was introduced in many parts of the former German Reich. 'Civil equality, religious liberty, the abolition of the tithe and of feudal rights, the sale of ecclesiastic holdings, the suppression of the guilds, the multiplication of the bureaucracy, and a "wise and liberal" administration, a constitution that brought with it the voting of taxes and of laws by the notables, all these were to weave a network of interest closely bound with the maintenance of French domination.'[1] The absurdly impotent Reich had been replaced by a number of sovereign states, especially in southern Germany. These states, to be sure, were only caricature forms of a modern sovereign state as we know it, but they nevertheless were a marked advance over the former terri-

[1] Georges Lefebvre, *Napoleon*, Paris 1935, p. 428.

torial subdivisions of the Reich, which had vainly sought to accommodate the development of capitalism to the old order of society. The new states were at least larger economic units; they had a centralized bureaucracy, a simpler system for administering justice, and a more rational method of taxation under some kind of public control. These innovations seemed to be in line with Hegel's demand for a more rational ordering of political forms to permit the development of the new intellectual and material forces unleashed by the French Revolution, and it is no wonder, therefore, that he at first viewed the struggle against Napoleon as a reactionary opposition. His reference to the 'War of Liberation' is, therefore, contemptuous and ironical. He went so far, in fact, that he could not acknowledge the defeat of Napoleon as final even after the Allies had triumphantly entered Paris.

Typical of Hegel's attitude to the political events of these years are the utterances in his lectures (1816) in which he defiantly emphasizes the purely intellectual values as against the actual political interests:

> We may hope that, in addition to the State, which has swallowed up all other interests in its own, the Church may now resume her high position—that in addition to the kingdom of the world to which all thoughts and efforts have hitherto been directed, the Kingdom of God may also be considered. In other words, along with the business of politics and the other interests of every-day life, we may trust that Science, the free rational world of mind, may again flourish.[2]

Truly, this was a strange attitude. The political philosopher who but one year later became the official ideological spokesman for the Prussian state and then declared the state's right to be the right of reason itself, now denounces political activity and interprets national libera-

[2] *Lectures on the History of Philosophy*, trans. E. S. Haldane, London 1892, pp. xi f.

tion to mean freedom for philosophical scholarship. Truth and reason he now sets far beyond the social and political whirl, in the realm of pure science.

We shall note that Hegel's new position stayed with him. As for his shift from a rather anti-nationalist to a nationalist position, we may recall a similar 'inconsistency' in the early days of modern philosophical writing. Hobbes, who may be called the most characteristic philosopher of the rising bourgeoisie, found his political philosophy compatible first with the monarchy of Charles I, then with Cromwell's revolutionary state, and finally with the Stuart reaction. It was irrelevant to Hobbes whether the sovereign state assumed the form of a democracy, oligarchy, or limited monarchy, as long as it asserted sovereignty in its relations with other states and maintained its own authority in relation to its citizens. So, too, for Hegel, differences in political form between nations did not matter so long as the underlying identity of social and economic relations was uniformly maintained as that of middle-class society. Modern constitutional monarchy seemed to him to serve quite well in preserving this economic structure. Upon the downfall of the Napoleonic system in Germany, he consequently was quite willing to hail the ensuing sovereign monarchy as the genuine heir of the Napoleonic system.

To Hegel, state sovereignty was a necessary instrument for preserving middle-class society. For, the sovereign state would remove the destructive competitive element from the individuals and make competition a positive interest of the universal; it would be capable of dominating the conflicting interests of its members. The point that is here implied is that where the social system requires the individual's existence to depend on competition with others, the only guarantee of at least a limited realization of the common interest would be the restriction of his freedom within the universal order of the state. Sovereignty of the state thus presupposes international competition among antagonistic political units, the power of each of which resides essentially in its undisputed authority over its members.

In his published report of 1817 on the debates of the Estates of Wurttemberg, Hegel's views are entirely dictated by this attitude. Wurttemberg had become a sovereign kingdom by act of Napoleon. A new constitution was necessary to replace the obsolescent semi-feudal system, and newly acquired territories had to be combined with the original state so as to form a centralized social and political whole. The king had drafted such a constitution and had submitted it to the assembled estates in 1815. The latter refused to accept it. Hegel, in his strong defense of the royal draft against the estates' opposition, interpreted the conflict between the two parties as a struggle between the old and new social principle, between feudal privilege and modern sovereignty.

His report shows throughout the guiding thread of the principle of sovereignty. Napoleon, he says, established the external sovereignty of the state—the historical task now is to establish its internal sovereignty, an undisputed authority of the government over its citizens. And this engenders a new conception of the relation of the state to its members. The idea of the social contract must be displaced by the idea of the state as an objective whole. The *Jenenser* system [8] had repudiated any application of the social contract to the state. Now, the main theme that shapes Hegel's philosophy is that the state is separate from society.

Out of the irreconcilable conflict of particular interests, which are the basis of modern society's relations,

[8] See above, p. 84.

the inherent mechanisms of this society can produce no common interest. The universal must be imposed upon the particulars, as it were, against their will, and the resulting relation between the individuals on the one hand and the state on the other cannot be the same as that between individuals. The contract might apply to the latter, but it cannot hold for the former. For, a contract implies that the contracting parties are 'equally independent of each other.' Their agreement is but a 'contingent relation' that originates from their subjective wants.[4] The state, on the other hand, is an 'objective, necessary relation,' essentially independent of subjective wants.

According to Hegel, civil society must finally generate an authoritarian system, a change that springs from the economic foundations of that society itself, and serves to perpetuate its framework. The change in form is supposed to save the threatened content. Hegel, we may recall, outlined an authoritarian system when he spoke of a 'government of discipline' at the conclusion of the *Jenenser* system of morality. That government form did not amount to a new order, but simply imposed a method on the prevailing system of individualism. Here, again, in elevating the state above society, Hegel follows the same pattern. He gives the state the supreme position because he sees the inevitable effects of the antagonisms within modern society. The competing individual interests are incapable of generating a system that would guarantee the continuance of the whole, hence an uncontrovertible authority must be imposed on them. The government's relation to the people is removed from the sphere of contract and made 'an original substantial unity.'[5] The individual bears primarily the relation of

[4] 'Verhandlungen in der Versammlung der Landstände des Königreichs Württemberg im Jahre 1815 und 1816,' in *Schriften zur Politik und Rechtsphilosophie*, p. 197.

[5] Ibid., p. 197.

duty to the state and his right is subordinate to this. The sovereign state takes shape as a disciplinary state.

Its sovereignty, however, must differ from that of the absolutistic state—the people must become a material part of the state power.[6] Since modern economy is founded on the individual's emancipated activity, his social maturity must be asserted and encouraged. It is notable in this connection that Hegel gave special criticism to one point in the royal constitution, that dealing with the restriction of suffrage. The king had provided, first, that officials of the state as well as members of the army, clergy, and medical profession were not to be elected and, secondly, that a net income of at least 200 florins from realties should be a prerequisite to suffrage. Hegel declared, on the first, that the consequent exclusion of state officials from the popular Chamber was extremely dangerous. For it was precisely those who were statesmen by profession and training who would be the ablest defenders of the common as against the particular interests. Every private business in this society, he declared, by its very nature sets the individual against the community.

'Realty owners as well as tradesmen and others who find themselves in possession of property or of a craft are interested in preserving the bourgeois order, but their direct aim therein is to preserve their private property.'[7]

They are prepared and determined to do as little as possible for the universal. He adds that this attitude is not a matter of ethics or of the personal character of some individuals, but is rooted 'in the nature of the case,'[8] in the nature of this social class. It can be counteracted by a stable bureaucracy as far removed as possible from the sphere of economic competition and thus capable of serving the state without any interference from private business.

[6] P. 161. [7] P. 169. [8] P. 170.

This essential function of bureaucracy in the state is a material element of Hegel's political thought. Historical developments have borne out his conclusions, though in a form quite different from his expectations.

Hegel also repudiates the second restriction of the franchise, that by property qualifications. For property is the very factor that makes the individual oppose the universal and follow the ties of his private interest instead. In Hegel's terminology, property is an 'abstract' qualification that has nothing to do with human attributes. The political influence of the mere quantity of holdings, he declares, is a negative heritage of the French Revolution; as a criterion of privileges it must eventually be overcome, or, at least, must no longer constitute 'the sole condition for one of the most important political functions.'[9] The abolition of property qualifications as prerequisites for political rights would strengthen rather than weaken the state. For, the strong bureaucracy that would be made possible would set this state on much firmer ground than the interests of relatively small proprietors can provide.

Describing the struggle between the king and the estates in Wurttemberg, Hegel depicts it as that between 'rational State law' (*vernünftiges Staatsrecht*) and the traditional code of positive law.[10] Positive law comes down to an outmoded code of old privileges held to be eternally valid only because valid for hundreds of years. 'Positive law,' he argues, 'must rightly perish when it loses that basis which is the condition of its existence.'[11] The old privileges of the estates have about as much basis in modern society as have 'sacrificial murder, slavery, feudal despotism, and countless other infamies.'[12] These have been done with as 'rights,'—reason has been a historical reality ever since the French Revolution. The recognition of the

[9] P. 177. [10] P. 198. [11] P. 199. [12] Ibid.

rights of man has overthrown old privilege and has laid down 'the everlasting principles of established legislation, government, and administration.'[13] At the same time, the rational order that Hegel is here discussing is gradually stripped of its revolutionary implications and adapted to the requirements of the society of his time. It now indicates for him the furthest limits within which this society can be reasonable without being negated in principle. He holds up the revolutionary terror of 1793 as brutal warning that the existing order must be protected with all available means. The princes ought to know 'as a result of the experiences of the past twenty-five years, the dangers and horrors connected with the establishment of new constitutions, and with the criterion of a reality that conforms to thought.'[14]

Hegel generally praised the endeavor to fashion reality in accordance with thought. This was man's highest privilege and the sole way to materialize the truth. But when such an attempt threatened the very society that originally hailed this as man's privilege, Hegel preferred to maintain the prevailing order under all circumstances. We may again cite Hobbes to show how anxiety for the existing order unites even the most disparate philosophies: 'The state of man can never be without some incommodity or other,' but 'the greatest, that in any form of government can possibly happen to the people in general, is scarce sensible, in respect of the miseries, and horrible calamities, that accompany a civil war . . .' 'The present ought always to be preferred, maintained, and accounted best; because it is against both the law of nature, and the divine positive law, to do anything tending to the subversion thereof.'[15]

[13] P. 185. [14] Pp. 161-2.

[15] Hobbes, *Leviathan,* in *Works,* edited by Molesworth, vol. III, pp. 170, 548.

It is not an inconsistency in Hegel's system that individual freedom is thus overshadowed by the authority vested in the universal, and that the rational finally comes forward in the guise of the given social order. The apparent inconsistency reflects the historical truth and mirrors the course of the antagonisms of individualist society, which turn freedom into necessity and reason into authority. Hegel's *Philosophy of Right,* to a considerable extent, owes its relevance to the fact that its basic concepts absorb and consciously retain the contradictions of this society and follow them to the bitter end. The work is reactionary in so far as the social order it reflects is so, and progressive in so far as it is progressive.

Some of the gravest misunderstandings that obscure the *Philosophy of Right* can be removed simply by considering the place of the work in Hegel's system. It does not treat with the whole cultural world, for the realm of right is but a part of the realm of mind, namely, that part which Hegel denotes as objective mind. It does not, in short, expound or deal with the cultural realities of art, religion, and philosophy, which embody the ultimate truth for Hegel. The place that the *Philosophy of Right* occupies in the Hegelian system makes it impossible to regard the state, the highest reality within the realm of right, as the highest reality within the whole system. Even Hegel's most emphatic deification of the state cannot cancel his definite subordination of the objective to the absolute mind, of the political to the philosophical truth.

The content to come is announced in the Preface, often attacked as a document of utmost servility to the Restoration and of uncompromising hostility to all the liberal and progressive tendencies of the time. Hegel's denunciation of J. F. Fries, one of the leaders of the insurgent German youth movement, his defense of the *Karlsbader Beschlüsse* (1819), with their wholesale persecutions of every liberal act or utterance (arbitrarily labeled with the then current term of abuse, 'demagogic'), his apologia for strong censorship, for the suppression of academic freedom, and for restricting all trends towards some form of truly representative government have all been quoted in confirmation of the charge. There is, of course, no justification for Hegel's personal attitude at the time. In the light of the historical situation, however, and especially of the later social and political development, his position and the whole Preface assume quite another significance. We must briefly examine the nature of the democratic opposition that Hegel criticizes.

The movement sprang from the disappointment and disillusionment of the petty bourgeoisie after the war of 1813-15. The liberation of the German states from French rule was accompanied by an absolutist reaction. The promise of political recognition for popular rights and the dream of an adequate constitution remained unfulfilled. The response was a surge of propaganda for the political unification of the German nation, a propaganda that did contain in large measure a truly liberalist hostility to the newly established despotism. Since, however, the upper classes were capable of holding their own within the absolutist framework, and since no organized working class existed, the democratic movement was, to a large extent, made up of resentment on the part of the powerless petty bourgeoisie. This resentment received striking expression in the program of the academic *Burschenschaften* and of their precursors, the *Turnvereine*. There was much talk of freedom and of equality, but it was a freedom that would be the vested privilege of the Teutonic race alone, and an equality that meant general poverty and privation. Culture was looked upon as the holding of the rich and of the alien, made to corrupt and soften the people. Hatred of the French went along with hatred of Jews,

Catholics, and 'nobles.' The movement cried for a truly 'German war,' so that Germany might unfold 'the abundant wealth of her nationality.' It demanded a 'savior' to achieve German unity, one to whom 'the people will forgive all sins.' It burned books and yelled woe to the Jews. It believed itself above the law and the constitution because 'there is no law to the just cause.' [16] The state was to be built from 'below,' through the sheer enthusiasm of the masses, and the 'natural' unity of the *Volk* was to supersede the stratified order of state and society.

It is not difficult to recognize in these 'democratic' slogans the ideology of the Fascist *Volksgemeinschaft*. There is, in point of fact, a much closer relation between the historical role of the *Burschenschaften,* with their racism and anti-rationalism, and National Socialism, than there is between Hegel's position and the latter. Hegel wrote his *Philosophy of Right* as a defense of the state against this pseudo-democratic ideology, in which he saw a more serious threat to freedom than in the continued rule of the vested authorities. There can be no doubt that his work strengthened the power of these authorities and thus assisted an already victorious reaction, but, only a relatively short time later, it turned out to be a weapon against reaction. For, the state Hegel had in mind was one governed by the standards of critical reason and by universally valid laws. The rationality of law, he says, is the life element of the modern state. 'The law is . . . the Shibboleth, by means of which are detected the false brethren and friends of the so-called people.' [17] We shall see that Hegel wove the theme through his mature political philosophy. There is no concept less compatible with

[16] See Heinrich von Trietschke, *Deutsche Geschichte im Neunzehnten Jahrhundert,* 3rd edition, 1886, vol. II, pp. 383-443, especially pp. 385, 391, 427, 439.

[17] *Philosophy of Right,* trans. S. W. Dyde, George Bell and Sons, London 1896, p. xxiii.

Fascist ideology than that which founds the state on a universal and rational law that safeguards the interests of every individual, whatever the contingencies of his natural and social status.

Hegel's attack on the democratic opponents of the Restoration is, moreover, inseparable from his even sharper criticism of the reactionary representatives of the organic theory of the state. His criticism of the *Volksbewegung* is linked with his polemic against K. L. von Haller's *Restauration der Staatwissenschaft* (first published in 1816), a work that exerted great influence on political romanticism in Germany. Haller there had considered the state to be a natural fact and at the same time a divine product. As such, he had accepted without justification the rule of the strong over the weak, which every state implies, and had rejected any interpretation of the state as representing the institutionalized rights of free individuals or as subject to the demands of human reason. Hegel characterized Haller's position as nothing short of 'fanaticism, mental imbecility, and hypocrisy.' [18] If supposedly natural values and not those of reason are fundamental principles of the state, then hazard, injustice, and the brute in man replace the rational standards of human organization.

Both the democratic and feudal opponents of the state agreed in repudiating the rule of law. Hegel held, against both of them, that the rule of law is the only adequate political form of modern society. Modern society, he said, is not a natural community or an order of divinely bestowed privileges. It is based on the general competition of free owners of property who get and hold their position in the social process through their self-reliant activity. It is a society in which the common interest, the per-

[18] Ibid., § 258, p. 244, *note*.

petuation of the whole, is asserted only through blind chance. Conscious regulation of the social antagonisms, therefore, by a force standing above the clash of particular interests, and yet safeguarding each of them, could alone transform the anarchic sum-total of individuals into a rational society. The rule of law was to be the lever of that transformation.

At the same time, Hegel rejected political theory as such, and denied that it had any use in political life. The rule of law was at hand; it was embodied in the state and constituted the adequate historical realization of reason. Once the given order was thus accepted and acquiesced in, political theory was rendered superfluous, for 'theories now set themselves in opposition to the existing order and make as though they were absolutely true and necessary.'[19] Hegel was impelled to renounce theory because he maintained that theory was necessarily *critical*, especially in the form it had taken in Western history. Ever since Descartes, it was claimed that theory could plumb the rational structure of the universe and that reason could through its efforts become the standard of human life. Theoretical and rational knowledge of the truth thus implied recognition of the 'untruth' of a reality not yet up to standard. The inadequate nature of the given reality forced theory to transcend it, to become idealistic. But, Hegel now says, history has not stood still; mankind has reached the stage where all the means are at hand for realizing reason. The modern state is the reality of that realization. Hence, any further application of theory to politics would now make theory Utopian. When the given order is taken as rational, idealism has reached its end. Political philosophy must henceforth refrain from teaching what the state ought to be. The state is, is rational, and there's the finale. Hegel adds that his philosophy will

[19] Ibid., p. xx, *note*.

instead counsel that the state must be recognized as a moral universe. The task of philosophy becomes that of 'reconciling men to the actual.'

A strange reconciliation, indeed. There is hardly another philosophical work that reveals more unsparingly the irreconcilable contradictions of modern society, or that seems more perversely to acquiesce in them. The very Preface in which Hegel renounces critical theory seems to be calling for it by stressing 'the conflict between what is and what ought to be.'

The content to which reason pointed was within reach, Hegel said. The realization of reason could no longer be philosophy's task, nor could it be allowed to dissipate itself in Utopian speculations. Society as actually constituted had brought to fruition the material conditions for its change, so that the truth that philosophy contained at its core might once for all be brought into being. Freedom and reason could now be seen as more than inner values. The given condition of the present was a 'cross' to be borne, a world of misery and injustice, but within it blossomed the potencies of free reason. The recognition of these potencies had been the function of philosophy, the attainment of the true order of society was now the function of practice. Hegel knew that 'one form of life has become old' and that it could never be rejuvenated by philosophy.[20] The concluding passages of the Preface set the tone for the entire *Philosophy of Right*. They mark the resignation of a man who knows that the truth he represents has drawn to its close and that it can no longer invigorate the world.

Nor can it invigorate the social forces he understood and represented. The *Philosophy of Right* is the philosophy of middle-class society come to full self-consciousness.

[20] Ibid., p. xxx.

It holds up the positive and the negative elements of a society that has grown mature and that sees full well its insurmountable limitations. All the fundamental concepts of modern philosophy are reapplied in the *Philosophy of Right* to the social reality from which they sprang, and all reassume their concrete form. Their abstract and metaphysical character disappears; their actual historical content shows forth. The notion of the subject (the ego) now discloses that it has an intrinsic connection with the isolated economic man, the notion of freedom with property, the notion of reason with the lack of real universality or community in the competitive sphere; natural law now becomes the law of competitive society—and all this social content is not the product of a forced interpretation, or of an external application of these concepts, but the final unfolding of their original meaning. At its roots, the *Philosophy of Right* is materialist in approach. Hegel exposes in paragraph after paragraph the social and economic under-structure of his philosophic concepts. True, he derives all the social and economic realities from the idea, but the idea is conceived in terms of them and bears their marks in all its moments.

The *Philosophy of Right* does not expound a specific theory of the state. It is not only a philosophic deduction of right, state, and society, or an expression of Hegel's personal opinions on their reality. What is essential in the work is the self-dissolution and self-negation of the basic concepts of modern philosophy. They share the fate of the society they explain. They lose their progressive character, their promising tone, their critical impact, and assume the form of defeat and frustration. It is this inner happening in the work rather than its systematic construction that we shall strive to develop.

In the Introduction, the general framework is set for

an elaboration of right, civil society, and state. The realm of right is the realm of freedom.[21] The thinking subject is the free being; freedom is an attribute of nis will. It is the *will* that is free, so that freedom is its substance and essence.[22] This assertion should not be taken to contradict the conclusion in the *Logic* that *thought* is the sole realm of freedom. For, the will is 'a special way of thinking,' namely, it is 'thought translating itself into reality' and becoming practice. Through his will, the individual can determine his acts in accord with his free reason. The entire sphere of right, the right of the individual, of the family, of society and of the state, derive from and must conform to the free will of the individual. To this extent, then, we are restating the conclusions of Hegel's earlier writings, that state and society are to be constructed by the critical reason of the emancipated individual. But that point is soon brought into question. The emancipated individual of modern society is not capable of such a construction. His will, expressive of particular interests, does not contain that 'universality' which would give common ground to both the particular and the general interest. The individual will is not of itself part and parcel of the 'general will.' The philosophical basis for social contract must be denied for this reason.

The will is a unity of two different aspects or moments: first, the individual's ability to abstract from every specific condition and, by negating it, to return to the absolute liberty of the pure ego; [23] secondly, the individual's act of freely adopting a concrete condition, freely affirming his existence as a particular, limited ego.[24] The first of these Hegel calls the universal aspect of will, because through constant abstraction from and negation of every determinate condition the ego asserts its identity as against

[21] § 1, Addition. [22] § 4. [23] § 5. [24] § 6.

the diversity of its particular states. That is, the individual ego is a true universal in the sense that it can abstract from and transcend every particular condition and remain at one with itself in the process. The second sense recognizes that the individual cannot in fact negate every particular condition, but must choose some one in which he carries on his life. He is in this respect a particular ego.

The fixation on either mode of will results in a negative liberty. If the individual abstracts from every particular condition and retreats into the pure will of his ego, he will constantly be rejecting all established social and political forms and will get to something like the abstract liberty and equality exalted in the French Revolution. The same was done in Rousseau's theory of the state and society, which predicated an original state of man where the living unit was the abstract individual possessing certain arbitrarily selected qualities such as good and evil, private owner or member of a community without private property, and so on. Rousseau, Hegel says, made 'the will and the spirit of the particular individual in his peculiar caprice . . . the substantive and primary basis' in society.[25]

Hegel's notion of the will aims to demonstrate that the will is of a dual character, consisting of a fundamental polarity between particular and universal elements. It aims, moreover, to show that this will is not adequate to give rise to a social and political order, but that the latter requires other factors that can be made harmonious with the will only through the long process of history. The individual's free will of necessity asserts his private interest; it can therefore never of itself will the general or common interest. Hegel shows, for example, that the free man becomes the property owner who, as such, stands

[25] § 29, p. 35.

against other property owners. His will is 'by nature' determined by his immediate 'impulses, appetites, and inclinations,' and is directed to satisfying these.[26] Satisfaction means that he has made the object of his will his own. He cannot fulfill his wants except by appropriating the objects he wants, thus excluding other individuals from the use and enjoyment of the same. His will necessarily takes 'the form of individuality [*Einzelheit*].'[27] The object is to the ego something 'which may or may not be mine.'[28] And the individual will has nothing in its nature that would overpass this mutual exclusion of 'mine' and 'thine' and unify the two in some common third. In its natural dimension, then, the free will is license, forever bound up with the arbitrary processes of appropriation.[29]

We have here a first example of Hegel's identifying a law of nature with the law of competitive society. The 'nature' of free will is conceived in such a way that it refers to a particular historical form of the will, that of the individual as private owner, with private property serving as the first realization of freedom.[30]

How, then, can the individual will, expressing the divided claims of 'mine' and 'thine,' with no common ground between, ever become the will of 'our' and thus express a common interest? The social-contract hypothesis cannot serve, for no contract between individuals transcends the sphere of private law. The contractual basis that is presumed for the state and society would make the whole subject to the same arbitrariness that governs private interests. At the same time, the state cannot base itself on any principle that implies an annulment of the rights of the individual. Hegel stands firmly by this thesis, which was enunciated in all the political philosophy of

[26] § 11. [27] § 12. [28] § 14, p. 24. [29] § 15. [30] § 41 *et seq.*

the rising middle class. The time had passed when the absolutist state described in the *Leviathan* could be said best to preserve the interests of the new middle class. A long process of discipline had since borne fruit—the individual had become the decisive unit of the economic order and, what is more, now demanded his rights in the political scheme. Hegel sets forth that demand and is true to it in all his political theory.

We have stated that Hegel represented the 'universality' of the will as a universality of the ego, meaning thereby that the universality consists in the fact that the ego integrates all existential conditions into its self-identity. The result is paradoxical: the universal is set in the most individual element in man, in his ego. Socially, the process is quite understandable. Modern society does not unite individuals so that they can carry on autonomous yet concerted activities for the good of all. They do not reproduce their society consciously, by collective activity, that is. Given such a situation as prevails, the abstract equality of the individual ego becomes the sole refuge for freedom. The freedom it wills is negative, a constant negation of the whole. The attainment of a positive freedom requires that the individual leave the monadic sphere of his private interest and settle himself in the essence of the will, which aims not at some particular end but at freedom as such. The will of the individual must become a will to general freedom. It can become such, however, only if he has actually become free. Only the will of the man who is himself free aims at positive freedom. Hegel puts this conclusion into the cryptic formula that 'freedom wills freedom,' or, 'the free will . . . wills the free will.' [31]

The formula contains concrete historical life in what

[31] § 21, Addition, p. 30, and § 27, p. 34.

seems to be an abstract philosophical pattern. It is not any individual, but the free individual who 'wishes freedom.' Freedom in its true form can be recognized and willed only by an individual who *is* free. Man cannot know freedom without possessing it; he must be free in order to become free. Freedom is not simply a status he has, but an action he undertakes as a self-conscious subject. So long as he knows no freedom, he cannot attain it by himself; his lack of freedom is such that he might even voluntarily choose or acquiesce in his own bondage. In that case, he has no interest in freedom, and his liberation must come about against his will. In other words, the act of liberating is taken out of the hands of individuals who themselves, because of their fettered status, cannot choose it as their own course.

The notion of freedom in the *Philosophy of Right* refers back to the essential relation between freedom and thought set forth in the *Logic.* The root of that relation is now laid bare in the social structure, and with it the connection is revealed between idealism and the principle of ownership. In the working out of the analysis, Hegel's conception loses its critical content and comes to serve as a metaphysical justification of private property. We shall attempt to follow out this turn of the discussion.

The process whereby the will 'purifies' itself to a point where it desires freedom is the laborious one of education through history. The education is an activity and product of thought. 'The self-consciousness, which purifies its object, content or end, and exalts it to universality, is thought carrying itself through into will. It is at this point that it becomes clear that the will is true and free only as thinking intelligence.' [32] Freedom of the will depends on thought, upon knowledge of truth. Man can be free

[32] § 21, pp. 29-30.

only when he knows his potentialities. The slave is not free for two reasons: first, because he is actually in bondage; secondly, because he has no experience or knowledge of freedom. Knowledge, or, in Hegel's language, the self-consciousness of freedom, is 'the principle of right, morality, and all forms of social ethics.'[33] The *Logic* had founded freedom on thought; the *Philosophy of Right*, recapitulating, gets at the socio-historical conditions for this conclusion. The will is free if it is 'wholly by itself, because it refers to nothing but itself, and all dependence upon any other thing falls away.'[34]

Of its very nature, the will aims at appropriating its object, making the latter part of its own being. This is a prerequisite for perfect freedom. But material objects offer a definite limit to such appropriation. Essentially, they are external to the appropriating subject, and their appropriation is hence necessarily imperfect. The only object that can become my property *in toto* is the mental object, for it has no autonomous reality apart from the thinking subject. 'It is the Mind I can appropriate in the most complete manner.'[35] Mental appropriation is different from property in material objects because the *comprehended* object does not remain external to the subject. Property is thus consummated by the free will, which represents the fulfillment of freedom as well as of appropriation.

The *Logic* had concluded that freedom consists in the subject's having complete power over its 'other.' The concrete form of such freedom is perfect and perennial ownership. The union of the principle of idealism with the principle of ownership is thus consummated. Hegel goes on to make the identification thoroughgoing for his philosophy. He states that 'only the will is the unlimited and

[33] § 21, p. 30. [34] § 23, p. 31. [35] § 52.

absolute, while all other things in contrast with the will are merely relative. To appropriate is at bottom only to manifest the majesty of my will towards things, by demonstrating that they are not self-complete and have no purpose of their own. This is brought about by my instilling into the object another end than that which it primarily had. When the living thing [Hegel is referring to the example of an animal as a potential object of will] becomes my property it gets another soul than it had. I give it my will.' [36] And, he concludes, 'free will is thus the idealism which refuses to hold that things as they are can be self-complete.'

The principle of idealism, that objective being depends upon thought, is now interpreted as the basis for the potential property-character of things. At the same time, it is the most veritable being, mind, that idealism conceives as fulfilling the idea of ownership.

Hegel's analysis of free will gives property a place in the very make-up of the individual, in his free will. The free will comes into existence as the pure will to freedom. This is 'the idea of right' and is identical with freedom as such. But it is only the *idea* of right and of freedom. The materialization of the idea begins when the emancipated individual *asserts* his will as a freedom to appropriate. 'This first phase of freedom we shall know as property.' [37]

The deduction of property from the essence of the free will is an analytical process in Hegel's discussion; what he does is draw the consequences of his former conclusions about the will. At first, the free will is 'the single will of a subject,' replete with aims that are directed to the variety of objects of a world to which the subject is related as an exclusive individual. He becomes actually free

[36] § 44, Addition, pp. 51-2.

[37] § 33, Addition, p. 41.

in a process of testing his freedom by excluding others from the objects of his will and making the latter exclusively his. By virtue of his exclusive will, the subject is 'a person.' That is, personality begins when there is a self-conscious power to make the objects of one's will one's own.[38]

Hegel has stressed that the individual is free only when he is recognized as free, and that such recognition is accorded him when he has proved his freedom. Such proof he can furnish by showing his power over the objects of his will, through appropriating them. The act of appropriation is completed when other individuals have assented to or 'recognized' it.[39]

We have also seen that for Hegel the subject's substance rests in an 'absolute negativity' in so far as the ego negates the independent existence of objects and turns them into media for its own fulfillment. The activity of the property owner is now the driving power of this negation. 'A person has the right to direct his will upon any object, as his real and positive end. The object thus becomes his. As it has no end in itself, it receives its meaning and soul from his will. Man has the absolute right to appropriate all that is a thing.' [40] Mere appropriation, however, results in mere possession (*Besitz*). But possession is property only if made objective for other individuals as well as for the owner. 'The form of mere subjectivity must be removed from the objects'; they must be held and used

[38] § 39. [39] § 44, p. 51.

[40] Hegel's concept of 'mutual recognition' of persons has three distinct elements in it:

a. the positivistic element—the mere acceptance of the fact of appropriation.
b. the dialectical element—the proprietor recognizes that the labor of those expropriated is the condition for the perpetuation and enjoyment of his property.
c. the historical element—the fact of ownership has to be confirmed by society.

The *Jenenser* system and the *Phenomenology of Mind* emphasized the

as the generally recognized property of a definite person.[41] That person must in turn recognize himself in the things he possesses, must know and handle them as the fulfillment of his free will. Then and then only does possession become an actual right.[42] Free will is of necessity the 'single will' of a definite person, and property has 'the quality of being private property.'[43]

The institution of private property has rarely been so consistently developed from and founded in the isolated individual's nature. Thus far, no universal order has entered Hegel's deduction, nothing that bestows the sanction of a universal right upon individual appropriation. No God has been invoked to ordain and justify it, nor have men's needs been cited as responsible for producing it. Property exists solely by virtue of the free subject's power. It is derived from the free person's essence. Hegel has removed the institution of property from any contingent connection and has hypostatized it as an ontological relation. He emphasizes over and over that it may not be justified as a means of satisfying human wants. 'The rationale of property does not consist in its satisfaction of needs but rather in the fact that the institution overcomes the mere subjectivity of the person, and, at the same time, fulfills the determination of the latter. The person exists as Reason only in property.'[44] Property is prior to the contingent needs of society. It is 'the first embodiment of freedom and therefore a substantial end in itself.' 'In

first two elements; the *Philosophy of Right* is mainly constructed upon the first and third. The deduction of private property in the latter work gives distinct indication of all the factors peculiar to modern philosophy, notably its respect for the prime authority of facts together with its demand that the basis for those facts be rationally justified.

The withdrawal of the dialectical element in this discussion shows an increasing influence of reification that sets in among Hegel's concepts. The *Jenenser* system and the *Phenomenology* had treated property as a relationship among men; the *Philosophy of Right* treats it as a relationship between subject and the objects.

[41] § 51, Addition.

[42] § 45.

[43] § 46.

[44] § 41, Addition (our translation).

man's relation to external objects, the rational element consists in the possession of property.' What and how much a person possesses, however, is a matter of chance and, from the standpoint of right, entirely contingent.[45] Hegel explicitly admits that the prevailing distribution of property is the product of accidental circumstances, quite at odds with rational requirements. On the other hand, he absolves reason from the task of passing judgment on this distribution. He makes no effort to apply the philosophical principle of the equality of men to the inequalities of property, and in fact rejects this step. The only equality that might be derived from reason is 'that everybody should possess property,'[46] but reason is entirely indifferent to the quality and quantity of ownership. It is in this connection that Hegel presents his striking definition, 'Right is unconcerned about differences in individuals.'[47]

The definition combines the progressive and regressive features of his philosophy of right. Unconcern about individual differences, as we shall see, is characteristic of the abstract universality of law, which sets a minimum of equality and rationality upon an order of irrationality and injustice. On the other hand, that same unconcern typifies a social practice wherein the preservation of the whole is reached only by disregarding the human essence of the individual. The object of the law is not the concrete individual, but the abstract subject of rights.

The process of transforming the relations between men into relations of things operates in Hegel's formulation. The person is submerged in his property and is a person only by virtue of his property. Consequently, Hegel denotes all Law of Persons as Law of Property. 'Clearly it is only personality that gives us a right to things, and there-

[45] § 49. [46] Ibid. Addition. [47] Ibid.

fore personal right is in essence real right [*Sachenrecht*].'[48]

The process of reification continues to permeate Hegel's analysis. He derives the entire Law of Contracts and Obligations from the Law of Property. Since the freedom of the person is exercised in the external sphere of things, the person can 'externalize' himself, that is, deal with himself as an external object. He can of his own free will 'alienate' himself and sell his performances and services. 'Mental endowments, science, art, even such matters of religion as sermons, masses, prayers, blessings, also inventions and so forth become objects of a contract; they are recognized and treated in the same way as the objects for purchase, sale, and so on.'[49] The alienation of the person, however, must have a limit in time, so that something remains of the 'totality and universality' of the person. If I were to sell 'the entire time of my concrete labor, and the totality of my produce, my personality would become the property of someone else; I would no longer be a person and would place myself outside of the realm of right.'[50] The principle of freedom, which was to demonstrate the absolute supremacy of the person over all things, has not only turned this person into a thing, but has also made him a function of time. Hegel struck upon the same fact that impelled Marx later to stipulate 'the shortening of the labor day' as the condition for man's passing into 'the realm of freedom.' Hegel's conceptions carry far enough, also, to touch upon the hidden force of labor-time and to reveal that the difference between the ancient slave and the 'free' worker can be expressed in terms of the quantity of time belonging to the 'lord.'[51]

The institution of private property has been derived from the free will of the person. This will, however, has

[48] § 40, *note*. [49] § 43. [50] § 67. [51] Ibid. Addition.

a definite limit, the private property of other persons. I am and I remain proprietor only in so far as I willingly renounce my right to appropriate other people's property. Private property thus leads beyond the isolated individual to his relations with other likewise isolated individuals. The instrument that makes the institution of property secure in this dimension is the *Contract*.[52] Here again, the ontological idea of reason is adjusted to the commodity-producing society and given its concrete embodiment there. 'It is just as much a necessity of reason that men make contracts, exchange, trade, as that they have property.' Contracts constitute that 'mutual recognition' which is required to transform possession into private property. Hegel's originally dialectical concept of 'recognition' now describes the state of affairs in the acquisitive society.[53]

Contracts, however, merely regulate the particular interests of proprietors and nowhere transcend the domain of private law. Hegel once more repudiates the doctrine of a social contract, because, he holds, it is false to say that men have an arbitrary choice to secede from the state or not to do so; 'rather is it absolutely necessary for everyone to be in a State.' The 'great progress' of the modern state over the feudal one is due to the fact that the former is 'an end in itself' and no man may make private arrangements with regard to it.[54]

The implications of private property drive Hegel ever deeper into the dark paths of the foundations of right. The Introduction had already announced that crime and punishment essentially pertain to the institution of private property,[55] and therefore also to the institution of right. The rights of property owners must of necessity clash since each stands against the other, the subject of his own particular will. Each depends in his acts upon 'the caprice

[52] § 72.
[53] See note 40, above.
[54] § 75, Addition.
[55] § 33, Addition.

and erratic choice' dictated by his knowledge and volition,[56] and the agreement of his private will with the general will is only an accident that bears the germs of new conflict. Private right is thus necessarily wrong, for the isolated individual must offend against the general right. Hegel declares that 'fraud and crime' are an 'unpremeditated or civil wrong [*unbefangenes oder bürgerliches Unrecht*],' denoting that they are a material part of civil society. The right in civil society originates from the fact that there is an abstract generalization of particular interests. If the individual, in pursuit of his interest, collides with the right, he can claim for himself the same authority that the others claim against him, namely, that he acts to preserve his own interest. The right, however, holds the higher authority because it also represents—though in an inadequate form—the interest of the whole.

The right of the whole and that of the individual do not have the same validity. The former codifies the demands of the society on which depend the maintenance and welfare of the individuals as well. If the latter do not recognize this right, they not only offend against the universal but also against themselves. They are wrong, and the punishment of their crime restores their actual right.

This formulation, which guides Hegel's theory of punishment, entirely detaches the idea of wrong from all moral considerations. The *Philosophy of Right* does not place wrong in any moral category, but introduces it under the head of Abstract Right. Wrong is a necessary element in the relationship of individual owners to one another. Hegel's exposition contains this strong mechanistic element, again a striking parallel with Hobbes's materialist political philosophy. To be sure, Hegel holds that free reason governs the will and act of individuals, but this

[56] § 81.

reason seems to behave in the manner of a natural law and not as an autonomous human activity. Reason rules over man instead of operating through his conscious power. When, therefore, Hegel identifies the Law of Reason (*Vernunftrecht*) with the Law of Nature (*Naturrecht*), this formula assumes a sinister significance, quite against Hegel's intention. He meant it to emphasize that reason is the very 'nature' of society, but the 'natural' character of the Law of Reason comes much closer to being the blind necessity of nature than the self-conscious freedom of a rational society. We shall see that Hegel repeatedly stresses the 'blind necessity' of reason in civil society. The same blind necessity that Marx later denounced as the anarchy of capitalism thus was placed in the center of the Hegelian philosophy when it set out to demonstrate the free rationality of the prevailing order.

The free will, the actual motor of reason in society, necessarily creates wrong. The individual must clash with the social order that claims to represent his own will in its objective form. But the wrong and the 'avenging justice' that remedies it not only express a 'higher logical necessity,' [57] but also prepare the transition to a higher social form of freedom, the transition from abstract right to morality. For, in committing a wrong, and in accepting punishment for his deed, the individual becomes conscious of the 'infinite subjectivity' of his freedom.[58] He learns that he is free only as a private person. When he collides with the order of right, he finds that this mode of freedom he has practiced has reached insurmountable limits. Repelled in the external world, the will now turns inward, to seek absolute freedom there. The free will enters the second realm of its fulfillment: the subject who appropriates becomes the *moral* subject.

[57] § 81.

[58] § 104, p. 103.

The transition from the first to the second part of Hegel's work thus traces a decisive trend in modern society, that in which freedom is internalized (*verinnerlicht*). The dynamics of the will, which Hegel puts forward as an ontological process, correspond to a historical process that began with the German Reformation. We indicated this in our Introduction. Hegel cites one of the most important documents that set this message forth, Luther's paper *On Christian Liberty,* wherein Luther maintained that 'the soul will not be touched nor affected if the body is maltreated, and the person subjected to another man's power.' Hegel terms this statement 'senseless sophistic reasoning,' but at the same time agrees that such a condition is possible, that man can be 'free in fetters.' This, he holds, is true only if it is the result of the man's free will, and then only in regard to himself. With regard to an other, one is unfree if his body is enslaved and free only if he actually and concretely exists as free.[59] Inner freedom, for Hegel, is only a transitory stage in the process of achieving outer freedom. The tendency to abolish the inner realm of freedom may be said to foreshadow that stage of society in which the process of internalizing values no longer proves efficient as a means of restraining the individual's demands. Inner freedom does at least reserve to the individual a sphere of unconditional privacy with which no authority may interfere, and morality does place him under some universally valid obligations. But when society turns to totalitarian forms, in accordance with the needs of monopolist imperialism, the entirety of the person becomes a political object. Even his innermost morality is subjugated to the state and his privacy abolished. The same conditions that previously called for the internalizing of values now demand that they be fully externalized.

[59] § 48.

Hegel's *Philosophy of Right* still shows a balance between these two polar developments. Hegel maintains that the subjectivity of the will 'remains the ground of the existence of freedom,'[60] and he lets freedom terminate in an all-powerful state. Morality, the realm of inner freedom, however, loses all its splendor and glory in Hegel's work and becomes a mere joint between Private and Constitutional Law, between abstract right and societal life.

It has often been stressed that Hegel's system contains no real ethics. His moral philosophy is absorbed in his political philosophy. But the submersion of ethics in politics conforms to his interpretation and valuation of civil society. It is not an accident that his section on Morality is the most brief and the least significant of any in his work.

We shall pass to the last portion of the *Philosophy of Right*, that treating social and political ethics (*Sittlichkeit*). This part of the work deals with the family, civil society, and the state, and we must first sketch the systematic connection that it has with the two preceding sections of the *Philosophy of Right*. The will here turns outward to the external realm of social reality. An individual who rejoices in the inner freedom and truth of his morality, we find, has not reached freedom and truth. The 'abstract good' is 'devoid of power'; it is compatible with any given content.[61] The *Science of Logic* had demonstrated that the idea is fulfilled only in actuality. Similarly, the free will must overcome the diremption between inner and outer world, between subjective and universal right, and the individual must achieve his will in objective social and political institutions, which in turn must accord with his will. The entire third part of the *Philosophy of Right* presupposes that no objective institution ex-

[60] § 106, p. 152. [61] § 141, p. 154.

ists that is not based upon the free will of the subject, and no subjective freedom that is not visible in the objective social order.

The opening paragraphs state precisely this. Promise is given, moreover, that the ideal will be shown as an actual existent. Mankind has reached the stage of maturity and possesses all the means that render the realization of reason possible. But these very means have been developed and employed by a society the organizing principle of which is the free play of private interests, and which is therefore unable to use them in the interest of the whole. The *Philosophy of Right* claims that private property is the material reality of the free subject and the realization of freedom. From his earliest writings, however, Hegel had seen that private property relations militate against a truly free social order. The anarchy of self-seeking property owners could not produce from its mechanism an integrated, rational, and universal social scheme. At the same time, a proper social order, Hegel maintained, could not be imposed with private property rights denied, for the free individual would be annulled thereby. The task of making the necessary integration devolved, therefore, upon an institution that would stand above the individual interests and their competing relationships, and yet would preserve their holdings and activities.

Hegel copes with the problem along the lines he followed when he raised the problem of natural law. The natural-law doctrine had struggled with the question of how a state of anarchic appropriation (the state of nature) could be transformed into one in which property is generally secure. Civil society was supposed to establish such a state of general security. Hegel now puts the same question, but takes one step beyond the traditional pattern in answering it. The two stages of development, that of the state of nature and that of civil society are overarched by a third, the state. Hegel holds the doctrine of natural law to be inadequate, because it makes civil society an end in itself. Even in Hobbes's political philosophy, absolute sovereignty was made subordinate to the need of an adequate safeguard for the securities and properties of civil society, and the fulfillment of this latter condition was made the content of sovereignty. Hegel says that civil society cannot be an end in itself because it cannot, by virtue of its intrinsic contradictions, achieve true unity and freedom. The independence of civil society is therefore repudiated by Hegel and made subordinate to the autonomous state.

Hegel shifts the task of materializing the order of reason from civil society to the state. The latter, however, does not displace civil society, but simply keeps it moving, guarding its interests without changing its content. The step beyond civil society thus leads to an authoritarian political system, which preserves intact the material content of the society. The authoritarian trend that appears in Hegel's political philosophy is made necessary by the antagonistic structure of civil society.

But it is not the only trend. The dialectic follows the structural transformation of civil society to the point of its final negation. The concepts that point to this negation are at the very root of the Hegelian system: Reason and freedom, conceived as genuine dialectical concepts, cannot be fulfilled in the prevailing system of civil society. Elements thus appear in Hegel's notion of the state that are incompatible with the order of civil society and outline the picture of a future social organization for mankind. This applies particularly to Hegel's basic requirement for a state, that it must preserve and satisfy the true interest of the individual and cannot be conceived except in terms of the perfect unity between the individual and the universal. The abstract determinations of the *Logic* once again show forth in their historical significance. The veritable being, the *Logic* had said, is the universal, which is in itself individual and contains the particular in itself. This veritable being, which the *Logic* called the notion, now returns as the state embodying reason and freedom. It is 'the Universal which has unfolded its actual rationality,' [62] and represents 'the identity of the general and particular will.' [63] The state is the 'embodiment of concrete freedom, in which the person and his particular interests have their complete development, and receive adequate recognition of their rights.' [64] The particular interests of individuals are in no circumstances to be set aside or suppressed; 'everything depends on the union of universality and particularity in the State.' [65]

The true dialectical content of reason and freedom repeatedly shows through Hegel's authoritarian formula for saving the given social scheme. The urge to preserve the prevailing system impels him to hypostatize the state as a domain in itself, situated above and even opposed to the rights of the individual. The state 'has an absolute authority or force.' [66] It is a matter of indifference to the state 'whether the individual exists or not.' [67] On the other hand, Hegel insists that the family, civil society, and state 'are not something foreign to the subject,' but part and parcel 'of his own essence.' [68] He calls the relation of the individual to these institutions a 'duty and obligation,' which necessarily restricts his liberty. But he maintains that it restricts only his 'abstract freedom' and therefore rather means the liberation of his 'substantial freedom.' [69]

The same dynamic that tears Hegel's concepts from their ties with the structure of middle-class society and drives the dialectical analysis beyond this social system

[62] § 152.
[63] § 155.
[64] § 260.
[65] § 261, Addition.
[66] § 146.
[67] § 145, Addition.
[68] § 147.
[69] § 148-9.

recurs in every portion of the last section of the *Philosophy of Right*. Family, civil society, and state are justified by a method that implies their negation. The discussion of the family that opens this section is entirely animated by this paradox. The family is a 'natural' foundation for the order of reason that culminates in the state, but at the same time it is such only in so far as it dissolves. The family has its 'external reality' in property, but property also destroys the family. Children grow up and establish property-holding families of their own.[70] The 'natural' unit of the family thus breaks up into a multitude of competing groups of proprietors, who essentially aim at their particular egoistic advantage. These groups make for the entry of civil society, which comes on the scene when all ethics has been lost and negated.[71]

Hegel bases his analysis of civil society on the two material principles of modern society: (1) The individual aims only at his private interests, in the pursuit of which he behaves as a 'mixture of physical necessity and caprice'; (2) Individual interests are so interrelated that the assertion and satisfaction of the one depends upon the assertion and satisfaction of the other.[72] This is so far simply the traditional eighteenth-century description of modern society as a 'system of mutual dependence' in which every individual, in pursuit of his own advantage, 'naturally' also promotes the interest of the whole.[73] Hegel, however, follows the negative rather than the positive aspects of this system. The civil community appears, only to disappear at once in a 'spectacle of excess, misery, and physical and social corruption.'[74] We know that from the beginning Hegel maintained that a true society, which is the free subject of its own progress and reproduction, can only be conceived as one that materializes conscious free-

[70] § 177. [71] § 181. [72] § 182. [73] § 184, Addition. [74] § 185.

dom. The complete lack of such within civil society at once denies to it the title of a final realization of reason. Like Marx, Hegel emphasizes the fact that the integration of the private interests in this society is the product of chance and not of free rational decision. The totality appears, therefore, not as liberty 'but as necessity.'[75] 'In Civil Society universality is nothing but necessity.'[76] It gives an order to a process of production in which the individual finds his place not according to his needs and abilities, but according to his 'capital.' The term 'capital' here refers not only to the proper economic power of the individual, but also to that part of his physical power that he expends in the economic process, that is, to his labor-power.[77] The specific wants of individuals are satisfied by means of abstract labor,[78] which is the 'general and permanent property' of men.[79] Because the possibility of sharing in the general wealth depends on capital, this system produces increasing inequalities.[80] It is a short step from this point to the famous paragraphs that set forth the intrinsic connection between the accumulation of wealth on the one hand and the growing impoverishment of the working class on the other:

> By generalizing the relations of men by way of their wants, and by generalizing the manner in which the means of meeting these wants are prepared and procured, large fortunes are amassed. On the other side, there occur a repartition and limitation of the work of the individual labourer and, consequently, dependence and distress in the artisan class . . .
>
> When a large number of people sink below the standard of living regarded as essential for the members of society, and lose that sense of right, rectitude and honour which is derived from self-support, a pauper class arises, and wealth accumulates disproportionately in the hands of a few.[81]

75 § 186.
76 § 229, Addition.
77 § 199-200.
78 § 196, 198.
79 § 199.
80 § 200.
81 § 243-4.

Hegel envisages the rise of a vast industrial army and sums up the irreconcilable contradictions of civil society in the statement that 'this society, in the excess of its wealth, is not wealthy enough . . . to stem excess of poverty and the creation of paupers.'[82] The system of estates that Hegel outlines as the proper organization of civil society is not of itself able to resolve the contradiction. The external unity attempted among competing individuals through the three estates—the peasantry, the traders (including craftsmen, manufacturers, and merchants), and the bureaucracy—merely repeats Hegel's earlier attempts in this direction; the idea sounds less convincing here than ever before. All the organizations and institutions of civil society are for 'the protection of property,'[83] and the freedom of that society means only 'the right of property.' The estates must be regulated by external forces that are more powerful than the economic mechanisms. These prepare the transition to the political ordering of society. This transition occurs in the sections on the Administration of Justice, the Police, and the Corporation.

The administration of justice makes abstract right into law and introduces a conscious universal order into the blind and contingent processes of civil society. We have said that the concept of law is central to the *Philosophy of Right,* so much so in fact that the title of the work might better be 'Philosophy of Law.' The entire discussion in it assumes that right actually exists as law, an assumption that follows from the ontological principles of Hegel's philosophy. Right, as we have seen, is an attribute of the free subject, of the person. The person, in turn, is what he is only by virtue of thought, *qua* thinking subject. Thought establishes a true community for otherwise isolated individuals, gives them a universality. Right ap-

[82] § 245.

[83] § 208.

plies to individuals in so far as they are universal; it may not be possessed because of any particular accidental qualities. This means that he who possesses right does so as 'the individual in the form of the universal, the ego *qua* universal person,' [84] and that the universality of right is essentially an abstract one. The idealist principle that thought is the true being is thus seen to imply that right is universal in the form of universal law, for the law abstracts from the individual and treats him as 'universal person.' 'Man has his value in his being man, not in his being a Jew, Catholic, Protestant, German, or Italian.' [85] The rule of law pertains to the 'universal person' and not to the concrete individual, and it embodies freedom precisely in so far as it is universal.

Hegel's legal theory is definitely aligned with the progressive trends in modern society. Anticipating later developments in jurisprudence, he rejects all doctrines bestowing the right on judicial decision rather than on the universality of the law, and he criticizes points of view that make judges 'the permanent law-givers' or leave to their discretion the ultimate decision as to right and wrong.[86] In his time the social forces in power had not yet come to agree that the abstract universality of the law, like the other phenomena of liberalism, interferes with their designs, and that the need is for a more direct and effective ruling instrument. Hegel's concept of law is adapted to an earlier phase of civil society, characterized by free competition among individuals more or less equally endowed materially, so that 'everyone is an end in himself . . .' and 'to each particular person others are a means to the attainment of his end.' [87] Within this system, Hegel says, even the common interest, the universal, 'appears as a means.'

[84] § 209. [85] Ibid. [86] § 211. [87] § 182, Addition.

Such is the social scheme that produced civil society. The scheme cannot perpetuate itself unless it harmonizes the antagonistic interests, of which it is made up, into a form that is more rational and calculable than the operations of the commodity market that governs it. Unrestricted competition requires a minimum of equal protection for the competitors and a reliable guarantee for contracts and services. This minimum of harmony and integration, however, cannot be had except by abstracting from each one's concrete existence and its variations. 'The right does not deal with man's specific determinations. Its purpose is not to advance and protect him' in his 'necessary wants and special aims and drives [such as his thirst for knowledge or his desire to maintain life, health, and so on].' [88] Man enters into contracts, exchange relations, and other obligations simply as the abstract subject of capital or of labor-power or of some other socially necessary possession or device. Accordingly, the law can be universal and treat individuals as equals only in so far as it remains abstract. Right is hence a form rather than a content. The justice dispensed by law gets its cue from the *general form* of transaction and interaction, while the concrete varieties of individual life enter only as a sum-total of attenuating or aggravating circumstances. The law as a universal thus has a negative aspect. It of necessity involves an element of chance, and its application to a particular case will engender imperfection and cause injustice and hardship. These negative elements, however, cannot be eliminated by extending the discretionary powers of the judge. The law's abstract universality is a far better guarantee of right, despite all the shortcomings, than is the individual's concrete and specific self. In civil society all individuals have private interests by which they are set

[88] *Philosophische Propaedeutik*, I, § 22 (*Sämtliche Werke*, ed. Hermann Glockner, Stuttgart 1927, vol. III, p. 49).

against the whole, and none of them can claim to be a source of right.

It is true at the same time that the abstract equality of men before the law does not eliminate their material inequalities or in any sense remove the general contingency that surrounds the social and economic status they possess. But by force of the fact that it disregards the contingent elements, the law is more just than the concrete social relations that produce inequalities, hazard, and other injustices. Law is at least based on a few essential factors common to all individuals. (We must bear in mind that private ownership is one of these 'essential factors' to Hegel, and that human equality means to him also an equal *right* of all to property.) In standing by its principle of fundamental equality, the law is able to rectify certain flagrant injustices without upsetting the social order that demands the continuance of injustice as a constitutive element of its existence.

This, at least, is the philosophical construction, valid only in so far as the rule of law gives greater security and protection to the weak than does the system that has since replaced it, the rule of authoritarian decree. Hegel's doctrine is the product of the liberalistic era and embodies its traditional principles. For laws to be obeyed they must be known to all, he says, citing the fact that tyranny would 'hang up the laws so high that no citizen could read them.' By the same token, he excludes retroactive legislation. The judge's power of decision, too, he states, must be restricted as far as possible through the calculable terms of the law itself. Public trial, for example, is essential as one such restrictive device, and is justified by the fact that the law requires the confidence of the citizenry and that the right, as essentially universal, belongs to all.[89]

[89] § 224, Addition.

Hegel's conception implies that the body of law is what free men would themselves establish of their own reason. He assumes, in line with the tradition of democratic political philosophy, that the free individual is the original legislator who gave the law to himself, but the assumption does not prevent Hegel from saying that law is materialized in the 'protection of property through the administration of justice.' [90]

This insight into the material connection between the rule of law and the rule of property compels Hegel, in contrast to Locke and his successors, to go beyond the liberalist doctrine. Because of this connection, the law cannot be the final point of integration for civil society, nor can it represent its real universality. The rule of law merely embodies the 'abstract right' of property. 'The function of judicial administration is only to actualize into necessity the abstract side of personal liberty in Civil Society . . . The blind necessity of the system of wants is not yet lifted up to consciousness of the universal, and worked from that point of view.' [91] The law must therefore be supplemented and even supplanted by a much stronger and stricter force which will govern individuals more directly and more visibly. The *Police* emerge.

Hegel's notion of the police adopts many features of the doctrine with which absolutism used to justify the regulations it practised upon social and economic life. The police not only interfered in the productive and distributive process, not only restricted freedom of trade and profit and watched over prices, poverty, and vagrancy, but also supervised the private life of the individual wherever

[90] § 208. See Locke, *Of Civil Government*, Book II, § 134: Locke's concept of property includes in its meaning the basic rights of the individuals, that is 'their lives, liberties and estates'! This concept still operates in Hegel's work. According to Hegel, everything that is other than and separable from the 'free mind' may be made property.

[91] *Encyclopædia of the Philosophical Sciences*, § 532 (*Hegel's Philosophy of Mind*, trans. W. Wallace, London 1894, p. 261).

the public welfare could be affected. There is, however, an important difference between the police who did all this during the rise of modern absolutism, and the police of the Restoration.[92] To a considerable extent, Hegel's *Philosophy of Right* expresses the official theory of the latter. The police is supposed to represent the interest of the whole against social forces that are not too weak but too strong to guarantee an undisturbed functioning of the social and economic process. The police does not any longer have to organize the process of production for want of private power and knowledge to achieve this. The task of the police is a negative one, rather, to safeguard 'the security of person and property' in the contingent sphere that is not covered by the universal stipulations of the law.[93]

Hegel's statements about the function of the police show, however, that he goes beyond the doctrine held during the Restoration, especially in his emphasis that the growing antagonisms of civil society increasingly make the social organism a blind chaos of selfish interests and necessitate the establishment of a powerful institution to control the confusion. Significantly enough, it is in this discussion of the police that Hegel makes some of his most pointed and far-reaching remarks about the destructive course that civil society is bound to take. And he concludes with the statement that 'by means of its own dialectic the civil society is driven beyond its own limits as a definite and self-complete society.' It must seek to open new markets to absorb the products of an increasing over-production, and must pursue a policy of economic expansion and systematic colonization.[94]

[92] See Kurt Wolzendorff, *Der Polizeigedanke des modernen Staates*, Breslau 1918, pp. 100-130.

[93] *Philosophy of Right*, § 230-31.

[94] Ibid. § 246-8.

The difficulties in relating the police to the external policy of the state disappear if we take into consideration the fact that the police for Hegel is a product of the growing antagonisms of the civil order and is introduced to cope with these contradictions. Accordingly, the line between the police and the state (which fulfills what the police begins) is not sharp. Hegel envisages a final situation wherein 'the labor of all will be subject to administrative regulation.'[95] This, he says, will 'shorten and alleviate the dangerous upheavals' to which civil society is prone. In other words, a totalitarian social organization will leave less time 'for conflicts to adjust themselves merely by unconscious necessity.'[96]

The police, however, is not the only remedy. The unruliness of civil society is to be bridled by yet another institution, the *Corporation,* which Hegel conceives along the lines of the old guild system, with some features added of the modern corporate state. The corporation is an economic as well as a political unit, with the following dual function: (1) to bring unity to the competing economic interests and activities within the estates, and (2) to champion the organized interests of civil society as against the state. The corporation is supervised by the state,[97] but it aims to safeguard the material concerns of trade and industry. Capital and labor, producer and consumer, profit and general welfare meet in the corporation, where the special interests of economic subjects are purified of mere self-seeking so that they can fit into the universal order of the state.

Hegel does not explain how all this is possible. It seems that the corporation selects its members according to their actual qualifications and that it guarantees their business and their assets, but this appears to be all. The

95 § 236. 96 Ibid. 97 § 255, Addition.

corporation remains an ideological agency above all, an entity that exhorts the individual to work for an ideal that doesn't exist, 'the unselfish end of the whole.'[98] Moreover, the corporation is to bestow upon him approbation as a recognized member of society. Actually, however, it is not the individual but the economic process that does the recognizing. The individual, therefore, obtains only an ideological good; his compensation is the 'honor' of belonging to the corporation.[99]

The corporation leads from the section on civil society to that on the state. The state is essentially separate and distinct from society. The decisive feature of civil society is 'the security and protection of property and personal freedom,' 'the interest of the individual' its ultimate purpose. The state has a totally different function, and is related to the individual in another way. 'Union as such is itself the true content and end' for the state. The integrating factor is the universal, not the particular. The individual may 'pass a universal life' in the state; his particular satisfactions, activities, and ways of life are here regulated by the common interest. The state is a subject in the strict sense of the word, namely, the actual carrier and end of all individual actions that now stand under 'universal laws and principles.'[100]

The laws and principles of the state guide the activities of free-thinking subjects, so that their element is not nature, but mind, the rational knowledge and will of associated individuals. This is the meaning of Hegel's terming the state 'Objective Mind.' The state creates an order that does not depend, as civil society did, on the blind interrelation of particular needs and performances for its own perpetuation. The 'system of wants' becomes a conscious scheme of life controlled by man's autonomous

98 § 253. 99 Ibid. 100 § 258, *note*.

decisions in the common interest. The state therefore can be denoted as the 'realization of freedom.' [101]

We have mentioned that for Hegel the state's fundamental task is to make the specific and the general interest coincide, so as to preserve the individual's right and freedom. Yet such a demand presupposes the identification of state and society, not their separation. For, the wants and interests of the individual exist in society and, no matter how they may be modified by the demands of the common welfare, they arise in and remain bound up with the social processes governing individual life. The demand that freedom and happiness be fulfilled thus eventually falls back upon society, and not upon the state. According to Hegel, the state has no aim other than 'association as such.' In other words, it has no aim at all if the social and economic order constitutes a 'true association.' The process of bringing the individual into harmony with the universal would engender the 'withering away' of the state, rather than the opposite.

Hegel, however, separated the rational order of the state from the contingent interrelations of the society because he looked upon society as civil society, which is not a 'true association.' The critical character of his dialectic forced him to see society as he did. Dialectical method understands the existent in terms of the negativity it contains and views realities in the light of their change. Change is a historical category.[102] The objective mind, with which the *Philosophy of Right* deals, unfolds itself in time,[103] and the dialectical analysis of its content has to be guided by the forms that this content has taken in

101 § 258, Addition and § 260.

102 Hegel, *Philosophie der Weltgeschichte*, ed. Georg Lasson, 1920, vol. I, p. 10.

103 See below, p. 224.

history. The truth thus appears as a historical achievement, so that the stage man has reached with civil society fulfills all preceding historical efforts. Some other form of association may come in the future, but philosophy, as the science of the actual, does not enter into speculations over it. The social reality, with its general competition, selfishness, and exploitation, with its excessive wealth and excessive poverty, is the foundation on which reason must build. Philosophy cannot jump ahead of history, for it is a son of its time, 'its time apprehended in thought.' [104]

The times are those of a civil society wherein has been prepared the material basis for realizing reason and freedom, but a reason distorted by the blind necessity of the economic process and a freedom perverted through competition of conflicting private interests. Yet this selfsame society has much that makes for a truly free and rational association: it upholds the inalienable right of the individual, increases human wants and the means for their satisfaction, organizes the division of labor, and advances the rule of law. These elements must be freed from private interests and submitted to a power that stands above the competitive system of civil society, in a specially exalted position. This power is the state. Hegel sees the state as 'an independent and autonomous power' in which 'the individuals are mere moments,' as 'the march of God in the world.' [105] He thought this to be the very essence of the state, but, in reality, he was only describing the historical type of state that corresponded to civil society.

We reach this interpretation of Hegel's state by placing his concept in the socio-historical setting that he himself implied in his description of civil society. Hegel's idea of the state stems from a philosophy in which the liberal-

[104] *Philosophy of Right,* p. xxviii.
[105] § 258, Addition.

istic conception of state and society has all but collapsed. We have seen that Hegel's analysis led to his denying any 'natural' harmony between the particular and the general interest, between civil society and the state. The liberalist idea of the state was thus demolished. In order that the framework of the given social order may not be broken, the common interest has to be vested in an autonomous agency, and the authority of the state set above the battle-ground of competing social groups. Hegel's 'deified' state, however, by no means parallels the Fascist one. The latter represents the very level of social development that Hegel's state is supposed to avoid, namely, the direct totalitarian rule of special interests over the whole. Civil society under Fascism rules the state; Hegel's state rules civil society. And in whose name does it rule? According to Hegel, in the name of the free individual and in his true interest. 'The essence of the modern state is the union of the universal with the full freedom of the particular, and with the welfare of individuals.' [106] The prime difference between the ancient and the modern world rests on the fact that in the latter the great questions of human life are to be decided not by some superior authority, but by the free 'I will' of man. 'This I will . . . must have its peculiar niche in the great building of State.' [107] The basic principle of this state is the full development of the individual.[108] Its constitution and all its political institutions are to express 'the knowledge and the will of its individuals.'

At this point, however, the historical contradiction inherent in Hegel's political philosophy determines its fate. The individual who knows and wishes his true interest in the common interest—this individual simply doesn't exist. Individuals exist only as private owners, subjects of the fierce processes of civil society, cut off from the com-

[106] § 260, Addition. [107] § 279, Addition. [108] § 260 and 261.

mon interest by selfishness and all it entails. As far as civil society reaches, none is free of its toils.

Outside of society, however, lies nature. If there could be found someone who possesses his individuality by virtue of his *natural* and not his social existence, and who is what he is simply by nature and not by the social mechanisms, he might be the stable point from which the state could be ruled. Hegel finds such a man in the monarch, a man chosen to his position 'by natural birth.' [109] Ultimate freedom can rest with him, for he is outside a world of false and negative freedom and is 'exalted above all that is particular and conditional.' [110] The ego of everyone else is corrupted by the social order that molds all; the monarch alone is not so influenced and is hence able to originate and decide all his acts by reference to his pure ego. He can cancel all particularity in the 'simple certainty of his self.' [111]

We know what the 'self-certainty of the pure ego' means to Hegel's system: it is the essential property of the 'substance as subject,' and thus characterizes the true being.[112] The use of this principle historically to yield the monarch's natural person again points up the frustration of idealism. Freedom becomes identical with the inexorable necessity of nature, and reason terminates in an accident of birth. The philosophy of freedom again turns into a philosophy of necessity.

Classical political economy described modern society as a 'natural system' whose laws appeared to have the necessity of physical laws. This point of view soon lost its magic. Marx showed how the anarchic forces of capitalism assume the quality of natural forces as long as they are not made subject to human reason, that the natural element in society is not a positive but a negative one. Hegel seems to

109 § 280. 110 § 279. 111 Ibid. 112 See above, pp. 155 f.

have had some inkling of this. He sometimes seems to be smiling at his own idealization of the monarch, declaring that the decisions of the monarch are only formalities. He is 'a man who says yes and so puts the dot upon the i.' [113] He notes that monarchs are not remarkable for intellectual or physical strength and that, despite this, millions permit themselves to be ruled by them.[114] Nevertheless, the intellectual weakness of the monarch is preferable to the wisdom of civil society, Hegel feels.

The fault with Hegel lies much deeper than in his glorification of the Prussian monarchy. He is guilty not so much of being servile as of betraying his highest philosophical ideas. His political doctrine surrenders society to nature, freedom to necessity, reason to caprice. And in so doing, it mirrors the destiny of the social order that falls, while in pursuit of its freedom, into a state of nature far below reason. The dialectical analysis of civil society had concluded that society was not capable of establishing reason and freedom of its own accord. Hegel therefore put forward a strong state to achieve this end and tried to reconcile that state with the idea of freedom by giving a strong constitutional flavoring to monarchy.

The state exists only through the medium of law. 'Laws express the content of objective freedom . . . They are an absolute final end and a universal work.' [115] Hence the state is bound by laws that are the opposite of authoritarian decrees. The body of laws is 'a universal work' that incorporates the reason and the will of associated men. The constitution expresses the interests of all (now, of course, their true, 'purified' interests), and the executive, legislative and judiciary powers are but the organs of constitutional law. Hegel repudiates the traditional division

[113] § 280, Addition. [114] § 281, Addition.

[115] *Encyclopædia of the Philosophical Sciences* (trans. W. Wallace, as Hegel's *Philosophy of Mind*), p. 263.

of these powers, as detrimental to the state's unity; the three functions of government are to work in permanent actual collaboration. The emphasis on the state's unity is so strong that it occasionally leads Hegel to formulations that come close to the organicist theory of the state. He declares, for instance, that the constitution, though 'begotten in time, should not be contemplated as made' by man, but rather as 'divine and perpetual.' [116] Such utterances spring from the same motives that impelled the most far-seeing philosophers to set the state above any danger of criticism. They recognized that the tie that most effectively binds the conflicting groups of the ruling class is the fear of any subversion of the existing order.

We shall not spend time upon Hegel's outline of the constitution, since it hardly adds essentially to his earlier writings on the same subject, although some important features of his system are worthy of brief notice. The traditional trinity of political powers is altered to consist of the monarchic, the administrative, and the legislative power. These overlap so that the executive power belongs to the first two and includes the judicial, while the legislative power is exercised by the government together with the estates. The entire political system again converges towards the idea of sovereignty, which, though now rooted in the 'natural' person of the monarch, still pervades the whole structure. Alongside the state's sovereignty over the antagonisms of civil society, Hegel now stresses its sovereignty over the people (*Volk*). The people 'is that part of the State which does not know what it wants,' and whose 'movement and action would be elemental, void of reason, violent, and terrible' [117] if not regulated. Here again, Hegel may have been thinking of the *Volksbewegung* of his time; the Prussian monarchy may well have seemed a

[116] *Philosophy of Right*, § 273, *note*.
[117] § 301 and 303, *note*.

paragon of reason compared to that Teutonic movement from 'below.' Yet, Hegel's advocacy of a strong hand over the masses is part of a more general trend, which threatens the whole constitutional structure of his state.

The state provides a unity for the particular and the general interest. Hegel's view of this unity differs from the liberalistic, inasmuch as his state is imposed upon the social and economic mechanisms of civil society and is vested in independent political powers and institutions. 'The objective will is in itself rational in its very conception, whether or not it be known by the individuals or willed as an object of their caprice.' [118]

Hegel's exaltation of the state's political power has, however, some clearly critical traits. Discussing the relation between religion and the state, he points out that 'religion is principally commended and resorted to in times of public distress, disturbance, and oppression; it is taught to furnish consolation against wrong and the hope of compensation in the case of loss.' [119] He notes the dangerous function of religion in its tendency to divert man from his search for actual freedom and to pay him fictitious damages for real wrongs. 'It would surely be regarded as a bitter jest if those who were oppressed by any despotism were referred to the consolations of religion; nor is it to be forgotten that religion may assume the form of a galling superstition, involving the most abject servitude, and the degradation of man below the level of the brute.' Some force has to interfere to rescue the individual from religion in such a case. The state comes to champion 'the rights of reason and self-consciousness.' 'It is not strength, but weakness which has in our times made religion a polemical kind of piety'; the struggle for man's historical fulfillment is not a religious but a so-

[118] § 258.

[119] § 270, *note*.

cial and political struggle, and its transplantation to an inner sanctum of the soul, of belief and morality, means regression to a stage long since past.

Nevertheless, these critical qualities are dwarfed by the oppressive trends inherent in all authoritarianism, which manifest their full force in Hegel's doctrine of external sovereignty. We have already shown how Hegel elevated the national interests of the particular state to the place of highest and most indubitable authority in international relations. The state puts forward and asserts the interests of its members by welding them into a community, in this way fulfilling their freedom and their rights and transforming the destructive force of competition into a unified whole. Undisputed *internal* authority of the state is a prerequisite for successful competition, and the latter necessarily terminates in *external* sovereignty. The life and death struggle of individuals in civil society for mutual recognition has its counterpart among sovereign states in the form of war. War is the inevitable issue of any test of sovereignty. It is neither an absolute evil nor an accident, but an 'ethical element,' for war achieves that integration of interests that civil society cannot establish by itself. 'Successful wars have prevented civil broils and strengthened the internal power of the State.' [120]

Hegel was thus as cynical as Hobbes on the subject of the bourgeois state, ending in a complete rejection of International Law. The state, the final subject that perpetuates competitive society, cannot be bound by a higher law, for such a law would amount to an external restriction of sovereignty and destroy the life-element of civil society.[121]

[120] § 324, *note.*

[121] Fascist ideology has made this intrinsic connection between sovereignty, war, and competition a decisive argument against liberal capitalism. 'An entire community can practice competition in an orderly way only in war or in competition with an outside community. Thus, in war-

No contract is valid among states. Sovereignty cannot be circumscribed by treaties that imply in their very nature a mutual dependence of the parties involved. Sovereign states stand outside the world of civil interdependence; they exist in a 'state of nature.'

We note again that blind nature enters and elbows aside the self-conscious rationality of objective mind:

> States find themselves in a natural more than a legal relation to each other. There is hence a continuous struggle between them. They conclude treaties and therewith establish a legal relation between themselves. On the other hand, however, they are autonomous and independent. Right, therefore, cannot be real as between them. They may break treaties arbitrarily, and they must constantly find themselves distrusting one another. Since they are in a state of nature, they act according to violence. They maintain and procure their rights through their own power and must as a matter of necessity plunge into war.[122]

Hegel's idealism comes to the same conclusion as did Hobbes's materialism. The rights of sovereign states 'have reality not in a general will which is constituted as a superior power, but in their particular wills.' [123] Accordingly, disputes among them can be settled only by war. International relations are an arena for 'the wild play of particular passions, interests, aims, talents, virtues, force, wrong, vice, and external contingency'—the moral end itself, 'the State's autonomy, is exposed to chance.' [124]

time, each warring community operates internally on the basis of cooperation and externally on the basis of competition. In this way there is order within and anarchy without. It is obviously an inevitable condition of any society of sovereign nations that it be characterized by anarchy. Multiple sovereignties are merely a synonym for anarchy. International anarchy is a corollary of national sovereignty.' This paragraph from Lawrence Dennis's book *The Dynamics of War and Revolution* (1940, p. 122) is an exact restatement of Hegel's doctrine of sovereignty.

122 *Philosophische Propädeutik*, I, § 31, in *Sämtliche Werke*, op. cit., vol. III, p. 74.

123 *Philosophy of Right*, § 333.

124 § 340.

But is this drama of chance and violence really final? Does reason terminate in the state and in that play of reckless natural forces in which the state must perforce engage? Hegel has repudiated such conclusions throughout the *Philosophy of Right*. The state right, though not bound by international law, is still not the final right, but must answer to 'the right of the World Mind which is the unconditional absolute.'[125] The state has its real content in universal history (*Weltgeschichte*), the realm of the world mind, which holds 'the supreme absolute truth.'[126] Furthermore, Hegel emphasizes that any relation between autonomous states 'must be external. A third must therefore stand above and unite them.' 'This third is the Mind which materializes itself in world history, and constitutes itself absolute judge over States.'[127] The state, even laws and duties, are merely 'a determinate reality'; they pass up into and rest upon a higher sphere.[128]

What, then, is this final sphere of state and society? How are state and society related to the world mind? These questions can only be answered if we turn to an interpretation of Hegel's *Philosophy of History*.

125 § 30. 126 § 33. 127 § 259, Addition. 128 § 270, *note*.

VII

The Philosophy of History

BEING, for dialectical logic, is a process through contradictions that determine the content and development of all reality. The *Logic* had elaborated the timeless structure of this process, but the intrinsic connection, between the *Logic* and the other parts of the system, and, above all, the implications of the dialectical method destroy the very idea of timelessness. The *Logic* had shown that the true being is the idea, but the idea unfolds itself 'in space' (as nature) and 'in time' (as mind).[1] Mind is of its very essence affected by time, for it exists only in the temporal process of history. The forms of the mind manifest themselves in time, and the history of the world is an exposition of mind in time.[2] The dialectic thus gets to view reality temporally, and the 'negativity' that, in the *Logic,* determined the process of thought appears in the *Philosophy of History* as the destructive power of time.

The *Logic* had demonstrated the structure of reason; the *Philosophy of History* expounds the historical content of reason. Or, we may say, the content of reason here is the same as the content of history, although by content we refer not to the miscellany of historical facts, but to what makes history a rational whole, the laws and tendencies to which the facts point and from which they receive their meaning.

'Reason is the sovereign of the world,' [3]—this, according to Hegel, is a hypothesis, and the only hypothesis in the

[1] *Philosophy of History,* p. 72.
[2] *Philosophie der Weltgeschichte,* ed. G. Lasson, op. cit., p. 134.
[3] *Philosophy of History,* p. 9.

philosophy of history. This hypothesis, which distinguishes the philosophic method of treating history from any other method, does not imply that history has a definite end. The teleological character of history (if indeed history has such) can only be a conclusion from an empirical study of history and cannot be assumed *a priori.* Hegel states emphatically that 'in history, thought must be subordinate to what is given, to the realities of fact; this is its basis and guide.'[4] Consequently, 'we have to take history as it is. We must proceed historically—empirically,' an odd approach for an idealistic philosophy of history.

The laws of history have to be demonstrated in and from the facts—thus far, Hegel's is the empirical method. But these laws cannot be known unless the investigation first has the guidance of proper theory. Facts of themselves disclose nothing; they only answer adequate theoretical questions. True scientific objectivity requires the application of sound categories that organize data in their actual significance, and not a passive reception of given facts. 'Even the ordinary, the "impartial" historiographer, who believes and professes that he maintains a simply receptive attitude, surrendering himself only to the data supplied him—is by no means passive as regards the exercise of his thinking powers. He brings his categories with him, and sees the phenomena . . . exclusively through these media.'[5]

But how does one recognize the sound categories and the proper theory? Philosophy decides. It elaborates those general categories that direct investigation in all special fields. Their validity in these fields, however, must be verified by the facts, and the verification is had when the given facts are comprehended by the theory in such a way that they appear under definite laws and as moments of definite

[4] Ibid., p. 8.

[5] Ibid., p. 11.

tendencies, which explain their sequence and interdependence.

The dictum that philosophy should provide the general categories for understanding history is not arbitrary, nor did it originate with Hegel. The great theories of the eighteenth century all took the philosophic view that history was progress. This concept of progress, soon to degenerate into a shallow complacency, originally pointed sharp condemnatory criticism on an obsolete social order. The rising middle class used the concept of progress as a means to interpret the past history of mankind as the prehistory of its own reign, a reign that was destined to bring the world to maturity. When, they said, the new middle class would get to shape the world in accordance with its interests, an unheard-of spurt in material and intellectual forces would make man master of nature and would initiate the true history of humanity. As long as all this had not yet materialized, history was still in a state of struggle for truth. The idea of progress, an integral element in the philosophy of the French Enlightenment, interpreted historical facts as signposts marking man's path to reason. The truth still lay outside the realm of fact—in a state to come. Progress implied that the given state of affairs would be negated and not continued.

This pattern still prevails in Hegel's *Philosophy of History*. Philosophy is the material as well as the logical *a priori* of history, so long as history has not yet won the level adequate to human potentialities. We know, however, that Hegel thought history had reached its goal and that idea and reality had found common ground. Hegel's work thus marks the apogee and end of the critical philosophic historiography. He still looks to freedom's interest in his dealing with historical facts, and still views the struggle for freedom as the only content of history. But this interest has lost its vigor and the struggle has come to an end.

The concept of freedom, as the *Philosophy of Right* has shown, follows the pattern of free ownership. As a result, the history of the world that Hegel looks out upon exalts and enshrines the history of the middle class, which based itself on this pattern. There is a stark truth in Hegel's strangely certain announcement that history has reached its end. But it announces the funeral of a class, not of history. At the close of the book, Hegel writes, after a description of the Restoration, 'This is the point which consciousness has attained.' [6] This hardly sounds like an end. Consciousness is historical consciousness, and when we read in the *Philosophy of Right* that 'one form of life has grown old,' it is one form, not all forms of life. The consciousness and the aims of his class were open to Hegel. He saw they contained no new principle to rejuvenate the world. If this consciousness was to be mind's final form, then history had entered a realm beyond which there was no progress.

Philosophy gives historiography its general categories, and these are identical with the basic concepts of the dialectic. Hegel has summarized them in his introductory lectures.[7] We shall get to them later. First, we must discuss the concepts he calls specific historical categories.

The hypothesis on which the *Philosophy of History* rests has already been verified by Hegel's *Logic:* the true being is reason, manifest in nature and come to realization in man. The realization takes place in history, and since reason realized in history is mind, Hegel's thesis implies that the actual subject or driving force of history is mind.

[6] P. 456.

[7] Georg Lasson has published the various forms of this introduction in his edition of Hegel's *Philosophie der Weltgeschichte,* 1920-22. See particularly vol. 1, p. 10 *et seq.* and p. 31 *et seq.*

Of course, man is also part of nature and his natural drives and impulses play a material role in history. Hegel's *Philosophy of History* does more justice to this role than do many empirical historiographies. Nature, in the form of the sum-total of natural conditions for human life, remains the primary basis of history throughout Hegel's book.

As a natural being, man is confined to particular conditions—he is born in this or that place or time, a member of this or that nation, bound to share the fate of the particular whole to which he belongs. Yet, despite all this, man is essentially a thinking subject, and thought, we know, constitutes universality. Thought (1) lifts men beyond their particular determinations and (2) also makes the multitude of external things the medium for the subject's development.

This double universality, subjective and objective, characterizes the historical world wherein man unfolds his life. History, as the history of the thinking subject, is of necessity universal history (*Weltgeschichte*) just because 'it belongs to the realm of Mind.' We apprehend the content of history through general concepts, such as nation, state; agrarian, feudal, civil society; despotism, democracy, monarchy; proletariat, middle class, nobility, and so on. Caesar, Cromwell, Napoleon are for us Roman, English, French citizens; we understand them as members of their nation, responding to the society and the state of their time. The universal asserts itself in them. Our general concepts grasp this universal to be the actual subject of history, so that, for example, the history of mankind is not the life and battles of Alexander the Great, Caesar, the German emperors, the French kings, the Cromwells and Napoleons, but the life and battles of that universal which unfolds itself in different guises through the various cultural wholes.

The essence of this universal is mind, and 'the essence of Mind is freedom . . . Philosophy teaches that all the qualities of Mind exist only through freedom; that all are but means for attaining freedom; that all seek and produce this and this alone.' [8] We have discussed these qualities, and we have seen that freedom terminates in the self-assurance of complete appropriation; that the mind is free if it possesses and knows the world as its property. It is therefore quite understandable that the *Philosophy of History* should end with the consolidation of middle-class society and that the periods of history should appear as necessary stages in the realization of its form of freedom.

The true subject of history is the universal, not the individual; the true content is the realization of the self-consciousness of freedom, not the interests, needs, and actions of the individual. 'The history of the world is none other than the progress of the consciousness of freedom.' [9] Yet, 'the first glance at history convinces us that the actions of men proceed from their needs, their passions, their characters and talents; and impresses us with the belief that such needs, passions and interests are the sole springs of action—the efficient agents in this scene of activity.' [10] To explain history thus means 'to depict the passions of mankind, its genius, its active powers.' [11] How does Hegel resolve the apparent contradiction? There can be no question that the needs and interests of individuals are the levers of all historical action, and that in history it is the individual's fulfillment that should come to pass. Something else asserts itself, however—historical reason. As they follow out their own interests, individuals promote the progress of mind, that is, perform a universal task that advances freedom. Hegel cites the example of Caesar's struggle for power. In his overthrow of the tra-

[8] *Philosophy of History*, p. 17.
[9] P. 19.
[10] P. 20.
[11] P. 13.

ditional form of Roman state, Caesar was certainly driven by ambition; but, in satisfying his personal drives he fulfilled 'a necessary destiny in the history of Rome and of the world'; through his actions, he achieved a higher, more rational form of political organization.[12]

A universal principle is thus latent in the particular aims of individuals—universal because 'a necessary phase in the development of truth.' [13] It is as if mind uses individuals for its unwitting tool. Let us take an example from Marxian theory that may elucidate the connection between Hegel's *Philosophy of History* and the subsequent evolution of the dialectic. Marx held that during a developed industrial capitalism individual capitalists are compelled to adapt their enterprises to the rapid progress of technology in order to assure their profits and outdo their competitors. They thereby reduce the amount of labor-power they employ and thus, since their surplus value is produced only by labor-power, reduce the rate of profit at the disposal of their class. In this way they accelerate the disintegrating tendencies of the social system they want to maintain.

The process of reason working itself out through individuals, however, does not occur with natural necessity, nor does it have a continuous and unilinear course. 'There are many considerable periods in history in which this development seems to have been intermitted; in which, we might rather say, the whole enormous gain of previous culture appears to have been entirely lost; after which, unhappily, a new commencement has been necessary.' [14] There are periods of 'retrocession' alternating with periods of steady advance. Regress, when it occurs, is not an 'external contingency' but, as we shall see, is part of the dialectic of historical change; an advance to a higher plane

[12] P. 30. [13] P. 29. [14] P. 56.

of history first requires that the negative forces inherent in all reality get the upper hand. The higher phase, however, is finally to be reached; every obstacle on the road to freedom is surmountable, given the efforts of a self-conscious mankind.

This is the universal principle of history. It is not a 'law,' in the scientific sense of the term, such, for example, as governs matter. Matter in its structure and motion has unchangeable laws that carry on and maintain it, but matter is nowhere the subject of its processes, nor has it any power over them. A being, on the other hand, that is the active and conscious subject of its existence stands under quite different laws. Self-conscious practice becomes part of the very content of the laws, so that the latter operate as laws only in so far as they are taken into the subject's will and influence his acts. The universal law of history is, in Hegel's formulation, not simply progress to freedom, but progress 'in the self-consciousness of freedom.' A set of historical tendencies becomes a law only if man comprehends and acts on them. Historical laws, in other words, originate and are actual only in man's conscious practice, so that if, for instance, there is a law of progress to ever higher forms of freedom, it ceases to operate if man fails to recognize and execute it. Hegel's philosophy of history might amount to a deterministic theory, but the determining factor is at least freedom. Progress depends on man's ability to grasp the universal interest of reason and on his will and vigor in making it a reality.

But if the *particular* wants and interests of men are the sole springs of their action, how can self-consciousness of freedom ever motivate human practice? To answer this question we must again ask, Who is the actual subject of history? Whose practice is historical practice? Individuals, it would seem, are merely agents of history. Their consciousness is conditioned by their personal interest; they make business, not history. There are some individuals, however, who rise above this level; their actions do not repeat old patterns but create new forms of life. Such men are men of history *kat'exochen, welthistorische Individuen,* like Alexander, Caesar, Napoleon.[15] Their acts, too, spring from personal interests, but in their case these become identical with the universal interest and the latter far transcends the interest of any particular group: they forge and administer the progress of history. Their interest must necessarily clash with the particular interest of the prevailing system of life. Historical individuals are men of a time when 'momentous collisions' arise 'between existing, acknowledged duties, laws, and rights, and those potentialities which are adverse to this fixed system; which assail and even destroy its foundations and existence.' [16] These potentialities appear to the historical individual as choices for his specific power, but they involve a 'universal principle' in so far as they are the choice of a higher form of life that has ripened within the existing system. Historical individuals thus anticipated 'the necessary . . . sequent step in progress which their world was to take.' [17] What they desired and struggled for was 'the very truth for their age, for their world.' Conscious of 'the requirements of the time' and of 'what was ripe for development,' they acted.

Even these men of history, however, are not yet the actual subjects of history. They are the executors of its will, the 'agents of the World Mind,' no more. They are victims of a higher necessity, which acts itself out in their lives; they are still mere instruments for historical progress.

The final subject of history Hegel calls the world mind (*Weltgeist*). Its reality lies in those actions, tendencies, ef-

[15] P. 29. [16] Ibid. [17] P. 30.

forts, and institutions that embody the interest of freedom and reason. It does not exist separate from these realities, and acts through these agents and agencies. The law of history, which the world mind represents, thus operates behind the backs and over the heads of individuals, in the form of an irresistible anonymous power. The transition from Oriental culture to that of the Greek world, the rise of feudalism, the establishment of bourgeois society—all these changes were not man's free work, but the necessary results of objective historical forces. Hegel's conception of the world mind emphasizes that in these previous periods of recorded history man was not the self-conscious master of his existence. The divine power of the world mind appeared then an objective force that rules over the actions of men.

The sovereignty of the world mind, as Hegel portrays it, exhibits the dark traits of a world that is controlled by the forces of history instead of controlling them. While these forces are as yet unknown in their true essence, they bring misery and destruction in their wake. History then appears as 'the slaughter-bench at which the happiness of peoples, the wisdom of States, and the virtue of individuals have been victimized.' [18] Hegel at the same time extols the sacrifice of individual and general happiness that results. He calls it 'the *cunning of reason.*' [19] Individuals lead unhappy lives, they toil and perish, but though they actually never win their goal, their distress and defeat are the very means by which truth and freedom proceed. A man never reaps the fruits of his labor; they always fall to future generations. His passions and interests, however, do not succumb; they are the devices that keep him working in the service of a superior power and a superior interest. 'This may be called the *cunning of*

[18] P. 21. [19] P. 33.

reason—that it sets the passions to work for itself, while that which develops its existence through such impulsion pays the penalty, and suffers loss.' [20] Individuals fail and pass away; the idea triumphs and is eternal.

The idea triumphs precisely because individuals perish in defeat. It is not the 'Idea that is implicated in opposition and combat, and that is exposed to danger. It remains in the background, untouched and uninjured' while 'individuals are sacrificed and abandoned. The Idea pays the penalty of existence and of transitoriness not from itself, but from the passions of individuals.' [21] But can this idea still be regarded as the incarnation of truth and freedom? Kant had emphatically insisted that it would contradict man's nature to use him as a mere means. Only a few decades later Hegel declares himself in favor of 'the idea that individuals, their desires and the gratification of them, are . . . sacrificed, and their happiness given up to the empire of chance, to which it belongs; and that as a general rule, individuals come under the category of means.' [22] He confesses that where man is simply an object of superior historical processes he can be an end in himself only in the domain of morality and religion.

The world mind is the hypostatic subject of history; it is a metaphysical substitute for the real subject, the unfathomable God of a frustrated humanity, hidden and awful, like the God of the Calvinists; the mover of a world in which all that occurs does so despite the conscious actions of man and at the expense of his happiness. 'History . . . is not the theater of happiness. Periods of happiness are blank pages in it.' [23]

This metaphysical subject, however, assumes concrete form as soon as Hegel raises the question of how the world mind materializes itself. 'In what material is the idea of

[20] Ibid. [21] Ibid. [22] Ibid. [23] P. 26.

Reason wrought out?' The world mind strives to realize freedom and can materialize itself only in the real realm of freedom, that is, in the *state*. Here, the world mind is, as it were, institutionalized; here it finds the self-consciousness through which the law of history operates.

The *Philosophy of History* does not discuss (as did the *Philosophy of Right*) the *idea* of the state; it discusses its various concrete historical forms. Hegel's well-known schema distinguishes three main historical stages in the development of freedom: the Oriental, the Greco-Roman, and the German-Christian.

> The Orientals have not attained the knowledge that Mind—man *as such*—is free; and because they do not know this, they are not free. They only know that *one is free*. But on this very account, the freedom of that one is only caprice . . . That *one* is therefore only a Despot, not a free man. The consciousness of freedom first arose among the Greeks, and therefore they were free; but they, and the Romans likewise, knew only that *some* are free—not man as such . . . The Greeks, therefore, had slaves; and their whole life and the maintenance of their splendid liberty, was implicated with the institution of slavery . . . The German nations, under the influence of Christianity, were the first to attain the consciousness, that man, as man, is free: that it is the *freedom* of Mind which constitutes its essence.[24]

Hegel distinguishes three typical state forms to correspond to the three main phases in the development of freedom: 'The East knew and to the present day knows only that One is free; the Greek and Roman world, that some are free; the German world knows that all are free. The first political form, therefore, which we observe in history, is despotism, the second democracy and aristocracy, the third monarchy.' At first, this is no more than the Aristotelian typology applied to universal history. The monarchic holds first rank as the perfectly free state form,

[24] P. 18; see also pp. 104-10.

by virtue of its rule of right and law under constitutional guarantees. 'In monarchy, . . . there is one lord and no serf, for servitude is abrogated by it; and in it Right and Law are recognized; it is the source of real freedom. Thus in monarchy, the caprice of individuals is kept under, and a common gubernatorial interest established.'[25] Hegel's judgment here is based on the fact that he regards the modern absolutist state to be an advance over the feudal system. He has reference to the strongly centralized bourgeois state that overcame the revolutionary terror of 1793. Freedom, he has shown, begins with property, unfolds itself in the universal rule of law that acknowledges and secures the equal right to property, and terminates in the state, which is able to cope with the antagonisms that attend freedom of property. Consequently, the history of freedom comes to an end with the advent of modern monarchy, which, in Hegel's time, achieved this goal.

The *Philosophy of Right* had concluded with the statement that the right of the state is subordinate to the right of the world mind and to the judgment of universal history. Hegel now develops this point. He gives the various state forms their place in the course of history, first coordinating each with its representative historical period. Hegel does not mean to say that the Oriental world knew only despotism, the Greco-Roman only democracy, and the German only monarchy. His scheme rather implies that despotism is the political form most adequate to the material and intellectual culture of the Orient, and the other political forms respectively to the other historical periods. He then proceeds to assert that the unity of the state is conditioned by the prevailing national culture; that is, the state depends on such factors as the geographical location and the natural, racial, and social qualities of the nation.

[25] P. 399.

This is the purport of his concept of national mind (*Volksgeist*).[26] The latter is the manifestation of the world mind at a given stage of historical development; it is the subject of national history in the same sense as the world mind is the subject of universal history. National history must be understood in terms of universal history. 'Each particular National genius is to be treated as only one individual in the process of Universal History.'[27] The history of a nation has to be judged according to its contribution to the progress of all mankind towards the self-consciousness of freedom.[28] The various nations do not contribute equally; some are active promoters of this progress. These are the world-historical nations (*welthistorische Volksgeister*). The decisive jumps to new and higher forms of life occur in their history, while other nations play more minor roles.

The question as to the relation of a particular state to the world mind may now be answered. Every form of state must be evaluated according to whether it is adequate to the stage of historical consciousness that mankind has reached. Freedom does not and cannot mean the same thing in the different periods of history, for in each period one type of freedom is the true one. The state must be built on the acknowledgment of this freedom. The German world, through the Reformation, produced in its course that kind of freedom which recognized the essential equality of men. Constitutional monarchy expresses and integrates this form of society. It is for Hegel the consummation of the realization of freedom.

Let us now consider the general structure of the histori-

[26] Pp. 50-54; see also p. 64. [27] P. 53.

[28] The decisive difference between Hegel's concept of the *Volksgeist* and the use made of the same concept by the *Historische Schule* consists in this: that the latter school conceived of the *Volksgeist* in terms of a natural rather than a rational development and set it against the higher values posited in universal history. We shall see later that the *Historische Schule's* conception belongs to the positivist reaction against Hegelian rationalism.

cal dialectic. Since Aristotle, historical change has been contrasted with changes in nature. Hegel held to the same distinction. He says historical change is 'an advance to something better, more perfect,' whereas mutation in nature 'exhibits only a perpetually self-repeating cycle.' [29] It is only in historical changes that something new arises. Historical change is therefore *development*. 'Everything depends on apprehending the principle of this development.' The principle implies first that there exists a latent 'destiny,' 'a potentiality striving to realize itself.' This is obvious in the case of the living being whose life is the unfolding of potentialities contained in the germ, and their constant actualization, but the highest form of development is reached only when self-consciousness exercises mastery over the whole process. The life of the thinking subject is the only one that may be called a self-realization, in the strict sense. The thinking subject 'produces itself, expands itself *actually* to what it always was *potentially*.' [30] And it achieves this result in so far as every particular existential condition is dissolved by the potentialities that are inherent in it and transformed into a new condition, which fulfills these potentialities. How is this process manifested in history?

The thinking subject lives in history, and the state furnishes in large part the existential conditions of its historical life. The state exists as the universal interest amid individual actions and interests. Individuals experience this universal in various forms, each of which is an essential phase in the history of every state. The state appears first as an immediate, 'natural' unity. At this stage, social antagonisms have not yet intensified and individuals find satisfaction in the state without consciously opposing their individualities to the commonwealth. This is the golden

[29] Ibid., p. 54. [30] P. 55.

youth of every nation, and the golden youth of universal history. Unconscious freedom prevails, but because it is unconscious, it is a stage of mere potential freedom; actual freedom comes only with the self-consciousness of freedom. The prevailing potentiality has to actualize itself; in doing so it shatters the unconscious stage of human organization.

Thought is the vehicle of this process. The individuals become conscious of their potentialities and organize their relations in accordance with their reason. A nation composed of such individuals has 'apprehended the principle of its life and condition, the science of its laws, right and morality, and has consciously organized the state.' [81]

This state, also, is subject to thought, the element that leads ultimately to its destruction, the same element that has given this state its form. Social and political reality cannot, for any length of time, conform to the demands of reason, for the state seeks to maintain the interest of that which is, and thus to fetter the forces that tend to a higher historical form. Sooner or later, the free rationality of thought must come into conflict with the rationalizations of the given order of life.

Hegel saw in this process a general law of history, as unalterable as time itself. No power whatsoever could, in the long run, stop the march of thought. Thinking was not a harmless activity but a dangerous one, which, as soon as it would flow among citizens and determine their practice, would drive them to question and even to subvert the traditional forms of culture. Hegel illustrated this destructive dynamics of thought by means of an ancient myth.

The god Kronos first ruled over the lives of men, and his rule signified a Golden Age during which men lived

[81] P. 76.

in immediate unity among themselves and with nature. But Kronos was the god of time, and time devoured its own children. Everything that man had accomplished was destroyed; nothing remained. Then, Kronos himself was devoured by Zeus, a power greater than time. Zeus was the god who brought forth reason and promoted the arts; he was the 'political god' who created the state and made it the work of self-conscious and moral individuals. This state was generated and maintained by reason and morality; it was something that could persist and endure,—reason's productive power seemed to bring time to a standstill. This moral and rational community, however, was dissolved by the same force that had created it. The principle of thought, of reasoning and knowledge destroyed the beautiful work of art that was the state, and Zeus, who had put an end to the devouring force of time, was himself swallowed up. The work of thought was destroyed by thought. Thought is thus drawn into the process of time, and the force that compelled knowledge in the *Logic* to negate every particular content is disclosed, in the *Philosophy of History*, as the negativity of time itself. Hegel says: 'Time is the negative element in the sensuous world. Thought is the same negativity, but it is the deepest, the infinite form of it . . .' [82]

Hegel connected the destructive dynamics of thought with *historical* progress towards 'universality.' The dissolution of a given form of the state is, at the same time, the crossing to a higher form of state that is more 'universal' than the preceding form. Man's self-conscious activity on the one hand 'destroys the reality, the permanence of what is, but at the same time it gains, on the other side, the essence, the notion, the universal.' [83] According to Hegel, historical progress is preceded and guided by a progress

[82] P. 77.

[83] P. 77.

of thought. As soon as thought is emancipated from its attachment to the prevailing state of affairs, it goes beyond the face value of things and tries for their notion. The notion, however, comprehends the essence of things as distinguished from their appearance—the prevailing conditions appear as limited particularities that do not exhaust the potentialities of things and men. Those who adhere to principles of reason, if they succeed in establishing new social and political conditions, will endeavor, through their higher conceptual knowledge, to incorporate more of these potentialities into the order of life. Hegel saw history progressing at least so much that the essential freedom and equality of men was being increasingly recognized, and the particular limitations on this freedom and equality were being increasingly removed.

When thought becomes the vehicle of practice it realizes the universal content of the given historical conditions by shattering its particular form. Hegel viewed the development of mankind as a process to real universality in state and society. 'The history of the world is the discipline [*Zucht*] of the uncontrolled natural will to universality and to subjective freedom.' [34] In the *Logic,* Hegel had designated the notion as the unity of the universal and the particular, and as the realm of subjectivity and freedom. In the *Philosophy of History,* he applied these selfsame categories to the final goal of historical development, that is, to a state in which the freedom of the subject is in conscious union with the whole. The progress of conceptual thinking, the comprehension of the notion, was here linked to the progress of freedom. The *Philosophy of History* thus gave a historical illustration of this essential connection between freedom and the notion, which had been explained in the *Logic.* Hegel elucidated

[34] P. 104.

this connection by analyzing the work of Socrates. Instead of surveying the content of Hegel's *Philosophy of History*, we shall discuss his analysis of the Socratic contribution.

Hegel begins with a description of the early period of the Greek city-state during which 'the subjectivity of will' was not yet awake within the natural unity of the *polis*. Laws existed and the citizenry obeyed them, but they looked upon them as having 'a necessity of nature.' [85] This period was the one of the great constitutions (Thales, Bias, Solon). The laws were held valid because they were laws; freedom and right existed only in the form of custom (*Gewohnheit*). The natural, continuous character of this state made 'the democratic constitution . . . here the only possible one; the citizens were still unconscious of particular interests, and therefore of a corrupting element . . .' [86] The absence of conscious subjectivity was the condition for an undisturbed functioning of democracy. The interest of the community could be 'intrusted to the will and resolve of the citizens' because these citizens did not yet have an autonomous will that could at any moment turn against the community. Hegel makes this point general for all democracy. True democracy, he holds, expresses an early phase in human development, a phase prior to that in which the individual is emancipated, and one incompatible with emancipation. His evaluation is obviously based on the conviction that the progress of society will necessarily engender a conflict between the interest of the individual and that of the community. Society cannot free the individual without separating him from the community and opposing his wish for subjective liberty to the demands of the whole. The reason the Greek city-state could be a democracy, Hegel implies, is that it was made up of citizens who were not yet conscious of

[85] P. 252. [86] Ibid.

their essential individuality. Hegel held that a society of emancipated individuals conflicted with democratic homogeneity.

Any recognition of individual freedom consequently seemed to involve tearing down the ancient democracy. 'That very subjective freedom which constitutes the principle and determines the peculiar form of freedom in *our* world—which forms the absolute basis of our political and religious life, could not manifest itself in Greece otherwise than as a *destructive* element.' [37]

This destructive element was brought into the Greek city-state by Socrates, who taught precisely the 'subjectivity' that Hegel calls the destructive element for the ancient democracy. 'It was in Socrates that . . . the principle of subjectivity [*Innerlichkeit*]—of the absolute independence of thought—attained free expression.' [38] Socrates taught that 'man has to discover and recognize in himself that which is Right and Good, and that this Right and Good is in its nature universal.' There are beautiful things in the state, good and brave deeds, true judgments, just judges—but something exists that is the beautiful, the good, the brave, etc.; it is more than all these particulars and common to all of them. Man has an idea of the beautiful, the good, etc., in his *notion* of beauty, goodness, etc. The notion comprises what is truly beautiful and good, and Socrates charged the thinking subject to discover this truth and to maintain it against all external authority. Socrates thus set the truth apart as a universal and attributed the knowledge of this universal to the autonomous thought of the individual. By so doing he 'set the individual up as the subject of all final decisions, against the fatherland and customary morality.' [39] Socrates's principles thus show 'a revolutionary opposition to the Athenian

[37] Ibid. [38] P. 269. [39] Pp. 269-70.

State.'[40] He was condemned to death. This act was justified in so far as the Athenians were condemning their 'absolute foe.' On the other hand, the death sentence contained the 'deeply tragical' element that the Athenians thereby also condemned their society and their state. For, their sentence recognized that 'what they reprobated in Socrates had already struck firm root among themselves.'[41]

A decisive *historical* turn thus followed upon a turn in the development of *thought*. Philosophy began to elaborate universal concepts, and this was the prelude of a new phase in state history. Universal concepts, however, are abstract concepts, and 'the construction of the State in the abstract' struck at the very foundations of the existing state. The homogeneity of the city-state was achieved through the exclusion of slaves, other Greek citizens, and 'barbarians.' Though Socrates himself may not have developed this implication, abstract universal concepts of their very nature imply a crossing beyond every particularity and a championing of the free subject, of man as man.

The same process that made abstract thought into truth's abode emancipated the individual as a real 'subject.' Socrates could not teach men to think in the abstract without making them free from the traditional standards of thought and existence. The free subject—as the *Logic* had maintained—is indeed intrinsically connected with the notion. The free subject arises only when the individual no longer accepts the given order of things but stands up to it because he has learned the notion of things and learned that the truth does not lie in the current norms and opinions. He cannot know this unless he has ventured into abstract thought. It gives him the necessary 'detachment' from the prevailing standards, and, in the form of critical, oppositional thought, it constitutes the medium in which the free subject moves.

[40] P. 270.

[41] Ibid.

When the principle of subjectivity first appeared, with Socrates, it could not be concretized and made the foundation of the state and society. The principle made its real debut with Christianity and thus 'arose first in religion.'

> [Its introduction into] the various relations of the actual world involves a more extensive problem than its simple implantation; a problem whose solution and application require a severe and lengthened process of culture. In proof of this, we may note that slavery did not cease immediately on the reception of Christianity. Still less did liberty predominate in states; or governments and constitutions adopt a rational organization; or recognize freedom as their basis. That application of the principle of Christianity to political relations; the thorough moulding or interpenetration of society by it, is a process identical with history itself.[42]

The German Reformation marks the first successful attempt to introduce the principle of subjectivity into changing social and political relations. It placed the sole responsibility for his deeds on the free subject and challenged the traditional system of authority and privilege in the name of Christian freedom and human equality. 'While, then, the individual knows that he is filled with the Divine Spirit, all [the hitherto prevailing external relations] . . . are *ipso facto* abrogated; there is no longer a distinction between priests and laymen; we no longer find one class in possession of the substance of the truth, as of all spiritual and temporal treasures of the Church.' The inmost subjectivity of man was recognized 'as that which can and ought to come into possession of the truth; and this subjectivity is the common property of *all mankind.*'[43]

Hegel's picture of the Reformation is fully as erroneous as his description of the subsequent social development,

[42] P. 18. [43] P. 416.

confusing the ideas by which modern society glorified its rise for the reality of this society. He was thus led to a harmonistic interpretation of history, according to which the crossing to a *new* historical form is at the same time a progress to a *higher* historical form—a preposterous interpretation, because all the victims of oppression and injustice are witness against it, as are all the vain sufferings and sacrifices of history. The interpretation is the more preposterous because it denies the critical implications of the dialectic and establishes a harmony between the progress of thought and the process of reality.

Hegel did not, however, consider the historical realization of man to be an *unswerving* progress. The history of man was to him at the same time the history of man's alienation (*Entfremdung*).

'What Mind really strives for is the realization of its notion; but in doing so, it hides that goal from its own vision, and is proud and well satisfied in this alienation from its own essence.'[44] The institutions man founds and the culture he creates develop laws of their own, and man's freedom has to comply with them. He is overpowered by the expanding wealth of his economic, social, and political surrounding and comes to forget that he himself, his free development, is the final goal of all these works; instead he surrenders to their sway. Men always strive to perpetuate an established culture, and in doing so perpetuate their own frustration. The history of man is the history of his estrangement from his true interest and, by the same token, the history of its realization. The concealment of man's true interest in his societal world is part of the 'cunning of reason' and is one of those 'negative elements' without which there is no progress to higher forms. Marx was the first to explain the origin and sig-

[44] P. 55.

nificance of this estrangement; Hegel had little more than a general intuition of its meaning.

Hegel died in 1831. The preceding year had brought the first revolutionary concussion to the political system of the Restoration—the same system that Hegel thought signified the realization of reason in civil society. The state began to totter. The Bourbons in France were overthrown by the July revolution. British political life was rent with heated discussions of the Reform Bill, which provided for far-reaching changes in the English electoral system, changes that favored the city bourgeoisie, and for the strengthening of Parliament at the expense of the crown. The French and the English movements resulted merely in an adjustment of the state to the prevailing power relationships so that the process of democratization that went on in political forms nowhere crossed beyond the social system of civil society. Nevertheless, Hegel knew full well the dangers of even the small transformations that were going on. He knew that the dynamics inherent in civil society, once loosed from the protective mechanisms of the state, could, at any moment, release forces to shake the whole system.

One of Hegel's latest writings, published the year of his death, was an extended paper on the English Reform Bill. It contained a severe criticism of the bill, claiming that it weakened the sovereignty of the monarch by setting up a Parliament that would place the 'abstract principles' of the French Revolution in opposition to the concrete hierarchy of the state. The strengthening of Parliament, he warns, will eventually unleash the terrifying power of the 'people.' Reform, in the given social situation, might suddenly turn into revolution. Were the bill to succeed,

. . . the struggle would threaten to become even more dangerous. There would no longer exist any higher power mediating between the interest of positive privilege and the demand for more real freedom, a higher power that might restrict and reconcile these. For, in England, the monarchic element does not have the power that other states have and through which they could effect transition from legislation based merely on positive rights to one based on the principles of real freedom. Other states have been able to effect transformations without upheaval, violence and robbery; in England, the transformation would have to be carried through by another force, by the people. An opposition building itself on a program hitherto foreign to Parliament and feeling itself unable to expand its influence among the other parties in Parliament might be induced to seek its strength among the people; then, instead of achieving a reform it would bring forth a revolution.[45]

Rudolf Haym, who interpreted Hegel according to German liberalism, recognized that Hegel's article was a document of fear and anxiety rather than of reactionary political philosophy, for 'Hegel did not disapprove of the tendency and content of the Reform Bill, but feared the danger of reform as such.'[46] Hegel's belief in the stability of the Restoration state was seriously shaken. Reform might be a good thing, but this state could not afford the liberty of reform without endangering the system of power on which it rested. Hegel's article on the Reform Bill is not a document expressive of any faith or confidence that the existing form of the state will eternally endure, any more than is his Preface to the *Philosophy of Right*. Here, too, Hegel's philosophy ends in doubt and resignation.[47]

[45] 'Ueber die Englische Reformbill' in *Schriften zur Politik und Rechtsphilosophie*, p. 326.

[46] *Hegel und seine Zeit*, Berlin 1857, p. 456.

[47] See Hegel's letters to Göschel (December 13, 1830) and to Schultz (January 29, 1831); cf. F. Rosenzweig, *Hegel und der Staat*, München 1920, vol. II, p. 220.

PART II

The Rise of Social Theory

Introduction

From Philosophy to Social Theory

The transition from philosophy to the domain of state and society had been an intrinsic part of Hegel's system. His basic philosophic ideas had fulfilled themselves in the specific historical form that state and society had assumed, and the latter became central to a new theoretical interest. Philosophy had in this way devolved upon social theory. To understand the impact of Hegel's philosophy on subsequent social theory, we must deviate from the usual explanation.

The traditional account of the post-history of Hegelian philosophy begins by pointing to the fact that the Hegelian school after Hegel's death split into a right and a left wing. The right wing, consisting of Michelet, Göschel, Johann Eduard Erdmann, Gabler, and Rosenkranz, to name only the most representative thinkers of this group, took up and elaborated the conservative trends in the Hegelian system, particularly in the Logic, Metaphysic and the Philosophies of Right and of Religion. The left wing, made up of David Friedrich Strauss, Edgar and Bruno Bauer, Feuerbach, and Ciszkowski, among others, developed the critical tendencies in Hegel, beginning this with a historical interpretation of religion. This latter group came into greater and greater social and political conflict with the Restoration and ended either in out-and-out socialism and anarchism, or in a liberalism of the petty-bourgeois stamp.

By the middle of the nineteenth century, the influence

of Hegelianism was almost dead. It got its rebirth in the last decades of the century in British Hegelianism (Green, Bradley, Bosanquet) and, later still, gained a new political impetus in Italy, where the interpretation of Hegel was used as a preparation for Fascism.

In a totally different form, the Hegelian dialectic also became an integral part of Marxian theory and its Leninist interpretation. Apart from these main lines, certain of Hegel's concepts found employment in sociology (in Lorenz von Stein's work, for example), in jurisprudence (the historical school; Lasalle) and in the field of history (Droysen, Ranke).

Such an account as this, though formally accurate, is a little too schematic, and obliterates certain important distinctions. The historical heritage of Hegel's philosophy, for instance, did not pass to the 'Hegelians' (neither of the right nor of the left)—they were not the ones who kept alive the true content of this philosophy. The critical tendencies of the Hegelian philosophy, rather, were taken over by, and continued in, the Marxian social theory, while, in all other aspects, the history of Hegelianism became the history of a struggle *against* Hegel in which he was used as a symbol for all that the new intellectual (and to a considerable extent even the practical political) efforts opposed.

Hegel's system brings to a close the entire epoch in modern philosophy that had begun with Descartes and had embodied the basic ideas of modern society. Hegel was the last to interpret the world as reason, subjecting nature and history alike to the standards of thought and freedom. At the same time, he recognized the social and political order men had achieved as the basis on which reason had to be realized. His system brought philosophy to the threshold of its negation and thus constituted the sole link between the old and the new form of critical theory, between philosophy and social theory.

Before we attempt to show how the inner workings of Western philosophy necessitated the transition to the critical theory of society, we must indicate the way in which the historical efforts that distinguish the modern era entered into and shaped the philosophic interest. The social forces at work in this historical surge used philosophy in its predominantly rationalistic form, and the idea of reason might well serve again as the starting point for our discussion.

Beginning with the seventeenth century, philosophy had quite definitely absorbed the principles of the rising middle class. Reason was the critical slogan of this class, with which it fought all who hampered its political and economic development. The term saw service in the war of science and philosophy against the Church, in the attack of the French Enlightenment on absolutism, and in the debate between liberalism and mercantilism. No clear-cut definition of reason, and no single meaning for it, ran through these periods. Its meaning changed with the changing position of the middle class. We shall try to gather up its essential elements and evaluate its varying historical impact.

The idea of reason is not necessarily anti-religious. Reason allows the possibility that the world might be the creature of God and that its order might be divine and purposive, but this should not exclude man's right to mold it in accordance with his needs and knowledge. The meaning of the world as rational implied, first, that it could be comprehended and changed by man's knowingful action. Nature was regarded as rational in its very structure, with subject and object meeting in the medium of reason.

Secondly, human reason, it was explained, is not once and for all restricted to a pre-established order, whether social or otherwise. The multitude of talents that man possesses all originate and develop in history, and he may employ them in many ways for the best possible satisfaction of his desires. Satisfaction itself will depend on the extent of his control over nature and society. The standard of reason was ultimate in this wide range of control. That is to say, nature and society alike were to be organized so that existing subjective and objective endowments freely unfolded. Bad organization in society was to a considerable extent held responsible for the harmful and iniquitous forms that institutions had assumed. With the advance towards a rational social order, these, it was held, would lose their vitiating character. Man would by education become a rational being in a rational world. The completion of the process would see the laws of his individual and social life all derived from his own autonomous judgment. The realization of reason thus implied an end to all external authority such as set man's existence at odds with the standards of free thought.

Thirdly, reason involves universality. For, the emphasis on reason declares that man's acts are those of a *thinking* subject guided by conceptual knowledge. With concepts as his instruments, the thinking subject can penetrate the contingencies and recondite devices of the world and reach universal and necessary laws that govern and order the infinitude of individual objects. He thus discovers potentialities that are common to multitudes of particulars, potentialities that will explain the changing forms of things and dictate the range and direction of their course. Universal concepts will become the organon of a practice that alters the world. They might arise only through this practice and their content might change with its progress, but they will not depend on chance. Genuine abstraction is not arbitrary, nor is it the product of free imagination; it is strictly determined by the objective structure of reality.

The universal is as real as the particular; it only exists in a different form, namely, as force, *dynamis,* potentiality.

Fourthly, thought unites the manifold not only of the natural but of the socio-historical world. The subject of thought, the source of conceptual universality, is one and the same in all men. The specific contents of universal concepts and their connotations may vary, but the thinking ego that is their source is a totality of pure acts, uniform in all thinking subjects. To say, then, that the rationality of the thinking subject is the ultimate basis for the rational organization of society is, in the last analysis, to recognize the essential equality of all men. Moreover, the thinking subject, as the creator of universal concepts, is necessarily free, and its freedom is the very essence of subjectivity. The mark of this essential freedom is the fact that the thinking subject is not chained to the immediately given forms of being, but is capable of transcending them and changing them in line with his concepts. The freedom of the thinking subject, in turn, involves his moral and practical freedom. For, the truth he envisions is not an object for passive contemplation, but an objective potentiality calling for realization. The idea of reason implies the freedom to act according to reason.

Fifthly, this freedom to act according to reason was regarded as exercised in the practice of natural science. A mastery of nature and of its recently unearthed resources and dimensions was a requisite of the new process of production that strove to transform the world into a huge commodity market. The idea of reason came under the sway of technical progress, and the experimental method was seen as the model of rational activity, that is, as a procedure that alters the world so that its inherent potencies become free and actual. Modern rationalism, as a result, had a tendency to pattern individual as well as social life on the model of nature. We point, for instance, to

Descartes's mechanistic philosophy, Hobbes's materialist political thought, Spinoza's mathematical ethics, and Leibniz's monadology. The human world was presented as governed by objective laws, analogous or even identical with the laws of nature, and society was set forth as an objective entity more or less unyielding to subjective desires and goals. Men believed their relations to each other to result from objective laws that operate with the necessity of physical laws, and their freedom to consist in adapting their private existence to this necessity. A strikingly conformist skepticism thus accompanied the development of modern rationalism. The more reason triumphed in technology and natural science, the more reluctantly did it call for freedom in man's social life. Under the pressure of this process, the critical and ideal elements slowly vanished and took refuge in heretical and oppositional doctrines (for example, in atheistic materialism during the French Enlightenment). The representative philosophers of the middle class (particularly Leibniz, Kant, and Fichte) reconciled their philosophical rationalism with the flagrant irrationality of the prevailing social relations, and inverted human reason and freedom so that they became ramparts of the isolated soul or mind, internal phenomena quite compatible with external realities, even if these contradicted reason and freedom.

We have already indicated the motives that prompted Hegel to break with the tendency of introversion and to proclaim the realization of reason in and through given social and political institutions. We have stressed the role of the dialectic in the process that brought philosophy to grips with social reality. It resulted in the dissolution of the harmonious world of fixed objects posited by common sense and in the recognition that the truth philosophy sought was a totality of pervasive contradictions. Philosophical concepts now came to reflect the actual movement of reality, but since they were themselves patterned on its social content, they stopped where the content stopped, that is, in the state that governed civil society, while the ideas and values that pointed beyond this social system were stowed away in the realm of the absolute mind, in the system of dialectical philosophy.

The method, however, that operated in this system reached farther than the concepts that brought it to a conclusion. Through the dialectic, history had been made part of the very content of reason. Hegel had demonstrated that the material and intellectual powers of mankind had developed far enough to call upon man's social and political practice to realize reason. Philosophy itself thus made direct application to social theory and practice, not as to some external force but as to its legitimate heir. If there was to be any progress beyond this philosophy, it had to be an advance beyond philosophy itself and, at the same time, beyond the social and political order to which philosophy had tied its fate.

This is the intrinsic connection that compels us to abandon chronological order and to discuss the foundations of Marxian theory before dealing with the early French and German sociology. The impact of the Hegelian philosophy upon social theory, and the specific function of modern social theory cannot be understood except from the fully unfolded form of Hegel's philosophy and its critical tendencies, as they went over to Marxian theory.

I

The Foundations of the Dialectical Theory of Society

1. The Negation of Philosophy

THE transition from Hegel to Marx is, in all respects, a transition to an essentially different order of truth, not to be interpreted in terms of philosophy. We shall see that all the philosophical concepts of Marxian theory are social and economic categories, whereas Hegel's social and economic categories are all philosophical concepts. Even Marx's early writings are not philosophical. They express the negation of philosophy, though they still do so in philosophical language. To be sure, several of Hegel's fundamental concepts crop up in the development from Hegel to Feuerbach to Marx, but the approach to Marxian theory cannot be made by showing the metamorphosis of old philosophical categories. Every single concept in the Marxian theory has a materially different foundation, just as the new theory has a new conceptual structure and framework that cannot be derived from preceding theories.

As a first approach to the problem, we may say that in Hegel's system all categories terminate in the existing order, while in Marx's they refer to the negation of this order. They aim at a new form of society even when describing its current form. Essentially they address themselves to a truth to be had only through the abolition of civil society. Marx's theory is a 'critique' in the sense that all concepts are an indictment of the totality of the existing order.

Marx considered Hegel's philosophy to be the most advanced and comprehensive statement of bourgeois principles. The German middle class of Hegel's day had not yet reached the level of economic and political power held by the middle classes of the western European nations. Hegel's system therefore unfolded and completed 'in thought' all those bourgeois principles (completed 'in reality' in other Western nations) that were not yet part of social reality. It made reason the sole universal standard of society; it recognized the role of abstract labor in integrating divergent individual interests into a unified 'system of wants'; it discovered the revolutionary implications of the liberalist ideas of freedom and equality; it described the history of civil society as the history of the irreconcilable antagonisms inherent in this social order.

Marx lays particular stress on the decisive contributions of Hegel's concept of labor. Hegel had said that the division of labor and the general interdependence of individual labor in the system of wants alike determine the system of state and society. Moreover, the process of labor likewise determines the development of consciousness. The 'life and death struggle' between master and servant opens the path to self-conscious freedom.

Furthermore, we must recall that Hegel's philosophy rests upon a specific interpretation of the subject-object relation. The traditional epistemological antagonism between subject (consciousness) and object, Hegel makes into a reflection of a definite historical antagonism. The object first appears as an object of desire, something to be worked up and appropriated in order to satisfy a human want. In the course of the appropriation, the object becomes manifest as 'the otherness' of man. Man is not 'with himself' when he deals with the objects of his desire and labor, but is dependent on an external power. He has to cope with nature, chance, and the interests of other proprietors. Development beyond this point of the relation between consciousness and the objective world is a social process. It leads first to the total 'estrangement' of consciousness; man is overpowered by things he has himself made. The realization of reason therefore implies the overcoming of this estrangement, the establishment of a condition in which the subject knows and possesses itself in all its objects.

This demonstration of the role of labor, and of the process of reification and its abolition, is, Marx declares, the greatest achievement of Hegel's *Phenomenology of Mind*. But the weight of the demonstration is lost. For, Hegel makes the claim that the unity of subject and object has already been consummated and the process of reification overcome. The antagonisms of civil society are set at rest in his monarchic state, and all contradictions are finally reconciled in the realm of thought or the absolute mind.

Did 'the truth' actually coincide with the given social and political order? Had history, then, discharged theory from any need to transcend the given system of life in society? Hegel's affirmative answer rested on the assumption that social and political forms had become adequate to the principles of reason, so that the highest potentialities of man could be developed through a development of existing social forms. His conclusion implied a decisive change in the relation between reality and theory: reality was held to coincide with theory. In the form Hegel finally gave it, theory, the adequate repository of the truth, seemed to give welcome to the facts as they were and hailed them as conforming to reason.

The truth, Hegel maintained, is a whole that must be present in every single element, so that if one material element or fact cannot be connected with the process of reason, the truth of the whole is destroyed. Marx said there was such an element—the *proletariat.* The existence of the proletariat contradicts the alleged reality of reason, for it sets before us an entire class that gives proof of the very negation of reason. The lot of the proletariat is no fulfillment of human potentialities, but the reverse. If property constitutes the first endowment of a free person, the proletarian is neither free nor a person, for he possesses no property. If the exercises of the absolute mind, art, religion, and philosophy, constitute man's essence, the proletarian is forever severed from his essence, for his existence permits him no time to indulge in these activities.

Furthermore, the existence of the proletariat vitiates more than just the rational society of Hegel's *Philosophy of Right;* it vitiates the whole of bourgeois society. The proletariat originates in the labor process and is the actual performer or subject of labor in this society. Labor, however, as Hegel himself showed, determines the essence of man and the social form it takes. If the existence of the proletariat, then, bears witness to 'the complete loss of man,' and this loss results from the mode of labor on which civil society is founded, the society is vicious in its entirety and the proletariat expresses a total negativity: 'universal suffering' and 'universal injustice.' [1] The reality of reason, right, and freedom then turns into the reality of falsehood, injustice and bondage.

The existence of the proletariat thus gives living witness to the fact that the truth has not been realized. History and social reality themselves thus 'negate' philosophy. The critique of society cannot be carried through by philosophical doctrine, but becomes the task of socio-historical practice.

1 Marx, 'Zur Kritik der Hegelschen Rechtsphilosophie,' in *Marx-Engels Gesamtausgabe,* ed. Marx-Engels Institute, Moskou, vol. 1, Frankfurt M. 1927, p. 619.

Before we outline the development of Marxian theory, we have to distinguish it from the other contemporary forms that were built on 'the negation of philosophy.' The deep surge of conviction that philosophy had come to an end colored the first decades after Hegel's death. The assurance spread that the history of thought had reached a decisive turn and that there was only one medium left in which 'the truth' could be found and put into operation, namely, man's concrete material existence. Philosophical structures had hitherto domiciled 'the truth,' setting it apart from the historical struggle of men, in the form of a complex of abstract, transcendental principles. Now, however, man's emancipation could become man's own work, the goal of his self-conscious practice. The true being, reason, and the free subject could now be transformed into historical realities. Hegel's successors accordingly exalted the 'negation of philosophy' as 'the realization of God' through the deification of man (Feuerbach), as 'the realization of philosophy' (Feuerbach, Marx), and as the fulfillment of the 'universal essence' of man (Feuerbach, Marx).

2. Kierkegaard

Who and what will fulfill the essence of man? Who will realize philosophy? The different answers to these questions exhaust the trends of post-Hegelian philosophy. Two general types may be distinguished. The first, represented by Feuerbach and Kierkegaard, seizes upon the isolated individual; the second, represented by Marx, penetrates to the origins of the individual in the process of social labor and shows how the latter process is the basis of man's liberation.

Hegel had demonstrated that the fullest existence of the individual is consummated in his social life. Critical employment of the dialectical method tended to disclose that individual freedom presupposes a free society, and that the true liberation of the individual therefore requires the liberation of society. Fixation on the individual alone would thus amount to adopting an abstract approach, such as Hegel himself set aside. Feuerbach's materialism and Kierkegaard's existentialism, though they embody many traits of a deep-rooted social theory, do not get beyond earlier philosophical and religious approaches to the problem. The Marxian theory, on the other hand, focuses down as a critical theory of society and breaks with the traditional formulations and trends.

Kierkegaard's individualistic interpretation of 'the negation of philosophy' inevitably developed a fierce opposition to Western rationalism. Rationalism was essentially universalistic, as we have shown, with reason resident in the thinking ego and in the objective mind. The truth was lodged either in the universal 'pure reason,' which was untouched by the circumstances of individual life, or in the universal mind, which could flourish though individuals might suffer and die. Man's material happiness was deserted in both cases, by the introversion of reason as well as by its premature adequation to the world as it is.

Rationalist philosophy, the individualists contended, was not concerned with man's actual needs and longings. Though it claimed to respond to his true interests, it gave no answer to his simple quest for happiness. It could not help him in the concrete decisions he constantly had to make. If, as the rationalists maintained, the real unique existence of the individual (which could never be reduced to a universal) was not the primary subject matter of philosophy, and the truth could not be found in or related to this unique existence, all philosophical efforts were superfluous, nay, dangerous. For they served to divert man from the only realm in which he seeks and needs the truth. Only one criterion, therefore, held for a genuine philosophy, its capacity to save the individual.

According to Kierkegaard, the individual is not the knowing but only the 'ethically existing subjectivity.' The sole reality that matters to him is his own 'ethical existence.' [2] Truth lies not in knowledge, for sense perception and historical knowledge are mere semblance, and 'pure' thought is nothing but a 'phantom.' Knowledge deals only with the possible and is incapable of making anything real or even of grasping reality. Truth lies only in action and can be experienced only through action. The individual's own existence is the sole reality that can actually be comprehended, and the existing individual himself the sole subject or performer of this comprehension. His existence is a thinking existence, but his thought is determined by his individual living, so that all his problems arise and are resolved in his individual activity.

Every individual, in his innermost individuality, is isolated from all others; [3] he is essentially unique. There is no union, no community, no 'universality' to contest his dominion. Truth is forever the outcome of his own decision (*Entscheidung*) and can be realized only in the free acts that spring from this decision. The sole decision open to the individual is that between eternal salvation and eternal damnation.

Kierkegaard's individualism turns into the most emphatic absolutism. There is only one truth, eternal happiness in Christ; and only one proper decision, to live a Christian life. Kierkegaard's work is the last great attempt to restore religion as the ultimate organon for liberating humanity from the destructive impact of an oppressive social order. His philosophy implies throughout a strong

[2] Kierkegaard, *Abschliessende unwissenschafliche Nachschrift,* in his *Werke,* Jena 1910, vol. VII, p. 15.

[3] Ibid., p. 21.

critique of his society, denouncing it as one that distorts and shatters human faculties. The remedy was to be found in Christianity, and the fulfillment in the Christian way of life. Kierkegaard knew that in this society such a way of life involved incessant struggle and ultimate humiliation and defeat, and that a Christian existence within current social forms was ever an impossibility. The church had to be separated from the state, for, any dependence on the state would betray Christianity. The true role of the church, freed of any restrictive force, was to denounce prevailing injustice and bondage and to point up the individual's ultimate interest, his salvation.

Salvation could not rely upon external institutions and authorities, nor could it ever be attained by pure thought. Consequently, Kierkegaard now shifts the burden of achieving a life in truth to the concrete individual, the same individual who is the basic concern of Christianity. The *individual* is 'the truth,' not reason or mankind or the state—for the individual is the only reality. 'That which exists is always an individual; the abstract does not exist.'[4]

Kierkegaard returns to the original function of religion, its appeal to the destitute and tormented individual. He thus restores to Christianity its combative and revolutionary force. The appearance of God again assumes the terrifying aspect of a historical event suddenly breaking in upon a society in decay. Eternity takes on a temporal aspect, while the realization of happiness becomes an immediately vital matter of daily life.

Kierkegaard, however, was holding to a content that could no longer take a religious form. Religion was doomed to share the fate of philosophy. The salvation of mankind could not any longer rest in the realm of faith, especially since advancing historical forces were in motion,

[4] P. 28.

bearing forward the revolutionary core of religion in a concrete struggle for social liberation. In these circumstances the religious protest was weak and impotent, and religious individualism could even turn against the individual it set out to save. If left to the inner world of the individual, 'the truth' gets separated from the social and political vortex in which it belongs.

Kierkegaard's attack on abstract thought led him to assail certain universal concepts that uphold the essential equality and dignity of man. He holds humanity (*reine Menschheit*) to be a 'negativity,' a mere abstraction from the individual and a leveling of all existential values.[5] The 'totality' of reason, in which Hegel saw the completion of the truth, is also a 'mere abstraction.'[6] We can best see how far from a purely philosophical matter is this focusing of philosophy on the uniqueness of the individual and how much it entails his social and political isolation, when we consider Kierkegaard's attitude to the socialist movement. There is no doubt, he says, that 'the idea of socialism and community (*Gemeinschaft*) cannot save this age.'[7] Socialism is just one among many attempts to degrade individuals by equalizing all so as to 'remove all organic, concrete differentiations and distinctions.'[8] It is a function of resentment on the part of the many against the few who possess and exemplify the higher values; socialism is thus part of the general revolt against extraordinary individuals.

The anti-rationalist attack on universals becomes increasingly important in the subsequent development of European thought. The assault upon the universal reason was easily swung to an attack on the positive social impli-

[5] *Zur Kritik der Gegenwart.* Innsbruck 1922, p. 34.
[6] Ibid., p. 42. [7] P. 61. [8] P. 64.

cations of this universal. We have already indicated that the concept of reason was connected with advanced ideas, like the essential equality of men, the rule of law, the standard of rationality in state and society, and that Western rationalism was thus definitely linked with the fundamental institutions of liberalist society. In the ideological field, the struggle against this liberalism began with the attack on rationalism. The position called 'existentialism' played an important part in this attack. First, it denied the dignity and reality of the universal. This led to a rejection of any universally valid rational norms for state and society. Later, it was claimed that no bond joins individuals, states, and nations into a whole of mankind, that the particular existential conditions of each cannot be submitted to the general judgment of reason. Laws, it was held, are not based upon any universal qualities of man in whom a reason resides; they rather express the needs of individual people whose lives they regulate in accordance with their existential requirements. This demotion of reason made it possible to exalt certain particularities (such as the race or the folk) to the rank of the highest values.

3. Feuerbach

Feuerbach starts with the fact Kierkegaard had failed to recognize, namely, that in the present age the human content of religion can be preserved only by abandoning the religious, other-worldly form. The realization of religion requires its negation. The doctrine of God (theology) must be changed into the doctrine of man (anthropology). Everlasting happiness will begin with the transformation of the kingdom of heaven into a republic of earth.

Feuerbach agrees with Hegel that mankind has reached maturity. The earth is ready to be transformed, through the collective and conscious practice of men, into a domain of reason and freedom. He therefore sketches a 'Philosophy of the Future,' which he regards as the logical and historical fulfillment of Hegel's philosophy. 'The new philosophy is the realization of the Hegelian,—moreover, of the entire preceding philosophy.' [9] The negation of religion had begun with Hegel's transformation of theology into logic; it ends with Feuerbach's transformation of logic into anthropology.[10] Anthropology, to Feuerbach, is a philosophy aiming at the concrete emancipation of man, outlining therefor the conditions and qualities of an actually free human existence. Such a philosophy cannot be idealist, for the means are at hand for carrying through a free human existence by liberation in fact. Hegel's great error was that he stuck to idealism at a time when a materialistic solution of the problem was at hand. The new philosophy, then, is a realization of Hegelian philosophy only as its negation.

When he accepted the given state of the world as adequate to the standard of reason, Hegel contradicted his own principles and hitched philosophy to an external content, that given in his day. His critical distinctions are in the end merely distinctions within that given, and his philosophy has a 'critical, but not a genetico-critical significance.' [11] The latter type of philosophy would not simply demonstrate and understand its object, but would investigate its origin and thus question its right to exist. The prevailing state of man is the result of a long historical process in which all transcendental values have been 'secularized' and made the aims of man's empirical life. The happiness he sought in heaven and in pure thought can now be satisfied on earth. Only a 'genetic' analysis will

[9] *Grundsätze der Philosophie der Zukunft,* in *Sämmtliche Werke,* Leipzig 1846, vol. II, § 20; see also § 31.

[10] *Vorläufige Thesen zur Reform der Philosophie,* op. cit., vol. II, p. 247.

[11] *Kritik der Hegelschen Philosophie* in op. cit., pp. 221-2.

enable philosophy to furnish the ideas that might help man in his *real* liberation. Hegel, Feuerbach insists, undertook no such analysis. His construction of history presupposed throughout that the prevailing stage of development reached in his time was the immanent end of all preceding stages.

Moreover, genetic analysis is not only a matter of the philosophy of history, but of logic and psychology as well. Here, Hegel failed the more, for thought receives no genetic analysis in his system. Being is conceived as thought from the outset. It enters the system not as the 'fact' of the external world, which is at first simply 'given' and other than thought, but as notion. And in the elaboration of the system being becomes a derivative mode of thought, or, as Feuerbach says, 'the predicate of thought.' Consequently, nature is derived from the structure and movement of thought—a complete reversal of the true state of affairs.

Feuerbach's genetic analysis of thought starts, *per contra,* from the obvious fact that nature is the primary and thought the secondary reality. 'The true relation of thought to Being is this; Being is subject, thought is predicate. Thought springs from Being, but Being does not spring from thought.' [12]

Philosophy must thus begin with being, not Hegel's abstract being-as-such, but with being in the concrete, that is, with nature. 'The essence of Being *qua* Being is the essence of nature.' [13] The new philosophy is not, however, to be a philosophy of nature in the traditional sense. Nature becomes relevant only in so far as it conditions human existence; man is to be the proper content and interest. The liberation of man requires the liberation of nature, of man's natural existence. 'All science must be founded

[12] *Vorläufige Thesen zur Reform der Philosophie,* p. 263.
[13] Ibid.

on nature. Theory is a mere hypothesis as long as the natural basis of theory has not been established. This holds especially true for the theory of freedom. The new philosophy will succeed in "naturalizing" freedom, the same that was hitherto merely an anti-natural and supranatural hypothesis.' [14]

Feuerbach joins the great tradition of materialist philosophers who, taking as the point of departure for their views man's actual state in nature and in society, could see that the idealistic solutions were illusory. The hard fact that man's natural drives were permitted no satisfactory outlet showed freedom and reason to be a myth, as far as social realities were concerned. Hegel had committed the unpardonable offense against the individual of constructing a realm of reason on the foundations of an enslaved humanity. Despite all historical progress, Feuerbach cries out, man is still in need, and the pervasive fact philosophy encounters is 'suffering.' This, and not cognition, is primary in man's relation to the objective world. 'Thought is preceded by suffering.' [15] And no realization of reason is in the offing until that suffering has been eliminated.

We have mentioned that 'the universal suffering' that Marx saw in the existence of the proletariat negated for him the reality of reason. The 'principle of suffering,' Marx held, was rooted in the historical form of society and required social action for its abolition. Feuerbach, *per contra,* introduces nature as the basis and medium for liberating mankind. Philosophy is negated and fulfilled by nature. Man's suffering is a 'natural' relation of the living subject to its objective environment, for the subject is opposed and overwhelmed by the object. Nature shapes and determines the ego from without, making it essentially 'passive.' The process of liberation cannot elimi-

[14] Ibid., p. 267. [15] P. 253.

nate this passivity, but can transform it from a source of privation and pain to one of abundance and enjoyment.

Feuerbach's conception of the ego reverses the traditional conception of it, which motivated modern philosophy since Descartes. The ego, according to Feuerbach, is primarily receptive, not spontaneous; determined, not self-determining; the passive subject of perception, not the active subject of thought. 'True objective thought, true objective philosophy arises only out of the *negation* of thought, out of *being determined* by the object, out of *passion,* the source of all pleasure and need.' [16] Feuerbach's naturalism thus maintains that perception, sensuousness (*Sinnlichkeit*), sensation (*Empfindung*) are the proper organon of philosophy. 'The object, in its true meaning, is given only by the senses'; [17] 'nothing is unquestionably and immediately certain except the object of the senses, of perception and sensation.' [18]

This is the point at which Marx's critique of Feuerbach begins. Marx upholds Hegel on this point, as against Feuerbach. Hegel had denied that sense-certainty is the final criterion of the truth, on the ground that, first, the truth is a universal that cannot be won in an experience that conveys particulars, and, second, that truth finds fulfillment in a historical process carried forward by the collective practice of men. The latter is basic, with sense-certainty and nature alike drawn into the movement so that they change their content in its course.[19]

Hegel's point was that labor brings sense-certainty and

[16] P. 258.

[17] *Grundsätze der Philosophie der Zukunft,* § 32.

[18] Ibid., § 37.

[19] Feuerbach discusses Hegel's critique of sense-certainty in his *Kritik der Hegelschen Philosophie,* op. cit., pp. 211-15. He isolates the standpoint of sense-certainty from the more comprehensive modes of understanding with which sense-certainty is psychologically and historically linked. The authority of common sense is upheld, as against a truth that is made manifest only when there is freedom from this authority.

nature into the historical process. Because he conceived human existence in terms of sense, Feuerbach disregarded this material function of labor altogether. 'Not satisfied with abstract thought, Feuerbach appeals to sense-perception [*Anschauung*]; but he does not understand our sensuous nature as practical, human-sensuous activity.' [20]

Labor transforms the natural conditions of human existence into social ones. By omitting the labor process from his philosophy of freedom, therefore, Feuerbach omitted the decisive factor through which nature might become the medium for freedom. His interpretation of man's free development as a 'natural' development neglected the historical conditions for liberation and made freedom into an event within the framework of the given order. His 'perceptual materialism' perceives only 'separate individuals in bourgeois society.' [21]

Marx focused his theory on the labor process and by so doing held to and consummated the principle of the Hegelian dialectic that the structure of the content (reality) determines the structure of the theory. He made the foundations of civil society the foundations of the theory of civil society. This society operates on the principle of universal labor, with the labor process decisive for the *totality* of human existence; labor determines the value of all things. Since the society is perpetuated by the continued universal exchange of the products of labor, the totality of human relations is governed by the immanent laws of the economy. The development of the individual and the range of his freedom depend on the extent to which his labor satisfies a social need. All men are free, but the mechanisms of the labor process govern the free-

[20] Marx, 'Theses on Feuerbach,' v; see *The German Ideology*, ed. R. Pascal, International Publishers, New York 1939, p. 198, and Sidney Hook, *From Hegel to Marx*, New York 1936, p. 293.

[21] Marx, 'Theses on Feuerbach,' IX; see *The German Ideology*, op. cit., p. 199, and Sidney Hook, op. cit., p. 299.

dom of them all. The study of the labor process is, in the last analysis, absolutely necessary in order to discover the conditions for realizing reason and freedom in the real sense. A critical analysis of that process thus yields the final theme of philosophy.

4. Marx: Alienated Labor

Marx's writings between 1844 and 1846 treat the form of labor in modern society as constituting the total 'alienation' of man. The employment of this category links Marx's economic analysis with a basic category of the Hegelian philosophy. The social division of labor, Marx declares, is not carried out with any consideration for the talents of individuals and the interest of the whole, but rather takes place entirely according to the laws of capitalist commodity production. Under these laws, the product of labor, the commodity, seems to determine the nature and end of human activity. In other words, the materials that should serve life come to rule over its content and goal, and the consciousness of man is completely made victim to the relationships of material production.

The materialistic proposition that is the starting point of Marx's theory thus states, first, a *historical fact,* exposing the materialistic character of the prevailing social order in which an uncontrolled economy legislates over all human relations. At the same time, Marx's proposition is a *critical* one, implying that the prevailing relation between consciousness and social existence is a false one that must be overcome before the true relation can come to light. The truth of the materialist thesis is thus to be fulfilled in its negation.

Marx emphasizes time and again that his materialistic starting point is forced upon him by the materialistic quality of the society he analyzes. He states that he begins with a 'fact,' an 'economic fact' recognized even by classical political economy.[22] As modern society runs its course, 'the worker becomes the poorer the more wealth he produces and the more his production increases in power and extent. The worker becomes a cheaper commodity the more commodities he produces. Hand in hand with the exploitation (*Verwertung*) of the objective world goes the depreciation of the human world.'[23] Classical political economy (Marx quotes Adam Smith and J. B. Say) admits that even great social wealth means nothing but 'stationary poverty' for the worker.[24] These economists had shown that poverty is not at all the result of adverse external circumstance, but of the prevailing mode of labor itself. 'In the progressing condition of society the destruction and impoverishment of the worker is the product of his own labor and of the wealth he has himself produced. Misery thus springs from the *nature* of the prevailing mode of labor' and is rooted in the very essence of modern society.[25]

What significance does this mode of labor have as far as the development of man is concerned? With this question, the Marxian theory leaves 'the plane of political economy.'[26] The totality of economic relations, laws, and institutions may not be treated simply as an isolated objective cluster of facts, but as making up a historical form within which men carry on their lives. Freed from the limitations of a specialized science, the economic categories are seen to be determining factors for human existence (*Daseinsformen, Existenzbestimmungen*), even if they denote objective economic facts (as in the case of

22 'Ökonomisch-philosophische Manuskripte' (1844), in *Marx-Engels Gesamtausgabe,* edited by the Marx-Engels Institute, vol. III, Berlin 1932, pp. 80-81, 89-90.

23 Ibid., p. 82. 24 P. 43. 25 P. 45. 26 P. 45.

commodity, value, ground rent).[27] Far from being a mere economic activity (*Erwerbstätigkeit*), labor is the 'existential activity' of man, his 'free, conscious activity'—not a means for maintaining his life (*Lebensmittel*) but for developing his 'universal nature.' [28] The new categories will evaluate the economic reality with a view to what it has made of man, of his faculties, powers, and needs. Marx summarizes these human qualities when he speaks of the 'universal essence' of man; his examination of the economy is specifically carried on with the question in mind whether that economy realizes man's *Gattungswesen* (*universelles Wesen*).

These terms point back to Feuerbach and to Hegel. Man's very nature lies in his universality. His intellectual and physical faculties can be fulfilled only if all men exist as men, in the developed wealth of their human resources. Man is free only if all men are free and exist as 'universal beings.' When this condition is attained, life will be shaped by the potentialities of the genus, Man, which embraces the potentialities of all the individuals that comprise it. The emphasis on this universality brings nature as well into the self-development of mankind. Man is free if 'nature is his work and his reality,' so that he 'recognizes himself in a world he has himself made.' [29]

All this has an obvious resemblance to Hegel's idea of reason. Marx even goes so far as to describe the self-realization of man in terms of the unity between thought and being.[30] The whole problem is, however, no longer a philosophical one, for the self-realization of man now requires the abolition of the prevailing mode of labor, and philosophy cannot deliver this result. The critique does begin in philosophic terms, because the enslavement

27 *A Contribution to the Critique of Political Economy*, trans. N. I Stone, Charles H. Kerr and Co., Chicago 1904, p. 302.
28 'Ökonomisch-philosophische Manuskripte,' pp. 87-8.
29 P. 89. 30 P. 117.

of labor and its liberation are alike conditions that go beyond the framework of traditional political economy and affect the very foundations of human existence (which are the proper domain of philosophy), but Marx departs from the philosophical terminology as soon as he has elaborated his own theory. The critical, transcendental character of the economic categories, hitherto expressed by philosophical concepts, later, in his *Capital,* is demonstrated by the economic categories themselves.

Marx explains the alienation of labor as exemplified in, first, the relation of the worker to the product of his labor and, second, the relation of the worker to his own activity. The worker in capitalist society produces commodities. Large-scale commodity production requires capital, large aggregations of wealth used exclusively to promote commodity production. The commodities are produced by independent private entrepreneurs for purposes of profitable sale. The worker labors for the capitalist, to whom he surrenders, through the wage contract, the product of his labor. Capital is power to dispose over the products of labor. The more the worker produces, the greater the power of capital becomes and the smaller the worker's own means for appropriating his products. Labor thus becomes the victim of a power it has itself created.

Marx summarizes this process as follows: 'The object which labor produces, its product, is encountered as an *alien entity,* a force that has become *independent* of its producer. The realization of labor is its objectification. Under the prevailing economic conditions, this realization of labor appears as its opposite, the negation [*Entwirklichung*] of the laborer. Objectification appears as loss of and enslavement by the object, and appropriation as alienation and expropriation.' [31] Once turned to the laws of

[31] P. 83.

capitalist commodity production, labor is inevitably impoverished. For, 'the more the worker toils, the more powerful becomes the alien world of objects he produces to oppose him, and the poorer he himself becomes . . .' [32] Marx shows this mechanism at work in the movement of wages. The laws of commodity production, without any external aids, maintain wages at the level of stationary poverty.[33]

> [As a result,] the realization of labor appears as negation to such an extent that the worker is negated to the point of starvation. The objectification appears as a loss of the objects to such an extent that the worker is deprived of the most necessary objects of life and labor. Moreover, labor itself becomes an object of which he can make himself master only by the greatest effort and with incalculable interruptions. Appropriation of the object appears as alienation to such an extent that the more objects the worker produces the less he possesses and the more he comes under the sway of his product, of capital.[34]

The worker alienated from his product is at the same time alienated from himself. His labor itself becomes no longer his own, and the fact that it becomes the property of another bespeaks an expropriation that touches the very essence of man. Labor in its true form is a medium for man's true self-fulfillment, for the full development of his potentialities; the conscious utilization of the forces of nature should take place for his satisfaction and enjoyment. In its current form, however, it cripples all human faculties and enjoins satisfaction. The worker 'does not affirm but contradicts his essence.' 'Instead of developing his free physical and mental energies, he mortifies his body and ruins his mind. He therefore first feels he is with himself when he is free from work and apart from himself when he is at work. He is at home when he does

32 Ibid. 33 Pp. 39-44. 34 P. 83.

not work and not at home when he does. His working is, therefore, not done willingly but under compulsion. It is forced labor. It is, therefore, not the satisfaction of a need, but only a *means* for the satisfaction of wants outside of it.' [35]

In consequence, 'Man [the worker] feels himself acting freely only in his animal functions like eating, drinking and begetting . . . whereas in his human functions he is nothing but an animal. The animal becomes the human and the human the animal.' [36] This holds alike for the worker (the expropriated producer), and for him who buys his labor. The process of alienation affects all strata of society, distorting even the 'natural' functions of man. The senses, the primary sources of freedom and happiness according to Feuerbach, are reduced to one 'sense of possessing.' [37] They view their object only as something that can or cannot be appropriated. Even pleasure and enjoyment change from conditions under which men freely develop their 'universal nature' into modes of 'egoistic' possession and acquisition.[38]

Marx's analysis of labor under capitalism is thus quite deep seated, going further than the structure of economic relationships to the actual human content. Relations such as those between capital and labor, capital and commodity, labor and commodity, and those between commodities are understood as human relations, relations in man's social existence. Even the institution of private property appears as 'the product, result and inevitable consequence of the alienated mode of labor,' and derives from the mechanisms of the social mode of production.[39] The alienation of labor leads to the division of labor so characteristic of all forms of class society: 'Each man has a particular, exclusive sphere of activity, which is forced upon him

[35] Pp. 85-6. [36] P. 86. [37] P. 118. [38] P. 119.
[39] Pp. 90-91; see also *The German Ideology*, op. cit., p. 44.

and from which he cannot escape' [40]—a division that is not overcome when the abstract freedom of the individual is proclaimed in bourgeois society. Labor separated from its object is, in the last analysis, an 'alienation of man from man'; the individuals are isolated from and set against each other. They are linked in the commodities they exchange rather than in their persons. Man's alienation from himself is simultaneously an estrangement from his fellow men.[41]

Marx's early writings are the first explicit statement of the process of reification (*Verdinglichung*) through which capitalist society makes all personal relations between men take the form of objective relations between things. Marx expounds this process in his *Capital* as 'the Fetishism of Commodities.' The system of capitalism relates men to each other through the commodities they exchange. The social status of individuals, their standard of living, the satisfaction of their needs, their freedom, and their power are all determined by the value of their commodities. The capacities and needs of the individual have no part in the evaluation. Even man's most human attributes become a function of money, the general substitute for commodities. Individuals participate in the social process as owners of commodities only. Their mutual relations are those of their commodities.[42] Capitalist commodity production has this mystifying result, that it transforms the social relations of individuals into 'qualities of . . . things themselves [commodities] and still more pronouncedly transforms the interrelations of production themselves into a thing [money].' [43] The mystifying result arises from the specific mode of labor in commodity production, with its

[40] *The German Ideology*, p. 22.
[41] 'Ökonomisch-philosophische Manuskripte,' p. 89.
[42] *A Contribution to the Critique of Political Economy*, p. 41.
[43] *Capital*, vol. III, trans. E. Untermann, Charles H. Kerr and Co., Chicago 1909, p. 962; cf. p. 966.

separate individuals working independently of each other, and fulfilling their own needs only through those of the market:

> The Fetishism of commodities has its origin . . . in the peculiar social character of the labor that produces them.
>
> As a general rule, articles of utility become commodities, only because they are products of the labor of private individuals or groups of individuals who carry on their work independently of each other. The sum-total of the labor of all these private individuals forms the aggregate labor of society [*gesellschaftliche Gesamtarbeit*]. Since the producers do not come into contact with each other until they exchange their products, the specific social character of each producer's labor does not show itself except in the act of exchange. In other words, the labor of the individual asserts itself as a part of the labor of society, only by means of the relations which the act of exchange establishes directly between the products, and indirectly, through them, between the producers. To the latter, therefore, the relations connecting the labor of one individual with that of the rest appear, not as direct social relations between individuals at work, but as what they really are, material relations between persons [*sachliche Verhältnisse von Personen*] and social relations between things.[44]

What does this reification accomplish? It sets forth the actual social relations among men as a totality of objective relations, thereby concealing their origin, their mechanisms of perpetuation, and the possibility of their transformation. Above all, it conceals their human core and content. If wages, as the reification process would indicate, express the value of labor, exploitation is at best a subjective and personal judgment. If capital were nothing other than an aggregate of wealth employed in commodity production, then capital would appear to be the cumulative result of productive skill and diligence. If the creation of profits were the peculiar quality of utilized capital,

[44] *Capital,* trans. S. Moore and E. Aveling, vol. I, Chicago 1906, pp. 83-4.

such profits might represent a reward for the work of the entrepreneur. The relation between capital and labor on this basis would involve neither iniquity nor oppression; it would rather be a purely objective, material relationship, and economic theory would be a specialized science like any other. The laws of supply and demand, the fixing of value and prices, the business cycles, and so on, would be amenable to study as objective laws and facts, regardless of their effect on human existence. The economic process of society would be a natural process, and man, with all his needs and desires, would play in it the role of an objective mathematical quantum rather than that of a conscious subject.

Marxian theory rejects such a science of economics and sets in its place the interpretation that economic relations are existential relations between men. It does this not by virtue of any humanitarian feeling but by virtue of the actual content of the economy itself. Economic relations only seem to be objective because of the character of commodity production. As soon as one delves beneath this mode of production, and analyzes its origin, one can see that its natural *objectivity* is mere semblance while in reality it is a specific historical form of existence that man has given himself. Moreover, once this content comes to the fore, economic theory would turn into a *critical* theory. 'When one speaks of private property one thinks he is dealing with something outside of man. When one speaks of labor, one has to do immediately with man himself. The new formulation of the question already involves its solution.'[45] As soon as their mystifying character is uncovered, economic conditions appear as the complete negation of humanity.[46] The mode of labor perverts all

[45] 'Ökonomisch-philosophische Manuskripte,' p. 93.
[46] The fact that a particular form of social life is 'negative' does not prevent its having progressive qualities. Marx frequently emphasized that

human faculties, accumulation of wealth intensifies poverty, and technological progress leads to 'the rule of dead matter over the human world.'[47] Objective facts come alive and enter an indictment of society. Economic realities exhibit their own inherent negativity.

We are here touching upon the origins of the Marxian dialectic. For Marx, as for Hegel, the dialectic takes note of the fact that the negation inherent in reality is 'the moving and creative principle.' The dialectic is the 'dialectic of negativity.'[48] Every fact is more than a mere fact; it is a negation and restriction of real possibilities. Wage labor is a fact, but at the same time it is a restraint on free work that might satisfy human needs. Private property is a fact, but at the same time it is a negation of man's collective appropriation of nature.

Man's social practice embodies the negativity as well as its overcoming. The negativity of capitalist society lies in its alienation of labor; the negation of this negativity will come with the abolition of alienated labor. Alienation has taken its most universal form in the institution of private property; amends will be made with the abolition of private property. It is of the utmost importance to note that Marx views the abolition of private property entirely as a means for the abolition of alienated labor, and not as an end in itself. The socialization of the means of production is as such merely an economic fact, just like any other

the capitalist mode of labor has had a distinctly progressive character in the sense that it has made possible the rational exploitation of all kinds of material resources, it has constantly increased the productivity of labor, and has emancipated a hitherto unknown multitude of human capacities. But progress in class society does not imply increasing happiness and liberty. Until the alienated form of labor is abolished, all progress will continue to be more or less technical, denoting more rational methods of production and a more rational domination of men and nature. With all these qualities, progress only aggravates the negativity of the social order, which perverts and restricts the forces of technical progress. Here, again, Hegel's philosophy was right: the progress of reason is no progress of happiness.

47 Ibid., p. 77.

48 P. 156.

economic institution. Its claim to be the beginning of a new social order depends on what man does with the socialized means of production. If these are not utilized for the development and gratification of the free individual, they will amount simply to a new form for subjugating individuals to a hypostatized universality. The abolition of private property inaugurates an essentially new social system only if free individuals, and not 'the society,' become masters of the socialized means of production. Marx expressly warns against such another 'reification' of society: 'One must above all avoid setting "the society" up again as an abstraction opposed to the individual. The individual *is* the social entity [*das gesellschaftliche Wesen*]. The expression of his life . . . is therefore an expression and verification of the *life of society*.'[49]

The true history of mankind will be, in the strict sense, the history of free individuals, so that the interest of the whole will be woven into the individual existence of each. In all prior forms of society, the interest of the whole lay in separate social and political institutions, which represented the right of society as against the right of the individual. The abolition of private property will do away with all this once and for all, for it will mark 'man's return from family, religion, state, etc., to his *human*, that is, *social* existence.'[50]

It is, then, the free individuals, and not a new system of production, that exemplify the fact that the particular and the common interest have been merged. The individual is the goal. This 'individualistic' trend is fundamental as an interest of the Marxian theory. We have shown the role of the universal in the traditional theories, placing stress on the fact that human fulfillment, what we have called 'the truth' exemplified, could only be conceived in

[49] P. 117.

[50] P. 115.

terms of the abstract universal concept so long as society retained the form it had. Shot through with a conflict at every hand among individual interests, the concrete conditions of social life made a mockery of 'the universal essence' of man and nature. And since the prevailing social realities contradicted that essence, and hence contradicted 'the truth,' the latter had no refuge save the mind, where it was hypostatized as an abstract universal.

Marx explains how this state of affairs came about, showing its origin in the division of labor of class society, and particularly in the divorce that was entailed between the intellectual and material forces of production.

> The forces of production, the state of society, and consciousness, can and must come into contradiction with one another, because the division of labor implies the possibility, nay the fact that intellectual and material activity—enjoyment and labor, production and consumption—devolve on different individuals . . . The division of labor . . . manifests itself also in the ruling class as the division of mental and material labor, so that inside this class one part appears as the thinkers of the class . . . while the others' attitude to these ideas and illusions is more passive and receptive, because they are in reality the active members of this class and have less time to make up illusions and ideas about themselves . . . It is self-evident that phantoms like 'the Higher Being,' 'Notion' . . . are merely the idealistic, spiritual expression, the conception apparently of the isolated individual, the image of very empirical fetters and limitations, within which the mode of production of life, and the form of intercourse coupled with it, move.[51]

Just as materially the reproduction of the social whole was the result of blind forces over which man's conscious powers exercised no guidance, so mentally, the universal came forth as a reality that was independent and creative. The groups governing society were compelled to hide the

[51] *The German Ideology,* pp. 21, 39-40, 21.

fact that their interests were private by cloaking them in the 'dignity of the universal.' 'Each new class which puts itself in the place of one ruling before it, is compelled, merely in order to carry through its aim, to represent its interest as the common interest of all the members of society . . . It will give its ideas the form of universality, and represent them as the only rational, universally valid ones.'[52] The claim of universality for the ideas of a ruling class is thus part of the mechanisms of class rule, and the critique of class society will also destroy its philosophical claims.

The universal concepts employed are at first those hypostatizing desired forms of human existence—concepts like reason, freedom, justice, and virtue, and also state, society, democracy. All of these envisage that man's universal essence is materialized either within the prevailing social conditions or beyond them in a supra-historical realm. Marx also points to the fact that such concepts become increasingly universal in scope with the advance of the society. The ideas of honor, loyalty, and so on, which characterized medieval times and which were the dominant ideas of the aristocracy, were far more restricted in appeal and applied to fewer persons than the ideas of freedom, equality, and justice, of the bourgeoisie, which reflect the more far-reaching base of that class. The development of dominant ideas thus keeps step with and mirrors an increasing social and economic integration. 'The most general abstractions commonly arise only where there is the highest concrete development, where one feature seems to be jointly possessed by many, and to be common to all. Then it cannot be thought of any longer in one particular form.'[53] The more society advances, the

[52] Pp. 40-41.
[53] *A Contribution to the Critique of Political Economy*, pp. 298-9.

more do 'abstract ideas hold sway, that is, ideas which increasingly take on the form of universality.' [54]

This process, however, turns into its opposite as soon as classes are abolished and the interest of the whole is fulfilled in the existence of every individual, for then 'It is no longer necessary to represent a particular interest as general or "the general interest" as ruling.' [55] The individual becomes the actual subject of history, in such a way that he is himself the universal and manifests the 'universal essence' of man.

Communism, with its '*positive* abolition of private property,' is thus of its very nature a new form of individualism, and not only a new and different economic system, but a different system of life. Communism is 'the real appropriation [*Aneignung*] of the essence of man by and for man, therefore it is man's complete conscious . . . return to himself as a social, that is, human being.' It is the 'true solution of man's conflict with nature and with man, of the strife between existence and essence, reification and self-determination, liberty and necessity, individual and genus.' [56] The contradictions that lay beneath the philosophy of Hegel and all traditional philosophy will dissolve in this new form of society. For these are historical contradictions rooted in the antagonisms of class society. Philosophical ideas express material historical conditions, which cast off their philosophical form as soon as they are subjected to the scrutiny of critical theory and are seized by conscious social practice.

Hegel's philosophy revolved about the universality of reason; it was a rational system with its every part (the subjective as well as the objective spheres) integrated into

[54] *The German Ideology*, p. 40.
[55] Ibid., p. 41.
[56] 'Ökonomisch-philosophische Manuskripte,' p. 114.

a comprehensive whole. Marx shows that capitalist society first put such a universality into practice. Capitalism developed the productive forces for the totality of a uniform social system. Universal commerce, universal competition, and the universal interdependence of labor were made to prevail and transformed men into 'world-historical, empirically universal individuals.' [57]

This universality, however, as we have explained, is a negative one, for the productive forces are used, as are the things man produces with them, in a way that makes them seem the products of an uncontrolled alien power. It is 'an empirical fact that separate individuals have, with the broadening of their activity into world-historical activity, become more and more enslaved under a power alien to them . . . a power which has become more and more enormous and, in the last instance, turns out to be the *world market.*' [58] The distribution of supply under international commodity production is a blind and anarchic universal process, wherein the demand of the individual is satisfied only if he can meet the requirements of exchange. Marx calls this anarchic relation of supply to demand a 'natural' form of social integration, meaning that it seems to have the force of a natural law instead of operating, as it should, under the joint control of all men.

5. The Abolition of Labor

The realization of freedom and reason requires a reversal of this state of affairs. 'Universal dependence, this natural form of the world-historical cooperation of individuals, will be transformed by this communist revolution into the control and conscious mastery of these powers, which, born of the action of men on one another, have

[57] *The German Ideology*, p. 25. [58] Ibid., p. 27.

till now overawed and governed men as powers completely alien to them.' [59]

Moreover, since the state of affairs that has prevailed 'till now' is a universal negativity, affecting all spheres of life everywhere, its transformation requires a *universal* revolution, that is to say, a revolution that would reverse, first, the *totality* of prevailing conditions and, secondly, would replace this with a new *universal* order. The material elements of complete revolution must be present so that the convulsion grips not specific conditions in the existent society, but the very 'production of life' prevailing in it, the 'total activity' on which it has been based.[60] This totalitarian character of the revolution is made necessary by the totalitarian character of the capitalist relations of production. 'Modern universal intercourse can be controlled by individuals . . . only when controlled by all.' [61]

The revolutionary convulsion that ends the system of capitalist society sets free all the potentialities for general satisfaction that have developed in this system. Marx accordingly calls the communist revolution an act of 'appropriation' [*Aneignung*], meaning that with the abolition of private property men are to obtain true ownership over all those things that have hitherto remained estranged from them.

Appropriation is determined by the object to be appropriated, that is, by 'the productive forces, which have been developed to a totality and which only exist within a universal intercourse. From this aspect alone, therefore, this appropriation must have a universal character . . .' [62] The universality that exists in the present state of society will be transposed to the new social order, where, however, it will have a different character. The universal will

[59] Ibid., pp. 27-8. [60] P. 29. [61] P. 67. [62] P. 66.

no longer operate as a blind natural force once men have succeeded in subjecting the available productive forces 'to the power of individuals united.' Man will then for the first time in history consciously treat 'all natural premises as the creatures of men.' [63] His struggle with nature will pursue 'a general plan' formulated by 'freely combined individuals.' [64]

The appropriation is also determined by the persons appropriating. The alienation of labor creates a society split into opposing *classes*. Any social scheme that effects a division of labor without taking account of the abilities and needs of individuals in assigning them their roles tends to shackle the activity of the individual to external economic forces. The mode of social production (the way in which the life of the whole is maintained) circumscribes the life of the individual and harnesses his entire existence to relations prescribed by the economy, without regard to his subjective abilities or wants. Commodity production under a system of free competition has aggravated this condition. The commodities allotted to the individual for the gratification of his needs were supposed to be the equivalent of his work. Equality seemed to be guaranteed, at least in this respect. The individual could not, however, choose his work. It was prescribed for him by his position in the social process of production, which was in turn forced upon him by the prevailing distribution of power and wealth.

The fact of classes contradicts freedom, or, rather, transforms it into an abstract idea. The class circumscribes the actual range of individual freedom within the general anarchy, the arena of free play still open to the individual. Each is free to the extent that his class is free, and the development of his individuality is confined to

[63] P. 70. [64] P. 72.

the limits of his class: he unfolds himself as a 'class individual.'

The class is the actual social and economic unit, not the individual. It 'achieves an independent existence over against the individuals, so that the latter find their conditions of existence predestined, and hence have their position in life and their personal development assigned to them by their class, [and] become subsumed under it.'[65] The existent form of society accomplishes a universal order only by negating the individual. The 'personal individual' becomes a 'class individual,'[66] and his constituent properties become universal properties that he shares with all other members of his class. His existence is not his, but that of his class. We recall Hegel's statement that the individual *is* the universal, that he acts historically not as a private person but as a citizen of his state. Marx understands this negation of the individual to be the historical product of class society, effectuated not by the state but by the ordering of labor.

The subsumption of individuals under classes is the same phenomenon as their subjection to the *division of labor*.[67] By division of labor Marx here means the process of separating various economic activities into specialized and delimited fields: first, industry and commerce separated from agriculture; then industry separated from commerce; and finally the latter subdivided into different branches.[68] This entire differentiation takes place under the requirements of commodity production in its capitalistic form, accelerated by the progress of technology. It is a blind and 'natural' process. The totality of labor required to perpetuate society appears as an *a priori* given body of work that is organized in a definite way. The specific division of labor that prevails seems an unalterable

[65] P. 49. [66] P. 77. [67] P. 49. [68] Pp. 8 and 48.

necessity that drags the individuals into its toils. Business becomes an objective entity that gives men a certain standard of living, a set of interests, and a range of possibilities that mark them off from men engaged in other businesses. The conditions of labor mold the individuals into groups or classes, and are class conditions converging upon the fundamental division into capital and wage labor.

The two fundamental classes, however, are not classes in the same sense. The proletariat is distinguished by the fact that, as a class, it signifies the negation of all classes. The interests of all other classes are essentially one-sided; the proletariat's interest is essentially universal. The proletariat has neither property nor profit to defend. Its one concern, the abolition of the prevailing mode of labor, is the concern of society as a whole. This is expressed in the fact that the communist revolution, in contrast to all previous revolutions, can leave no social group in bondage because there is no class below the proletariat.

The universality of the proletariat is, again, a negative universality, indicating that the alienation of labor has intensified to the point of total self-destruction. The labor of the proletarian prevents any self-fulfillment; his work negates his entire existence. This utmost negativity, however, takes a positive turn. The very fact that he is deprived of all assets of the prevailing system sets him beyond this system. He is a member of the class 'which is really rid of all the old world and at the same time stands pitted against it.'[69] The 'universal character' of the proletariat is the final basis for the universal character of the communist revolution.

The proletariat is the negation not only of certain particular human potentialities, but also of man as such. All

[69] P. 57; see also p. 67.

specific distinguishing marks by which men are differentiated lose their validity. Property, culture, religion, nationality, and so on, all things that might set one man off from another, make no such mark among proletarians. Each lives in society only as the bearer of labor power, and each is thus the equivalent of all others of his class. His concern to exist is not the concern of a given group, class, or nation, but is truly universal and 'world historical.' 'The proletariat can thus only exist *world-historically* . . .' [70] The communist revolution, its movement, is therefore necessarily a world revolution.[71]

The prevailing social relations that the revolution upsets are everywhere negative because they everywhere result from a negative ordering of the labor process that perpetuates them. The labor process itself is the life of the proletariat. Abolition of the negative ordering of labor, alienated labor as Marx terms it, is hence at the same time the abolition of the proletariat.

The abolition of the proletariat also amounts to the abolition of labor as such. Marx makes this an express formulation when he speaks of the achievement of revolution. Classes are to be abolished 'by the abolition of private property and of labor itself.' [72] Elsewhere, Marx says the same thing: 'The communistic revolution is directed against the preceding *mode* of activity, does away with *labor.*' [73] And again, 'the question is not the liberation but the abolition of labor.' [74] The question is not the liberation of labor because labor has already been made 'free'; free labor is the achievement of capitalist society. Communism can cure the 'ills' of the bourgeois and the distress of the proletarian only 'by removing their cause, namely, "labor." ' [75]

[70] P. 26. [71] P. 25. [72] P. 49. [73] P. 69.
[74] *Sankt Max*, in the *Marx-Engels Gesamtausgabe*, op. cit., vol. v, p. 185.
[75] Ibid., p. 198.

These amazing formulations in Marx's earliest writings all contain the Hegelian term *Aufhebung,* so that abolition also carries the meaning that a content is restored to its true form. Marx, however, envisioned the future mode of labor to be so different from the prevailing one that he hesitated to use the same term 'labor' to designate alike the material process of capitalist and of communist society. He uses the term 'labor' to mean what capitalism actually understands by it in the last analysis, that activity which creates surplus value in commodity production, or, which 'produces capital.' [76] Other kinds of activity are not 'productive labor' and hence are not labor in the proper sense. Labor thus means that free and universal development is denied the individual who labors, and it is clear that in this state of affairs the liberation of the individual is at once the negation of labor.

An 'association of free individuals' to Marx is a society wherein the material process of production no longer determines the entire pattern of human life. Marx's idea of a rational society implies an order in which it is not the universality of labor but the universal satisfaction of all individual potentialities that constitutes the principle of social organization. He contemplates a society that gives to each not according to his work but his needs. Mankind becomes free only when the material perpetuation of life is a function of the abilities and happiness of associated individuals.

We can now see that the Marxian theory has developed a full contradiction to the basic conception of idealist philosophy. The idea of reason has been superseded by the idea of happiness. Historically, the first was interlaced into a society in which the intellectual forces of production were detached from the material ones. Within this

[76] *Theorien über den Mehrwert,* ed. Karl Kautsky, Stuttgart 1905, vol. I, pp. 258, 260 ff.

framework of social and economic iniquities, the life of reason was a life of higher dignity. It dictated individual sacrifice for the sake of some higher universal independent of the 'base' impulses and drives of individuals.

The idea of happiness, on the other hand, roots itself firmly in the demand for a social ordering that would set aside the class structure of society. Hegel had emphatically denied that the progress of reason would have anything to do with the satisfaction of individual happiness. Even the most advanced concepts of the Hegelian philosophy, as we have shown, preserved and in the last analysis condoned the negativity of the existing social system. Reason could prevail even though the reality shrieked of individual frustration: idealist culture and the technological progress of civil society bear witness of that. Happiness could not. The demand that free individuals attain satisfaction militated against the entire set-up of traditional culture. The Marxian theory consequently rejected even the advanced ideas of the Hegelian scheme. The category of happiness made manifest the positive content of materialism. Historical materialism appeared at first as a denunciation of the materialism prevalent in bourgeois society, and the materialist principle was in this respect a critical instrument of exposé directed against a society that enslaved men to the blind mechanisms of material production. The idea of the free and universal realization of individual happiness, *per contra,* denoted an *affirmative* materialism, that is to say, an affirmation of the material satisfaction of man.

We have dwelt rather extensively upon Marx's early writings because they emphasize tendencies that have been attenuated in the post-Marxian development of his critique of society, namely, the elements of communistic individualism, the repudiation of any fetishism concerning the socialization of the means of production or the growth of the productive forces, the subordination of all these factors to the idea of the free realization of the individual. Under all aspects, however, Marx's early writings are mere preliminary stages to his mature theory, stages that should not be overemphasized.

6. The Analysis of the Labor Process

Marx rests his theories on the assumption that the labor process determines the totality of human existence and thus gives to society its basic pattern. It now remains for him to give the exact analysis of this process. The early writings took labor to be the general form of man's struggle with nature. 'Labor is at first a process between man and nature, a process in which man mediates, regulates, and controls the material reactions between himself and nature by his own action.'[77] In this respect labor is basic to all forms of society.

The capitalistic ordering of labor is designated in Marx's early essays as 'alienation,' and hence as an 'unnatural,' degenerated form of labor. The question arises, how has such a degeneration become possible? And this is more than a *quaestio facti,* since alienated labor appears as a fact only in the light of its abolition. The analysis of the prevailing form of labor is simultaneously an analysis of the premises of its abolition.

In other words, Marx views the existing conditions of labor with an eye to their negation in an actually free society. His categories are negative and at the same time positive: they present a negative state of affairs in the light of its positive solution, revealing the true situation in existing society as the prelude to its passing into a new form. All the Marxian concepts extend, as it were, in these two dimensions, the first of which is the complex of

[77] *Capital,* op. cit., vol. I, p. 197 (our version).

given social relationships, and the second, the complex of elements inherent in the social reality that make for its transformation into a free social order. This twofold content determines Marx's entire analysis of the labor process. We shall now deal with the conclusions he draws.[78]

In the prevailing social system, labor produces commodities. Commodities are use-values to be exchanged on the market. Every product of labor is, as a commodity, exchangeable for every other product of labor. It has an exchange value that equates it with all other commodities. This universal homogeneity, by which all commodities are equated with all others, cannot be ascribed to the use-values of commodities, for, as use-values, they are exchanged only in so far as they are different from one another. Their exchange value, on the other hand, is a 'purely quantitative relation.' 'As exchange value, one kind of use-value is worth as much as another kind, if taken in the right proportion. The exchange value of a palace can be expressed in a certain number of boxes of shoe blacking. Vice versa, London manufacturers of shoe blacking have expressed the exchange value of their many boxes of blacking, in palaces. Thus, entirely apart from their natural forms, and without regard to the specific kind of wants for which they serve as use-values, commodities in certain quantities equal each other, take each other's place in exchange, pass as equivalents, and, in spite of their variegated appearance,' [79] are all of a piece. The reason for this homogeneity must be sought in the nature of labor.

All commodities are products of human labor; they are 'materialized [*vergegenständlichte*] labor.' As embodi-

[78] The fundamental tendencies of Marxian economic theory are best expounded by Henryk Grossmann in his *Das Akkumulations- und Zusammenbruchsgesetz des kapitalistischen Systems*, Leipzig 1929.

[79] *A Contribution to the Critique of Political Economy*, p. 21.

ments of social labor, 'all commodities are the crystallization of the same substance.'[80] At first this labor appears to be just as diversified as the use-values produced by it. Labor performed in the production of wheat is quite different from that used in the production of shoes or cannon. 'What in reality appears as a difference in use-values is, in the process of production, a difference in the work creating those use-values.'[81] If, then, the property common to all commodities is labor, it must be labor stripped of all qualitative distinctions. That would leave labor as the quantity of *labor-power* expended in the production of a good. This quantity is 'indifferent to the form, content, and individuality' of the labor; it is therefore ready for a purely quantitative measurement, equally applicable to all kinds of individual labor. The standard of such measurement is given by *time*. 'Just as the quantitative existence of motion is time, so the quantitative existence of labor is labor-time.' If all specificity of labor is abstracted, one act of labor is distinguished from another only by its duration. In this 'abstract, universal' form, labor represents the common property of all commodities that becomes constitutive of their exchange value. 'Labor creating exchange value is . . . *abstract, general labor.*'[82]

But even the time-measurement of labor still leaves an individual factor. The amount of labor-time spent by different workers in the production of one and the same kind of commodity varies according to their physical and mental condition and their technical equipment. These individual variations are cancelled in a further step of reduction. The labor-time is computed for the average technical standard prevailing in production, hence, the time that determines exchange value is 'socially necessary labor time.' The 'labor time contained in a commodity

[80] Ibid., p. 22. [81] P. 22. [82] P. 23.

is the labor-time *necessary* for its production, i.e. it is the labor-time which is required for the production of another specimen of the same commodity under the same general conditions of production.' [83]

Marx thus comes to the fact that the phenomenon of labor covers two entirely different kinds of labor: (1) *concrete specific labor,* correlative to concrete specific use-values (carpentry, shoemaking, agricultural labor, etc.) and (2) *abstract universal labor,* as expressed in the respective exchange values of commodities.[84] Every single act of labor in commodity production comprises both abstract and concrete labor—just as any product of social labor represents both exchange value and use-value. The social process of production, however, when it determines the value of commodities, sets aside the variety of concrete labor and retains as the standard of measurement the proportion of necessary abstract labor contained in a commodity.

Marx's conclusion that the value of commodities is determined by the quantity of abstract labor socially necessary for their reproduction is the fundamental thesis of his *labor theory of value.* It is introduced not as a theorem, but as the description of a historical process. The reduction of concrete to abstract labor 'appears to be an abstraction, but it is an abstraction that takes place daily in the social process of production.' [85] Since it is the theoretical conception of a historical process, the labor theory of value cannot be developed in the manner of a pure theory.

It is a well-known fact that Marx considered the discovery of the twofold character of labor to be his original contribution to economic theory, and to be pivotal for a clear comprehension of political economy.[86] His distinc-

[83] P. 26. [84] P. 33. [85] P. 24. [86] *Capital,* vol. I, p. 48.

tion between concrete and abstract labor allows him insights to which the conceptual apparatus of classical political economy was necessarily blind. The classical economists designated 'labor' as the sole source of all social wealth, and overlooked the fact that it is only abstract, universal labor that *creates* value in a commodity-producing society, while concrete particular labor merely preserves and transfers already existing values. In the production of cotton, spinning, for example, the concrete activity of the individual worker merely transfers the value of the means of production to the product. His concrete activity does not increase the value of the product. The product, however, does appear on the market with a new value in addition to that of the means of production. This new value results from the fact that a certain quantity of abstract labor-power, that is, labor-power irrespective of concrete form, has been added in the process of production to the object of labor. Since the worker does not do double work in the same time, the double result (preservation of value and the creation of new value) can be explained only by the dual character of his labor. 'By the simple addition of a certain quantity of labor, new value is added, and by the quality of this added labor, the original values of the means of production are preserved in the product.' [87]

The process in which labor-power becomes an abstract quantitative unit characterizes a 'specifically *social* form of labor' to be distinguished from that form which is 'the *natural* condition of human existence,' [88] namely, labor as productive activity directed to the adaptation of nature. This specifically social form of labor is that prevalent in capitalism.

Under capitalism, labor produces commodities, that is,

[87] Ibid., p. 223.
[88] *A Contribution to the Critique of Political Economy*, p. 33.

the products of labor appear as exchange values. But how does this system of universal commodity production, which is not directly oriented to the satisfaction of individual needs, tend to fulfill these needs? How do the independent producers know that they produce actual *use-values?*

Use-values are means for the gratification of human wants. Since every form of society must satisfy the needs of its members in some degree, in order to maintain their lives, 'the use-value of things remains a prerequisite' to commodity production. Under the commodity system, the individual's need is a fraction of the 'social need' made manifest on the market. The distribution of use-values takes place according to the social distribution of labor. The satisfaction of a demand presupposes that the use-values are available on the market, while the latter will appear on the market only if society is willing to devote a portion of its labor-time to producing them. A certain amount of production and consumption goods is required to reproduce and maintain society at its prevailing level. 'The social need, that is the use-value on a social scale, appears here as a determining factor for the amount of social labor which is to be supplied by the various particular spheres' of production.[89] A definite quota of labor-time is spent in the production of machines, buildings, roads, textiles, wheat, cannon, perfumes, etc. Marx says that 'society' allots the available labor-time needed for these. Society, however, is not a conscious subject. Capitalist society provides for no complete association or planning. How, then, does it distribute labor-time to various types of production in accordance with social needs?

The individual is 'free.' No authority may tell him how he is to maintain himself; everyone may choose to work at what he pleases. One individual may decide to produce

[89] *Capital*, vol. III, p. 745.

shoes, another books, a third rifles, a fourth golden buttons. But the goods each produces are commodities, that is, use-values not for himself but for other individuals. Each must exchange his products for the other use-values that will satisfy his own needs. In other words, the satisfaction of his own needs presupposes that his own products fill a social need. But he cannot know this in advance. Only when he brings the products of his labor to the market will he learn whether or not he expended *social* labor-time. The exchange value of his goods will show him whether or not they satisfy a social need. If he can sell them at or above his production cost, society was willing to allot a quantum of its labor-time to their production; otherwise, he wasted or did not spend socially necessary labor-time. The exchange value of his commodities decides his social fate. The 'form in which this proportional distribution of labor operates, in a state of society where the interconnection of social labor is manifested in the *private exchange* of the individual products of labor, is precisely the exchange value of these products,' [90] and thus determines the proportional fulfillment of the social need.

Marx calls this mechanism by which the commodity producing society distributes the labor-time at its disposal among the different branches of production the *law of value*. The different branches that have been made independent in the development of modern society are integrated through the market, where the exchange value of the commodities produced yields the measure of the social need they satisfy.

The supplying of society with use-values is thus governed by the law of value, which has superseded the freedom of the individual. He depends, for the gratification

[90] Marx, *Letters to Dr. Kugelmann,* International Publishers, New York 1934, July 11, 1868 (pp. 73-4).

of his needs, on the market, for he buys the means for this gratification in the form of exchange values. And he finds the exchange values of the goods he desires to be a pre-given quantity over which he, as an individual, has no power whatever.

Moreover, the social need that appears on the market is not identical with the real need, but only with 'solvent social need.' The various demands are conditional upon the buying power of the individuals, and therefore, upon 'the mutual relations of the different social classes and their relative economic position.' [91] The individual's desires and wants are shaped and, with the vast majority, restricted by the situation of the class to which he belongs, in such a way that he cannot express his real need. Marx summarizes this state of affairs when he says: 'The *need for commodities on the market,* the demand, differs quantitatively from the *actual social need.*' [92]

Even if the market were to manifest the actual social need, the law of value would continue to operate as a blind mechanism outside the conscious control of individuals. It would continue to exert the pressure of a 'natural law' (*Naturgesetz*),[93] the necessity of which, far from precluding, would rather insure the rule of chance over society. The system of relating independent individuals to one another through the necessary labor-time contained in the commodities they exchange may seem to be one of utmost rationality. In reality, however, this system organizes only waste and disproportion.

Society buys the articles which it demands by devoting to their production a portion of its available labor-time. That means, society buys them by spending a definite quantity of the labor-time over which it disposes. That part of society, to which the division of labor assigns the task of employing its

[91] *Capital,* vol. III, p. 214. [92] Ibid., p. 223.
[93] *Letters to Kugelmann,* July 11, 1868.

labor in the production of the desired article, must be given an equivalent for it of other social labor, incorporated in articles which *it* wants. There is, however, no necessary, but only an accidental, connection between the volume of society's demand for a certain article and the volume represented by the production of this article in the total production, or the quantity of social labor spent on this article . . . True, every individual article, or every definite quantity of any kind of commodities, contains, perhaps, only the social labor required for its production, and from this point of view the market-value of this entire mass of commodities of a certain kind represents only necessary labor. Nevertheless, if this commodity has been produced in excess of the temporary demand of society for it, so much of the social labor has been wasted, and in that case this mass of commodities represents a much smaller quantity of labor on the market than is actually incorporated in it.[94]

From the point of view of the individual, the law of value asserts itself only *ex post;* waste of labor is inevitable. The market provides a correction and a punishment for individual freedom; any deviation from the socially necessary labor-time means defeat in the economic competitive struggle through which men maintain their lives in this social order.

The guiding question of Marx's analysis was, How does capitalist society supply its members with the necessary use-values? And the answer disclosed a process of blind necessity, chance, anarchy and frustration. The introduction of the category of use-value was the introduction of a forgotten factor, forgotten, that is, by the classical political economy which was occupied only with the phenomenon of exchange value. In the Marxian theory, this factor becomes an instrument that cuts through the mystifying reification of the commodity world. For, restoration of the category of use-value to the center of economic

[94] *Capital,* vol. III, pp. 220-21.

analysis means a sharp questioning of the economic process as to whether and how it fills the real needs of individuals. Behind the exchange-relations of capitalism it shows the actual human relations, warped to a 'negative totality' and ordered by uncontrolled economic laws.[95] Marx's analysis showed him the law of value as the general 'form of Reason' in the existent social system. The law of value was the form in which the common interest (the perpetuation of society) asserted itself through individual freedom. That law, though it manifested itself on the market, was seen to originate in the process of production (the socially necessary labor-time that lay at its root was production time). For this reason, it was only an analysis of the process of production that would yield a yes or no answer to the question, Can this society ever fulfill its promise: individual liberty within a rational whole?

Marx's analysis of capitalist production assumes that capitalist society has actually emancipated the individual, that men enter the productive process free and equal, and that the process turns from its own inner rationale. Marx grants the most favorable conditions to civil society, disregards all complicating disturbances. The abstractions that underlie the first volume of *Capital* (for example, that all commodities are exchanged according to their values, that external trade is excluded, etc.) put the reality so that it 'conforms with its notion.'[96] This methodological procedure is in keeping with the dialectical conception. The inadequacy between existence and essence belongs to the very core of reality. If the analysis were to confine itself

[95] When Marx declares that use-values lie outside the scope of economic theory, he is at first describing the actual state of affairs in classical political economy. His own analysis begins by accepting and explaining the fact that, in capitalism, use-values appear only as the 'material depositories of exchange value' (op. cit., vol. I, p. 43). His critique then refutes the capitalist treatment of use-values and sets its goal on an economy in which this relation is entirely abolished.

[96] See e.g. *Capital*, vol. III, pp. 169, 206, 223.

to the forms in which reality appears, it could not grasp the essential structure from which these forms and their inadequacy originate. Unfolding the essence of capitalism requires that provisional abstraction be made from those phenomena that might be attributed to a contingent and imperfect form of capitalism.

From the beginning, Marx's analysis takes capitalist production as a historical totality. The capitalist mode of production is a specifically historical form of commodity production that originated under the conditions of 'primary accumulation,' such as the wholesale expulsion of peasants from their land, the transformation of arable soil into pasture in order to furnish wool for a rising textile industry, the accumulation of large pools of wealth through the plunder of new colonies, the breakdown of the guild system when it met the power of the merchant and industrialist. There arose in the process the modern laborer, freed of all dependence on feudal lords and guild masters, but likewise cut off from the means and instruments through which he might utilize his labor-power for his own ends.[97] He was free to sell his labor-power to those who held these means and instruments, to those who owned the soil, the materials of labor, and the proper means of production. Labor-power and the means for its material realization became commodities possessed by different owners. This process took place in the fifteenth and sixteenth centuries and resulted, with the universal expansion of commodity production, in a new stratification of society. Two main classes faced each other: the beneficiaries of primary accumulation and the impoverished masses deprived of their previous means of subsistence.

They were really emancipated. The 'natural' and personal dependencies of the feudal order had been abol-

[97] Vol. I, pp. 632-3.

ished. 'The exchange of commodities of itself implies no other relations of dependence than those which result from its own nature.'[98] Everyone was free to exchange the commodities he owned. The first group exercised this freedom when it used its wealth to appropriate and utilize the means of production, whereas the masses enjoyed the freedom of selling the only good left to them, namely, their labor-power.

The primary conditions of capitalism were herewith at hand: free wage labor and private property in the means of commodity production. From this point on, capitalist production could go its course entirely under its own power. Commodities are exchanged by the free will of their owners who enter the market free of all external compulsion, in the full joy of knowledge that their commodities will exchange as equivalents, and that perfect justice will prevail. Also, the exchange value of every commodity is determined by the necessary labor-time required for its production; and the measurement of this labor-time is apparently the most impartial social standard. What is more, production starts with a free contract. One party sells his labor-power to the other. The labor-time necessary for the production of this labor-power is the labor-time that goes into making enough commodities to reproduce the worker's existence. The buyer pays the price of this commodity. Nothing interferes with the perfect justice of the labor contract; both parties are treated equally as free commodity owners. They 'deal with each other as on the basis of equal rights, with this difference alone, that one is buyer, the other seller; both, therefore, equal in the eyes of the law.' The labor contract, the basis of capitalist production, is ostensibly the realization of freedom, equality, and justice.

[98] Vol. I, p. 186.

But labor-power is a peculiar kind of commodity. It is the only commodity whose use-value it is to be *'a source not only of value, but of more value than it has itself.'* [99] This 'surplus value,' created by the abstract universal labor hidden behind its concrete form, falls to the buyer of labor-power without any equivalent, since it does not appear as an independent commodity. The value of the labor-power sold to the capitalist is replaced in *part* of the time the laborer actually works; the rest of this time goes unpaid. Marx's statement of the way surplus value arises may be summarized in the following argument: that the production of the commodity, labor-power, requires part of a labor day, whereas the laborer really works a full day. The value paid by the capitalist is part of the actual value of the labor-power in use, while the other part of the latter is appropriated by the capitalist without remuneration. This argument, however, if isolated from Marx's entire conception of labor, retains an accidental element. Actually, Marx's presentation of the production of surplus value is intrinsically connected with his analysis of the twofold character of labor and must be interpreted in the light of this phenomenon.

The capitalist pays the exchange value of the commodity, labor-power, and buys its use-value, namely, labor. 'The value of labor-power, and the value which that labor-power creates in the labor process, are two entirely different magnitudes.' [100] The capitalist puts the labor-power he bought to work at the machinery of production. The labor process contains both an objective and a subjective factor: the means of production on the one hand and labor-power on the other. The analysis of the twofold character of labor has shown that the objective factor creates no new value—the value of the means of production

[99] P. 216. [100] Pp. 215-16.

simply reappears in the product. 'It is otherwise with the subjective factor of the labor process, with labor-power in action. While the laborer, by virtue of his labor being of a specialized kind that has a special object (*durch die zweckmässige Form der Arbeit*), preserves and transfers to the product the value of the means of production, he at the same time, by the mere act of working, creates each instant an additional or new value.'[101] The quality of preserving value by adding new value is, as it were, a 'natural gift' of labor-power, 'which costs the laborer nothing, but which is very advantageous to the capitalist.'[102] This property possessed by abstract, universal labor, hidden behind its concrete forms, though it is the sole source of new value, itself has no proper value. The labor contract thus necessarily involves exploitation.

The twofold character of labor, then, is the condition that makes surplus value possible. By virtue of the fact that labor has this dual form, the private appropriation of labor-power inevitably leads to exploitation. The result issues from the very nature of labor whenever labor-power becomes a commodity.

For labor-power to become a commodity, however, there must be 'free' labor: the individual must be free to sell his labor-power to him who is free and able to buy it. The labor contract epitomizes this freedom, equality, and justice for civil society. This historical form of freedom, equality, and justice is thus the very condition of exploitation. Marx summarizes the whole in a striking paragraph:

> [The area] within whose boundaries the sale and purchase of labor-power goes on, is in fact a very Eden of the innate rights of man. There alone rule Freedom, Equality, Property and Bentham. Freedom, because both buyer and seller of a commodity, say of labor-power, are constrained only by their

101 P. 231.

102 P. 230.

own free will. They contract as free agents, and the agreement they come to, is but the form in which they give legal expression to their common will. Equality, because each enters into relation with the other, as with a simple owner of commodities, and they exchange equivalent for equivalent. Property, because each disposes only of what is his own. And Bentham, because each looks only to himself. The only force that brings them together and puts them in relation with each other, is the selfishness, the gain and the private interests of each. Each looks to himself only, and no one troubles himself about the rest, and just because they do so, do they all, in accordance with the pre-established harmony of things, or under the auspices of an all-shrewd providence, work together to their mutual advantage, for the common weal and in the interest of all.[108]

The labor contract, from which Marx derives the essential connection between freedom and exploitation, is the fundamental pattern for all relations in civil society. Labor is the way men develop their abilities and needs in the struggle with nature and history, and the social frame impressed on labor is the historical form of life mankind has bestowed upon itself. The implications of the free labor contract lead Marx to see that labor produces and perpetuates its own exploitation. In other words, in the continuing process of capitalist society, freedom produces and perpetuates its own opposite. The analysis is in this wise an immanent critique of individual freedom as it originates in capitalist society and as it develops *pari passu* with the development of capitalism. The economic forces of capitalism, left to their devices, create enslavement, poverty, and the intensity of class conflicts. The truth of this form of freedom is thus its negation.

'Living' labor, labor-power, is the only factor that increases the value of the product of labor beyond the value of the means of production. This increase in value trans-

[108] P. 195.

forms the products of labor into components of capital. Labor, therefore, produces not only its own exploitation, but also the means for this exploitation, namely, capital.[104]

Capital, on the other hand, requires that the surplus value be converted anew into capital. If the capitalist were to consume his surplus value instead of reinvesting it in the process of production, the latter would cease to yield him any profit, and the incentive of commodity production would vanish. 'Accumulation resolves itself into the reproduction of capital on a progressively increasing scale,' [105] and this in turn is rendered possible only by a progressively increasing utilization of labor-power for commodity production. Capitalist production on a progressively increasing scale is identical with exploitation developing on the same scale. The accumulation of capital means growing impoverishment of the masses, 'increase of the proletariat.' [106]

With all these negative features, capitalism develops the productive forces at a rapid pace. The inherent requirements of capital demand that surplus value be increased through increase in the productivity of labor (rationalization and intensification). But technological advance diminishes the quantity of living labor (the subjective factor) used in the productive process, in proportion to the quantity of the means of production (the objective factor). The objective factor increases as the subjective factor decreases. This change in the technical composition of capital is reflected in the change of its 'value-composition': the value of labor-power diminishes as the value of the means of production increases. The net result is an increase in 'the organic composition of capital.' With the progress of production goes an increase in the mass of capital in the hands of individual capitalists. The weaker

104 P. 633. 105 P. 636. 106 P. 673.

is expropriated by the stronger in the competitive struggle, and capital becomes centralized in an ever smaller circle of capitalists. Free individual competition of the liberalist stamp is transformed into monopolist competition among giant enterprises. On the other hand, the increasing organic composition of capital tends to decrease the *rate* of capitalist profit, since the utilization of labor-power, the sole source of surplus value, diminishes in ratio to the means of production employed.

The danger of the falling rate of profit aggravates the competitive struggle as well as the class struggle: political methods of exploitation supplement the economic ones, which slowly reach their limit. The requirement that capital be utilized, that there be production for production's sake, leads, even under ideal conditions, to inevitable disproportions between the two spheres of production, that of production goods and that of consumption goods, resulting in constant overproduction.[107] The profitable investment of capital becomes increasingly difficult. The struggle for new markets plants the seed of constant international warfare.

We have just summarized some of the decisive conclusions of Marx's analysis of the laws of capitalism. The picture is that of a social order that progresses through the development of the contradictions inherent in it. Still, it progresses, and these contradictions are the very means through which occur a tremendous growth in the productivity of labor, an all-embracing use and mastery of natural resources, and a loosing of hitherto unknown capacities and needs among men. Capitalist society is a union of contradictions. It gets freedom through exploitation, wealth through impoverishment, advance in production through restriction of consumption. The very structure

[107] Cf. Henryk Grossmann, op. cit., pp. 179 ff.

of capitalism is a dialectical one: every form and institution of the economic process begets its determinate negation, and the crisis is the extreme form in which the contradictions are expressed.

The law of value, which governs the social contradictions, has the force of a natural necessity. 'Only as an internal law, and from the point of view of the individual agents as a blind law, does the law of value exert its influence here and maintain the social equilibrium of production in the turmoil of its accidental fluctuations.' [108] The results are of the same blind sort. The falling rate of profit inherent in the capitalist mechanism undermines the very foundations of the system and builds the wall beyond which capitalist production cannot advance. The contrast between the abundant wealth and power of a few and the perpetual poverty of the mass becomes increasingly sharper. The highest development of the productive forces coincides with oppression and misery in full flood. The real possibility of general happiness is negated by the social relationships posited by man himself. The negation of this society and its transformation become the single outlook for liberation.

7. The Marxian Dialectic

We may now attempt to summarize the qualities that distinguish the Marxian from the Hegelian dialectic. We have emphasized that Marx's dialectical conception of reality was originally motivated by the same datum as Hegel's, namely, by the negative character of reality. In the social world, this negativity carried forward the contradictions of class society and thus remained the motor of the social process. Every single fact and condition was

[108] *Capital,* vol. III, p. 1026.

drawn into this process so that its significance could be grasped only when seen in this totality to which it belonged. For Marx, as for Hegel, 'the truth' lies only in the whole, the 'negative totality.'

However, the social world becomes a negative totality only in the process of an *abstraction,* which is imposed upon the dialectical method by the structure of its subject matter, capitalist society. We may even say that the abstraction is capitalism's own work, and that the Marxian method only follows this process. Marx's analysis has shown that capitalist economy is built upon and perpetuated by the constant reduction of concrete to abstract labor. This economy step by step retreats from the concrete of human activity and needs, and achieves the integration of individual activities and needs only through a complex of abstract relations in which individual work counts merely in so far as it represents socially necessary labor-time, and in which the relations among men appear as relations of things (commodities). The commodity world is a 'falsified' and 'mystified' world, and its critical analysis must first follow the abstractions which make up this world, and must then take its departure from these abstract relations in order to arrive at their real content. The second step is thus the abstraction from the abstraction, or the abandonment of a false concreteness, so that the true concreteness might be restored. Accordingly, the Marxian theory elaborates first the abstract relations that determine the commodity world (such as commodity, exchange value, money, wages) and returns from them to the fully developed content of capitalism (the structural tendencies of the capitalist world that lead to its destruction).

We have said that for Marx, as well as for Hegel, the truth lies only in the negative totality. However, the totality in which the Marxian theory moves is other than that of Hegel's philosophy, and this difference indicates the decisive difference between Hegel's and Marx's dialectics. For Hegel, the totality was the totality of reason, a closed ontological system, finally identical with the rational system of history. Hegel's dialectical process was thus a universal ontological one in which history was patterned on the metaphysical process of being. Marx, on the other hand, detached dialectic from this ontological base. In his work, the negativity of reality becomes a *historical* condition which cannot be hypostatized as a metaphysical state of affairs. In other words, it becomes a social condition, associated with a particular historical form of society. The totality that the Marxian dialectic gets to is the totality of class society, and the negativity that underlies its contradictions and shapes its every content is the negativity of class relations. The dialectical totality again includes nature, but only in so far as the latter enters and conditions the historical process of social reproduction. In the progress of class society, this reproduction assumes various forms at the various levels of its development, and these are the framework of all the dialectical concepts.

The dialectical method has thus of its very nature become a historical method. The dialectical principle is not a general principle equally applicable to any subject matter. To be sure, every fact whatever can be subjected to a dialectical analysis, for example, a glass of water, as in Lenin's famous discussion.[109] But all such analyses would lead into the structure of the socio-historical process and show it to be constitutive in the facts under analysis. The dialectic takes facts as elements of a definite historical totality from which they cannot be isolated. In his reference to the example of a glass of water, Lenin states that 'the whole of human practice must enter the "definition"

[109] *Selected Works,* New York 1934, International Publishers, vol. IX, p. 62 ff.

of the object'; the independent objectivity of the glass of water is thus dissolved. Every fact can be subjected to dialectical analysis only in so far as every fact is influenced by the antagonisms of the social process.

The historical character of the Marxian dialectic embraces the prevailing negativity as well as its negation. The given state of affairs is negative and can be rendered positive only by liberating the possibilities immanent in it. This last, the negation of the negation, is accomplished by establishing a new order of things. The negativity and its negation are two different phases of the same historical process, straddled by man's historical action. The 'new' state is *the truth* of the old, but that truth does not steadily and automatically grow out of the earlier state; it can be set free only by an autonomous act on the part of men, that will cancel the whole of the existing negative state. Truth, in short, is not a realm apart from historical reality, nor a region of eternally valid ideas. To be sure, it transcends the given historical reality, but only in so far as it crosses from one historical stage to another. The negative state as well as its negation is a concrete event within the same totality.

The Marxian dialectic is a historical method in still another sense: it deals with a *particular stage* of the historical process. Marx criticizes Hegel's dialectic for generalizing the dialectical movement into a movement of all being, of being-as-such, and getting therefore merely 'the abstract, logical, speculative expression of the movement of history.'[110] Moreover, the movement to which Hegel gave such abstract expression, and which he thought was general, actually characterizes only a particular phase of man's history, namely, 'the history of his maturing' (*Entstehungsgeschichte*).[111] Marx's distinction between the

110 'Ökonomisch-philosophische Manuskripte,' op. cit., pp. 152-3.
111 Ibid., p. 153.

history of this maturing and the 'actual history' of mankind amounts to a delimitation of the dialectic. The *Entstehungsgeschichte* of mankind, which Marx calls his prehistory, is the history of class society. Man's *actual* history will begin when this society has been abolished. The Hegelian dialectic gives the *abstract logical* form of the pre-historical development, the Marxian dialectic its *real concrete* movement. Marx's dialectic, therefore, is still bound up with the pre-historical phase.

The negativity with which Marxian dialectic begins is that characterizing human existence in class society; the antagonisms that intensify this negativity and eventually abolish it are the antagonisms of class society. It is of the very essence of the Marxian dialectic to imply that, with the transition from the pre-history represented by class society to the history of classless society, the entire structure of historical movement will change. Once mankind has become the conscious subject of its development, its history can no longer be outlined in forms that apply to the prehistorical phase.

Marx's dialectical method still reflects the sway of blind economic forces over the course of society. The dialectical analysis of social reality in terms of its inherent contradictions and their resolution shows this reality to be overpowered by objective mechanisms that operate with the necessity of 'natural' (physical) laws—only thus can the contradiction be the ultimate force that keeps society moving. The movement is dialectical in itself inasmuch as it is not yet piloted by the self-conscious activity of freely associated individuals. The dialectical laws are the developed knowledge of the 'natural' laws of society, and therefore a step towards their annulment, but they are still a knowledge of 'natural' laws. To be sure, the struggle with the 'realm of necessity' will continue with man's passage to the stage of his 'actual history,' and the negativity and the contradiction will not disappear. Nevertheless, when society has become the free subject of this struggle, the latter will be waged in entirely different forms. For this reason, it is not permissible to impose the dialectical structure of pre-history upon the future history of mankind.

The concept that definitely connects Marx's dialectic with the history of class society is the concept of *necessity*. The dialectical laws are *necessary* laws; the various forms of class society *necessarily* perish from their inner contradictions. The laws of capitalism work with 'iron necessity towards inevitable results,' Marx says. This necessity does not, however, apply to the positive transformation of capitalist society. It is true, Marx assumed that the same mechanisms that bring about the concentration and centralization of capital also produce 'the socialization of labor.' 'Capitalist production begets, with the inexorability of a law of Nature, its own negation,' namely, property based 'on co-operation and the possession in common of the land and of the means of production.' [112] Nevertheless, it would be a distortion of the entire significance of Marxian theory to argue from the inexorable necessity that governs the development of capitalism to a similar necessity in the matter of transformation to socialism. When capitalism is negated, social processes no longer stand under the rule of blind natural laws. This is precisely what distinguishes the nature of the new from the old. The transition from capitalism's inevitable death to socialism is necessary, but only in the sense that the full development of the individual is necessary. The new social union of individuals, again, is necessary, but only in the sense that it is necessary to use available productive forces for the general satisfaction of all individuals. It is the realization of freedom and happiness that necessitates

[112] *Capital*, op. cit., vol. I, p. 837.

L*

the establishment of an order wherein associated individuals will determine the organization of their life. We have already emphasized that the qualities of the future society are reflected in the current forces that are driving towards its realization. There can be no blind necessity in tendencies that terminate in a free and self-conscious society. The negation of capitalism begins within capitalism itself, but even in the phases that precede revolution there is active the rational spontaneity that will animate the post-revolutionary phases. The revolution depends indeed upon a totality of objective conditions: it requires a certain attained level of material and intellectual culture, a self-conscious and organized working class on an international scale, acute class struggle. These become revolutionary conditions, however, only if seized upon and directed by a conscious activity that has in mind the socialist goal. Not the slightest natural necessity or automatic inevitability guarantees the transition from capitalism to socialism.

Capitalism has itself extended the scope and power of rational practices to a considerable degree. The 'natural laws' that make capitalism work have been counteracted by tendencies of another kind, which have retarded the effect of the necessary processes and thereby protracted the life of the capitalist order.[113] Capitalism has been subjected in certain areas to large-scale political and administrative regulations. Planning, for example, is not an exclusive feature of socialist society.[114] The natural necessity of the social laws Marx expounded implied the possibility of such planning under capitalism, when they referred to an interplay of order and chance, of conscious action and blind mechanisms. The possibility of rational planning under capitalism does not, of course, impair the validity of

[113] Ibid., vol. III, pp. 272-81.
[114] *Critique of the Gotha Program*, 1891, New York 1938.

the fundamental laws that Marx discovered in this system —the system is destined to perish by virtue of these laws. But the process might involve a long period of barbarism. The latter can be prevented only by free action. The revolution requires the maturity of many forces, but the greatest among them is the subjective force, namely, the revolutionary class itself.[115] The realization of freedom and reason requires the free rationality of those who achieve it.

Marxian theory is, then, incompatible with fatalistic determinism. True, historical materialism involves the determinist principle that consciousness is conditioned by social existence. We have attempted to show, however, that the necessary dependence enunciated by this principle applies to the 'pre-historical' life, namely, to the life of class society. The relations of production that restrict and distort man's potentialities inevitably determine his consciousness, precisely because society is not a free and conscious subject. As long as man is incapable of dominating these relations and using them to gratify the needs and desires of the whole, they will assume the form of an objective, independent entity. Consciousness, caught in and overpowered by these relations, necessarily becomes *ideological.*

Of course, the consciousness of men will continue to be determined by the material processes that reproduce their society, even when men have come to regulate their social relations in such a way that these contribute best to the free development of all. But when these material processes have been made rational and have become the conscious work of men, the blind dependence of consciousness on social conditions will cease to exist. Reason, when determined by rational social conditions, is determined by itself. Socialist freedom embraces both sides of

[115] *The Poverty of Philosophy*, trans. H. Quelch, Chicago 1910, p. 190.

the relation between consciousness and social existence. The principle of historical materialism leads to its self-negation.

The labor process, which shows forth as fundamental in the Marxian analysis of capitalism and its genesis, is the ground on which the various branches of theory and practice operate in capitalist society. An understanding of the labor process, therefore, is at the same time an understanding of the source for the separation between theory and practice, and of the element that re-establishes their interconnection. Marxian theory is of its very nature an integral and integrating theory of society. The economic process of capitalism exercises a totalitarian influence over all theory and all practice, and an economic analysis that shatters the capitalist camouflage and breaks through its 'reification' will get down to the subsoil common to all theory and practice in this society.

Marxian economics leaves no room for an independent philosophy, psychology, or sociology. 'Morality, religion, metaphysics, all the rest of ideology and their corresponding forms of consciousness, thus no longer retain the semblance of independence . . . When reality is depicted, philosophy, as an independent branch of activity loses its medium of existence. At the best its place can only be taken by a summing-up of the most general results, abstractions which arise from the observation of the historical development of men.' [116]

With the separation of theory from practice, philosophy became the sanctuary of true theory. Science was either pressed 'into the service of capital' [117] or degraded to the position of a leisurely pastime remote from any concern

[116] *The German Ideology*, pp. 14-15.
[117] *Capital*, vol. I, p. 397.

with the actual struggles of mankind, while philosophy undertook in the medium of abstract thought to guard the solutions to man's problem of needs, fears, and desires. 'Pure Reason,' reason purified of empirical contingencies, became the proper realm of truth.

Towards the conclusion of his *Critique of Pure Reason,* Kant raises the three questions with which human reason is most vitally concerned: How can I know? What shall I do? What may I hope? These questions and the attempts at their solution indeed comprise the very core of philosophy, its concern for the essential potentialities of man amid the deprivations of reality. Hegel had placed this philosophic concern in the historical context of his time, so that it became manifest that Kant's questions led into the actual historical process. Man's knowledge, activity, and hope were referred in the direction of establishing a rational society. Marx set out to demonstrate the concrete forces and tendencies that prevented and those that promoted this goal. The material connection of his theory with a definite historical form of practice negated not only philosophy but sociology as well. The social facts that Marx analyzed (for example, the alienation of labor, the fetishism of the commodity world, surplus value, exploitation) are not akin to sociological facts, such as divorces, crimes, shifts in population, and business cycles. The fundamental relations of the Marxian categories are not within the reach of sociology or of any science that is preoccupied with describing and organizing the objective *phenomena* of society. They will appear as facts only to a theory that takes them in the preview of their negation. According to Marx, the correct theory is the consciousness of a practice that aims at changing the world.

Marx's concept of truth, however, is far from relativism. There is only one truth and one practice capable of realizing it. Theory has demonstrated the tendencies that make for the attainment of a rational order of life, the conditions for creating this, and the initial steps to be taken. The final aim of the new social practice has been formulated: the abolition of labor, the employment of the socialized means of production for the free development of all individuals. The rest is the task of man's own liberated activity. Theory accompanies the practice at every moment, analyzing the changing situation and formulating its concepts accordingly. The concrete conditions for realizing the truth may vary, but the truth remains the same and theory remains its ultimate guardian. Theory will preserve the truth even if revolutionary practice deviates from its proper path. Practice follows the truth, not vice versa.

This absolutism of truth completes the philosophical heritage of the Marxian theory and once for all separates dialectical theory from the subsequent forms of positivism and relativism.

II

The Foundations of Positivism and the Rise of Sociology

1. Positive and Negative Philosophy

In the decade following Hegel's death, European thought entered an era of 'positivism.' This positivism announced itself as the system of *positive philosophy,* taking a form quite different from that which later positivism assumed. Comte's *Cours de philosophie positive* was published between 1830 and 1842, Stahl's positive philosophy of the state between 1830 and 1837, and Schelling began in 1841 his Berlin lectures on the *positive Philosophie* that he had been elaborating ever since 1827.

While there can be no doubt about Comte's contribution to positivism (Comte himself derived the positivistic method from the foundations of positive philosophy), it may seem preposterous to relate Schelling's and Stahl's positive philosophy to that movement. Was Schelling not an exponent of metaphysics in its most transcendent form, and did Stahl not expound a religious theory of the state? True, Stahl is recognized as a representative of positivism in legal philosophy, but what has Schelling's philosophy of mythology and revelation—which furnished some basic concepts for Stahl's doctrine—to do with positivism?

We find, however, in Schelling's *Philosophie der Offenbarung* the opinion that the traditional metaphysics, since it was occupied only with the notion of things and their pure essence, could not get at their actual existence and thus could not provide real knowledge. In contrast, Schelling's philosophy aims at the truly actual and existent, and by that token claims to be 'positive.' He raises the question whether the rationalistic metaphysics was not a purely 'negative' philosophy, and whether, following Kant's destruction of this metaphysics, 'the positive should not now organize itself, free and independent of the former, into a science of its own.'[1] Moreover, in 1827, at the conclusion of his lectures on the history of modern philosophy, Schelling undertook to justify the emphasis laid upon experience by the British and French philosophers and defended this empiricism against its German foes. He went so far as to declare that, 'if we had only a choice between empiricism and the oppressive apriorism [*Denknotwendigkeiten*] of an extreme rationalism, no free mind would hesitate to decide for empiricism.'[2] He ended by stating that the great task German philosophy would have would be to overcome aprioristic metaphysics through a 'positive system,' which would finally transform philosophy into a true 'science of experience.'

In its fundamental aspects, Schelling's positive philosophy is certainly greatly different from Comte's. The 'positives,' to Comte, are the matters of fact of observation, while Schelling stresses that 'experience' is not limited to the facts of outer and inner sense. Comte is oriented to physical science and to the necessary laws that govern all reality, while Schelling attempts to expound a 'philosophy of freedom' and maintains that free creative activity is the ultimate matter of fact of experience. Nevertheless, despite these essential differences, there is a common tendency in both philosophies to counter the sway of apriorism and to restore the authority of experience.[3]

[1] Schelling, *Sämmtliche Werke*, sect. 2, vol. III, Stuttgart 1858, p. 83.
[2] Ibid., sect. 1, vol. x. Stuttgart 1861, p. 198.
[3] Constantin Frantz, a leading German conservative political philosopher, already recognized in 1880 that the 'positivistic school in France' and Schelling's positive philosophy 'are, in a certain sense, directed to the same end' (*Schelling's positive Philosophie*, Cöthen 1880, Part III, p. 277).

This common tendency might best be understood by considering what the new positive philosophy was directed against. Positive philosophy was a conscious reaction against the critical and destructive tendencies of French and German rationalism, a reaction that was particularly bitter in Germany. Because of its critical tendencies, the Hegelian system was designated as *'negative philosophy.'* Its contemporaries recognized that the principles Hegel enunciated in his philosophy led him 'to a critique of everything that was hitherto held to be the objective truth.'[4] His philosophy 'negated'—namely, it repudiated any irrational and unreasonable reality. The reaction saw a challenge to the existing order in Hegel's attempt to measure reality according to the standards of autonomous reason. Negative philosophy, it was claimed, tries for the potentialities of things, but is incapable of knowing their reality. It stops short at their 'logical forms' and never reaches their actual content, which is not deducible from these forms. As a result, so the critique of Hegel ran, the negative philosophy can neither explain nor justify things as they are. This led to the most fundamental objection of all, that negative philosophy, because of its conceptual make-up, 'negates' things as they are. The matters of fact that make up the given state of affairs, when viewed in the light of reason, become negative, limited, transitory—they become perishing forms within a comprehensive process that leads beyond them. The Hegelian dialectic was seen as the prototype of all destructive negations of the given, for in it every immediately given form passes into its opposite and attains its true content only by so doing. This kind of philosophy, the critics said, denies to the given the dignity of the real; it contains 'the principle of revolution' (Stahl said). Hegel's statement that the real is

[4] Moses Hess, 'Gegenwärtige Krisis der deutschen Philosophie,' 1841, in *Sozialistiche Aufsätze,* Berlin 1921, pp. 9, 11.

rational was understood to mean that only the rational is real.

Positive philosophy made its counter-attack against critical rationalism on two fronts. Comte fought against the French form of negative philosophy, against the heritage of Descartes and the Enlightenment. In Germany, the struggle was directed against Hegel's system. Schelling received an express commission from Frederick William IV 'to destroy the dragon seed' of Hegelianism, while Stahl, another anti-Hegelian, became the philosophic spokesman of the Prussian monarchy in 1840. German political leaders clearly recognized that Hegel's philosophy, far from justifying the state in the concrete shape it had taken, rather contained an instrument for its destruction. Within this situation, positive philosophy offered itself as the appropriate ideological savior.

The history of post-Hegelian thought is characterized by this twofold thrust of positive philosophy, which we have just summarized.[5] Positive philosophy was supposed to overcome negative philosophy in its entirety, that is, to abolish any subordinating of reality to transcendental reason. Moreover, it was to teach men to view and study the phenomena of their world as neutral objects governed by universally valid laws. This tendency became particularly important in social and political philosophy. Hegel had considered society and the state to be the historical work of man and interpreted them under the aspect of freedom; in contrast, positive philosophy studied the social realities after the pattern of nature and under the aspect of objective necessity. The independence of matters of fact was to be preserved, and reasoning was to be di-

[5] In the following discussion, we shall disregard Schelling's positive philosophy, since it had no relevance to the development of social thought and influenced the political philosophy only through the use which Stahl made of it.

rected to an acceptance of the given. In this way positive philosophy aimed to counteract the critical process involved in the philosophical 'negating' of the given, and to restore to facts the dignity of the positive.

This is the point at which the connection between positive philosophy and positivism (in the modern sense of the term) becomes clear. Their common feature, apart from their joint struggle against metaphysical apriorism, is the orientation of thought to matters of fact and the elevation of experience to the ultimate in knowledge.

The positivist method certainly destroyed many theological and metaphysical illusions and promoted the march of free thought, especially in the natural sciences. The positivistic attack on transcendent philosophy was reinforced through great strides in these sciences around the first half of the last century. Under the impact of the new scientific temper positivism could claim, as Comte put it, to be the philosophic integration of human knowledge; the integration was to come through the universal application of the scientific method and through excluding all objectives that, in the last analysis, could not be verified by observation.

The positivistic opposition to the principle that the matters of fact of experience have to be justified before the court of reason, however, prevented the interpretation of these 'data' in terms of a comprehensive *critique of the given itself*. Such a criticism no longer had a place in science. In the end, positive philosophy facilitated the surrender of thought to everything that existed and manifested the power to persist in experience. Comte explicitly stated that the term 'positive' by which he designated his philosophy implied educating men to take a positive attitude towards the prevailing state of affairs. Positive philosophy was going to affirm the existing order against those who asserted the need for 'negating' it. We shall see that

Comte and Stahl emphatically stressed this implication of their work. The political aims thus expressed link the positive philosophy with the doctrines of the French counter-revolution: Comte was influenced by De Maistre, Stahl by Burke.

Modern social theory got its greatest impetus from positivism during the nineteenth century. Sociology originated in this positivism and through its influence developed into an independent empirical science. Before we continue this line of analysis, however, we must briefly consider the trend in social theory exemplified by the so-called early French socialists, who had different roots from those of the positivists and who led in another direction, although, in their beginnings, they associated themselves with the positivist position.

The early French socialists found the decisive motives for their doctrines in the class conflicts which conditioned the after-history of the French Revolution. Industry made great strides, the first socialist stirrings were felt, the proletariat began to consolidate. The social and economic conditions that prevailed were seen by these thinkers to constitute the real basis of the historical process. Saint-Simon and Fourier focused their theoretical implements upon the totality of these conditions, thus making society, in the modern sense of the word, the object upon which their theory worked. Sismondi concluded that the economic antagonisms of capitalism were the structural laws of modern society; Proudhon saw society as a system of contradictions. A number of English writers, beginning in 1821, carried their analyses of capitalism so far that they saw the class struggles as the driving motor of social development.[6]

All these doctrines aimed at a critique of the prevailing

[6] Marx, *Theorien über den Mehrwert*, Stuttgart 1921, vol. III, pp. 281 ff.

social forms, with the fundamental concepts serving as instruments for transforming and not for stabilizing or justifying the given order.

Between the positivist and the critical streams, however, there lay a connecting link in the form of a systematic attempt to fuse the principle of class struggle with the idea of objective scientific sociology. Von Stein's work, *Geschichte der sozialen Bewegung in Frankreich von 1789 bis auf unsere Tage* (1850) made this attempt. He conceived the social antagonisms in terms of the dialectic—the class struggle was the negative principle by which society proceeds from one historical form to another. Von Stein considered himself an orthodox Hegelian. Building on Hegel's separation of state from society, he found that the actual content of historic progress was made up of changes in social structure and that the objective of the warring classes was to possess state power. But he interpreted these tendencies as general sociological laws, so that it was by virtue of some 'natural' mechanism that the class conflicts were supposed to lead to social order and to progress on ever higher levels. The force of the dialectic was thus neutralized and made part of a sociological system in which social antagonisms were just means for establishing social harmony. In the end, von Stein's doctrine is not so far removed from the social theory of positive philosophy.

We shall begin our discussion of the development of post-Hegelian social thought with a brief sketch of the main trends in Saint-Simon's work and in the critical social theory that developed in France. We shall then turn to an analysis of the two most influential writings of the positivist social school: Comte's *Sociology* and Stahl's *Philosophy of Right*, ending with von Stein's study, which reconciles Hegel's dialectical conceptions with the system of positive philosophy.

2. Saint-Simon

Saint-Simon, like Hegel, begins with the assertion that the social order engendered by the French Revolution proved that mankind had reached the adult stage.[1] In contrast to Hegel, however, he described this stage primarily in terms of its economy; the industrial process was the sole integrating factor in the new social order. Like Hegel, again, Saint-Simon was convinced that this new order contains the reconciliation of the idea and reality. Human potentialities are no longer the concern of theory apart from practice; the content of theory has been transferred to a plane of rational activity carried on by individuals in direct association with one another. 'Politics, morals, and philosophy, instead of terminating in leisurely contemplation detached from practice, have eventually arrived at their veritable occupation, namely, to create social happiness. In a word, they are ready to realize that liberty is no longer an abstraction, nor society a fiction.'[2] The process of realizing this is an economic one. The new era is that of industrialism, which brings with it a guarantee that it can fulfill all human potentialities. 'Society as a whole is based on industry. Industry is the only guarantor of its existence, and the unique source of all wealth and prosperity. The state of affairs which is most favorable to industry is, therefore, most favorable to society. This is the starting point as well as the goal of all our efforts.'[3] The progress of economic conditions necessitates that philosophy pass into social theory; and the social theory is none other than political economy or 'the science of production.'[4]

At first Saint-Simon contented himself with proclaim-

[1] *Œuvres de Saint-Simon*, ed. Enfantin, Paris 1868 ff., vol. II, p. 118.
[2] Ibid., p. 13. [3] Ibid. [4] P. 188.

ing the principles of radical liberalism. Individuals had been set free in order that they might work, while society was the natural integer that sewed their independent efforts into a harmonious whole. Government was an evil necessary to cope with the danger of anarchy and revolution that lurk behind the mechanisms of industrial capitalism. Saint-Simon began with a predominantly optimistic view of industrial society—the rapid progress of all productive forces, he thought, would soon blot out the growing antagonisms and the revolutionary upheavals within this social system. The new industrial order was above all a positive one, representing the affirmation and fruition of all human endeavor for a happy and abundant life. It was not necessary to go beyond the given; philosophy and social theory needed but to understand and organize the facts. Truth was to be derived from the facts and from them alone. Saint-Simon thus became the founder of modern positivism.[5]

Social theory, Saint-Simon held, would use 'the same method that is employed in the other sciences of observation. In other words, reasoning must be based upon the facts observed and discussed, instead of following the method adopted by the speculative sciences, which refer all facts to reasoning.'[6] Astronomy, physics, and chemistry had already been established on this 'positive basis'; the time had now come for philosophy to join these special sciences and make itself entirely positive.

Saint-Simon promulgated this positivism as the ultimate principle of his philosophy: 'In all portions of my work, I shall be occupied with establishing series of facts, for I am convinced that this is the only solid part of our knowledge.'[7] Theology and metaphysics, and, moreover, all

[5] *Mémoire sur la science de l'homme,* written in 1813; op. cit., vol. XI; see Weill, *Saint-Simon et son œuvre,* Paris 1894, pp. 55 ff.

[6] *Saint-Simon,* op. cit., vol. XI, pp. 8 f.

[7] P. 22.

transcendental concepts and values were to be tested by the positivistic method of exact science. 'Once all our knowledge is uniformly founded on observations, the direction of our spiritual affairs must be trusted to [*conferée à*] the power of positive science.' [8]

The 'science of man,' another name for social theory, thus was launched on the pattern of a natural science; it had to be impressed with a positive 'character, by founding it on observation and by treating it with the method employed by the other branches [!] of physics.' [9] Society was to be treated like nature. This attitude involved the sharpest deviation from and opposition to Hegel's philosophic theory. The interest of freedom was removed from the sphere of the individual's rational will and set in the objective laws of the social and economic process. Marx considered society to be irrational and hence evil, so long as it continued to be governed by inexorable objective laws. Progress to him was equivalent to upsetting these laws, an act that was to be consummated by man in his free development. The positivist theory of society followed the opposite tendency: the laws of society increasingly received the form of natural objective laws. 'Men are mere instruments' before the omnipotent law of progress, incapable of changing or charting its course.[10] The deification of progress into an independent natural law was completed in Comte's positive philosophy.

Saint-Simon's own work did contain elements that ran counter to the tendencies of industrial capitalism. According to him, the progress of the industrial system presupposed that the struggle between classes was first transformed and diverted into a struggle against nature, in which all the social classes joined.[11] The form of government he envisaged was not one in which rulers command

[8] Vol. IV, p. 83.
[9] P. 187.
[10] P. 119.
[11] Vol. IV, pp. 147, 162.

their subjects, but one in which the government exercises a technical administration over the work to be done.[12] We might say that Saint-Simon's philosophy developed in just the reverse way to Hegel's. It began with the reconciliation of idea and reality and ended by viewing them as irreconcilable.

Economic crises and class struggles intensified in France as the revolution of 1830 approached. 'By 1826 it was evident that the nation and the monarchy were moving in opposite directions; the monarch was preparing to establish a despotism while the nation was drifting toward revolution.' [13] The lectures that Saint-Simon's pupil, Bazard, gave in these years on his master's doctrine turned it into a radical critique of the existing social order.

Bazard's presentation holds to the basic assumption that philosophy must be made identical with social theory, that society is conditioned by the structure of its economic process, and that rational social practice alone will eventually produce a genuine social form oriented to human needs. The given form of society is no longer adequate to progress and harmony as far as Bazard is concerned. He stigmatizes the industrial system as one of exploitation, as the last but by far not the least example of the 'exploitation of man by man,' which has run the gamut of civilization's history. In all its relations, the industrial system is molded by the inevitable struggle between the proletariat on the one hand and the owners of the instruments and machinery of production on the other.

> The whole mass of workers is today exploited by those whose property it utilizes . . . The entire weight of this exploitation falls upon the working class, that is, upon the immense majority who are workers. Under such conditions, the worker

[12] P. 150.

[13] Frederick B. Artz, *Reaction and Revolution*, New York 1934, Harper and Brothers, p. 230 f.

has become the direct descendant of the slave and the serf. He is, as a person, free, and no longer attached to the soil, but this is all the freedom he has got. He can exist in this state of legal freedom only under the conditions imposed upon him by that small class which a legislation born of the right to conquest has invested with the monopoly of wealth, with the power to command the instruments of labor at will and at leisure.[14]

Saint-Simon's positivism was thus turned into its opposite. Its original conclusions had glorified liberalism, but it now knew that the system underlying this liberalism holds within it the seed of its own destruction. Bazard showed, as Sismondi had before him, that the accumulation of wealth and the spread of poverty, with their attendant crises and growing exploitations, follow from the economic organization in which 'the capitalists and proprietors' are the ones to arrange the social distribution of labor. 'Every individual is left to his own devices' in the process of production, and no common interest or collective effort exists to combine and administer the multitude of works. When 'the instruments of labor are utilized by isolated individuals' subject to the rule of chance and the fact of power, industrial crises are made inevitable.[15]

The social order, then, Bazard said, has become general disorder 'as a result of the principle of unlimited competition.'[16] Progressive ideas like the ones with which capitalist society justified its social scheme at the beginning, ideas of general freedom and of the pursuit of happiness within a rational scheme of life, can reach fruition only with a new revolution 'that will finally do away with the exploitation of man by man in all its insidious forms. That revolution is inevitable, and until it is consummated all the glowing phrases so oft repeated about the light of

[14] *Doctrine Saint-Simonienne. Exposition.* Paris 1854, p. 123 f.
[15] P. 137. [16] P. 145.

civilization and the glory of the century will remain mere language for the convenience of privileged egoists.'[17] The institution of private property will have to come to an end, for if exploitation is to disappear the scheme of property by which exploitation is perpetuated must also disappear.[18]

The *Doctrine Saint-Simonienne* reflects the social upheavals caused by the progress of industrialism under the Restoration. During this period, machines were introduced on an ever larger scale (especially in the textile mills), and industry began to concentrate.—However, France experienced not only the industrial and commercial growth which Saint-Simon's early writings extoll, but the reverse of this as well. Costly crises shook the entire system in 1816-17 and in 1825-7. Workers banded together to destroy the machines that caused them so much misery and unemployment. 'There could be no doubt that the rise of large-scale industry had an unfavorable influence on the condition of the worker. Agrarian home labor suffered from factory competition. The introduction of machines rendered cheap female and child labor possible and these in turn served to depress wages. Migration to the cities created a scarcity of housing facilities, and this condition, together with a general lack of proper food, made for a breeding ground of rickets and tuberculosis. Epidemics like the cholera epidemic of 1832 took their toll particularly among workers. Misery fosters dipsomania and prostitution. Industrial centers have a mortality far above the average, especially among children.'[19]

Government intervened—with repressive measures against workers. The Lex Le Chapelier of 1789 had prohibited organization of workers. Strikes were now answered

[17] Pp. 125 f. [18] P. 127.

[19] Henri Sée, *Französische Wirtschaftsgeschichte,* Jena 1936, vol. II, p. 244.

with a call of the army. Leaders were given lengthy prison sentences. Increasing restrictions were placed on the freedom of workers.[20] 'While pledging the entire power of the state against the workers, the authorities are extremely lenient with the entrepreneurs.' In 1829 the ship owners of Grenouille associated themselves for the purpose of lowering the wages of their seamen. The judiciary and the ministry of the navy declared their procedure contrary to law, but refused any legal action because they feared 'that the seamen could be driven to rebellion.'[21]

Occurrences like these made it obvious that the economic process, or factors in it, reached its tentacles into the totality of social relations and held them in grip. Smith and Ricardo had treated this economic process as a specialized science, where wealth, poverty, labor, value, property, and all its other paraphernalia appeared as strictly economic conditions and relations, to be derived from or explained by economic laws. Saint-Simon had made the economic laws the foundation of the whole process of society. Now, when his socialist successors in France were building social theory on an economic base, they were changing the conceptual character of political economy. It ceased to be a 'pure' and specialized science, becoming instead an intellectual force for exposing the antagonisms of the modern social structure and for guiding action in the direction of resolving them. By the same token, the commodity world ceased to be conceived in terms of its own reification. When Sismondi, for instance, argued against Ricardo that 'political economy is not a science of calculus but a moral science,' he was not advocating a regress from scientific to moral criteria in reasoning, but was indicating that the focus of economic

[20] Pp. 250 f.

[21] Pp. 251 f.

theory should be upon human wants and desires.[22] Sismondi's statement belongs in the last analysis with the tendency that operated in Hegel when he gave to social theory a philosophic construction. Hegel was getting at the point that society, which was the historical stage in the self-development of men, had to be interpreted as the totality of human relations, and this with an eye to its role in advancing the realization of reason and freedom. It was precisely this philosophic interpretation of social theory that turned the latter into a *critical* theory of political economy. For, as soon as it was viewed in the light of reason and freedom, the prevailing form of society appeared as a complex of economic contradictions that bred an irrational and enslaved order. Because the philosophic interpretation of society carried the critical implications that it did, any disjunction between philosophy and social theory was held to weaken these critical motives, which pushed philosophical concepts to see beyond and to go beyond the given state of affairs. Proudhon saw the reason for the apologetic conclusions of economic theory and its consequent frustration of any principle of action to consist in 'the separation of philosophy from political economy.' 'Philosophy,' he said, 'is the algebra of society, and political economy is the application of this algebra.' Philosophy to him, then, was 'the theory of reason.'[23] Following out this beginning, Proudhon defined social theory as 'the accord between reason and social practice,'[24] and in stating the subject matter of social theory he placed great stress on its comprehensive area of application; it deals with 'the entire life of society,' with 'the

[22] *Nouveaux principes d'économie politique*, 2nd ed., Paris 1827, vol. I, p. 313.

[23] *Système des contradictions économiques*, ed. C. Bouglé and H. Moysset, Paris 1923, vol. II, pp. 392 f.

[24] Ibid., p. 391.

ensemble of its successive manifestations,'[25] thus reaching far beyond the range of the special science of economics.

Emphasis on the philosophic nature of social theory, however, does not attenuate the importance of its economic foundation. Quite the contrary, such emphasis would expand the scope of economic theory beyond the limits of a specialized science. 'The laws of economy are the laws of history,' Proudhon says.[26]

The new political economy was quite different from the classical objective science of Adam Smith and Ricardo. It differed from this in that it showed the economy to be contradictory and irrational throughout its structure, with crisis as its natural state and revolution as its natural end. Sismondi's work, the first thoroughgoing immanent critique of capitalism, amply illustrates the contrast. It held to the criterion of a truly critical theory of society. 'We shall take society in its actual organization, with its workers deprived of property, their wages fixed by competition, their labor dismissed by their masters as soon as they no longer have need of it—for it is to this very social organization that we object.'[27]

All forms of social organization, Sismondi declared, exist to gratify human wants. The prevailing economic system does so under continuous crisis and growing poverty amid accumulating wealth. Sismondi laid bare the mechanisms of early industrial capitalism that led to this result.[28] The necessity of recurring crises, he stated, is a consequence of the impact of capital on the productive process. The increasing exploitation and the persistent disproportion between production and consumption are

[25] Vol. I, p. 73.

[26] *De la création de l'ordre dans l'humanité,* ed. C. Bouglé and A. Cuvillier, Paris 1927, p. 369.

[27] *Nouveaux principes* . . ., vol. II, p. 417.

[28] See Henryk Grossmann, *Sismonde de Sismondi et ses theories économiques,* Bibliotheca universitatis liberae Poloniae, Warsaw 1924.

consequences of the system of commodity exchange. Sismondi went on to sketch the hidden relations behind exchange value and use-value and the various forms for appropriating surplus value. He demonstrated the connection between the concentration of capital, overproduction, and crisis. 'Through the concentration of wealth among a small number of proprietors the internal market continues to shrink and industry is ever increasingly compelled to sell on external markets where even greater concussions threaten.' [29] Free competition falls far short of giving full development to all productive capacities and to the greatest satisfaction of human needs; it brings wholesale exploitation and repeated destruction of the sources of wealth. To be sure, capitalism brought immense progress to society, but the advance resulted in 'a constant increase in the working population and in a labor supply that usually surpassed the demand.' [30] The economic mechanisms of commodity production is responsible for these antagonisms. Were the tendencies of the system given their full expression, the result would be 'to transform the nation into a huge factory' that, 'far from creating wealth, would cause general misery.' [31]

Only six years after Saint-Simon had inaugurated positivism, social theory gave this radical refutation to the social order by which he had justified his new philosophy. 'The system of industry' was seen as the system of capitalist exploitation. The doctrine of harmonious equilibrium was replaced by the doctrine of inherent crisis. The idea of progress was given a new meaning: economic progress did not necessarily mean human progress,—under capitalism, progress is made at the expense of freedom and reason. Sismondi repudiated the philosophy of progress together with the entire panoply of optimistic glorifi-

[29] *Nouveaux principes* . . . vol. I, p. 361.
[30] Ibid., p. 408.
[31] P. 78.

cation. He called upon the state to exert its protective authority in the interest of the oppressed mass. 'The fundamental dogma of free and general competition has made great strides in all civilized societies. It has resulted in a prodigious development of industrial power, but it has also brought terrifying distress for most classes of the population. Experience has taught us the need for the protective authority [of government], needed lest men be sacrificed for the advancement of a wealth from which they will derive no benefit.' [82]

Only a short decade after the publication of Sismondi's work, social philosophy fell back upon the dogma of progress, and, characteristically enough, relinquished political economy as foundational for social theory. Comte's positive philosophy ushered in this regress. We shall deal with it now.

3. The Positive Philosophy of Society: Auguste Comte

Comte severed social theory from its connection with the negative philosophy and placed it in the orbit of positivism. At the same time he abandoned political economy as the root of social theory and made society the object of an independent science of *sociology*. Both steps are interconnected: sociology became a science by renouncing the transcendent point of view of the philosophical critique. Society now was taken as a more or less definite complex of facts governed by more or less general laws—a sphere to be treated like any other field of scientific investigation. The concepts that explain this realm were to be derived from the facts that constitute it, while the farther-reaching implications of philosophical concepts were to be excluded. The term 'positive' was a polemical term that de-

[82] Pp. 52 f.

noted this transformation from a philosophic theory to a scientific one. To be sure, Comte wished to elaborate an all-embracing *philosophy,* as the title of his principal work indicates, but it is readily visible that, in the context of positivism, philosophy means something quite different from what it meant previously, so much so that it repudiates the true content of philosophy. 'Philosophie positive' is, in the last analysis, a contradiction *in adjecto.* It refers to the synthesis of all empirical knowledge ordered into a system of harmonious progress following an inexorable course. All opposition to social realities is obliterated from philosophic discussion.

Comte summarizes the contrast between the positivist and the philosophic theory as follows: positive sociology is to concern itself with the investigation of facts instead of with transcendental illusions, with useful knowledge instead of leisured contemplation, certainty instead of doubt and indecision, organization instead of negation and destruction.[1] In all these cases, the new sociology is to tie itself to the facts of the existing social order and, though it will not reject the need for correction and improvement, it will exclude any move to overthrow or negate that order. As a result, the conceptual interest of the positive sociology is to be apologetic and justificatory.

This has not been true of all positivist movements. At the beginning of modern philosophy, and again in the eighteenth century, positivism was militant and revolutionary. Its appeal to the facts then amounted to a direct attack on the religious and metaphysical conceptions that were the ideological support of the *ancien régime.* The positivist approach to history was developed then as proof positive that the right of man to alter the social and political forms of life accorded with the nature and progress

[1] *Discours sur l'esprit positif,* Paris 1844, pp. 41-2.

of reason. Again, the principle of sense-perception as the basis of verification was used by the French Enlightenment philosophers to protest the prevailing absolutistic system. They held that since the senses are the organon of truth and since the gratification of the senses is the proper motivation of human action, the advancement of man's material happiness is the proper end that government and society should serve. The given form of government and society patently contradicted this end; in the last analysis, this was the 'fact' to which the positivists of the Enlightenment made their appeal. They aimed not at a well-ordered science, but at a social and political practice, remaining rationalists in the genuine sense that they tested human practice by the standard of a truth transcendent to the given social order, the standard represented by a social ordering that did not exist as a fact but as a goal. The 'truth' they saw, a society wherein free individuals could use their aptitudes and fulfill their needs, was not derived from any existing fact or facts but resulted from a philosophic analysis of the historical situation, which showed an oppressive social and political system to them. The Enlightenment affirmed that reason could rule the world and men change their obsolete forms of life if they acted on the basis of their liberated knowledge and capacities.

Comte's positive philosophy lays down the general framework of a social theory that is to counteract these 'negative' tendencies of rationalism. It arrives at an ideological defense of middle-class society and, moreover, it bears the seeds of a philosophic justification of authoritarianism. The connection between positive philosophy and the irrationalism that characterized the later authoritarian ideology, ushered in with the decline of liberalism, is quite clear in Comte's writings. Hand in hand with the shackling of thought to immediate experience goes his constant widening of the realm of experience, so that it ceases to be restricted to the realm of scientific observation but claims also various types of supra-sensual power. In fact, the outcome of Comte's positivism turns out to be a religious system with an elaborate cult of names, symbols, and signs. He himself expounded a 'positive theory of authority' and became the authoritative leader of a sect of blind followers. This was the first fruit of the defamation of reason in positive philosophy.

It had been the fundamental conviction of idealism that truth is not given to man from some external source but originates in the process of interaction between thought and reality, theory and practice. The function of thought was not merely to collect, comprehend, and order facts, but also to contribute a quality that rendered such activity possible, a quality that was thus *a priori* to facts. A decisive portion of the human world therefore consisted, the idealists held, of elements that could not be verified by observation. Positivism repudiated this doctrine, slowly replacing the free spontaneity of thought with predominantly receptive functions. This was not merely a matter of epistemology. The idealistic idea of reason, we recall, had been intrinsically connected with the idea of freedom and had opposed any notion of a natural necessity ruling over society. Positive philosophy tended instead to equate the study of society with the study of nature, so that natural science, particularly biology, became the archetype of social theory. Social study was to be a science seeking social laws, the validity of which was to be analogous to that of physical laws. Social practice, especially the matter of changing the social system, was herewith throttled by the inexorable. Society was viewed as governed by rational laws that moved with a natural necessity. This position directly contradicted the view held by the dialectical social theory, that society is irrational precisely in that it is governed by natural laws.

The 'general dogma of the invariability of physical laws' Comte calls the 'true spirit' of positivism.[2] He proposes to apply this tenet to social theory as a means of freeing the latter from theology and metaphysics and giving it the status of a science. 'Theological and metaphysical philosophy do not hold sway today except in the system of social study. They must be excluded from this final refuge. Mainly, this will be done through the basic interpretation that social movement is necessarily subject to invariant physical laws, instead of being governed by some kind of will.'[3] The positivist repudiation of metaphysics was thus coupled with a repudiation of man's claim to alter and reorganize his social institutions in accordance with his rational will. This is the element Comte's positivism shares with the original philosophies of counter-revolution sponsored by Bonald and De Maistre. Bonald wished to demonstrate that 'man cannot give a constitution to religious or political society any more than he can give weight to a body or extension to matter,' and that his intervention only prevents society from attaining its 'natural constitution.'[4] De Maistre wished to show that 'human reason, or what is called philosophy, adds nothing to the happiness of states or of individuals,'[5] that '*creation* is beyond the capacities of man'[6] and that his reason 'is completely ineffectual not only for creating but also for conserving any religious or political association.'[7] The 'revolutionary spirit' was to be checked by spreading an-

[2] *Discours sur l'esprit positif,* p. 17.

[3] *Cours de philosophie positive,* 4th ed., vol. IV, Paris 1877, p. 267.

[4] Bonald, 'Théorie du pouvoir,' in *Œuvres,* Paris 1854, vol. I, p. 101.

[5] De Maistre, 'Etude sur la souveraineté,' in *Œuvres complètes,* Lyon 1884, vol. I, p. 367.

[6] Ibid., p. 373.

[7] Ibid., p. 375.

other teaching, that society possesses an immutable natural order to which man's will must submit.

Comte also charged sociology to make secure this teaching as a means of establishing 'the general limits of all political action.'[8] Assent to the principle of invariant laws in society will prepare men for discipline and for obedience to the existing order and will promote their 'resignation' to it.

'Resignation' is a keynote in Comte's writings, deriving directly from assent to invariable social laws. 'True resignation, that is, a disposition to endure necessary evils steadfastly and without any hope of compensation therefor, can result only from a profound feeling for the invariable laws that govern the variety of natural phenomena.'[9] The 'positive' politics that Comte advocates would tend, he declares, 'of its very nature to consolidate public order,' even as far as incurable political evils are concerned, by developing a 'wise resignation.'[10]

There is no doubt as to the social groups and purposes in whose behalf resignation is adduced. Rarely in the past has any philosophy urged itself forward with so strong and so overt a recommendation that it be utilized for the maintenance of prevailing authority and for the protection of vested interest from any and all revolutionary onset. Comte begins his propaganda for positivism by declaring that genuine science has no other general aim than 'constantly to establish and fortify the intellectual order which . . . is the indispensable basis of all veritable order.'[11] Order in science and order in society merge into an indivisible whole. The ultimate goal is to justify and fortify this social order. Positive philosophy is the only weapon able to combat 'the anarchic force of purely revolutionary principles'; it alone can succeed in 'absorbing

[8] *Cours de philosophie positive,* vol. IV, p. 281.
[9] Ibid., pp. 142 f. [10] P. 142. [11] P. 138.

the current revolutionary doctrine.' [12] 'La cause de l'ordre,' moreover, will bring even greater advantages. Positive politics will tend spontaneously 'to divert from the various existing powers . . . and from all their delegates the greatly exaggerated attention accorded to them by public opinion . . .' [13] The consequence of this diversion will be to concentrate all social effort on primarily a 'moral' renovation. Time and again, Comte stresses the 'serious and threatening dangers' that attend 'the predominance of purely material considerations' in social theory and practice.[14] The innermost interests of his sociology are much more sharply antimaterialistic than Hegel's idealism. 'The principal social difficulties are today essentially not political but moral ones,' and their solution requires a change in 'opinions and morals' rather than in institutions. Positivism is therefore urged to give aid 'in transforming political agitation into a philosophical crusade,' which would suppress radical tendencies as, after all, 'incompatible with any sane conception of history.' [15] The new philosophical movement will in due time teach men that their social order stands under eternal laws against which none may transgress without punishment. According to these laws all forms of government are 'provisional,' which means that they will painlessly adjust themselves to the irresistible progress of mankind. Revolution under such conditions is without sense.

The 'provisional powers' that govern society, Comte argues, will no doubt find their security effectively increased through the influence of 'positive politics which is alone able to imbue the people with the feeling that, in the present state of their ideas, no political change is of real importance.' [16] The lords of earth will learn, also,

12 P. 140. 13 P. 141. 14 See pp. 116, 118.
15 *Discours sur l'esprit positif*, p. 57.
16 *Cours de philosophie positive*, vol. IV, p. 141.

that positivism inclines 'to consolidate all power in the hands of those who possess this power—whoever they may be.' [17] Comte becomes even more outspoken. He denounces 'the strange and extremely dangerous' theories and efforts that are directed against the prevailing property order. These erect an 'absurd Utopia.' [18] Certainly, it is necessary to improve the condition of the lower classes, but this must be done without deranging class barriers and without 'disturbing the indispensable economic order.' [19] On this point, too, positivism offers a testimonial to itself. It promises to 'insure the ruling classes against every anarchistic invasion' [20] and to show the way to a proper treatment of the mass. Outlining the meaning of the term 'positive' in his philosophy, Comte summarizes the grounds for his recommendation of himself to the *cause de l'ordre* by stressing that his philosophy is of its very nature 'destined not to destroy but to organize' and that it will 'never pronounce an absolute negation.' [21]

We have devoted considerable space to the social and political role of Comte's sociology because the subsequent development of positivism has obliterated the strong connection between the social and methodological principles.

We now raise the question, Which of its principles makes positive philosophy the adequate guardian and defender of the exsiting order? In drawing our contrast between the positivist spirit of the Enlightenment and later positivist views,[22] we have already pointed to the latter's negation of metaphysics and to 'the subordination of imagination to observation,' [23] and we have shown that these signified a tendency to acquiesce in the given. All scientific concepts were to be subordinated to the facts. The

17 *Discours* . . . , p. 78.
18 *Cours* . . . , p. 151.
19 Ibid.
20 P. 152.
21 *Discours* . . . , pp. 42 f.
22 See above, p. 342.
23 *Cours de philosophie positive,* p. 214.

former were merely to make manifest the real connec tions among the latter. Facts and their connections represented an inexorable order comprising social as well as natural phenomena. The laws positivist science discovered and that distinguish it from empiricism, were positive also in the sense that they affirmed the prevailing order as a basis for denying the need to construct a new one. Not that they excluded reform and change—on the contrary, the idea of progress loomed large in the sociology of Comte—but the laws of progress were part of the machinery of the given order, so that the latter progressed smoothly to a higher stage without having to be destroyed first.

Comte had little difficulty in arriving at this result, for he saw the different stages of historical development as stages of a 'philosophic movement' rather than of a social process. Comte's law of three stages illustrates this quite clearly. History, he says, takes the inevitable path of first, theological rule, then, metaphysical rule, and finally, positivist rule. This conception permitted Comte to come forward as a brave warrior against the *ancien régime* at a time when the *ancien régime* had long been broken and the middle class had long consolidated its social and economic power. Comte interpreted the *ancien régime* primarily as the vestige of theological and metaphysical ideas in science.

Observation instead of speculation means, in Comte's sociology, an emphasis on order in place of any rupture in the order; it means the authority of natural laws in place of free action, unification in place of disorder. The idea of order, so basic to Comte's positivism, has a totalitarian content in its social as well as methodological meaning. The methodological emphasis was on the idea of a unified science, the same idea that dominates recent developments in positivism. Comte wanted to found his philosophy on a system of 'universally recognized principles' that will draw their ultimate legitimacy solely from 'the voluntary assent by which the public will confirm them to be the result of perfectly free discussion.' [24] 'The public,' just as in neo-positivism, turns out to be a forum of scientists who have the necessary equipment of knowledge and training. Social questions, because of their complicated nature, must be handled 'by a small group of an intellectual élite.' [25] In this way, the most vital issues that are of great moment to all are withdrawn from the arena of social struggle and bottled for investigation in some field of specialized scientific study. Unification is a matter of agreement among scientists whose efforts along this line will sooner or later yield 'a permanent and definite state of intellectual unity.' All the sciences will be poured into the same crucible and fused into a well-ordered scheme. All concepts will be put to the test of 'one and the same fundamental method' until, in the end, they issue forth ordered in 'a rational sequence of uniform laws.' [26] Positivism thus will 'systematize the whole of our conceptions.' [27]

The positivist idea of *order* refers to an ensemble of laws entirely different from the ensemble of dialectical laws. The former are essentially affirmatory and construct a stable order, the latter, essentially negative and destructive of stability. The former see society as a realm of natural harmony, the latter as a system of antagonisms. 'The notion of natural laws entails at once the corresponding idea of a spontaneous order, which is always coupled with the notion of some harmony.' [28] Positivist sociology is basically 'social statics,' quite in keeping with the positivist doctrine that there is a 'true and permanent

[24] P. 46. [25] P. 92; cf. pp. 144 f. [26] Ibid.

[27] *Système de politique positive*, Paris 1890, vol. I, p. 11; trans. J. H. Bridges as *A General View of Positivism*, new ed. F. Harrison, London 1908, pp. 11 f.

[28] *Cours de philosophie positive*, vol. IV, p. 248.

harmony between the various existential conditions in society.' [29] The harmony prevails, and, because it does so, the thing to do is 'contemplate the order, for the purpose of correcting it conveniently, but not and nowhere to create it.' [30]

A closer scrutiny of Comte's laws of social statics discloses their amazing abstractness and poverty. They center about two propositions. First, men need to work for their happiness; second, all social actions show that they are overwhelmingly motivated by selfish interests. The principal task of positivist political science is to strike the right balance between the different kinds of work to be done and the skilful employment of self-interest for the common good. In this connection, Comte stresses the need for strong authority. 'In the intellectual, no less than in the material order, men find above all the indispensable need for some supreme directing hand capable of sustaining their continuous activity by rallying and fixing their spontaneous efforts.' [31] When positivism reaches its dominant position in the world, in the last stage of human progress, it changes hitherto existing forms of authority, but it does not by any means abolish authority itself. Comte outlines a 'positive theory of authority,' [32] envisaging a society with all its activity based on the consent of individual wills. The liberalist tinge of this picture is shaded over, however. The instinct to submit triumphs, as the founder of positivist sociology renders a paean to obedience and leadership. 'How sweet it is to obey when we can enjoy the happiness . . . of being conveniently discharged, by sage and worthy leaders, from the pressing responsibility of a general direction of our conduct.' [33]

Happiness in the shelter of a strong arm—the attitude,

[29] Ibid., p. 232.
[30] P. 252.
[31] Pp. 241-2.
[32] P. 244.
[33] P. 439.

so characteristic today in Fascist societies, makes juncture with the positivist ideal of certainty. Submission to an all-powerful authority provides the highest degree of security. Perfect certainty of theory and practice, Comte claims, is one of the basic attainments of positivist method.

The idea of certainty did not, of course, emerge with positive philosophy, but had been a strong feature of rationalism ever since Descartes. Positivism did, however, reinterpret its meaning and function. As we have indicated, rationalism asserted that the ground of theoretical and practical certainty was the freedom of the thinking subject. On this foundation it constructed a universe that was rational precisely to the extent that it was dominated by the intellectual and practical power of the individual. Truth sprang from the subject, and the imprint of subjectivity was upon it whatever objective form it took. The world was real to the extent that it conformed to the subject's rational autonomy.

Positivism shifts the source of certainty from the subject of thought to the subject of perception. Scientific observation yields certainty here. The spontaneous functions of thought recede, while its receptive and passive functions gain predominance.

Comte's sociology, by virtue of the concept of order, is essentially 'social statics'; it is also 'social dynamics' by virtue of the concept of *progress*. The relation between the two basic concepts Comte has often explained. Order is 'the fundamental condition of progress'[34] and 'all progress ultimately tends to consolidate order.'[35] The principal reason for the fact that social antagonisms still prevail is that the idea of order and that of progress are still separated, a condition which has made it possible for anarchist revolutionaries to usurp the latter idea. Positive

[34] *Discours . . .*, p. 56.
[35] *Cours de philosophie positive*, vol. IV, p. 17.

philosophy aims to reconcile order and progress, to achieve a 'common satisfaction of the need for order and the need for progress.' [36] This it can do by showing that progress is in itself order—not revolution, but evolution.

His antimaterialistic interpretation of history facilitated Comte's undertaking. He retained the Enlightenment conception that progress is primarily intellectual progress, the continuous advance of positive knowledge.[37] He removed from the Enlightenment conception as much of its material content as he could, thus adhering to his promise 'to substitute an immense intellectual movement for a sterile political agitation.' [38] Servant of the pre-eminent need to safeguard the existing order, the idea of progress stands in the way of physical, moral, and intellectual development except along lines that the given 'system of circumstances' permits.[39] Comte's idea of progress excludes revolution, the total transformation of the given system of circumstances. Historical development becomes nothing more than a harmonious evolution of the social order under perennial 'natural' laws.

'Dynamic sociology' is to present the mechanics of this evolution. Its outlook is essentially 'to conceive each state of society as the necessary result of the preceding one and the indispensable motor of the succeeding one.' [40] Social dynamics deals with the laws governing this continuity; in other words, the 'laws of succession,' whereas social statics treats of the 'laws of co-existence.' [41] The former makes for 'the true theory of progress,' the latter, 'the true theory of order.' Progress is equated with a persistent growth of intellectual culture in history. The fundamental law of social dynamics is that increasing power accrues to

[36] Ibid., p. 148; cf. *Discours* . . . , pp. 53 f.
[37] *Discours* . . . , p. 59.
[38] Ibid., p. 76.
[39] *Cours de philosophie positive,* vol. IV, p. 262.
[40] P. 263. [41] P. 264.

those organic faculties by which man is differentiated in nature from lower organic beings, namely, 'intelligence and *sociabilité*.'[42] As civilization proceeds, it comes closer and closer to exhibiting the nature of mankind in the concrete; the highest grade of civilization is the one most in conformity with 'nature.'[43] Historical progress is a natural process and is, as such, governed by natural laws.[44] Progress *is* order.

The process of making social theory compatible with existing conditions is not complete as far as we have developed it. All elements that would transcend or point beyond the validity of the given matters of fact have yet to be excluded; this requires that social theory be made *relativistic.* The last decisive aspect of positivism, Comte states, as we would expect, is its tendency 'everywhere to substitute the relative for the absolute.'[45] From this 'irrevocable predominance of the relativist point of view' he derives his basic view that social development has a naturally harmonious character. Every historical stage of society is as perfect as the corresponding 'age of humanity' and system of circumstance permit.[46] A natural harmony prevails not only among the coexisting parts of the social scheme, but also between the potentialities of mankind revealed therein and the realization of these.

According to Comte, relativism is inseparable from the conception that sociology is an exact science dealing with the invariant laws of social statics and dynamics. These laws are to be discovered only by scientific observation, which, in turn, requires a constant progress in scientific technic to cope with the highly complicated phenomena it has to organize.[47] The attainment of complete knowledge coincides with the completion of scientific

[42] *Discours* . . . , p. 60.
[43] *Cours* . . . , p. 442.
[44] P. 267.
[45] *Discours* . . . , p. 43.
[46] *Cours* . . . , p. 279.
[47] Ibid., pp. 216 f.

progress itself; prior to such perfection, all knowledge and truth are inevitably partial and relative to the attained level of intellectual development.

So far, Comte's relativism is merely methodological, based on a necessary inadequacy in the methods of observation. Owing to the fact, however, that social development is interpreted primarily as intellectual development, his relativism posits a pre-established harmony between the subjective side of sociology (the method) and the objective (the content). All social forms and institutions, as we have mentioned, are provisional in the sense that, as intellectual culture advances, they will pass into others that will correspond with intellectual capacities of an advanced type. Their provisional character, though a sign of their imperfection, is at the same time the mark of their (relative) truth. The concepts of positivism are relativistic because all reality is relative.

Science, to Comte, is the field of theoretical relativism, and the latter the area from which 'value judgments' are excluded. Positivist sociology 'neither admires nor condemns political facts but looks upon them . . . as simple objects of observation.'[48] When sociology becomes a positivist science it is divorced from any concern with the 'value' of a given social form. Man's quest for happiness is not a scientific problem, nor is the question of the best possible fulfillment for his desires and talents. Comte boasts that he can easily treat the whole realm of social physics 'without once using the word "perfection," which is replaced forever by the purely scientific term "development."'[49] Each historical level represents a higher stage of development than the one preceding, by force of the fact that the later is the necessary product of the earlier one and contains a plus of experience and new knowledge.

[48] P. 293.

[49] P. 264.

Comte holds, however, that his concept of development does not exclude perfection.[50] The essential conditions of men and their capacities have improved with social development; this is incontestible. But the improvement of capacities takes place primarily in science, art, morals, and such, all of which, like the improvement in social conditions, move 'gradually, within convenient limits.' Accordingly, revolutionary efforts for a new order of society have no place in the scheme. They can be dispensed with. 'The vain search for better government' is not necessary,[51] for each established governmental form has its relative right, to be disputed only by those taking an absolutist point of view, which is false *per definitionem*. Comte's relativism thus terminates in the 'positive theory of authority.'

Comte's reverence for established authority was easily compatible with all-around tolerance. Both attitudes hold equally in this brand of scientific relativism. There is no room for condemnation. 'Without the slightest alteration of its proper principles' positivism can 'do exact and philosophical justice to all prevalent doctrines' [52]—a virtue that will make it acceptable 'to all the different existing parties.' [53]

The idea of tolerance had changed its content and function as positivism developed. The French Enlighteners who fought the absolute state gave no relativist framework to their demand for tolerance, but asserted that demand as part of their general effort to establish a better form of government—'better' in precisely the sense Comte repudiates. Tolerance did not mean justice to all existing parties. It meant, in fact, the abolition of one of the most influential of parties, that of the clergy allied with the feudal nobility, which was using intolerance as an instrument for domination.

[50] P. 275. [51] P. 224. [52] P. 149. [53] P. 153.

When Comte came on the scene, his 'tolerance' was not a slogan for opponents of the existing order, but for the opponents of these. As the concept of progress was formalized, tolerance was detached from the standard that had given it content in the eighteenth century. Earlier, the positivist standard had been a new society, while tolerance had been equivalent to intolerance towards those who opposed that standard. The formalized concept of tolerance, on the other hand, amounted to tolerating the forces of reaction and regress as well. The need for this kind of toleration resulted from the fact that all standards that go beyond given realities had been renounced—standards that in Comte's eyes were akin to those seeking an absolute. In a philosophy that justified the prevailing social system, the cry of toleration became increasingly useful to the beneficiaries of the system.

Comte, however, does not treat all parties equally. He says many times that there is an essential affinity between positivism and one large social group, the proletariat. Proletarians have an ideal disposition to positivism.[54] Comte has an entire section in the *Système de politique positive* dedicated to the proposition that 'the new philosophers will find their most energetic allies among our proletarians.'[55]

The fact of the proletariat worried Comte's sociology as well as it did its antithesis, the Marxian critique. There could be no positive theory of civil society unless the fact of the proletariat could be reconciled with the harmonious order of progress it so patently contradicts. For, if the proletariat is the foundational class in civil society, the laws of this society's advance are the laws of its destruction, and the theory of society must be a negative one. Sociology must, in the face of this, present a refutation of the dia-

[54] *Discours* . . . , p. 86.
[55] *Système de politique positive*, vol. I, p. 129.

lectical thesis that accumulation of wealth takes place alongside an intensification of poverty.

Comte regarded the latter thesis as a 'sinister and immoral prejudice,' [56] one that positivism had to eradicate if it would maintain the 'industrial discipline' the society needs in order to function. Comte held that the theory and practice of liberalism could not safeguard discipline. 'The vain and irrational disposition to allow for only that degree of order that comes of itself' (that is, that comes through the free play of economic forces) amounts to a 'solemn resignation' of social practice in the face of every real emergency in the social process.[57]

Comte's belief in the necessary laws of progress did not exclude practical efforts in the direction of such social reform as would remove any obstacles in the path of these laws. The positivist program of social reform foreshadows liberalism's turn into authoritarianism. In contrast to Hegel, whose philosophy showed a similar tendency, Comte slurred over the fact that the turn is made necessary because of the antagonistic structure of civil society. Classes in conflict, he held, are but vestiges of an obsolete régime, soon to be removed by positivism, without any threat to the 'fundamental institution of property.' [58]

The rule of positivism, Comte says, will improve the condition of the proletariat, first in education and second through 'the creation of work.' [59] The vision entails an all-embracing hierarchic state, governed by a cultural élite composed of all social groups and permeated by a new morality that unites all diverse interests into a real whole.[60] Notwithstanding the many declarations that this hierarchy will derive its authority from the free consent of its members, Comte's state resembles in many respects

[56] *Cours* . . . , pp. 201 f.

[57] P. 202.

[58] P. 201, *note*.

[59] *Discours* . . . , p. 93.

[60] Cf. especially *Cours de philosophie positive*, vol. IV, p. 150 ff

the modern authoritarian state. We find, for example, that there is to be a 'spontaneous union of the brain and the hand.'[61] Obviously, regulation from above plays an important part in the establishment of such a union. Comte makes the matter more explicit. He states that industrial development has already reached a point at which it becomes necessary 'to regulate the relation between entrepreneur and worker toward an indispensable harmony that is no longer sufficiently guaranteed in the free natural antagonism between them.'[62]

The act of combining entrepreneurs and workers, we are assured, is by no means intended as a step towards abolishing the inevitably inferior position of the worker. The latter's activity, Comte holds, is naturally less extensive and less responsible than that of the entrepreneur. Society is a 'positive hierarchy,' and submission to the social stratification is indispensable to the life of the whole.[63] Consequently, the new morality is to be primarily one of 'duty' to the whole. The justified claims of the proletariat become duties, too. The worker will receive 'first education and then work.' Comte does not elaborate on this 'work creation program,' but does speak of a system in which all private functions become public ones,[64] so that every activity is organized and exercised as a public service.

This 'nationalization' of labor has nothing to do, of course, with socialism. Comte stresses that in the 'positive order,' 'the various public enterprises can, to an increasing extent, be entrusted to private industry,' provided that such 'administrative change' does not tamper with the necessary discipline.[65] He refers in this connection to an agency that has become increasingly important in maintaining positive order—the army. His effort to do justice

61 Ibid., p. 152.
62 Ibid., vol. VI, pp. 433 f.
63 Vol. VI, p. 497.
64 P. 485.
65 P. 503.

to all social groups alike prompts him to recommend his philosophy to the 'military class,' with the reminder that positivism, though it approves of the slow disappearance of military action, 'directly justifies the important provisional function' of the army in the 'necessary maintenance of the material order.' [66] Because of the grave disturbances to which the social system is prone, 'the army has the increasingly essential task of participating actively . . . to maintain the constancy of public order.' [67] As national wars disappear, we shall witness that the army will more and more be entrusted with the 'social mission' of a great political gendarmerie (*une grande maréchaussée politique*).[68]

In one decisive aspect, however, Comte's system retains the emancipatory function of Western philosophy, for it tends to bridge the gulf between isolated individuals and to unite them in a real universal. We have attempted to show how the positivist method engendered the quest for unification, and we have stressed its negative implications. But the idea of a universal positive order drove Comte beyond the empty conception of a unified science and the oppressive vision of a government of positive high priests. There is still another universality prevalent in Comte's system, that of *society*. It emerges as the one arena in which man acts out his historical life, and, by the same token, it becomes the only object of social theory. The individual plays almost no part in Comte's sociology, he is entirely absorbed by society, and the state is a mere by-product of the inexorable laws that govern the social process.

On this point, Comte's sociology transcends the limits of Hegel's political philosophy. The positive theory of society sees no reason for confining human development within the boundaries of sovereign national states. Its idea

[66] P. 529. [67] P. 356. [68] P. 357.

of a universal order is consummated only through the union of all individuals in mankind, and the positivist destruction of obsolete theological and metaphysical standards comes to fruition in the recognition of *humanity* as the *être suprême*. Humanity, not the state, is the real universal, nay, it is the only reality.[69] It is the only entity that, in the age of mankind's maturity, is worthy of religious reverence. 'The great conception of Humanity will irrevocably eliminate that of God.' [70]

It is as if Comte had tried, with this idea of humanity, to make amends for the oppressive atmosphere in which his positivist sociology moved.

4. The Positive Philosophy of the State: Friedrich Julius Stahl

Notwithstanding its sinister aspects and anachronistic orientation (calling for a struggle against the *ancien régime* when that had already been replaced by the new middle-class regime symbolized quite clearly in the rule of the 'bourgeois king,' Louis Philippe), Comte's positivism expressed the consciousness of an advancing social class that had fought its triumphant way through two revolutions. The positive philosophy affirmed that the course of human history pressed towards ultimate subordination of all social relations to the interests of industry and science, implying that the state would be slowly absorbed by a society that would embrace the earth.

In contrast to its form in France, positive philosophy in Germany was of quite a different cast. The political aspirations of the German middle class had been defeated without a struggle:

[69] *Système de politique positive*, vol. I, p. 334.
[70] P. 329.

While in England and France feudalism was entirely destroyed, or, at least reduced, as in the former country, to a few insignificant forms, by a powerful and wealthy middle class, concentrated in large towns, and particularly in the capital, the feudal nobility in Germany had retained a great portion of their ancient privileges. The feudal system of tenure was prevalent almost everywhere. The lords of the land had even retained the jurisdiction over their servants . . . This feudal nobility, then extremely numerous and partly very wealthy, was considered, officially, the first 'Order' in the country. It furnished the higher Government officials, it almost exclusively officered the army.[1]

The Restoration strengthened absolutism to such an extent that the bourgeoisie found itself hampered at every turn.[2] The struggle against this absolutism, as against all German absolutism ever since the wars of liberation, had been confined to the demand upon the monarchy to grant a representative form of constitution. Eventually, a promise was wrung from Frederick William III that he would recognize some kind of popular sovereignty. This promise, however, materialized in the ridiculous reality of the Provincial Estates, about which one historian has made the following comment: 'This was an outmoded system of representing special interests, with the knights holding undisputed predominance, especially in the eastern provinces. The condition for membership in the Estates was *Grundeigentum!* Even in the provinces of the Rhine [the most industrialized areas] 55 representatives of the land stood against 25 representatives of the towns.'[3] The middle class was a hopeless minority throughout.

The interests of these Provincial Estates paralleled their impotence, and the whole is neatly shown in their level of

1 Engels, *Germany: Revolution and Counter-Revolution,* International Publishers, New York 1933, p. 11.

2 Karl Lamprecht, *Deutsche Geschichte,* vol. x, Berlin 1922, pp. 395 ff., 402 ff.

3 Veit Valentin, *Geschichte der Deutschen Revolution* 1848-9. Berlin 1930, vol. I, p. 27.

debate. Johann Jacoby, one of the leaders of the democratic opposition, said about them:

> It would be hard to find an institution which is less popular and which the healthy sense of the people regards as a more useless burden than the Provincial Estates. Everyone would gladly spare us the work of proving from the records that, among all the resolutions adopted there, not a single one could be found which was of any general interest. Flagrant abuses were not removed, nor were steps taken against any bureaucratic despotism. The entire work of the numerous sessions was confined to setting up houses of correction, institutions for deaf mutes and the insanes, fire insurance companies, and to writing laws about new roads, wagon tracks, dog taxes, and so on . . .[4]

When Frederick William IV's government came upon the scene, all aspirations to a liberal reform of the state made their exit.[5] Absolutism triumphed, accompanied by a complete transformation of culture. 'The Prussia of von Stein's reforms, of the wars of liberation, and of Humboldt's and Hardenberg's strivings for a constitution became the Prussia of romantic monarchy, of theistic irrationalism, and of the Christian idea of the State. Berlin ceased to be the university of Hegel and the Hegelians and became that of the philosophers of the Revelation, Schelling and Stahl.' [6]

The Hegelian system, which had viewed state and society as a 'negative' totality and had subjected both to the historical process of reason, could no longer be approved as the official philosophy. Nothing was more suspect than reason and freedom to the new government that now took its cues from the Russian Czar and Prince

[4] Quoted in Franz Mehring, *Zur Preussischen Geschichte von Tilsit bis zur Reichsgründung*, Berlin 1930, p. 241.

[5] Friedrich Schnabel, *Deutsche Geschichte im neunzehnten Jahrhundert*, vol. II, Freiburg 1933, p. 31.

[6] Erich Kaufmann, *Studien zur Staatslehre des monarchischen Prinzips*, Leipzig 1906, p. 54.

Metternich.[7] It needed a positive principle of justification that would protect the state from rebellious forces and shield it, more resolutely than Hegel did, from the onslaught of society. The positivist reaction that set in in Germany was, in the strict sense, a philosophy of the state and not of society. The slight breach in this development occurred when Lorenz von Stein, fusing the Hegelian tradition with the French movement, shifted the emphasis to the structure of society. Its effect on the development of social theory in Germany was negligible, however. The positive philosophy of the state continued to dominate German political theory and practice for decades.

Stahl's philosophy offered a compromise to those who counseled personal absolutism and to the weak demands of the German middle class. He advocated a constitutional system of representation (though not of the people as a whole, but only of estates), legal guarantees of civil liberties, inalienable personal freedom, equality before the law, and a rational system of laws. Stahl took great pains to distinguish his monarchic conservatism from any defense of arbitrary absolutism.[8]

The import of Stahl's philosophy lay definitely in its adjusting anti-rationalist authoritarianism to the social development of the middle class. For example, he combines the labor theory of property with the feudal doctrine that all property is, in the last analysis, held by the grant of the authorities.[9] He advocates the *Rechtsstaat*, but subordinates its guarantee of civil liberty to the authoritative sovereignty of the monarch.[10] He was antiliberal, yet he did not speak only for the feudal past, but

[7] Valentin, op. cit., pp. 37 f.

[8] Cf. *Das monarchische Prinzip*, Heidelberg 1845; and *Die gegenwärtigen Parteien in Staat und Kirche*, 2nd ed., Berlin 1868.

[9] *Philosophie des Rechts*, 3rd and 4th ed., Heidelberg 1854, vol. II, pp. 356, 360.

[10] Ibid., vol. III, pp. 137 ff.

for that period in the historical future when the middle class itself became anti-liberal. His arch-enemy was not the middle class, but the revolution that threatened this class along with the nobility and the monarchist state. His anti-rationalism served the cause of a ruling aristocracy that stood in the way of rational progress; it also served the interest of all rule that could not be justified on rational grounds.

The revolution, Stahl declared, is 'the world-historic mark of our age.' It would found 'the entire State on the will of man instead of on the commandment and ordinance of God.'[11] Significantly enough, the principle that the state rests on the will of men was precisely what the rising middle class had asserted when it carried on its fight against feudal absolutism. Stahl's doctrine repudiated the whole philosophy of Western rationalism[12] that had accompanied this struggle. He condemned modern rationalism as the matrix of revolution; this philosophy, he said, is in the 'internal, religious realm what revolution is in the external, political realm,'[13] namely, the 'estrangement of man from God.'

Since German rationalism had got its most representative expression through Hegel, Stahl concentrated his attack on the latter. He articulated the official reply of the ruling circles of Germany to the Hegelian philosophy. These circles had a far deeper insight into the true character of Hegel's philosophy than had those academic interpreters who saw it as giving unconditional glorification to the existing order. Hegel's doctrine is 'a hostile force,'

11 'Was ist die Revolution?', in *Siebzehn parlamentarische Reden*, Berlin 1862, p. 234.

12 The repudiation began in German political theory prior to Stahl, and Haller, the influence of Burke (F. Gentz), the romanticists, and *Historische Schule* contributed to it. It was only in Stahl's work, however, that the tendencies begun in these schools and movements obtained a systematic elaboration and a political sanction.

13 *Was ist die Revolution*, p. 240.

essentially 'destructive.'[14] His dialectic cancels the reality given, and his theory 'from the outset occupies the same ground as the revolution.'[15] His political philosophy, incapable of demonstrating the 'organic unity' between subjects and the 'one supreme personality [God-king-authority],'[16] undermines the foundations of the prevailing social and political system. We shall not quote more of the innumerable passages in which Stahl testifies to the subversive qualities of Hegelianism, but shall seek rather to set down the conceptions to which Stahl takes exception and on which he sees fit to heap condemnation.

Stahl indicts Hegel along with the most outstanding representatives of European rationalism since Descartes—a configuration that recurs in the ideological attacks of National Socialism.[17] Rationalism construes state and society on the pattern of reason, and in so doing lays down standards that must inevitably lead it to oppose 'all given truth and all given prestige.' It contains, he says, the principle of 'false freedom' and has 'entailed all those ideas which find their ultimate consummation in revolution.'[18] Reason is never satisfied with the truth that is 'given'; it 'spurns the nutriment offered to it.'[19]

Stahl saw the most dangerous embodiment of rationalism to be the theory of Natural Law. He summarized this theory as 'the doctrine that derives law and state from the nature or reason of the [individual] man.'[20] Stahl counterposed to it the thesis that the nature and reason of the individual could not serve as a norm for social organization, for it had always been in the name of the in-

[14] Stahl, *Philosophie des Rechts*, vol. I, pp. xiv and 455.
[15] Ibid., p. 473.
[16] Ibid., vol. III, p. 6.
[17] See particularly H. Heyse, *Idee und Existenz*, Hamburg 1935, and F. Böhm, *Anti-Cartesianismus*, Leipzig 1938.
[18] *Die gegenwärtigen Parteien in Staat und Kirche*, p. 11.
[19] *Philosophie des Rechts*, vol. I, p. 263.
[20] Ibid., p. 252.

dividual's reason that radical demands for a revolution had been advanced. Natural right could not be made to coincide with the given positive right, any more than Hegel's rational state could with the given form of state. Stahl took the idea of natural law in its critical meaning; he understood it to invest the individual with more and higher rights than those the positive right gave him. He therefore opposed to the thesis of natural law the view that 'right and positive right are equivalent [*gleichbedeutende*] concepts,' and to Hegel's 'negative' dialectic he opposed a 'positive philosophy' of authoritarianism.

We have sketched the disparagement of reason in the positive philosophy, and we have stated that the method of this philosophy implied a ready acceptance of the powers that be. Stahl's work verifies this assertion. He is a conscious positivist,[21] motivated by the desire 'to save the worth of the positive, the concrete, the individual, the worth of the facts.'[22] He reproaches Hegel's philosophy for its alleged inability to explain the particular facts that compose the order of reality.[23] Always preoccupied with the universal, Hegel never gets down to the individual contents of the given, which are its true contents.

The 'conversion of science' that Stahl advocates[24] means a turn to positivism—a peculiar brand of it, to be sure, represented, in Stahl's view, by Schelling's 'positive philosophy.'[25] Schelling is lauded for having set the right of 'the historical' against 'the logical, which is timeless and void of action.'[26] All that has grown in history, out of the eternal life of the nation, all that has been sanctioned by

21 Cf. Karl Mannheim, 'Das konservative Denken,' *Archiv für Sozialwissenschaft und Sozialpolitik*, vol. LVII, 1927, pp. 84 f.; and also E. Kaufmann, op. cit., pp. 58 ff.

22 *Philosophie des Rechts*, vol. II, p. 38.

23 Ibid., p. 37.

24 P. vii.

25 See the preface to the second edition of vol. II.

26 Vol. I, p. xvii.

tradition, possesses a truth of its own and is not answerable to reason. Stahl interprets Schelling in terms of the *Historische Schule,* which had used the special authority of the given to justify the existing positive right. In the article that set forth the program of this *Historische Schule,* Friedrich Karl von Savigny had written (1814): 'There can be no question of a choice between good and evil, as if the acceptance of the given were good while its repudiation was evil and at the same time possible. The repudiation of the given is, rather, strictly impossible. The given inevitably dominates us; we might be mistaken with regard to it, but we cannot change it.' [27] The prevailing law and the whole gamut of rights were part of 'the general life of the *Volk*' with which it had grown naturally throughout history; law and right could not be made subject to the critical standards of reason. The historical theory of Savigny rejected, as the later positivism did, the 'negative philosophy' of rationalism (and particularly the doctrine of Natural Law), claiming that that philosophy was hostile to the established order. It likewise shared with the later positivist sociology the penchant for interpreting social processes in terms of natural ones. Everything in the life of society was an organism, and every organism good and right in itself. Schelling described the legal order as a 'natural order,' so to speak, as a 'second nature,' and he denounced all attempts to transform it in accordance with freedom's interest. 'The legal order is not a moral but merely a natural order over which freedom has as little power and authority as it has over sensuous nature. It is therefore not surprising that all attempts to make the legal order a moral one present themselves in their own absurdity and in the most frightful form of

[27] Ernst Landsberg, *Geschichte der deutschen Rechtswissenschaft,* vol. III, München 1910, p. 201.

despotism which immediately follows from it.'[28] The claim that nature was pre-eminent over society was intended as an antidote against the claims of the 'rational will' to change given forms in accordance with the interest of free individuals.

Stahl embodied the principles of the 'naturalist' schools in his positive philosophy with the express purpose of using them as principles of justification. He did not hesitate to emphasize, at the beginning of his work, that his philosophy had a protective function:

'For a century and a half, philosophy has founded authority, marriage, and property not on God's commandment and ordinance, but on man's will and consent. The peoples have followed this doctrine by defying their rulers and the historical order, and ultimately by rising against the just institution of property.'[29] Any philosophy that 'derives the natural and moral universe from human reason, that is, from the laws and attributes of thought,'[30] undermines the given order and merits extermination. The positive philosophy that replaces it 'will foster deference to order and to authority, such as has been invoked by God to govern men, and to all rights and conditions that have become legitimate through His Will.'[31] Order and authority, the two pivotal terms of Comte's positivism, reappear in Stahl's political philosophy. He, too, offers his ideological services to the governing powers, no less persistently than did Comte.

Stahl is particularly sensitive on the score of justifying property. 'Should we give over the question, what is property to the Proudhons?' he demands.[32] If, as rationalism had it, property is to draw its right only from man's

[28] Schelling, *System des transcendentalen Idealismus*, in *Sämmtliche Werke*, Stuttgart 1858, vol. III, p. 583 f.
[29] *Philosophie des Rechts*, vol. II, p. x.
[30] Ibid., p. xviii. [31] P. xxii. [32] P. xvii.

will, it must follow 'that communism is right as against the philosophy of right laid down from Grotius to Hegel, . . . and is also right as against present-day society.' [33] Property and the whole system of social and political relations must be withdrawn from any rationalist handling and must be justified on a more solid ground. Stahl's political philosophy strives to posit all the data of the prevailing social scheme as the data of a true and just reality; its method is to bend human will and reason to the authority of those data.

We shall not dwell at length on the method. Essentially, it consists in tracing, by direct and indirect means, the entire social and political order to God's ordinance. The more vital the issue in question, the more direct the derivation. 'The distribution of wealth' is 'the work of God's ordinance.' [34] The institutions of society are based upon 'God's ordering of the world of mankind.' [35] Social inequality is God's will: 'There must be a different right for man, woman, and child, for the uneducated worker who is brought to law and the landlord who is free from trial. The right must differ in accordance with the vocation of the sex, age, estate or class.' [36] The state and its authorities comprise a 'divine institution,' and though men are free to live under this constitution or that, 'not only is the *state as such* God's command, but the *particular* constitution and the *particular* authorities everywhere possess divine sanction.' [37]

The method is associated with a personalistic philosophy [38] that is the more insidious because it embodies the progressive ideas of middle-class rationalism, interpreting them in an irrationalist context. The 'personality' is exalted to a 'primordial being' and a 'primordial concept.' [39]

[33] P. 375.
[34] P. 376.
[35] P. 191.
[36] Vol. I, p. 277.
[37] Vol. III, p. 177.
[38] Vol. II, Book I.
[39] P. 14.

The created world culminates in the existence of the personality; the latter is an 'absolute end' and the bearer of 'primordial right.'[40] This principle yields Stahl his notion of humanitarianism, namely, that the 'welfare, right, and honor of every individual, even the lowest, is the community's concern, that everyone must be considered, protected, honored, and provided for in accordance with his individuality, without distinction of descent, race, estate, gift . . .'[41] In the anti-rationalistic texture that is Stahl's philosophy, however, these progressive ideas take on the opposite of their original meaning. The radiance of 'personality' puts the drab realities of the social system into shade and shows them forth only as a totality of personal relations emanating from the Person of God and terminating, on earth, in the person of the sovereign monarch. State and society, which in reality are dominated by power relations and ruled by economic laws, appear as a moral Reich governed by ethical laws and rights and duties. The Restoration appears as a world made for the development of the personality.

Stahl's premature personalism illustrates a decisive truth about modern philosophy, that the standpoint of the concrete is frequently farther from the truth than the abstract. The reaction against German idealism saw an intellectual tendency gaining momentum, to merge philosophy with the concreteness of actual life. The demand was made that man's concrete locus in existence should replace abstract concepts in philosophy and become the standard of thought. But when his concrete existence bears witness of an irrational order, the defamation of abstract thought and the surrender to 'the concrete' amounts to a surrender of philosophy's critical motives, of its opposition to an irrational reality.

[40] P. 312. [41] P. 346.

Stahl offered his 'concrete personality' theory as a substitute for Hegel's abstract universalism. The substance of the world was to be the personality in its concrete existence, and not reason. But a universalism came to the fore that was far more dangerous than Hegel's. The totality of existing inequalities and distinctions in the given social and political reality were immediately posited and affirmed in the personality. The personality had its concrete existence in the specific relations of subordination and domination that held in the social reality, while in the social division of labor the personality was an object to be governed. All these inequalities, Stahl held, belong to the nature of personality and may not be questioned. The equality of men 'does not exclude distinctions and grades, inequality of actual rights, inequality even of legal status.'[42]

We shall indicate now only the fundamental tendencies of Stahl's positive philosophy of the state. The personalist principle in the universe implies that all domination has 'a personal character,' that is, has the character of conscious personal authority. In the civil order domination is vested in the many tentacles of the state organism that emanate from and center about the 'natural personality' of the monarch.[43] The state is essentially a monarchy. It may take the form of a representative government, but in any case the sovereignty of the monarch must stand above the various estates.[44]

Stahl accepts Hegel's separation of state from society, but renders it far less strict by interpreting all social relations as 'moral' ones. He advocates that the state exercise a far-reaching regulation of the economy; he is opposed

[42] Ibid., p. 331. [43] Ibid., vol. III, p. 2.
[44] *Das monarchische Prinzip*, pp. 12, 14, 16.

to unlimited freedom of trade and commerce.[45] The state is 'a union [*Verband*] of the people under authority [*Obrigkeit*].'[46] As a moral realm, the state has this twofold aim: 'on the one hand, domination as such, namely, the end that authority prevail among men,' and on the other hand, 'the protection and advancement of men, the development of the nation, and execution of God's command.'[47]

The state is no longer bound by the interest of the individual, but is 'a power and subject prior to and above the individual members.'[48] Authority is the force that, in the last analysis, binds the social and political relations to the whole. The entire system functions through obedience, duty, and acquiescence. 'All domination involves the acceptance of the ruler's thought and will in the existence of those ruled.'[49] This is a striking anticipation of the character-type urged and molded by the modern authoritarian state. Hegel would have regarded such a statement as a horror. The surrender of individual thought and will to the thought and will of some external authority runs counter to all the principles of his idealist rationalism.

Stahl entirely detaches the state from any connection with the autonomy of its individuals. State and society 'cannot originate from and depend on them'; its preservation requires a power that rests solely on ordinance, is independent of the will of individuals, nay, 'is opposed to it, and compelling it from without.'[50] Reason is displaced by obedience, which becomes 'the primary and irremissible motive and the foundation of all morality.'[51] The liberalist philosophy is relinquished even before the social and economic ground of liberalism has become a fact.

[45] *Philosophie des Rechts*, vol. III, pp. 61, 70.
[46] Ibid., p. 131.
[47] P. 144.
[48] P. 141.
[49] P. 9.
[50] Vol. II, p. 143.
[51] P. 106.

Whereas the French social economists could look upon the progress of industrial capitalism as a challenge calling for the transformation of existing social and political relations into an order that might develop individual potentialities, men like Stahl had to concern themselves with the salvation of a system oriented to the past and to some eternal and immutable hierarchy. When Stahl, therefore, criticizes the prevailing labor process—for example, when he appears shocked by the 'calamity of the factory system and machine production' [52]—and makes reference to Sismondi,[53] he is nevertheless far from drawing any consequences. State and society remain bound by divine command and historical tradition. They are as they ought to be. The people is a community stronger than all class stratification. *Volksgemeinschaft* is a fact; the community, not the individual, is the final subject of right. 'Only the *Volk* possesses the unity of *Lebensanschauung* and the germ of creative production.' [54] Tradition and custom ingrown among the people are the source of right. The individual's quest for freedom and happiness is diverted by being referred to the irrational community, which is always right. That which has germinated and become preserved in the 'natural' growth of history is true in itself. 'Man is not an absolutely free being. He is a created and limited one, hence dependent upon the power that gave him his existence and on the given order of life and the given authorities through whom this power let him into existence. The authorities, therefore, hold full power over him, even without his consent.' [55]

In all its aspects, the philosophy of Stahl stands out as having deserted the progressive ideas that Hegel's system had attempted to save for the society in which they had originated and in which they were later betrayed. Reason

[52] Vol. III, p. 73. [53] P. 59. [54] Vol. II, p. 193.
[55] *Die gegenwärtigen Parteien* . . . , p. 22.

N

is superseded by authority, freedom by submission, right by duty, and the individual is put at the mercy of the unquestionable claims of a hypostatized whole. Stahl's philosophy of right gathers together some of the fundamental conceptions that later guided the preparation of National Socialist ideology. Such are the implications of the 'positive philosophy' which claimed to supplant the negative philosophy of Hegel.

5. The Transformation of the Dialectic into Sociology: Lorenz von Stein

There still remains for consideration the important influence exerted by the Hegelian philosophy on the social theory of Lorenz von Stein. Stein's works were well known to Marx and Engels and received criticism in their writings prior to the *Communist Manifesto*. Some controversy has arisen as to whether and how far they took over Stein's conceptions in their own theory; this problem does not interest us here, however, for the question seems irrelevant in view of the fact that the structure and aims of the Marxian theory are quite different from those of Stein's sociology.

The influence of Stein's work on the development of social theory was slight; he was deemed a historian of the French Revolution and of French social theories, rather than a theoretician. The first edition of his *Der Socialismus und Communismus des heutigen Frankreichs*, published in 1842, gives little indication of his sociological concepts. The edition of 1850, however, published in three volumes under the title, *Geschichte der sozialen Bewegung in Frankreich von 1789 bis auf unsere Tage*,[1] gives full elaboration of these. The long introduction

[1] Edited by G. Salomon, München 1922. We quote from this new edition.

treats 'the concept of society and the laws of social movement.' It represents the first German sociology.

We are here using the term sociology in its exact sense, to designate the treatment of social theory as a special science, with a subject matter, conceptual framework, and method of its own. Social theory is taken as 'the science of society,' investigating the particularly social relations among men and the laws or tendencies operating in these.[2] This implies that such 'social' relations can be distinguished from physical, economic, political, or religious ones, though in reality they might never occur without these. Sociology as a special science, though 'concerned with the general study of society,' gives over a great number of social problems to other specialized sciences for treatment. 'Thus problems such as the production and distribution of wealth, the tariff and international trade and investment are handled by economics.'[3] Other groups of social problems are turned over to other special sciences, for example, to political science and education, and, above all, sociology is severed from any connection with *philosophy.*

The emancipation of sociology from philosophy must not be confused with the 'negation' and 'realization of philosophy,' as it occurs in Marxian social theory. Sociology does not 'negate' philosophy, in the sense of taking over the hidden content of philosophy and carrying it into social theory and practice, but sets itself up as a realm apart from philosophy, with a province and truth of its own. Comte is rightly held to be the inaugurator of this separation between philosophy and sociology. It is true that

[2] See Robert M. MacIver, *Society*, New York 1937, pp. vii f. and pp. 4-8; *The Fields and Methods of Sociology*, ed. L. L. Bernard, New York 1934, pp. 3 ff.; C. M. Case, *Outlines of Introductory Sociology*, New York 1934, p. xvii and pp. 25 ff.

[3] William F. Ogburn and Meyer F. Nimkoff, *Sociology*, Cambridge 1940, p. 14.

Comte and other thinkers in the same tradition made a formal equation between their social theory and philosophy: thus, John Stuart Mill outlined his logic of social science within a comprehensive general logic, and Spencer made the principles of sociology part of his System of Synthetic Philosophy. But these thinkers changed the meaning of philosophy, to make it quite different from the philosophy that originally gave birth to social theory. Philosophy to these men was merely a synopsis of the fundamental concepts and principles employed in the specialized sciences (with Comte: mathematics, astronomy, physics, chemistry, biology, and sociology; with Spencer: biology, psychology, sociology, and morals). The synoptic study of these sciences was 'philosophical' by virtue of its general positivistic character, its refutation of all transcendental ideas. Such philosophy thus amounted to the refutation of philosophy.

The anti-philosophical bent of sociology is of great significance. We have seen that, with Comte, society became the subject-matter of an independent field of investigation. The social relations and the laws governing them were no longer derived—as they had been in Hegel's system—from the essence of the individual; still less were they analyzed according to such standards as reason, freedom, and right. The latter now appeared unscientific; sociological method was oriented to describing observable facts and to establishing empirical generalities about them. In contrast to the dialectical conception, which viewed the world as a 'negative totality' and was therefore intrinsically *critical,* the sociological method was intrinsically *neutral,* viewing society in the same way physics viewed nature.

Ever since Comte, sociology has been patterned on the natural sciences. It has been held a science precisely in so far as its subject-matter was amenable to the same neutral treatment as that of the exact sciences. John Stuart Mill's characterization of the science of society remains typical for its subsequent development. Mill said,

> This science stands in the same relation to the social, as anatomy and physiology to the physical body. It shows by what principles of his nature man is induced to enter into a state of society; how this feature of his position acts upon his interests and feelings, and through them upon his conduct; how the association tends progressively to become closer, and the cooperation extends itself to more and more purposes; what those purposes are, and what the varieties of means most generally adopted for furthering them; what are the various relations which establish themselves among men as the ordinary consequence of the social union; what those which are different in different states of society; and what are the effects of each upon the conduct and character of man.[4]

According to this description, the science of society is, in principle, not to be distinguished from natural science. Social phenomena are 'exact' to a lesser degree and more difficult to classify than natural phenomena, but they can be subjected to the standard of exactness and to the principles of generalization and classification; for this reason the theory of society is a real science.[5] Sociology, moreover, has this in common with the other exact sciences: it proceeds from accumulating facts to classifying them successfully. This is the principle of its procedure. 'All knowledge that is not systematized according to this principle must be ruled out of the science of society.'[6]

The very principles, however, that make sociology a special science set it at odds with the dialectical theory of society. In the latter, generalization and classification of facts was at best an irrelevant undertaking. How could such procedure have any bearing on the truth, when all

[4] John Stuart Mill, *Essays on Some Unsettled Questions of Political Economy*, London 1844, p. 135.
[5] Herbert Spencer, *The Study of Sociology*, New York 1912, p. 40.
[6] Lester F. Ward, *Outlines of Sociology*, New York 1898, p. 163.

facts were regarded as constituted by the unique structure and movement of the social whole, in which the changing directions of human practice throughout history played an essential part? The dialectical theory of society emphasized the essential potentialities and contradictions within this social whole, thereby stressing what could be done with society, and also exposing the inadequacy of its actual form. Scientific neutrality was incompatible with the nature of the subject-matter and with the directions for human practice derived from an analysis of it. Furthermore, the dialectical social theory could not be a special science among other sciences, because it considered the social relations to embrace and condition all spheres of thought and existence. Society is the negative totality of all given human relations (including relations to nature), and not any part of these. For these reasons, the dialectic was a philosophical and not a sociological method, one in which every single dialectical notion held all of the negative totality and thus conflicted with any cutting off of a special realm of social relations.

Any attempt at sociology first had to refute the dialectical claim, as Stahl did, or to detach it from its philosophical ground, as did von Stein, who transformed dialectical laws and concepts into sociological ones. Von Stein called his work 'the first attempt to set up the concept of society as an independent concept, and to develop its content.'[7] Hegel's *Philosophy of Right* had exposed the destructive antagonisms within civil society (§§ 243-6) as inevitable products of this social order. To be sure, the Hegelian emphasis weakened the force of the social contradictions by interpreting them as ontological ones. Nevertheless, Hegel's dialectic had set up no inexorable 'natural' law of history, but had quite clearly indicated that the path

[7] *Geschichte der sozialen Bewegung* . . . , p. 6.

of man's historical practice lay in the direction of freedom. The dialectical movement of civil society in the work of von Stein appears much more as the movement of things (capital, property, labor) than as the movement of men. Social development is governed by natural laws rather than by human practice. Von Stein regards this state of affairs not as the product of capitalist reifications but as the 'natural' state of modern society. Reification is understood as a universal law, with which social theory and practice need perforce comply. The dialectic becomes part of an objective and impartial study of society.

Owing to the circumstances in which von Stein's work originated, however, these neutralizing tendencies were considerably counteracted. Stein was, after all, guided by his study of social struggles in post-revolutionary France and paid close attention to French social critics and theorists of the period. This concrete historical approach induced him to say that the economic process was basic to the social and political process, and that the class struggles were the true pivotal content of society. He saw and admitted for a time that the irreconcilable contradictions of modern society were the motor of its development, thus aligning himself with Hegel's dialectical analysis of society. But this focussing upon the antagonisms within the economic process had to be abandoned if sociology was to be secure as an objective science. Hence, von Stein himself renounced his own earlier position. As early as 1852 he foreswore the attempt to base social theory on political economy:

It is well known that the entire science of society originated from a study of the economic antagonism that exploitation and competition have induced between the fourth estate especially, or labor shorn of capital, and the owners of capital. This fact has led to a conclusion which, evident as it seemed, necessarily brought great jeopardy to the deeper foundations of this science. The author of these lines cannot deny that he himself contributed greatly to the acceptance of this conclusion. For, he assumed that since the *present* form [of society] is essentially conditioned by the economic relations, the social order as such could not be other than a print [*Abdruck*], as it were, of the economic order . . . From this opinion, then, followed the other that the entire movement of society is also exclusively governed by these laws which determine economic life, in such a manner that the whole science of society is eventually reduced to a mere reflex of the economic laws and developments.[8]

This statement professes that establishing sociology as a real science requires the abolition of its economic foundation. Stein's sociology henceforth set out to uphold social harmony in the face of the economic contradictions, and morality in the face of social struggles.

In 1856 Stein published his *Gesellschaftslehre*. The first book began the construction of a social ethics' and the last concluded with 'the principles of social harmony,' showing that 'the various orders of society and its classes are linked together so that they supplement and fulfill one another.'[9] In place of dealing with von Stein's final system of sociology,[10] we shall limit ourselves to a brief summary of the foundations of his sociology as expounded in the introduction to the *Geschichte der sozialen Bewegung in Frankreich*.[11] The preface to the edition of 1850 advances the assumption basic to the new science of society, that social dynamic is governed by a necessary law which it is sociology's task to discover. This law, Stein says, can be expressed in its most general form as the struggle of the ruling class to obtain full possession of state

[8] *Deutsche Vierteljahrsschrift*, Stuttgart 1852, p. 145; quoted by H. Nitzschke, *Die Geschichtsphilosophie Lorenz von Steins*, München 1932, pp. 132 f.

[9] *Gesellschaftslehre*, Stuttgart 1856, p. 430.

[10] See the bibliography in Nitzschke, op. cit.

[11] *Geschichte der sozialen Bewegung . . .*, vol. 1, p. 11 ff.

power and to exclude the other class from possessing such. The social process consists at root in the class war between capital and labor for state control.[12]

The antagonism between state and society is the basic idea of Stein's sociology. The two materialize two entirely different principles. Society is 'the organic unity of human life as conditioned by the distribution of wealth, regulated by the organism of labor, moved by the system of wants, and joined to succeeding generations by the family and its right.' [13] We can recognize Hegel in this definition, as well as the early French socialists. Stein clothes the skeleton conception that he took over from Hegel with the material got from the French critical analysis of modern society. In essence, society is class society. 'The general and inalterable relation in society is that between a dominant and a dependent class'; [14] the existence of classes is an 'inevitably given fact' [15] originating in the process of labor. 'Those who possess the material of labor as property herewith possess what those who have no property need in order to acquire it. In the utilization of their labor power, the latter are dependent on this prerequisite, namely, the material [of labor], and since this material is property which cannot be worked on [*bearbeitet*] without the consent of the proprietors, it follows that all who possess nothing but labor power are *dependent on those* who *possess property*.' [16] The social order is thus necessarily a class order; its prime feature is self-seeking, a general penchant of each to acquire 'the means for his own independence and the means for making others dependent.' [17]

In contrast to society, the *state* is 'the community of all individual wills elevated to a personal union.' The principle of the state is the development, progress, wealth,

[12] Ibid., p. 3.
[13] P. 29.
[14] P. 47.
[15] P. 71.
[16] P. 23.
[17] Pp. 42 f.

power, and intelligence of *all* individuals 'without distinction,' positing all individuals as free and equal.[18] The state preserves the common interest, reason, and freedom, from the conflicting private interests of society.[19]

Of utmost significance for the evolution of sociology is the manner in which Stein's separation of state and society disposes of the actual problem of modern social theory. In the first place, class antagonism is declared to be the 'general and unalterable' law of society, and accepted as an 'inevitable fact.' Despite the retention of Hegelian terminology, Stein succumbs to the positivist, affirmative tendencies of early sociology. Secondly, he neutralizes the basic contradictions of modern society by distributing them between two different domains, those of state and society. Freedom and equality are reserved to the *state,* while exploitation and inequality are delegated to the *'society,'* thus turning the inherent contradiction of society into an antagonism between state and society. Modern society is released from any obligation to fulfill human freedom—the responsibility belongs to the state. The state, on the other hand, exists only as the prize of the classes in struggle and is incapable of 'withstanding the power and the claims of society.' [20] The solution of the social antagonisms thus seems to revert to society again.

Stein declares that the process of enslavement and of liberation is, in entirety, a social process, and that bondage and freedom are sociological concepts.[21] Liberty means social independence, or the ownership of sufficient means to enable one to fix the conditions of another's labor. Liberty is necessarily connected with bondage; society is a class order and hence incompatible with freedom. Stein is thus faced with the following problem: the state is the true field of realization of human community, but it is

[18] P. 47. [19] P. 66. [20] P. 73. [21] P. 76.

impotent before class society. The latter, the actual field in which men fulfill themselves, 'cannot be free, owing to its principle.' The 'possibility of progress, therefore, must be sought in a factor' that stands above state and society and is more powerful than both.[22]

This ultimate factor, Stein decides, is 'the personality and its destiny.' The personality is more powerful than state or society; it is 'the foundation and spring-board for the development to freedom.'[23] This conception marks Stein's *volte-face* from the economic foundations of social theory and its achievements. He comes out with an idealist ethics. Not only is society, unfree in its very principle, discharged from the responsibility for freedom, but the state, which inevitably must come under the sway of society, is similarly discharged. The process of transforming philosophical into sociological concepts finally yields man's historical existence to the inalterable mechanisms of the social process and reserves his 'destiny' and goal to his moral personality. The coast is clear for treating social problems in the manner of *wertfreie* science.

We have seen that Stein views the social process as a struggle between state and society, or as a struggle on the part of the ruling social class for state power.[24] The state's principle is 'to elevate all individuals to perfect freedom'; the principle of the society, 'to subjugate some individuals to others.'[25] History is in reality the constant renewal of this conflict on different levels, and the progress of history takes place through the changes in social structure that result.

Stein proceeds to establish the 'natural laws' of this change. We have already mentioned the first law, that the ruling class strives to make possession of state power as exclusively its own as it can.[26] As soon as this goal is

[22] P. 75. [23] Ibid. [24] P. 32. [25] P. 45. [26] P. 49.

reached, a new dynamic begins, consisting in attempts 'to use the state power in the positive interest of the ruling class.' [27] There are different historic stages of this use and, consequently, different degrees of social domination or bondage. The first stage is characterized by 'absolute triumph of society over the state,' or the complete identification of the ruling class with 'the idea of the state.' Stein calls this 'absolute society.' [28] It begins with class appropriation of the means of labor and is accompanied by an increasing subjugation of the class deprived of these means. Hence, 'the development of all social order is a movement toward bondage.' [29]

Just as the class structure of society is necessarily the source of bondage, it is also as much the source of a development in the direction of freedom. The process sets in wherever the capitalist class has completed its organization of society in its own interest. We know that freedom is a 'social concept,' 'dependent on the acquisition of those goods' required for the individual's growth.[30] It follows that the subject class will strain towards getting possession of the wherewithal to gratify its cultural as well as material wants. This class will demand (1) general and equal education and (2) material freedom, that is, the opportunity to acquire property.[31] The latter demand will conflict with the interest of the established order, the vested interest of the ruling class.

In the last analysis, the possessor class aims to 'satisfy its wants and desires *without* labor.' [32] The possessor class, then, is a non-laboring class, and the opposition between property and lack of property is really one between unearned income and labor.[33] Since labor alone makes property a right and a value, and since unearned income is a 'dead weight' that cannot resist the onslaught of labor, it

[27] P. 56.
[28] P. 62.
[29] P. 66.
[30] P. 81.
[31] Pp. 85-7.
[32] P. 90.
[33] P. 91.

follows that the working class will increasingly become 'the master of all value,' that is, will increasingly acquire property in the means of production and finally take over the place of the former non-laboring class. When this occurs, the legal and political structures, which have been modelled on the interests of a non-laboring ruling class, will openly conflict with the actual new power relations and controls in society. 'Transformation of the established system of right becomes an intrinsic—soon also an extrinsic—necessity.' [84]

Two kinds of transformation are possible, political reform and revolution. In the first case, state power would have to yield to the demands of the dependent class and sanction the fact of social equality by recognizing legal equality. The major changes in history, however, have all been effected by revolution: 'The upper class does not grant the demand of the lower class, nor does it allow for a legal reorganization that would conform to the new distribution of social wealth.' [85] Revolution under such conditions is inevitable.

Stein places heavy stress on the fact that revolution contains in its principle a contradiction that at once determines the course it will take. Every revolution proclaims *general* equality for the whole class hitherto excluded from power, but actually establishes equal right only for that *part* of the class that has already got possession of economic wealth. When the class is victorious in its revolution, then, it splits into two conflicting strata. 'No revolutionary movement is able to avert this contradiction . . . According to its inalterable nature, every revolution uses a social class whose interest it will not and cannot serve. Every revolution, as soon as it is complete, thus encounters an enemy in the person of the very mass that

[84] P. 93.

[85] P. 97.

helped achieve the result.'[36] In other words, every revolution issues into a new class conflict and a new form of class society. The privileges of unearned income are abolished, and property based upon labor becomes the foundation of the new social order, but this same property, in the form of capital, soon stands against the potential of acquisition, labor-power. The earning power of capital comes to oppose capital-less labor.[37] Although this condition seems 'perfectly harmonious' and an adequate result of the process of free acquisition, it turns out to be the fountain of a new form of bondage, for in reality, 'labor is excluded from acquiring capital.'[38] The social position of the capitalist is a function of the aggregate of his capital. The growth of capital depends on the value of the product over and above its production cost. The competition of capitals requires a struggle for lower production costs and thus leads necessarily to constant pressure on wages; this is of the essence of capital. The interest of capital conflicts with the interest of labor; the original harmony is dissolved into contradiction.[39]

Stein emphasized that the mechanisms of the revolution operate in the form of unalterable natural laws, that moral indignation or similar evaluations are hence entirely out of place. Moreover, Stein knows that the contradictions he has just analyzed are distinctive of a society based on free labor and acquisition, and that the same may not be applied to other forms of social organization. 'It is precisely the activity of property owners that, taking the form of competition, renders it impossible for those who do not possess property to acquire it.'[40] He goes one step further to declare that the proletariat will need its own revolution to overthrow this society. The proletariat is the class that the middle-class revolution has deprived of all

[36] P. 100. [37] P. 106. [38] P. 107. [39] P. 108. [40] Pp. 109 f.

acquisitive power. Little wonder, then, that it claims the right to seize that power and to reorganize society on the pattern of real social equality. This proletarian act would constitute 'the social revolution' as distinguished from all preceding revolutions, which were 'political revolutions.' [41]

At this point, Stein's sociology veers from its dialectical direction and follows the ideas of positive sociology. The proletarian revolution would be a disaster, and the victory of the proletariat, the 'triumph of bondage.' [42] The reason is that the proletariat is not the stronger or the better part of the social whole. Moreover, it lacks the right to seize the state because it 'does not possess the material and intellectual goods which are prerequisite for true supremacy.' [43] The idea of proletarian rule is, therefore, a contradiction in itself. The proletariat is incapable of maintaining any such supremacy—the old ruling class will soon take revenge upon it and clamp down a dictatorship of violence. 'The successful revolution always leads to dictatorship. And this dictatorship, setting itself above society . . . proclaims itself an *independent state power* and takes the right, mantle and halo of such. This is the end of social revolution.' [44]

But is it likewise the end of social process? The 'personality,' exalted to the position of the decisive factor in social development, has prepared Stein's sudden departure from critical analysis. The acquisitive society preserves personality, for it establishes the principle that free personal development demands the universal opportunity to earn. If the opportunity has been restricted in the actual course capitalism took, it may still be restored by proper 'social reform.' In modern acquisitive society, capital expresses man's mastery over his external life. 'The quality of

[41] P. 126. [42] P. 127. [43] Ibid. [44] P. 131.

personal freedom here is therefore to be found in the fact that the most inferior grade of labor power is able to get possession of capital.'[45] Also, Stein recalls his critical analysis of the contradictions inherent in middle-class society. He asks whether it is at all possible in an acquisitive society so to organize the labor process 'that work alone achieves a possession corresponding to its amount and kind.'[46] The answer he gives is affirmative, resting on an appeal to man's true interest. Man requires freedom and will have it. It is particularly in the interest of the possessing class 'to work for social reform, through all its social forces, and with the aid of the state and its power.'[47]

Lorenz von Stein thus turned the dialectic into an ensemble of objective laws calling for social reform as the adequate solution of all contradictions and neutralized the critical elements of the dialectic.

[45] P. 136. [46] Ibid. [47] P. 138.

III

Conclusion
The End of Hegelianism

1. British Neo-idealism

Hegel's philosophy held to the progressive ideas in Western rationalism and worked out their historical destiny. It attempted to light up the right of reason, and its power, amid the developing antagonisms of modern society. There was a dangerous element in this philosophy, dangerous to the existing order, that is, which derived from its use of the standard of reason to analyze the form of the state. Hegel endorsed the state only in so far as it was rational, that is, in so far as it preserved and promoted individual freedom and the social potencies of men.

Hegel attached the realization of reason to a definite historical order, namely, the sovereign national state that had emerged on the Continent with the liquidation of the French Revolution. In so doing, he submitted his philosophy to a decisive historical test. For any basic change that might take place in this order would have to alter the relation between Hegel's ideas and the existing social and political forms. This means, for example, that when civil society develops forms of organization that deny the essential rights of the individual and abolish the rational state, the Hegelian philosophy must clash with this new state. On its side, the state will then also repudiate Hegel's philosophy.

One final test exists for this conclusion, that to be found in the Fascist and National Socialist attitudes to

Hegel. These state philosophies exemplify the abolition of the rational standard and the individual freedom on which Hegel's glorification of the state depended. There can be no meeting ground between them and Hegel. And yet, ever since the first World War, when the system of liberalism began to shape into the system of authoritarianism, a widespread opinion has blamed Hegelianism for the ideological preparation of the new system. We quote, for example, the dedication to L. T. Hobhouse's important book, *The Metaphysical Theory of the State:*[1]

> In the bombing of London I had just witnessed the visible and tangible outcome of a false and wicked doctrine, the foundations of which lay, as I believe, in the book before me [Hegel's *Phenomenology of Mind*] . . . With that work began the most penetrating and subtle of all intellectual influences which have sapped the rational humanitarianism of the eighteenth and nineteenth centuries, and in the Hegelian theory of the God-state all that I had witnessed lay implicit.

We shall later note the curious fact that the official defenders of the National Socialist state reject Hegel precisely on the ground of his 'rational humanitarianism.'

To decide more fully who is right in this controversy, however, we must sketch the role of Hegelianism in the later period of liberalist society. In Germany, the representative social and political philosophy of the last half of the nineteenth century remained anti-Hegelian or, at best, indifferent to Hegel. There were, however, apart from the employment of Hegelian philosophy in the Marxian theory, two great renaissances of Hegelianism, one in England, the other in Italy. The British movement was still connected with the principles and philosophy of liberalism and for this very reason lay much closer to the spirit of Hegel than did the Italian. The latter

[1] London (The Macmillan Company, New York) 1918, p. 6.

movement was drawing nearer to the approaching current of Fascism and was therefore becoming more and more of a caricature of Hegel's philosophy, especially in the case of Gentile.

At first glance, the tendencies in the British and Italian Hegelianism seem to bear out Hobhouse's interpretation. The political philosophy of the British idealists seized upon the anti-liberal ideas in Hegel's *Philosophy of Right.* From T. H. Green to Bernard Bosanquet the crescendo of emphasis fell increasingly upon the independent principle of the state and on the pre-eminence of the universal. The social interests of free individuals, on which the liberalist tradition had relied for its construction of the state, were disregarded. The state, according to Green, is based on an 'ideal principle of its own, and the common good, which the state embodies and guards, cannot result from the free play of individual interests. There are no individual rights separate from the universal right represented by the state. 'To ask why I am to submit to the power of the state, is to ask why I am to allow my life to be regulated by that complex of institutions without which I literally should not have a life to call my own, nor should be able to ask for a justification of what I am called to do.' [2]

Green comes much closer to the inner motives of Hegel's philosophy when he attempts to understand this universal as a historical force that operates through the deeds and passions of men. In the state, the actions of men 'whom in themselves we reckon bad, are "overruled" for good,' made to depend not on individual passion and motive but 'in some measure' on 'the struggle of mankind towards perfection.' [3] The tendencies in Green to reify the universal as against the individual are counteracted

[2] *Lectures on the Principles of Political Obligation,* Longmans, Green and Co., London 1895, p. 122. [3] Pp. 134 f.

by his adherence to the progressive tendencies of Western rationalism. He insists throughout his work that the state be submitted to rational standards, such as imply that the common good is best served through advancing the interest of free individuals. He grants men the right to dispute laws that violate their just claim to determine their own will, but he demands that all claims against the existing order 'must be founded on a reference to an acknowledged social good.'[4]

Far from being an apology for authoritarianism, Green's political philosophy can, in a certain sense, be designated as a super-liberalism. 'The general principle that the citizen must never act otherwise than as a citizen, does not carry with it an obligation under all conditions to conform to the law of his state, since those laws may be inconsistent with the true end of the state as the sustainer and harmonizer of social relations.'[5] Green thus grants to every individual (*qua* citizen) the liberty to assert an 'illegal right' provided that 'its exercise should be contributory to some social good which the public conscience is capable of appreciating.'[6] He has no doubt that there is such a thing as a 'public conscience,' always open to rational conviction and always willing to permit truth to progress.[7]

The material arena in which the common good has to be realized is not 'the state as such,' but 'this or that particular state,' which might, perhaps, not fulfill the purpose of a true state and, therefore, have to be 'swept away and superseded by another.' Hence, there is no ground for holding that a state is justified in doing 'whatever its

[4] P. 148. [5] P. 148. [6] P. 149.

[7] Green places responsibility for the antagonisms of capitalism (of which he is fully aware) not on the liberalist system but on the contingent historical conditions under which capitalism arose. (Ibid., pp. 225, 228.) He demands certain restrictions of liberalist freedom, especially in respect to freedom of contract, and a removal of conditions and relations occasioned by 'the power of class interests' (pp. 209 f.).

interests seem to require.' [8] In contrast to Hegel, Green holds war, even just war, to be a wrong against the individual's right to life and liberty.[9] And in opposition to Hegel's fundamental concept of supreme sovereignty of the national state, Green envisages an over-arching organization of mankind, which, through an increase in the free scope of the individual and an expansion of free trade, will make 'the motives and occasions of international conflict tend to disappear.' [10]

The point has sometimes been made that the development of British idealism from Green to Bosanquet was one in which the rationalist and liberalist ideas of earlier days were slowly abandoned.[11] We might venture to add to this a corollary: the more Hegelian in wording this idealism became, the further it removed itself from the true spirit of Hegel's thought. Bradley's metaphysics, notwithstanding its Hegelian concepts, has a strong irrationalist core that is entirely alien to Hegel. Bosanquet's *Philosophical Theory of the State* (1899) has features that make the individual a victim of the hypostatized state universal, so characteristic of the later Fascist ideology. The 'average individual is no longer accepted as the real self or individuality. The center of gravity is thrown outside him.' [12] 'Outside him' means to Bosanquet outside 'his own private interest and amusement,' outside the sphere of his immediate want and desire. From its beginnings, this renaissance of idealism showed a definite anti-materialist tendency,[13] a quality it shares with the tendencies accompanying the transition from liberalism to authoritarianism. The ideology accompanying this movement prepared the individual for more labor and less enjoyment,

[8] P. 173. [9] P. 169. [10] P. 177.

[11] Cf. R. Metz, *A Hundred Years of British Philosophy*, London 1938, pp. 283, 327 f.

[12] *The Philosophical Theory of the State*, The Macmillan Co., London 1899, p. 125.

[13] R. Metz, op. cit., pp. 249, 267.

a slogan of the authoritarian economy. Gratification of individual wants had to give way before duties to the whole. The duties, as they came, were found to jibe less and less with any rational standard, and the more true this situation became, the greater stress was laid on the doctrine that the individual's relation to the whole was a relation between two 'ideal' entities that overrule his empirical existence. 'We see that there is a meaning in the suggestion that our real self or individuality may be something which in one sense we are not, but which we recognize as imperative upon us.' [14] Liberty for the individual can be realized only through obedience to that 'imperative.' It is vested in the state which, as the guardian of our real 'self,' is 'the instrument of our greatest self-affirmation.' [15]

The juxtaposition of a real and an empirical self is an ambiguity. It might refer to a significant dualism, to the actual distress of men in their empirical reality as against a 'real' self that demands fulfillment for need and a remedy of distress. On the other hand, the same conception may signify a deprecation of the empirical life in favor of an unconditionally 'ideal' life of the state. Bosanquet's political philosophy runs from one to the other of these two poles. He adopts Rousseau's revolutionary principle of compulsory education towards freedom, but in the course of discussion, the goal, freedom, dissolves before the compulsory means. 'Force, automatism, and suggestion' are the very conditions for progress in intellect. 'In promoting the best life, these aids must be employed by society as exercising absolute power—viz. by the State.' [16] 'The realization of the best life' is the end set by state and society, but that end is so far overshadowed by the element of force involved in its attainment that the

[14] Bosanquet, op. cit., p. 126.
[15] P. 127.
[16] P. 183.

state must be defined as 'a unit, recognized as rightly exercising control over its members through absolute physical power,' or 'recognized as a unit lawfully exercising force.'[17] Hobhouse replies to this definition that it can properly fit into the scheme of any authoritarian absolutism.[18]

The question may now be answered how far the political theory of these British neo-idealists constitutes a genuine resumption of the Hegelian philosophy. One original motive of German idealism they certainly retained, namely, that true liberty cannot be achieved through the mind-set and daily practice of isolated individuals in the competitive vortex of modern society. Freedom is rather a condition to be sought beyond, in the state. The state alone fulfills their real wills and their real selves. Hegel thought that the particular kind of state that could serve this purpose was the one that retained the decisive achievements of the French Revolution and incorporated them into a rational whole.

When the British idealists elaborated their political doctrine, it was at least obvious that the historical form of the state that had come upon the scene was by no means 'the realization of freedom and reason.'

The great merit of Hobhouse's book lies in its exposure of the incompatibility between Hegel's conception and the material basis of the existing state. He points to the fact that Bosanquet's philosophy yields the individual into the clutches of a society *as such,* or to 'the state' generally, whereas in reality the individual always has to carry on his life in some particular historical form of society and state. This 'central fallacy' is of the utmost importance, for in it is implied the confusion between contingent

17 Pp. 184 f.

18 *The Metaphysical Theory of the State,* London 1918, p. 22.

power-relations and moral obligations.[19] State and society as they are cannot claim the dignity of being reason's embodiment: 'When we think of the actual inconsistencies of traditional social morality, the blindness and crudity of law, the elements of class-selfishness and oppression that have coloured it . . . we are inclined to say that no mere philosopher, but only the social satirist, could treat this conception as it deserves.' [20] To those who hold abstractly to Hegel's political philosophy, Hobhouse replies that the very fact of class society, the patent influence of class interests on the state, renders it impossible to designate the state as expressive of the real will of individuals as a whole. 'Wherever a community is governed by one class or one race, the remaining class or race is permanently in the position of having to take what it can get. To say that institutions of such a society express the private will of the subject class is merely to add insult to injury.' [21] In place of concern for the universal, Hobhouse puts concern for the actual welfare of the individual; in place of the *Weltgeist,* the infinite number of human lives irretrievably lost. 'If the world cannot be made incomparably better than it has hitherto been, then the struggle has no issue, and we had better strengthen the doctrine of the militant state and arm it with enough high explosive to bring life to an end.' [22]

Insistence on man's claim to universal happiness, which is always happiness for each, so frequently found in the pages of Hobhouse's book, renders it one of the great documents of liberalist philosophy.

> The happiness and misery of society is the happiness and misery of human beings heightened or deepened by its sense of common possession. Its will is their wills in the conjoint result. Its conscience is an expression of what is noble or ignoble in them when the balance is struck. If we may judge

[19] P. 77. [20] P. 80. [21] P. 85. [22] P. 117.

each man by the contribution he makes to the community, we are equally right to ask of the community what it is doing for this man. The greatest happiness will not be realized by the greatest or any great number unless in a form in which all can share, in which indeed the sharing is for each an essential ingredient. But there is no happiness at all except that experienced by individual men and women, and there is no common self submerging the soul of men. There are societies in which their distinct and separate personalities may develop in harmony and contribute to a collective achievement.[23]

Hobhouse is of course right as against the neo-idealists, just as liberalism is right as against any irrational hypostasis of the state that disregards the fate of the individual. On the other hand, the demands that Hobhouse advances are in line with the abstract principles of liberalism, but they conflict with the concrete form that liberalist society took. Hegel once defined liberalism as the social philosophy that 'sticks to the abstract' and is always 'defeated by the concrete.'[24] The principles of liberalism are valid, the common interest cannot be other in the last analysis than the product of the multitude of freely developing individual selves in society. But the concrete forms of society that have developed since the nineteenth century have increasingly frustrated the freedom to which liberalism counsels allegiance. Under the laws that govern the social process, the free play of private initiative has wound up in competition among monopolies for the most part:

An era of cut-throat competition, followed by a rapid process of amalgamation, threw an enormous quantity of wealth into the hands of a small number of captains of industry. No luxury of living to which this class could attain kept pace with its rise of income, and a process of automatic saving set in upon an unprecedented scale. The investment of these savings in other industries helped to bring these under the same concen-

[23] P. 133.
[24] *Philosophie der Weltgeschichte,* ed. G. Lasson, vol. II, p. 925.

trative forces . . . In the free competition of manufacturers preceding combination the chronic condition is one of 'over-production,' in the sense that all the mills or factories can only be kept at work by cutting prices down towards a point where the weaker competitors are forced to close down, because they cannot sell their goods at a price which covers the true cost of production.[25]

BOSANQUET'S *Philosophical Theory of the State* appeared when this transition from liberal to monopolistic capitalism had already begun. Social theory was faced with the alternative either of abandoning the principles of liberalism so that the existing social order might be maintained, or of fighting the system in order to preserve the principles. The latter choice was implied in the Marxian theory of society.

2. The Revision of the Dialectic

The Marxian theory, however, had itself begun to undergo fundamental changes. The history of Marxism has confirmed the affinity between Hegel's motives and the critical interest of the materialist dialectic as applied to society. The schools of Marxism that abandoned the revolutionary foundations of the Marxian theory were the same that outspokenly repudiated the Hegelian aspects of the Marxian theory, especially the dialectic. Revisionist writing and thought, which expressed the growing faith of large socialist groups in a peaceful evolution from capitalism to socialism, attempted to change socialism from a theoretical and practical antithesis to the capitalist system into a parliamentary movement within this system. The philosophy and politics of opportunism, represented by this movement, took the form of a struggle against

25 J. A. Hobson, *Imperialism,* London (The Macmillan Company, New York) 1938, pp. 74-5.

what it termed 'the remnants of Utopian thinking in Marx.' The result was that revisionism replaced the critical dialectic conception with the conformist attitudes of naturalism. Bowing to the authority of the facts, which indeed justified the hopes of a legal parliamentary opposition, revisionism diverted revolutionary action into the channel of a faith in the 'necessary natural evolution' to socialism. The dialectic, in consequence, was termed 'the treacherous element in the Marxian doctrine, the trap that is laid for all consistent thinking.'[1] Bernstein declared that the 'snare' of dialectic consists in its inappropriate 'abstraction from the specific particularities of things.'[2] He defended the matter-of-fact quality of fixed and stable objects as against any notion of their dialectical negation. 'If we wish to comprehend the world, we have to conceive it as a complex of ready-made objects and processes.'[3]

This amounted to the revival of common sense as the organon of knowledge. The dialectical overthrow of the 'fixed and stable' had been undertaken in the interest of a higher truth that might dissolve the negative totality of 'ready-made' objects and processes. This revolutionary interest was now renounced in favor of the secure and stable given state of affairs that, according to revisionism, slowly evolves towards a rational society. 'The class interest recedes, the common interest grows in power. At the same time, legislation becomes increasingly more powerful and regulates the struggle of economic forces, governing increasingly more realms which were previously left to the blind war of particular interests.'[4]

With the repudiation of the dialectic, the revisionists

[1] E. Bernstein, *Die Voraussetzungen des Sozialismus und die Aufgaben der Sozialdemokratie,* Stuttgart 1899, p. 26.

[2] E. Bernstein, *Zur Theorie und Geschichte des Sozialismus,* Berlin 1904, Part III, p. 75.

[3] Ibid., p. 74.

[4] Ibid., p. 69.

falsified the nature of the laws that Marx saw ruling society. We recall Marx's view that the natural laws of society gave expression to the blind and irrational processes of capitalist reproduction, and that the socialist revolution was to bring emancipation from these laws. In contrast to this, the revisionists argued that the social laws are 'natural' laws that guarantee the inevitable development towards socialism. 'The great achievement of Marx and Engels lay in the fact that they had better success than their predecessors in weaving the realm of history into the realm of necessity and thus elevating history to the rank of a science.' [5] The critical Marxist theory the revisionists thus tested by the standards of positivist sociology and transformed into natural science. In line with the inner tendencies of the positivist reaction against 'negative philosophy,' the objective conditions that prevail were hypostatized, and human practice was rendered subordinate to their authority.

Those anxious to preserve the critical import of the Marxian doctrine saw in the anti-dialectical trends not only a theoretical deviation, but a serious political danger that threatened the success of socialist action at every turn. To them the dialectical method, with its uncompromising 'spirit of contradiction,' was the essential without which the critical theory of society would of necessity become a neutral or positivist sociology. And since there existed an intrinsic connection between Marxian theory and practice, the transformation of the theory would result in a neutral or positivist attitude to the existing societal form. Plekhanov emphatically announced that 'without dialectic, the materialist theory of knowledge and practice is incomplete, one sided; nay more, it is impossible.' [6] The

[5] Karl Kautsky, 'Bernstein und die materialistische Geschichtsauffassung, in *Die Neue Zeit*, 1898-9, vol. II, p. 7.

[6] *Fundamental Problems of Marxism*, ed. D. Ryazanov, New York, n.d., p. 118.

method of dialectic is a totality wherein 'the negation and destruction of the existing' appears in every concept, thus furnishing the full conceptual framework for understanding the entirety of the existing order in accordance with the interest of freedom. Dialectical analysis alone can provide an adequate orientation for revolutionary practice, for it prevents this practice from being overwhelmed by the interests and aims of an opportunist philosophy. Lenin insisted on dialectical method to such an extent that he considered it the hallmark of revolutionary Marxism. While discussing the most urgent practical political matters, he indulged in analyses of the significance of the dialectic. The most striking example is to be found in his examination of Trotsky's and Bukharin's theses for the trade union conference, written on January 25, 1921.[7] In this tract Lenin shows how a poverty of dialectical thinking may lead to grave political errors, and he links his defense of dialectic to an attack on the 'naturalist' misinterpretation of Marxian theory. The dialectical conception, he shows, is incompatible with any reliance upon the natural necessity of economic laws. It is furthermore incompatible with the exclusive orientation of the revolutionary movement to economic ends, because all economic ends receive their meaning and content only from the totality of the new social order to which this movement is directed. Lenin regarded those who subordinated political aims and spontaneity to the purely economic struggle to be among the most dangerous falsifiers of Marxian theory. He held against these Marxists the absolute predominance of politics over economics: 'Politics cannot but have precedence over economics. To argue differently, means forgetting the ABC of Marxism.'[8]

[7] *Selected Works,* vol. IX, pp. 62 ff. See above, p. 314.
[8] Ibid., p. 54.

3. Fascist 'Hegelianism'

While the heritage of Hegel and the dialectic was being defended only by the radical wing among the Marxists, at the opposite pole of political thought a revival of Hegelianism was taking place that brings us to the threshold of Fascism.

The Italian neo-idealism was from the outset associated with the movement for national unification and, later, with the drive to strengthen the nationalist state against its imperialist competitors.[1] The fact that the ideology of the young national state looked to Hegelian philosophy for its support is to be explained by the particular historical development in Italy. In its first phase, Italian nationalism had to contend with the Catholic Church, which regarded the Italian aspirations as detrimental to Vatican interests. The protestant tendencies of German idealism provided efficient weapons for the justification of a secular authority in the struggle with the church. Furthermore, Italy's entry among the imperialist powers brought in an extremely backward national economy, with a middle class split into numerous competing groups, hardly fit to cope with the growing antagonisms that accompanied the adaptation of this economy to modern industrial expansion. Croce as well as Gentile emphasized that a petty 'positivism' and materialism held sway which made people feel satisfied with their small private interests and unable to understand the far-reaching sweep of nationalist aims. The state had to assert its imperialist interest under frequent opposition from the middle class. Also, it had yet to achieve what other national states had already achieved,

[1] For the historical position of Italian neo-idealism, see the following: Benedetto Croce, *History of Italy*, 1871-1915, New York 1929, chapter x; Giovanni Gentile, *Grundlagen des Faschismus*, Stuttgart 1936, pp. 14 f., 17 ff.; R. Michels, *Italien von Heute*, Zürich 1930, p. 172.

an efficient bureaucracy, a centralized administration, a rationalized industry, and a complete military preparedness against the external and internal enemy. This positive task of the state made Italian neo-idealism lean towards the Hegelian position.

The turn towards Hegel's conception was an ideological maneuver against the weakness of Italian liberalism. Sergio Panuncio, the official theoretician of the Fascist state, has shown that ever since Mazzini, Italian political philosophy was predominantly anti-liberal and anti-individualist. This philosophy found in Hegel a congenial demonstration of the state as an independent substance, existing *vis-à-vis* the petty interests of the middle class. Panuncio endorses Hegel's distinction between state and civil society and with it his remarks on the corporation, saying that 'those writers are right who relate so many aspects of the Fascist State to Hegel's organic State.' [2]

Italian idealism, however, was Hegelian only where it confined itself to expounding Hegel's philosophy. Spaventa and above all Croce made essential contributions to a new understanding of Hegel's system. Croce's *Logic* and *Esthetics* were attempts at a genuine revival of Hegelian thought. In contrast, the political exploitation of Hegel renounced the fundamental interests of his philosophy. Moreover, the closer Italian idealism drew to Fascism, the more it deviated from Hegelianism, even in the field of theoretical philosophy. Gentile's main philosophical works are a logic and a philosophy of mind. Although he also wrote a *Rifforma della Dialettica hegeliana,* proclaiming the mind as the only reality, his philosophy, when judged by its content and not its language, has nothing to do with Hegel's. The central conception of the *Theory of Mind as Pure Act* (1916) might remotely resemble Kant's

[2] *Allgemeine Theorie des Faschistischen Staates,* Berlin 1934, p. 25.

notion of the transcendental consciousness, but this resemblance, too, is in the wording rather than the meaning. We shall in our discussion limit ourselves to this work. Though it appeared long before the triumph of Fascism, it shows most clearly the affinity between Italian neo-idealism and this authoritarian system and provides a lesson as to what happens to a philosophy that fosters such affinity.

One important truth applies to both Gentile's works and to the later utterances of Fascist philosophy: they cannot be treated on a philosophic level. Comprehension and knowledge are made part of the course of political practice, not on any rational grounds, but because no truth is recognized apart from such practice. Philosophy is no longer declared to hold its truth in opposition to an untrue social practice, nor is philosophy supposed to agree only with such practice as is directed towards realizing reason. Gentile proclaims practice, no matter what form it may be taking, to be the truth as such. According to him the sole reality is the act of thinking. Any assumption of a natural and historical world separate from and outside this act is denied. The object is thus 'resolved' into the subject,[3] and any opposition between thinking and doing, or between mind and reality becomes meaningless. For, thinking (which is 'making,' real doing) is *ipso facto* true. 'The true is what is in the making.'[4] Recasting a sentence from Giambattista Vico, Gentile writes, 'verum et fieri convertuntur.'[5] And he sums up, 'the concept of truth coincides with the concept of fact.'[6]

There can be few statements more remote from Hegel's spirit. Despite his many assertions about the reality of mind, Gentile can be considered neither a Hegelian nor an idealist. His philosophy is much closer to positivism.

[3] *The Theory of Mind as Pure Act*, trans. H. Wildon Carr, London (The Macmillan Company, New York) 1922, p. 10.

[4] Ibid., p. 15. [5] P. 17. [6] P. 15.

The approach of the authoritarian state seems to announce itself in an attitude that submits all too readily to the authority of matters of fact. An integral part of totalitarian control is the attack on critical and independent thought. The appeal to facts is substituted for the appeal to reason. No reason can sanction a regime that uses the greatest productive apparatus man has ever created in the interest of an increasing restriction of human satisfactions—no reason except the fact that the economic system can be retained in no other way. Just as the Fascist emphasis on action and change prevents the insight into the necessity of *rational* courses of action and change, Gentile's deification of thinking prevents the liberation of thought from the shackles of 'the given.' The fact of brute power becomes the real god of the time, and as that power enhances itself, the surrender of thought to the fact shows forth the more. Lawrence Dennis, in his recent book defending Fascist policy, shows the same abdication of thought when he advocates 'a scientific and logical' method, the 'governing assumption' of which will be that 'facts are normative, that is to say, facts should determine rules, being paramount to rules. A rule which contradicts a fact is nonsense.' [7]

Gentile discards the fundamental principle of all idealism, namely, that there is an antagonism and strain between truth and fact, between thought or mind and reality. His whole theory is based upon the immediate identity of these polar elements, whereas Hegel's point had been that there is no such immediate identity but only the dialectical process of achieving it. Before we outline some of the implications of the new philosophy of 'mind,' we must review the factors that brought to Gentile the reputation of being an idealist philosopher. We shall find them in his use of Kant's transcendental ego.

[7] Lawrence Dennis, *The Dynamics of War and Revolution*, New York 1940, p. 25.

According to Gentile, the statement that the pure act of thinking is the only reality, does not apply to the empirical but only to the transcendental *I*.[8] All the qualifications of mind (its developing unity, its identity with its immediate manifestations, its being 'free' and 'the principle of space,' etc.) refer only to its transcendental activity. The distinction between empirical and transcendental ego, and the description of the transcendental point of view [9] follow Kant's pattern with fair accuracy. But the use to which Gentile puts the conception destroys the very meaning of transcendental idealism. The latter had assumed that a reality is given to consciousness but cannot be resolved into it; the reception of sense data is the condition for the spontaneous acts of pure understanding. Hegel, too, although he rejected the Kantian notion of a 'thing-in-itself,' did not abandon the objective foundations of transcendental idealism. His principle of 'mediation' retained them—the realization of mind was the continued working out of a process between reason and reality.

Gentile, on the other hand, claims to have 'got rid of the illusion of a natural reality.' [10] 'We do not suppose as a logical antecedent of knowledge the reality which is the object of knowledge; . . . we cancel that independent nature of the world, which makes it appear the basis of mind, by recognizing that it is only an abstract moment of mind.' [11] Kant's transcendental ego was distinguished by its unique relations to a pre-given reality. When this reality is 'cancelled,' the transcendental ego must, despite all assertions to the contrary, remain a mere word that obtains a certain meaning only by a generalization from the empirical ego. With the destruction of the objective barrier, man is delivered into a world supposedly his

[8] See particularly *Theory of Mind*, chapter 1.
[9] P. 6.
[10] P. 257.
[11] P. 273.

own, real only as his own act and doing. 'The individual is the real positive' and all that is positive is 'posited by us.'[12] To be sure, it is positive only in so far as 'we oppose it to ourselves,' recognize it 'not as our work but that of others.' But the opposition will dissolve as soon as we see that the individual, by virtue of the transcendental consciousness, is also the universal. The individual makes itself and the universal; the universal is 'the self-making of the universal.'[13]

Behind this rather confused heap of words, a significant process is working itself out, a process of breakdown for all rational laws and standards, an exaltation of action regardless of the goal, a veneration of success. In a sense, Gentile's philosophy retains the slight traces of the liberalist scheme in which idealism originated, especially in its insistence that 'the individual is the only positive.' But this individuality, oscillating between the meaningless transcendental and the empty concrete, has no other content than action. Its entire essence resolves into its acts, which have no supra-individual laws to restrain them and no valid principles to judge them. Gentile himself calls his doctrine 'absolute formalism': there is no 'matter' apart from the pure 'form' of acting. 'The only matter there is in the spiritual act is the form itself, as activity.'[14] Gentile's doctrine that true reality is action justified in itself clearly enunciates and glorifies the conscious and programmatic lawlessness of Fascist action. 'The mind itself . . . in its actuality is withdrawn from every preestablished law, and cannot be defined as a being restricted to a definite nature, in which the process of life is exhausted and completed.'[15] From the Hegelian dialectic Gentile borrows the idea that reality is a ceaseless process, but the process, detached from any pattern of universal

[12] Pp. 88 f. [13] P. 107. [14] P. 243. [15] P. 19.

reason, produces a wholesale destruction rather than any construction of the rational forms of life. 'True life . . . is made one by death . . .'[16]

Hegel's philosophy weaves the transitory nature of all historical forms into the world-historical web of reason in progress; the content of the transitory is still present at the final inauguration of freedom. Gentile's actualism is entirely indifferent to reason and greets prevailing evil and deficiency as a great good. 'Our mind's real need is not that error and evil should disappear from the world but that they should be eternally present,' for there is no truth without error and no good without evil.[17] Notwithstanding, then, the paradoxical interpretation of reality as 'mind,' Gentile accepts the world as it is and deifies its horrors. Finite things, whatever and however they may be, are 'always the very reality of God.' The philosophy that eventuates 'exalts the world into an eternal theogony which is fulfilled in the inwardness of our being.'[18] This inwardness, however, is no longer a refuge from a miserable reality, but justifies the final dissolution of all objective norms and values into the disorder of pure action.

All its fundamental motives show Gentile's to be the strict opposite of Hegel's philosophy, and it is by virtue of its being the opposite that it passes directly into the Fascist ideology. Identification of thought with action, and of reality with mind prevents thought from taking a position opposed to 'reality.' Theory becomes practice to such a degree that all thought is rejected if it is not immediate practice or immediately consummated in action. Gentile's theory of mind praises 'anti-intellectualism,'[19] foreshadowing the typically relativistic traits of Fascist philosophy, to be noted in the repudiation of all fixed

[16] P. 154. [17] P. 246. [18] P. 277. [19] Pp. 269, 271.

programs that go beyond the requirements of the immediate situation. Action sets its own aims and norms that may not be judged by any objective ends and principles. 'The Foundations of Fascism,' published by Gentile, announce the abolition of all 'programs' to be the very philosophy of Fascism. Fascism is bound by no principles; 'change of course,' to keep step with the changing constellations of power, is its sole unchanging program. No decision is valid for the future; 'the true decisions of the Duce are those which are simultaneously formulated and executed.' [20]

The statement discloses one essential attribute of the authoritarian state, the inconsistency of its ideology. Gentile's actualism asserts the totalitarian rule of practice over thought, the independence of the latter disappearing once and for all. Loyalty to any truth that lies outside or beyond the practical aims of Fascist politics is declared meaningless. Theory as such and all intellectual activity are made subservient to the changing requirements of politics.

4. National Socialism versus Hegel

We cannot understand the basic difference between the Hegelian and the Fascist idea of the state without sketching the historical foundations of Fascist totalitarianism.

Hegel's political philosophy was grounded on the assumption that civil society could be kept functioning without renouncing the essential rights and liberties of the individual. Hegel's political theory idealized the Restoration state, but he looked upon it as embodying the lasting achievements of the modern era, namely, the German Reformation, the French Revolution, and idealist culture.

[20] *Grundlagen des Faschismus,* p. 33; cf. Benito Mussolini, *Relativismo e Fascismo,* in *Diuturna, Scritti Politici,* ed. V. Morello, Milano 1924, pp. 374 ff.

The totalitarian state, on the other hand, marks the historical stage at which these very achievements become dangerous to the maintenance of civil society.

The roots of Fascism are traceable to the antagonisms between growing industrial monopolization and the democratic system.[1] In Europe after the first World War, the highly rationalized and rapidly expanding industrial apparatus met increasing difficulties of utilization, especially because of the disruption of the world market and because of the vast network of social legislation ardently defended by the labor movement. In this situation, the most powerful industrial groups tended to assume direct political power in order to organize monopolistic production, to destroy the socialist opposition, and to resume imperialist expansionism.

The emerging political system cannot develop the productive forces without a constant pressure on the satisfaction of human needs. This requires a totalitarian control over all social and individual relations, the abolition of social and individual liberties, and the incorporation of the masses by means of terror. Society becomes an armed camp in the service of those great interests that have survived the economic competitive struggle.

The anarchy of the market is removed, labor becomes compulsory service, and the productive forces are rapidly expanded—but the whole process serves only the interests of the ruling bureaucracy, which constitutes itself the heir of the old capitalist class.

The Fascist organization of society requires a change in the entire setting of culture. The culture with which German idealism was linked, and which lived on until

[1] See the analysis of National Socialism in Robert A. Brady, *The Spirit and Structure of German Fascism*, The Viking Press, New York 1937, and Franz L. Neumann, *Behemoth, The Origin and Practice of National Socialism*, to be published by Oxford University Press, New York 1941.

the Fascist era, accented private liberties and rights, so that the individual, at least as a private person, could feel safe in the state and in society. The total surrender of human life to the vested social and political powers was prevented not only by a system of political representation, legal equality, freedom of contracts, but also by the alleviating influence of philosophy, art, and religion. When Hegel divided man's social life among the family, civil society, and the state, he recognized that each of these historical stages had a relative right of its own. Moreover, he subordinated even the highest stage, the state, to the absolute right of reason asserted in the world history of mind.

When Fascism finally demolished the liberalist framework of culture, it in effect abolished the last field in which the individual could claim his right against society and the state.

Hegel's philosophy was an integral part of the culture which authoritarianism had to overcome. It is therefore no accident that the National Socialist assault on Hegel begins with the repudiation of his political theory. Alfred Rosenberg, official keeper of National Socialist 'philosophy,' opened the drive on Hegel's concept of the state. As a consequence of the French Revolution, he says, 'a doctrine of power, alien to our blood, arose. It reached its apogee with Hegel and was then, in a new falsification, taken over by Marx . . .'[2] This doctrine bestowed upon the state, he continues, the dignity of the absolute and the attribute of an end in itself. To the masses, the state came forth as a 'soul-less instrument of force.'[3]

The ideological attack of National Socialism upon the Hegelian conception of the state contrasts rather squarely

[2] Alfred Rosenberg, *Der Mythos des 20. Jahrhunderts*, 7th ed., München 1933, p. 525.
[3] Ibid.

with the Italian Fascists' seeming acceptance of it. The difference is to be explained in the different historical situations that the two Fascist ideologies had to meet. In contrast to Italy, the German state had been a powerful and firmly established reality, which even the Weimar Republic had not shaken in its foundations. It was a *Rechtsstaat,* a comprehensive rational political system with distinctly demarcated and recognized spheres of rights and liberties that could not be utilized by the new authoritarian regime. Moreover, the latter could discard the state form because the economic powers who stood behind the National Socialist movement were long since strong enough to govern directly, without the unneçessary mediation of political forms that would have to grant at least a minimum of legal equality and security.

Consequently, Rosenberg, like all the other National Socialist spokesmen, turns against 'the State' and denies its supreme authority. 'Today we view the State no longer as an independent idol before which men must kneel. The State is not even an end, but is only a means for preserving the people,' [4] and 'the authority of the *Volkheit* is above that of the State. He who does not admit this fact is an enemy of the people . . .' [5]

Carl Schmitt, the leading political philosopher of the Third Reich, likewise rejects the Hegelian position on the state, declaring it incompatible with the substance of National Socialism. Whereas the political philosophy of the last century had been based upon a dichotomy between state and society, National Socialism substitutes the triad of state, movement (the party), and people (*Volk*). The state is by no means the ultimate political reality in

[4] P. 526; see Hitler, *Mein Kampf,* Reynal and Hitchcock, New York 1939, p. 592: 'The basic realization is that the state represents not an end but a means.'

[5] Rosenberg, op. cit., p. 527.

the triad; it is superseded and determined by the 'movement' and its leadership.[6]

Alfred Rosenberg's statement sets the stage for the National Socialist rejection of Hegel's political philosophy. He says Hegel belonged to the line of development that produced the French Revolution and the Marxian critique of society. Here, as in many other instances, National Socialism reveals a far deeper understanding of the realities than many of its critics. Hegel's state philosophy held to the progressive ideas of liberalism to such an extent that his political position became incompatible with the totalitarian state of civil society. The state as reason—that is, as a rational whole, governed by universally valid laws, calculable and lucid in its operation, professing to protect the essential interest of every individual without discrimination—this form of state is precisely what National Socialism cannot tolerate.

This is the supplementary institution of economic liberalism that had to be crushed as soon as that form of economy went under. The Hegelian triad of family, society, and state has disappeared, and in its place is the over-arching unity that devours all pluralism of rights and principles. The government is totalitarian. The individual championed in the Hegelian philosophy, he who bore reason and freedom, is annihilated. 'The individual, so we teach today, has as such neither the right nor the duty to exist, since all rights and all duties derive only from the community.'[7] This community, in turn, is neither the union of free individuals, nor the rational whole of the Hegelian state, but the 'natural' entity of the race. National Socialist ideologists emphasize that the 'community' to which the individual is completely subordinate constitutes a natural reality bound together by

[6] *Staat, Bewegung, Volk*, Hamburg 1933, p. 12.
[7] Otto Dietrich, in the *Völkische Beobachter*, December 11, 1937.

'blood and soil' and subject to no rational norms or values.

The focussing upon 'natural' conditions serves to divert attention from the social and economic basis of totalitarianism. The *Volksgemeinschaft* is idolized as a natural community precisely because and in so far as there is no actual social community. Since the social relations demonstrate the lack of any community, the *Volksgemeinschaft* has to be set apart in the dimension of 'blood and soil,' which does not hamper the real play of class interests within society.

The elevation of the *Volk* to the position of the original and ultimate political entity shows once again how distant National Socialism is from the Hegelian conception. According to Hegel, the *Volk* is that part of the state that does not know its own will. This attitude of Hegel's, though it may seem a reactionary one, is closer to freedom's interest than the popular radicalism of the National Socialist utterances. Hegel rejects any notion that 'the people' are an independent political factor, because, he maintains, political efficacy requires the consciousness of freedom. The people, Hegel said time and again, have not as yet achieved this consciousness, they are still lacking the knowledge of their true interest, and constitute a rather passive element in the political process. The establishment of a rational society presupposes that the people have ceased to exist in the form of 'masses' and have been transformed into an association of free individuals. National Socialism, in contrast, glorifies the masses and retains the 'people' in their pre-rational, natural condition.[8] Even in this condition, however, the *Volk* is not

[8] See Otto Dietrich, *Die philosophischen Grundlagen des Nationalsozialismus*, Breslau 1935, p. 29; Otto Koellreutter, *Vom Sinn und Wesen der nationalen Revolution*, Tübingen 1933, pp. 29 f.; and the same author's *Volk und Staat in der Weltanschauung des Nationalsozialismus*, Berlin 1935, p. 10.

allowed to play an active political role. Its political reality is supposed to be represented by the unique person of the Leader, who is the source of all law and all right and the sole author of social and political existence.

The German idealism that culminated in the Hegelian teaching asserted the conviction that social and political institutions should jibe with a free development of the individual. The authoritarian system, on the other hand, cannot maintain the life of its social order except by forcible conscription of every individual, regardless of his interest, into the economic process. The idea of individual welfare gives way to the demand for sacrifice. 'The duty of sacrifice for the whole has no limit if we regard the people as the highest good on earth.' [9] The authoritarian system cannot considerably or permanently raise the standard of living, nor can it enlarge the area and means of individual enjoyment. This would undermine its indispensable discipline and, in the last analysis, would annul the Fascist order, which, of its very nature, must prevent any free development of productive forces. Consequently Fascism 'does not believe in the possibility of "happiness" on earth,' and it 'denies the equation that well-being equals happiness.' [10] Today, when all the technical potentialities for an abundant life are at hand, the National Socialists 'consider the decline of the standard of living inevitable' and indulge in panegyrics on impoverishment.[11]

The total victimization of the individual that takes place is encouraged for the specific benefit of the industrial and political bureaucracy. It therefore cannot be justified on the ground of the individual's true interest. National Socialist ideology simply states that true human

[9] Koellreutter, *Vom Sinn und Wesen . . .*, p. 27.
[10] Mussolini, *Fascism: Doctrine and Institutions,* Rome 1935, pp. 10, 21.
[11] *Volk im Werden,* ed. Ernst Krieck, 1933, No. 1, p. 24.

existence consists in unconditional sacrifice, that it is of the essence of the individual's life to obey and to serve—'service which never comes to an end because service and life coincide.' [12]

Ernst Krieck, one of National Socialism's representative spokesmen, devoted a considerable portion of his writing to a repudiation of German idealism. In his periodical, *Volk im Werden,* he published an article called *'Der Deutsche Idealismus zwischen den Zeitaltern,'* in which the following sweeping declaration occurs: 'German idealism must . . . be overcome in form and in content if we are to become a political and active nation.' [13] The reason for the condemnation is clear. German idealism protested the wholesale surrender of the individual to ruling social and political forces. Its exaltation of mind and its insistence on the significance of thought implied, National Socialism correctly saw, an essential opposition to any victimization of the individual. Philosophic idealism was part and parcel of idealist culture. And this culture recognized a realm of truth that was not subject to the authority of the order that is and of the powers that be. Art, philosophy, and religion envisioned a world that challenged the claims of the given reality. Idealist culture is incompatible with Fascist discipline and control. 'We live no longer in the age of education, culture, humanity, and pure spirit, but in the necessity for struggle, for political visions of reality, for soldiery, national discipline, for the national honor and future. It is, therefore, not the idealist but the heroic attitude which is demanded of men as the task and need of life in this epoch.' [14]

Krieck makes no attempt to point to any specific sins in the thought-structure of German idealism. Although a

[12] *Der Deutsche Student,* August 1933, p. 1.
[13] 1933, No. 3, p. 4. See Krieck, E., *Die deutsche Staatsidee,* Leipzig 1934.
[14] P. 1; see also No. 5, 1933; pp. 69, 71.

philosopher and holding Hegel's chair at the University of Heidelberg, he finds difficulty in coping with the simplest philosophical idea. We must turn for specific statements to those who by profession are still engaged in philosophical work. Franz Böhm's *Anti-Cartesianismus,* which offers a National Socialist interpretation of the history of philosophy, contains a chapter on '*Hegel und Wir.*' Hegel is here made the symbol of all that National Socialism abhors and rejects; the 'emancipation from Hegel' is hailed as forerunner of a return to a true philosophy. 'For a century, Hegel's universalistic conception . . . buried the motivations of the German history in philosophy.' [15] What is this anti-German orientation in Hegel? First, his stress on thought, his attack on action for action's sake. Böhm gets to the center of Hegelianism when he criticizes its 'humanitarian ideals.' He recognizes the intrinsic connection between the notions of reason and mind and the 'universalistic conception' of humanity.[16] To view the world as mind, he says, and to measure existing forms according to reason's standard is tantamount in the end to transcending contingent and 'natural' distinctions and conflicts among men, and passing beyond these to the universal essence of man. It is tantamount to upholding the right of humanity as against the particular claims of politics. Reason implies the unity of all men as rational beings. When reason finally fulfills itself in freedom, the freedom is the possession of all men and the inalienable right of every individual. Idealistic universalism thus implies individualism.

The National Socialist critique harps on the tendencies in Hegel's philosophy that contradict all totalitarianism. By virtue of these tendencies it declares Hegel to be the 'symbol of a centuries-old, superseded past' and 'the philosophic counter-will of our time.'

[15] Leipzig 1938, p. 25.

[16] Ibid., pp. 28 f.

Böhm's criticism recurs in a somewhat milder and more elaborate form in another representative document of the National Socialist philosophy, Hans Heyse's *Idee und Existenz,* which declares Hegel 'the source of all liberal, idealistic as well as materialistic philosophies of history.' [17] The National Socialists, in contrast to many Marxists, take the connection between Hegel and Marx seriously.

The fact that the development towards authoritarian forms was an about-face from Hegelian principles, rather than any consequence of these, was recognized within and outside of Germany as early as the period of the first World War. Muirhead in England declared at that time that 'it is not in Hegelianism, but in the violent reaction against the whole idealist philosophy that set in shortly after his death, that we have to look for the philosophical foundations of present-day militarism.' [18] The statement holds with all its implications. The ideological roots of authoritarianism have their soil in the 'violent reaction' against Hegel that styled itself the 'positive philosophy.' The destruction of the principle of reason, the interpretation of society in terms of nature, and the subordination of thought to the inexorable dynamics of the given operated in the romanticist philosophy of the state, in the Historical School, in Comte's sociology. These anti-Hegelian tendencies joined forces with the irrational philosophies of Life, history and 'existence' that arose in the last decade of the nineteenth century and built the ideological framework for the assault on liberalism.[19]

The social and political theory responsible for the development of Fascist Germany was, then, related to Hegelianism in a completely negative way. It was anti-

[17] Hamburg 1935, p. 224.

[18] J. H. Muirhead, *German Philosophy in Relation to the War,* quoted in R. Metz, op. cit., p. 282.

[19] See my article 'Der Kampf gegen den Liberalismus in der totalitären Staatsauffassung,' in *Zeitschrift für Sozialforschung,* 1934, pp. 161-94.

Hegelian in all its aims and principles. No better witness to this fact exists than the one serious political theorist of National Socialism, Carl Schmitt. The first edition of his *Begriff des Politischen* raises the question of how long 'the spirit of Hegel' lived in Berlin, and he replies, 'in any case, the school that became authoritative in Prussia after 1840 preferred to have the "conservative" philosophy of F. J. Stahl, while Hegel wandered from Karl Marx to Lenin and to Moscow.' [20] And he summarizes the entire process in the striking statement that on the day of Hitler's ascent to power 'Hegel, so to speak, died.' [21]

20 München 1932, p. 50.
21 *Staat, Bewegung, Volk,* op. cit., p. 32.

Bibliography

PART ONE

Hegel

Sämtliche Werke, ed. G. Lasson and J. Hoffmeister, Felix Meiner, Leipzig 1928 ff.

Sämtliche Werke, ed. H. Glockner, Jubiläumsausgabe, 26 vols., Fr. Frommann, Stuttgart 1927 ff.

Dokumente zu Hegels Entwicklung, ed. J. Hoffmeister, Fr. Frommann, Stuttgart 1936.

Hegels Theologische Jugendschriften, ed. H. Nohl, J. C. B. Mohr, Tübingen 1907.

Briefe von und an Hegel, ed. K. Hegel, 2 vols., Leipzig 1887.

Hegel-Archiv, ed. G. Lasson, 4 issues, F. Meiner, Leipzig 1912 ff.

The Phenomenology of Mind, transl. J. J. B. Baillie, 2 vols., Swan Sonnenschein (The Macmillan Co., New York), London 1910.

Science of Logic, transl. W. H. Johnston and L. G. Struthers, 2 vols., The Macmillan Co., New York 1929.

Hegel's Doctrine of Reflection, being a paraphrase and a commentary . . . of the second volume of Hegel's Larger Logic, by W. T. Harris. D. Appleton and Co., New York 1881.

Hegel's Doctrine of Formal Logic, being a translation of the first section of the Subjective Logic, by H. S. Macran, Clarendon Press, Oxford 1912.

Hegel's Logic of World and Idea, being a translation of the second and third parts of the Subjective Logic, by H. S. Macran, Clarendon Press, Oxford 1929.

The Logic of Hegel, transl. from the Encyclopaedia of the Philosophical Sciences, by W. Wallace, 2. ed., Clarendon Press, Oxford 1892.

Hegel's Philosophy of Mind, transl. from the Encyclopaedia of the Philosophical Sciences, by W. Wallace, Clarendon Press, Oxford 1894.

Philosophy of Right, transl. S. W. Dyde, George Bell and Sons, London 1896.

The Philosophy of History, transl. J. Sibree, The Colonial Press, New York 1899.

The Philosophy of Fine Arts, transl. F. P. R. Osmaston, 4 vols., George Bell and Sons, London 1920.

Lectures on the Philosophy of Religion, transl. E. B. Speirs and J. B. Sanderson, 3 vols., K. Paul, Trench, Trubner and Co., London 1895.

Lectures on the History of Philosophy, transl. E. S. Haldane and F. H. Simson, 3 vols., K. Paul, Trench, Trubner and Co., London 1892 ff.

SECONDARY WORKS

1. *General*

Besides the older standard works of Rosenkranz, Haym, Stirling, Caird, and Fischer, we mention only:

Croce, B., *What is Alive and What is Dead in Hegel's Philosophy,* transl. D. Ainslie, London 1915.

Hartmann, N., *Hegel,* Berlin 1929.

Heimann, B., *System und Methode in Hegels Philosophie,* Berlin 1927.

Kroner, R., *Von Kant zu Hegel,* 2 vols., Tübingen 1921-24.

Moog, W., *Hegel und die Hegelsche Schule,* München 1930.

Mure, G. R. G., *An Introduction to Hegel,* London 1940.

Stace, W. T., *The Philosophy of Hegel,* London 1924.

Steinbüchel, Th., *Das Grundproblem der Hegelschen Philosophie,* Bonn 1933.

The Philosophical Review, 1931, no. 3, Commemorative Issue, with articles by R. M. Cohen, S. Hook, and G. H. Sabine.

2. *On Hegel's Early Writings*

Dilthey, W., *Die Jugendgeschichte Hegels* (*Gesammelte Schriften,* vol. IV), Leipzig 1921.

Haering, Th., *Hegel. Sein Wollen und Werk.* 2 vols., Leipzig 1929-38.

Maier, J., *On Hegel's Critique of Kant,* New York 1939.

Schwarz, J., *Hegels Philosophische Entwicklung,* Frankfurt M. 1938.

Wacker, H., *Das Verhältnis des jungen Hegel zu Kant,* Berlin 1932.

3. *On the Phenomenology of Mind*

Busse, M., *Hegels Phaenomenologie des Geistes und der Staat,* Berlin 1931.

Loewenberg, J., 'The Exoteric Approach to Hegel's Phenomenology of Mind.' 'The Comedy of Immediacy in Hegel's Phenomenology of Mind,' in: *Mind,* vol. XLIII and XLIV, 1934-35.

Purpus, W., *Zur Dialektik des Bewusstseins nach Hegel,* Berlin 1908.

4. *On the Science of Logic*

Baillie, J. B., *The Origin and Significance of Hegel's Logic,* London 1901.

Günther, G., *Grundzüge einer neuen Theorie des Denkens in Hegels Logik,* Leipzig 1933.

MacTaggert, J. E., *Studies in the Hegelian Dialectics,* Cambridge 1896.

—— *A Commentary on Hegel's Logic,* Cambridge 1931.

Marcuse, H., *Hegels Ontologie und die Grundzüge einer Theorie der Geschichtlichkeit,* Frankfurt M. 1932.

Noël, G., *La logique de Hegel,* Paris 1933.

Wallace, W., *Prolegomena to the Study of Hegel's Philosophy and Especially of his Logic,* 2. ed., Oxford 1894.

5. *On the Political Philosophy and the Philosophy of History*

Heller, H., *Hegel und der nationale Machtstaatsgedanke,* Berlin 1921.

Löwenstein, J., *Hegels Staatsidee; ihr Doppelgesicht und ihr Einfluss im neunzehnten Jahrhundert,* Berlin 1927.

Rosenzweig, F., *Hegel und der Staat,* 2 vols., München 1920.

The chapters on Hegel in: Sabine, G. H., *History of Political Theory,* New York 1937, and Vaughan, C. A., *Studies in the History of Political Philosophy Before and After Rousseau,* 2 vols., Manchester 1939.

'La Révolution de 1789 et la pensée moderne.' Special issue of the *Revue philosophique de la France et de l'étranger,* Paris 1939.

6. *From Hegel to Marx*

Hess, M., *Sozialistische Aufsätze,* ed. Th. Zlocisti, Berlin 1921.
Hook, S., *From Hegel to Marx,* New York 1935.
Löwith, K., *Von Hegel zu Nietzsche,* Zürich 1940.
Lukács, G., *Geschichte und Klassenbewusstsein,* Berlin 1923.
Plenge, J., *Marx und Hegel,* Tübingen 1911.
Vogel, P., *Hegels Gesellschaftsbegriff und seine geschichtliche Fortbildung durch Lorenz Stein, Marx, Engels und Lassalle,* Berlin 1925.

PART TWO

Schelling, F., W. J. v., *Sämmtliche Werke,* 14 vols., Stuttgart 1856 ff.
Kierkegaard, S., *Gesammelte Werke,* ed. H. Gottsched and Ch. Schrempf, 12 vols., Jena 1913 ff.
Feuerbach, L., *Sämmtliche Werke,* 10 vols., Leipzig 1846 ff.

Marx-Engels Gesamtausgabe, ed. Marx-Engels Institute Moscow, Frankfurt M. 1927 ff.
Marx-Engels, *Selected Works,* 2 vols., ed. Marx-Engels Institute, Moscow 1935.
Marx, K., *Capital,* transl. S. Moore, E. Aveling, and E. Untermann, 3 vols., Charles H. Kerr and Co., Chicago 1906-09.
—— *A Contribution to the Critique of Political Economy,* transl. N. I. Stone, Charles H. Kerr and Co., Chicago 1904.
—— *Letters to Dr. Kugelmann,* International Publishers, New York 1934.
—— *The Poverty of Philosophy,* transl. H. Quelch, Charles H. Kerr and Co., Chicago 1910.
—— *Theorien über den Mehrwert,* ed. K. Kautsky, 3 vols., Stuttgart 1905 ff.
—— and Engels, F., *Critique of the Gotha Program,* International Publishers, New York 1933.
—— —— *The German Ideology,* ed. R. Pascal, International Publishers, New York 1933.
—— —— *Germany: Revolution and Counter-Revolution,* International Publishers, New York 1933.

Lenin, *Selected Works*, 12 vols., International Publishers, New York 1934 ff.

Saint-Simon, *Œuvres*, ed. Enfantin, 11 vols., Paris 1868-76.
Doctrine Saint-Simonienne. Exposition. Paris 1854.
Sismondi, S., *Nouveaux principes d'économie politique*, 2 vols., 2. ed., Paris 1827.
Proudhon, P.-J., *Système des contradictions économiques*, ed. C. Bouglé and H. Moysset, 2 vols., Paris 1923.
—— *De la création de l'ordre dans l'humanité*, ed. C. Bouglé and A. Cuvillier, Paris 1927.
Comte, A., *Discours sur l'esprit positif*, Paris 1844.
—— *Cours de philosophie positive*, 4. ed., ed. E. Littré, 6 vols., Paris 1877.
—— *Système de politique positive*, 4 vols., Paris 1890 (English translation London 1870-75).
—— *The Positive Philosophy of Auguste Comte*, freely transl. and condensed by H. Martineau, 3. ed., 2 vols., London 1893.
Mill, J. St., *A System of Logic, Ratiocinative and Inductive*, 8. ed., New York 1884.
—— *Essays on Some Unsettled Questions of Political Economy*, London 1844.
—— *Auguste Comte and Positivism*, 3. ed., London 1882.
Spencer, H., *The Study of Sociology*, New York 1912.
—— *The Principles of Sociology*, 3 vols., New York 1884-97.

Stahl, F. J., *Philosophie des Rechts*, 3. and 4. ed., 3 vols., Heidelberg 1854.
—— *Das monarchische Prinzip*, Heidelberg 1845.
—— *Die gegenwärtigen Parteien in Staat und Kirche*, 2. ed., Berlin 1868.
—— *Siebzehn parlamentarische Reden*, Berlin 1862.

Stein, L. v., *Geschichte der sozialen Bewegung in Frankreich von 1789 bis auf unsere Tage*, ed. G. Salomon, 3 vols., München 1923.
—— *Gesellschaftslehre*, Stuttgart 1856.
Green, L. T., *Lectures on the Principles of Political Obligation*, Longmans, Green and Co., London 1895.
Bosanquet, B., *The Philosophical Theory of the State*, London (The Macmillan Co., New York) 1899.

Hobhouse, L. T., *The Metaphysical Theory of the State*, London (The Macmillan Co., New York) 1918.

Gentile, G., *The Theory of Mind as Pure Act*, transl. H. Wildon Carr, The Macmillan Co., London-New York 1922.
—— *Grundlagen des Fascismus*, Stuttgart 1936.
Panuncio, S., *Allgemeine Theorie des faschistischen Staates*, Berlin 1934.
Mussolini, B., *Fascism: Doctrine and Institutions*, Rome 1935.
Hitler, A., *Mein Kampf*, Reynal and Hitchcock, New York 1939.
Rosenberg, A., *Der Mythos des 20. Jahrhunderts*, 7. ed., München 1933.
—— *Gestaltung der Idee*, München 1936.

SECONDARY WORKS

1. *On the Dialectical Theory of Society*

Adams, H. P., *Karl Marx in his Earlier Writings*, London 1940.
Adoratsky, V., *Dialectical Materialism*, New York 1934.
Bukharin, N. I., *Historical Materialism*, New York 1925.
Cornu, A., *Karl Marx. De L'hégélianisme au matérialisme historique*, Paris 1934.
Croce, B., *Historical Materialism and the Economics of Karl Marx*, transl. C. M. Meredith, New York 1914.
Hook, S., *Towards the Understanding of Karl Marx*, New York 1933.
Jackson, T. H., *Dialectics. The Logic of Marxism and its Critics*, London 1936.
Korsch, K., *Marxismus und Philosophie*, 2. ed., Leipzig 1930.
—— *Karl Marx*, London 1938.
Lenin, *Aus dem philosophischen Nachlass*, ed. V. Adoratski, Wien-Berlin 1932.
Lukács, G., *Geschichte und Klassenbewusstsein*, Berlin 1923.
Paschukanis, E., *Allgemeine Rechtslehre und Marxismus*, Wien-Berlin 1929.
Plekhanov, G. V., *Fundamental Problems of Marxism*, ed. D. Ryazanov, New York 1929.
Troeltsch, E., Die marxistische Dialektik, in *Gesammelte Schriften*, vol. III, Tübingen 1922.

Revisionism

Bernstein, E., *Die Voraussetzungen des Sozialismus und die Aufgaben der Sozialdemokratie,* Stuttgart 1899.
—— *Zur Theorie und Geschichte des Sozialismus,* Berlin 1904.
Kautsky, K., Bernstein und die materialistische Geschichtsauffassung, in *Die Neue Zeit,* 1898-99, vol. II.

2. *On the Foundations of Positivism*

Artz, F. B., *Reaction and Revolution,* 1814-32, Harper and Brothers, New York and London 1934.
Booth, A., *Saint-Simon and Saint-Simonism,* London 1871.
Caird, E., *The Social Philosophy and Religion of Auguste Comte,* 2. ed., Glasgow 1893.
Grossmann, H. *Sismonde de Sismondi et ses theories économiques,* Warsaw 1925.
Lévy-Bruhl, L., *La philosophie d'Auguste Comte,* Paris 1900 (English transl. New York 1903).
Sée, H., *Französische Wirtschaftsgeschichte,* vol. II, Jena 1936.
—— *La vie économique de la France sous la monarchie censitaire,* Paris 1927.
Weill, G., *Saint-Simon et son œuvre,* Paris 1894.

3. *On the Philosophy of the Restoration*

Brie, S., *Der Volksgeist bei Hegel und in der historischen Rechtsschule,* Berlin 1909.
Frantz, C., *Schelling's positive Philosophie,* 3 parts, Cöthen 1880.
Kantorowicz, H., Volksgeist und historische Rechtsschule, in *Historische Zeitschrift,* vol. 108, 1912.
Kaufmann, E., *Studien zur Staatslehre des monarchischen Prinzips,* Leipzig 1906.
Landsberg, E., *Geschichte der deutschen Rechtswissenschaft,* vol. II, München 1910.
Mannheim, K., Das konservative Denken, in *Archiv für Sozialwissenschaft und Sozialpolitik,* vol. LVII, 1927.
Mehring, F., *Zur preussischen Geschichte von Tilsit bis zur Reichsgründung,* Berlin 1930.
Schnabel, F., *Deutsche Geschichte im neunzehnten Jahrhundert,* 4 vols., Freiburg 1933-7.

Treitschke, H. v., *Deutsche Geschichte im neunzehnten Jahrhundert,* 5 vols., Leipzig 1890-96.

Valentin, V., *Geschichte der deutschen Revolution von 1848-49,* 2 vols., Berlin 1930.

4. *Philosophy under Fascism and National Socialism*

Brady, R. A., *The Spirit and Structure of German Fascism,* The Viking Press, New York 1937.

Croce, B., *History of Italy,* 1871-1915, New York 1929.

Hobson, J. A., *Imperialism,* The Macmillan Co., London 1938.

Michels, R., *Italien von Heute,* Zürich 1930.

Silone, I., *Der Fascismus,* Zürich 1934.

Bäumler, A., *Studien zur deutschen Geistesgeschichte,* Berlin 1937.

Böhm, F., *Anti-Cartesianismus. Deutsche Philosophie im Widerstand,* Leipzig 1938.

Der Deutsche Student, 1933 ff.

Dietrich, O., *Die philosophischen Grundlagen des Nationalsozialismus,* Breslau 1935.

Heidegger, M., *Die Selbstbehauptung der deutschen Universität,* Breslau 1933.

Heyse, H., *Idee und Existenz,* Hamburg 1935.

Koellreutter, O., *Vom Sinn und Wesen der nationalen Revolution,* Tübingen 1933.

—— *Volk und Staat in der Weltanschauung des Nationalsozialismus,* Berlin 1935.

Krieck, E., *Nationalpolitische Erziehung,* Leipzig 1932.

—— *Die deutsche Staatsidee,* Leipzig 1934.

—— *Völkisch-politische Anthropologie,* part III, Leipzig 1938.

—— (ed.) *Volk im Werden,* Leipzig 1933 ff.

Schmitt, C., *Der Begriff des Politischen,* München 1932.

—— *Staat, Bewegung, Volk,* Hamburg 1933.

—— *Ueber die drei Arten des rechtswissenschaftlichen Denkens,* Hamburg 1934.

Dennis, L., *The Dynamics of War and Revolution,* New York 1940.

Kolnai, A., *The War Against the West,* New York 1938.

Marcuse, H., Der Kampf gegen den Liberalismus in der totalitären Staatsauffassung, in *Zeitschrift fur Sozialforschung,* vol. III, Paris 1935.

Index

SUPPLEMENTARY EPILOGUE

WRITTEN IN 1954

Epilogue*

The defeat of Fascism and National Socialism has not arrested the trend toward totalitarianism. Freedom is on the retreat – in the realm of thought as well as in that of society. Neither the Hegelian nor the Marxian idea of Reason have come closer to realization; neither the development of the Spirit nor that of the Revolution took the form envisaged by dialectical theory. Still, the deviations were inherent in the very structure which this theory had discovered —they did not occur from outside; they were not unexpected.

From the beginning, the idea and the reality of Reason in the modern period contained the elements which endangered its promise of a free and fulfilled existence: the enslavement of man by his own productivity; the glorification of delayed satisfaction; the repressive mastery of nature in man and outside; the development of human potentialities within the framework of domination. In Hegel's philosophy, the triumph of the Spirit leaves the State behind in the reality – unconquered by the Spirit and oppressive in spite of its commitment to Right and Freedom. Hegel accepted Civil Society and its State as the adequate *historical* realization of Reason – which meant that they were not the *ultimate* realization of Reason. The latter was relegated to metaphysics: Hegel concluded the encyclopedic presentation of his system with Aristotle's description of the *Nous* as *Theos.* At the beginning and at the end, Western philosophy's answer to the quest for Reason and Freedom is the same. The deification of the Spirit implies acknowledgment of its defeat in the reality. Hegel's philosophy was the last which could dare to comprehend reality as manifestation of the Spirit. The subsequent history made such an attempt impossible.

Hegel saw in the "power of *negativity*" the life element of the Spirit and thereby of Reason. This power of Negativity was in the last analysis the power to comprehend and

*Written in 1954

alter the given facts in accordance with the developing potentialities by rejecting the "positive" once it had become a barrier to progress in freedom. Reason is in its very essence contra-diction, opposition, negation as long as freedom is not yet real. If the contradictory, oppositional, negative power of Reason is broken, reality moves under its own positive law and, unhampered by the Spirit, unfolds its repressive force. Such decline in the power of Negativity has indeed accompanied the progress of late industrial civilization. With the increasing concentration and effectiveness of economic, political, and cultural controls, the opposition in all these fields has been pacified, co-ordinated, or liquidated. The contradiction has been absorbed by the affirmation of the positive. In 1816, when the wars of national liberation had ended, Hegel exhorted his students against the "business of politics" and the State which had "swallowed up all other interests into its own," to uphold the "courage of truth," of thought, the power of the Spirit as the highest value. Today, the Spirit seems to have a different function: it helps to organize, administer, and anticipate the powers that be, and to liquidate the "power of Negativity." Reason has identified itself with the reality: what is actual is reasonable although what is reasonable has not yet become actuality.

Has the other, the Marxian attempt to redefine Reason suffered a similar fate? Marx believed that industrial society had created the preconditions for the realization of Reason and Freedom while only its capitalistic organization prevented this realization. Full maturity of the productive forces, mastery over nature, and a material wealth great enough to fulfil at least the basic needs of all members of society at the attained cultural level were the prerequisites for socialism, and these prerequisites had been created. However, in spite of this substantive link between capitalist productivity and socialist freedom, Marx thought that only a revolution and a revolutionary social class could accomplish the transition. For in this transition, far more was involved than the liberation and rational utilization of the productive forces, namely, the liberation of man himself: abolition of his enslavement to the instruments of his labor, and thereby the complete transvaluation of all prevailing values. Only this "more" would turn quantity into quality and establish a different, non-repressive society — the determinate *negation* of capitalism. These new principles and values could only be realized by a class which was *free from* the old and repressive principles and values, whose existence embodied the very negation of the capitalist system and therefore the historical possibility of opposing and overcoming this system. Marx' idea of the proletariat as the absolute negation of capitalist society telescopes in one notion the historical relation between the preconditions and the realization of freedom. In a strict sense, liberation *presupposes* freedom: the former can be accomplished only if undertaken and sustained by free individuals — free from the needs and interests of domination and repression. Unless the revolution itself progresses through freedom, the need for domination and repression would be carried over into the new society, and the fateful separation between the "immediate" and the "true" interest of the individuals would be almost inevitable; the individuals would become the objects of their own liberation, and freedom would be a matter of administration and decree. Progress would be progressive repression, and the "delay" in freedom would threaten to become self-propelling and self-perpetuating.

The decisive importance of the relation between the pre-revolutionary and post-revolutionary proletariat has been demonstrated only after the death of Marx, in the transformation of free into organized capitalism. It was this development which transformed Marxism into Lenism and determined the fate of Soviet Society — its progress under a new system of repressive productivity. Marx' conception of the "free" proletariat as the absolute negation of the established social order belonged to the model of "free" capitalism: a society in which the free operation of the basic economic laws and relations would increase the internal contradictions and make the industrial proletariat their principal victim as well as the self-conscious agent of their revolutionary solution. When Marx envisaged the transition to socialism from the advanced industrial countries, he did so because not only the maturity of the productive forces, but also the irrationality of their use, the maturity of the internal contradictions of capitalism and of the will to their abolition were essential to his idea of socialism. But precisely in the advanced industrial countries, since about the turn of the century, the internal contradictions became subject to increasingly efficient organization, and the negative force of the proletariat was increasingly whittled down. Not only a small "labor aristocracy" but the larger part of the laboring classes were made into a positive part of the established society. It was not simply the overflow of productivity into a rising standard of living which caused this transformation. When Engels died in 1895, the living and working conditions of the laboring classes in the advanced capitalist countries had shown a long range tendential improvement far above the level described and anticipated in Marx' *Capital*. Still, Engels saw no reason for a fundamental revision of the Marxian prediction. Engels' emphasis on the growing legal-parliamentary power of organized labor seems to indicate that he counted on a further improvement in the condition of labor, as the direct result of growing working class power within the functioning capitalist system. Nor did the trend seem to refute the Marxian conception. The "supra-profits" of the monopolistic period could serve as an explanation for the rise in real wages — at the expense of "supra-exploited" groups and regions, and at the cost of recurrent war-preparation and wars. Not just impoverishment, but impoverishment in the face of growing social productivity was supposed to make the proletariat a revolutionary force. Marx' notion of impoverishment implies consciousness of the arrested potentialities of man and of the possibility of their realization – consciousness of alienation and de-humanization. But then the development of capitalist productivity stopped the development of revolutionary consciousness. Technological progress multiplied the needs and satisfactions, while its utilization made the needs as well as their satisfactions repressive: they themselves sustain submission and domination. Progress in administration reduces the dimension in which individuals can still be "with themselves" and "for themselves" and transforms them into total objects of their society. The development of consciousness becomes the dangerous prerogative of outsiders. The sphere in which individual and group transcendence was possible is thus being eliminated – and with it the life element of oppostion. Here we can indicate only a few of the principal factors which enabled late industrial civilization to absorb its negativity.

The increase in the apparatus of production and distribution outgrew individual and group control and generated a hierarchy of public and private bureaucracies, with a high degree of neutralization of responsibility. Even at the top of the hierarchy, where responsibility is identifiable and final, the specific individual and group interest can assert itself only within the overriding interest of the preservation and expansion of the apparatus as a whole. The latter is indeed the incarnation of the general will, the collective need. Since it keeps, at least in the advanced industrial countries, society going under improving conditions and with better satisfaction of needs, the rationality of opposition appears even more spurious, if not senseless. Considering the given facts and tendencies, there is no reason to assume that further progress demands the destruction of its present basis. This reconciliation of the opposition was operative long before the first World War revealed the extent to which the "objectively" revolutionary classes had been integrated into the national interest.

The tremendous rise in the productivity of labor within the framework of the prevailing social institutions made mass production inevitable – but also mass manipulation. The result was that the standard of living rose with the concentration of economic power to monopolistic proportions. Concurrently, technological progress fundamentally changed the balance of social power. The scope and effectiveness of the instruments of destruction controlled by the government made the classical forms of the social struggle old-fashioned and romantic. The barricade lost its revolutionary value just as the strike lost its revolutionary content. The economic and cultural co-ordination of the laboring classes was accompanied and supplemented by the obsolescence of their traditional weapons.

The consolidation of the capitalist system was greatly enhanced by the development of Soviet society. This development influenced the situation of the Western world in two ways: (1) The failure of the Central European revolutions after the first World War isolated the Bolshevik Revolution from its anticipated economic and political base in the advanced capitalist countries and led it on the road of terroristic industrialization by virtue of its own resources. What Marx had branded as the repressive and exploitative features of capitalist industrialization was thus reproduced, on a new basis, in Soviet society in order to obtain as rapidly as possible the achievements of Western industrialization. Compared with the Marxian idea of socialism, Stalinist society was not less repressive than capitalist society – but much poorer. The image of freedom which Marxism had upheld against the prevailing unfreedom seemed to have lost its realistic content. In the Western world, Communism came to be identified, not with a higher but with a lower stage of the historical development, and with a hostile foreign power. As against this power, the national cause also appeared as the cause of freedom. (2) Then the Soviet state grew into a highly rationalized and industrialized society, outside the capitalist world and powerful enough to compete with the latter on its own terms, challenging its monopoly in progress and its claim to shape the future of civilization. The Western world answered with total mobilization, and it was this mobilization which completed national and international control over the danger zones of society. The Western world was unified to an extent unknown in its long history. The common interest, which had already successfully organized the internal contradictions, now proceeded to organize the external ones. The international co-ordination in turn helped to intensify the national co-ordination. Conformity becomes a question of life and death – not only for individuals but also for nations.

The tendencies which were here just enumerated have been often and amply described in terms of "mass democracy," "popular culture," etc. Such terminology lends itself easily to a wrong focus: as if these tendencies were due to the rise of "masses," or to the decline of certain cultural values and institutions. They rather seem to grow out of the historical structure of late industrial society once this society had succeeded in controlling its own dialectic on the ground of its own productivity. Nor are these tendencies confined to any specific cultural or political area. The pre-conditioning of the individuals, their shaping into objects of administration, seem to be universal phenomena. The idea of a different form of Reason and Freedom, envisioned by dialectical idealism as well as materialism, appears again as Utopia. But the triumph of regressive and retarding forces does not vitiate the truth of this Utopia. The total mobilization of society against the ultimate liberation of the individual, which constitutes the historical content of the present period, indicates how real is the possibility of this liberation.

SUPPLEMENT TO THE BIBLIOGRAPHY

HEGEL

The only real event in the recent history of Hegel's philosophy is the post-war revival of Hegel-studies in France. Focussed on the "Phenomenology" and the actual content of its dialectic, the new French Hegel-interpretation shows clearer than any previous one the inner connection between the idealistic and materialistic dialectic:

Hyppolite, Jean, *Genèse et Structure de la Phénomenologie de l'Esprit de Hegel.* Aubier, Paris 1946

Hyppolite, Jean, "Situation de l'Homme dans la Phénomenologie Hegelienne", in *Les Temps Modernes,* II, 19, 1947

Kojève, Alexandre, *Introduction à la Lecture de Hegel.* Lecons sur la Phénomenologie de l'Esprit, ed. R. Queneau. Gallimard, Paris 1947

Tran-Duc-Thao, "La 'Phénomenologie de l'Espirit' et son contenu réel," in: *Les Temps Modernes,* III, 36, 1948

On Hegel's political philosophy:

Popper, Karl, *The Open Society and Its Enemies.* 2 vols. G. Routledge, London 1945; Princeton 1950.
vol. II: The High Tide of Prophecy: Hegel, Marx, and the Aftermath

Weil, Eric, *Hegel et l'Etat.* J. Vrin. Paris 1950

Hegel's philosophy plays a decisive part in the foundation of Sartre's existentialism:

Sartre, Jean-Paul, *L'Etre et le Néant,* Gallimard, Paris 1943

Heidegger's Hegel-interpretation:

Heidegger, Martin, "Hegels Begriff der Erfahrung," in: *Holzwage, Klostermann,* Frankfurt/Main 1950

Lukács, George, *Der junge Hegel.* Ueber die Beziehungen von Dialektik und Oekonomie. Europa Verlag, Zurich 1948

MARX

Most important is the first publication of Marx' manuscript "Grundrisse der Kritik der politischen Oekonomie" written in 1857-1858. This is actually the first version, previously unknown, of *Das Kapital.* It is far more "philosophical" than the final version and shows how Marx' mature economic theory grows out of his philosophical conception.

Marx, Karl, *Grundrisse der Kritik der politischen Oekonomie.* Marx-Engels-Lenin Institut Moskau, 2 vols. 1939 and 1941. Re-issued in one volume by Dietz Verlag, Berlin 1953

(See: Rosdolsky, R., "Das 'Kapital im allgemeinen und die vielen Kapitalien'", in: *Kyklos,* VI, no 2.)

The following titles are relevant to the problems of Marxian theory discussed in this volume. Literature on the post-Marxian development of Marxian theory is not included:

Bekker, Konrad, *Marx' philosophische Entwicklung, sein Verhaltnis zu Hegel.* Zúrich and New York 1940

Cornu, Auguste, *Karl Marx et la Pensée Moderne.* Paris 1948

Cornu, Auguste, Essai de Critique Marxiste. Paris 1951

Morf, Otto, *Das Verhaltnis von Wirtschaftstheorie und Wirtschaftsgeschichte bei Karl Marx.* Bern 1951

Popitz, Heinrich, *Der entfremdete Mensch.* Basel 1953

Schlesinger, Rudolph, *Marx, His Time and Ours.* London 1950

Somerhausen, Luc, *L'Humanisme Agissant de Karl Marx.* Paris 1946

Thier, Erich, "Die Anthropologie des jungen Marx", introduction to Marx, *Nationalekonomie und Philosophie,* Koln-Berlin 1950

Venable, Vernon, *Human Nature: the Marxian View.* New York 1946

(See also the 2 volume of Karl Popper's *The Open Society* quoted above)